*Imagining the Nation in Nature*

# Imagining the Nation in Nature

*Landscape Preservation and*
*German Identity, 1885–1945*

Thomas M. Lekan

HARVARD UNIVERSITY PRESS
Cambridge, Massachusetts
London, England
2004

*Library of Congress Cataloging-in-Publication Data*

Lekan, Thomas M.
Imagining the nation in nature : landscape preservation and German identity, 1885–1945 /
Thomas M. Lekan.
   p.  cm.
Includes bibliographical references and index.
ISBN 0-674-01070-1 (alk. paper)
1. Landscape protection—Social aspects—Germany—History—20th century.
2. Landscape—Psychological aspects—Germany—History—20th century.
3. National socialism and science. I. Title.

QH77.G3L44  2003
333.72′0943′0904—dc22      2003056641

# Contents

*Imagining the Nation in Nature*

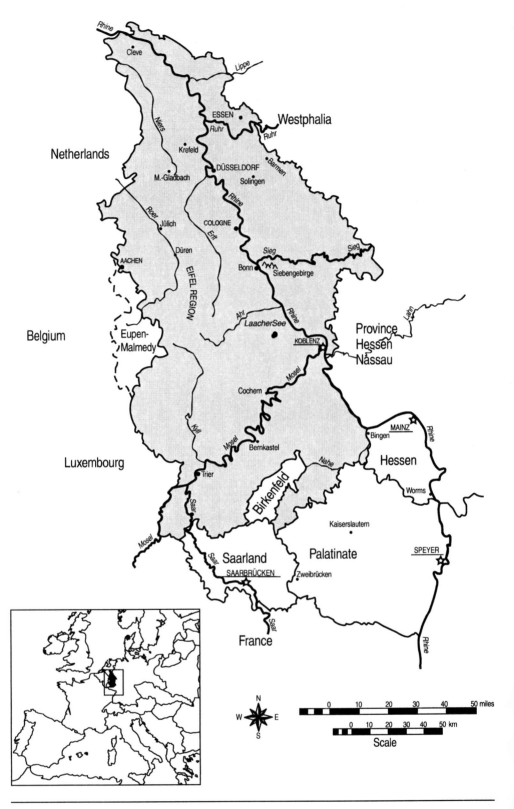

Map of the Rhine Province, 1936. *Source:* Landeshauptmann of the Rhine Province, ed.,
*Rheinprovinz und angrenzende Landesteile, Verwaltungsatlas 1936* (Düsseldorf, 1937).

# Introduction

"The German landscape seems very German to me," wrote the British author Stephen Spender on his journey through Germany in 1946, "because it is reflected in so many German poems and pictures, and often in the minds of the Germans."[1] Commenting on the visual impact of this landscape, Spender noted that it was

> as varied as that of any other country, yet much of it has in common a mental quality, less sensuous and luminous than France, less earthy than England. It is possible to think of it abstractly and it is possible to imagine it as full of intentions, moods. It doesn't suggest the gods and nymphs of Greece, nor is it haunted with the sense of individuals like England or France, but it is full of impulses, some warm and friendly, some sinister. It has been shaped and thought of and thought into, rather than civilized.[2]

Spender's words evoke one of the most powerful rhetorical means for grounding national identities in modern Europe: the assertion that there is an organic link between a people and its landscape. In Germany, the nineteenth-century Romantic cult of nature had saturated the landscape with symbolic meanings, creating a sublime naturalism running through the poetry of Heinrich Heine, the philosophy of Gottfried Herder, the visual art of Caspar David Friedrich, and the music of Richard Wagner. Romantic nationalists also used geographic features to endow the nation with a sense of longevity and permanence. When Ernst Moritz Arndt declared the Rhine in 1813 as "Germany's River, but not Germany's Border," he imagined the nation as an organic entity with a territorial foundation outside the vicissitudes of history, whose essence stood above class, religious, and regional divisions.

In his 1946 travels, Spender described a cultural landscape impregnated by this heady Romantic tradition, an environment with a "mental quality" distinguishing it from both the "sensuous" French countryside and the "earthy" English moors. Yet the debacle of Nazism and World War II had given the German landscape an ominous import not found in those other countries' nationalized topographies. In the war-ravaged German countryside, Spender could no longer simply appreciate the natural scenery as an aesthetic tableau; he found it instead "full of impulses, some warm and friendly, some sinister." In the textures of the landscape, Spender hoped to find clues that might resolve what had become a central question of German identity: how did the same culture that had inspired Heine and Friedrich also generate Adolf Hitler? Had the Nazi appeal to "Blood and Soil" perverted the Romantics' appreciation of nature, or had Romantic mysticism itself endowed the landscape with volatile moods and menacing intentions? For Spender, geography and history were intertwined; in the physical landscape lay the essence of the nation's identity.

When Spender wrote that the German landscape was "shaped and thought of and thought into, rather than civilized," he suggested that its visual impact reflected Germans' *conscious* efforts to maintain a balance between human priorities and unspoiled nature. British visitors such as Spender had been appreciating Germany's landscape since the late eighteenth century, when Britain emerged as the "workshop of the world" and the growth of cities such as London and Manchester spurred English Romantics to seek sublime nature along the banks of the Rhine. As Germany's own late-nineteenth-century industrialization and urbanization threatened to destroy the country's scenic landmarks, middle-class Germans were among the first in Europe to call on both the state and private citizens to protect their nation's environment. New associations formed, under the headings of *Naturschutz* (nature protection) and *Heimatschutz* (homeland protection), that transformed turn-of-the-century back-to-the-land impulses into a concrete environmental reform movement that by 1914 included tens of thousands of members located in every German state and province.³ These organizations dedicated themselves to a variety of nature preservation activities, including researching and creating inventories of Germany's natural features, lobbying government agencies to pass regulations designed to protect the *Heimat* landscape, and raising public awareness about both the beauty of nature and the need to care for the natural environment. As part of the modernizing efforts of the Weimar Republic, these organizations also began in the 1920s to involve themselves in regional landscape conservation, known as *Landschaftspflege,* that advocated future-oriented, environmentally sensitive planning, a forerunner of today's sustainable development. Long before the ecological activism and Green movements of the 1970s and 1980s, Germany had a highly organized nature protection movement that criticized industrial capitalism's destruction of the natural environment and laid the institutional foundation for modern environmental regulation.⁴

The beneficial aesthetic and ecological results of these early movements' efforts to protect nature and to plan development were evident in the German landscape that Spender experienced in 1946, as they are today. They included nature preserves such as the Siebengebirge along the Rhine near Bonn and the Lüneburger Heath near Hamburg, the green belts and urban parks surrounding Cologne and Berlin that created "lungs" for the city, and the compact villages in Bavaria that were built around their medieval cores rather than being allowed to sprawl into the surrounding countryside. Despite the aesthetic and ecological benefits of these measures, however, their political legacy and cultural significance remain as problematic today as they were for Spender in the immediate postwar era. The same groups that supported environmental reform in Germany became some of the most ardent supporters of National Socialism in 1933, abandoning the perceived materialism and instability of liberal democracy in favor of a dictatorship that promised to return Germany to its roots in Blood and Soil. Unlike the American environmental movement, which looks back proudly on a century of progressive environmental reform, the German movement is thus burdened with an ambiguous political and moral legacy. Here environmentalism has appeared in shades of both green and brown.⁵ Landscape preservationists' support for Nazism poses a dilemma for German environmental historians: did preservationists' admirable efforts to set German industrialization on a more sustainable environmental path also help to push the country on a "special path" *(Sonderweg)* that rejected modernity and rationality altogether in favor of Nazism's mystical appeal to Blood and Soil? Or were preservationists' efforts to protect their homeland environment a reflection of regional and local identities divorced from these larger political concerns, which modern environmentalists might applaud as harbingers of a greener future? By studying German nature protection between 1885 and 1945, this book shows that the contradictory "intentions" and ominous "moods" Spender detected in the German landscape found expression in these movements' varied reformist impulses, political aims, and popular reception during the period.

Landscape preservation movements first emerged in Germany in the 1880s as a form of cultural politics that articulated educated middle-class Germans' anxieties about their national identity, the pace and scope of industrialization and urbanization, and the aesthetic deterioration of the rural countryside. Their concerns were not "ecological" in a modern sense; these early defenders of nature rarely spoke about such environmental issues as acid rain, the health effects of unseen toxic pollutants, the resource strain caused by overpopulation, or the intrinsic value of nonhuman species. Instead, they interpreted environmental destruction through a nationalist lens, arguing that nature's aesthetic "disfigurement" *(Verunstaltung)* would surely erode Germany's distinctive national character, destroying the balance of nature within its borders and leading to its population's moral decline. German preservationists imagined the country's rural landscapes, scenic landmarks, and indigenous flora and fauna as "natural monuments" that anchored the organic foundation of national identity. They served as tactile and perdurable markers of the primordial homeland first settled by Germanic tribes and destined to hold the German nation.

Such evidence of national longevity was especially important to Germany, the so-called belated nation, which had been unified only since 1871 and whose pathway to modernity was punctuated by political instability. During the period between 1871 and 1945 Germans organized themselves into three different political communities, mobilized their natural and intellectual resources to become the Continent's leading industrial power, and provoked two world wars that resulted in millions of casualties and unprecedented destruction on the home front. Amid this turmoil, preservationists offered a stable and supposedly apolitical vision of German nationhood that was rooted in the natural landscape, even as Germans reinvented their political community as an authoritarian constitutional monarchy (the so-called Second Empire, the Kaiserreich of 1871–1918), a parliamentary democracy (the Weimar Republic, 1919–1933), and a racist dictatorship (the National Socialist era, 1933–1945). Behind the rhetoric of organic permanence were fundamental changes in the goals, practice, and meaning of both *Naturschutz* and *Heimatschutz*. The aims of landscape preservation—indeed what counted as *natural* in preservationist discourse—shifted radically as preservationists tried to articulate their vision of environmental reform in this ever-changing political terrain.

Landscape preservationists' attempts to imagine Germany in the natural landscape reveal the close ties between environmental perception and nationalism that existed during this period. As recent scholarship on the formation of national identities has demonstrated, European nation-states were products of cultural innovation and social engineering rather than autonomous collective identities that existed prior to their discursive and symbolic articulation. Initiated by Romantic intellectuals in the early nineteenth century and then "mass produced" between 1880 and 1914, the nation as a social identity soon transformed ordinary men and women, peasants and workers, bourgeois and aristocrats, into Germans, Frenchmen, or Italians.[6] Eric Hobsbawm has characterized this period as the "heyday of invented traditions," a time when Europeans reinvigorated or even created new dynastic lineages, ancient rituals, and time-honored festivals.[7] Such practices provided nation-states with cultural legitimacy and a sense of heritage in an age of rapid industrialization and social change. This study extends Hobsbawm's analysis to the organic world, arguing that landscape preservationists participated actively in the cultural construction of nationhood by envisioning natural landmarks as touchstones of emotional identification, symbols of national longevity, and signs of a new form of environmental stewardship. As Anthony Smith has argued, natural features "can delimit and locate a community in the landscape" by recalling symbolic crises, dramatic events, or turning points in the history of the community and by endowing the group with "foci of creative energy."[8] German landscape preservation organizations, like parallel movements in Great Britain, France, and the United States in this period, helped to shape this cultural nationalization of landscape. Preservationists argued that nature, unlike art works, historic buildings, or royal monuments, required no education, breeding, or taste to interpret; it was a cultural good whose aesthetic immediacy and accessibility were available to all Germans, regardless of class, gender, or religious background.

To popularize nature protection and outdoor experiences, preservationists published newsletters, wrote newspaper editorials, participated in school curriculum reform efforts, and established youth camps to train the masses in a new mode of seeing and experiencing natural features as facets of a shared homeland topography. Modern technologies that mechanically reproduced nature in postcards, journals, photographs, and stories also shaped ordinary consumption and recreation toward nationalist ends. Even ordinary practices such as hiking took on new cultural meaning after 1890. Natural vistas along walking trails above "Father Rhine," for example, allowed wanderers to visualize the connections between local natural monuments and the far corners of the German fatherland. Preservationists' efforts to set aside natural monuments from industrialization did not merely prevent environmental destruction but *produced* new political identities by naturalizing modern political borders and schooling local citizens in the aesthetic beauties of nature.

Of greatest concern to Germany's landscape preservationists was the effect of industrial modernity on the character and contours of *Heimat,* a word that signifies a deep emotional attachment to place.[9] Many German preservationists embraced the views of Wilhelm Heinrich Riehl, a conservative social theorist of the mid-nineteenth century, who insisted that environmental stewardship and nature conservation were essential to preserving national character.[10] In the first volume of Riehl's monumental *Natural History of the German People,* which he titled *Land and People (Land und Leute),* Riehl disparaged the French Enlightenment view that nationhood was a product of written constitutions, abstract natural rights, or the protection of private property; instead he proposed that national character emerged organically, from the topography and culture of a particular territory.[11] Like his intellectual predecessors Herder and Arndt, Riehl proposed that each landscape, be it national, regional, or local, reflected centuries of interaction between an area's human inhabitants and their natural environment. The resulting cultural landscape mirrored the inhabitants' unique settlement patterns and formed a repos-

itory of collective memory that anchored the *Heimat* community in
space and time. Riehl's "sociology of habitat" thus created a new
moral geography that charged ordinary features of the *Heimat* landscape—including forests, rivers, rock formations, and heaths—with
symbolic meaning.[12] He argued that Germany's strength lay in the diversity and health of its regional landscapes, and he elevated emotional identification with one's local region to a form of national patriotism. Following Riehl, many nineteenth-century observers recast
the aesthetic enjoyment of forests, meadows, and rock formations
as a form of sacred patriotic devotion, arguing that such landmarks
needed to be revered and protected as the very essence of
Germanness. More important, they asserted that nature conservation
served a real purpose: guarding the roots of national character and
stabilizing the society. As Riehl once remarked, "We must retain the
forest not only to keep our stoves from growing cold in winter, but
also to keep the pulse of our nation beating warmly and happily. We
need it to keep Germany German."[13]

Despite the politically conservative origins of *Heimat* discourse,
the historian Celia Applegate has noted that the concept has been
used in such a diverse array of political contexts and ideological debates in German culture that it is impossible to describe it as inherently reactionary.[14] Though ethnic-racialist or *völkisch* discourses
of *Heimat* flourished in late nineteenth- and early twentieth-century
Germany, these potentially xenophobic understandings of homeland
coexisted with local, regional, pluralist, and even democratic meanings, especially in the west-central Rhineland and parts of southern
Germany.[15] As Applegate's research has shown, Germany's status as a
"nation of provincials," a country forged by Bismarck's agglomera-
tion of once-independent provinces, cities, and kingdoms in 1871,
led to a decentralized conception of homeland within regional *Heimat*
movements.[16] *Heimat* provided a framework for negotiating the differences between national, regional, and local identities in German
society, in which Rhinelanders, Swabians, and Saxons retained their
provincial distinctiveness while contributing to the German nation
as a whole. Far from being antithetical to nation building, in other
words, *Heimat* created what Alon Confino has termed a "common
denominator of variousness" that gave the newly created German nation the emotional accessibility of the familiar hometown, linking
an individual's lifeworld to Bismarck's political creation.[17] Provin-

cial *Heimat* advocates also proposed that homeland sentiments super-ceded political, social, and religious differences, providing common ground in the fractious political scene of Second Empire Germany and beyond. Most important, *Heimat* provided a touchstone of identity amid the maelstrom of change ushered in by rapid modernization, affixing personal memory to the mental map of the homeland.

Though *Heimat* provided a malleable "system of sentiments" that called for attachment to place amid the displacements of modernity, it was not an empty, sentimental metaphor used to divert provincial Germans from "real" political engagement or to buttress regional elites' cultural authority. *Heimat* societies' activities included the creation of local heritage and natural history museums, research into local folklore and dialects, the publication of regional histories, and historic preservation. Such endeavors gave the homeland a concrete existence that attracted a broad spectrum of German society to civic engagement in the community: urban professionals, the petite bourgeoisie, and white-collar workers.[18] Nature- and landscape-protection activities linked such *Heimat* sentiments to a familiar topography, offering venues for bourgeois civic participation in this regional and local institutional milieu. Most landscape preservation organizations developed as branches of regional natural history groups, beautification societies, and hiking clubs; many even received funds from provincial officials interested in galvanizing regional loyalty. Landscape preservationists fortified the ability of *Heimat* to bridge the local and the national by envisioning German strength emanating upward from the country's mosaic of unique regional landscapes, rather than downward from the Reich capital of Berlin. By hiking in the *Heimat,* studying a local bird species, or creating a plaque marking a unique natural landmark, individuals gave the nation a tangible, emotive quality that linked individual life stories to the collective memory of *Heimat,* enabling provincial Germans to visualize, touch, and even smell their particular region as part of a larger geographical entity: the German nation. Preservationists trusted that individuals would thereby experience the landscape as "Germans," members of a community tied to a particular place, rather than as citizens of an abstract political territory.

To understand this regionalist inflection of *Heimat* and landscape preservation, this study focuses on one of Germany's most recognized districts: the west-central Rhineland, particularly the former Prussian

Rhine Province. This region provides an ideal site of investigation because of the tensions that emerged there between rapid industrialization and urbanization, on the one hand, and the desire to protect the area's symbolic landscapes, particularly the scenic Rhine Valley, on the other. Though cultural historians have often identified the forest as the quintessential symbol of German identity, many Romantics saw the nation's origins as fluvial rather than sylvan, with the Rhine serving as the lifeblood of German culture in much the same way that the Nile and the Ganges had nourished Egyptian and Indian civilizations. As the former border between the Roman Empire to the west and Germanic tribes to the east, the Rhine River was rhetorically cast in the nineteenth century as the geographic birthplace of German national consciousness. The German *Volk* had expelled Napoleon's armies across Father Rhine, claiming both sides of the river as German territory and rebuffing French claims to the waterway as France's "natural border."[19] Not surprisingly, this history charged the region's natural scenery with added emotional significance; as Simon Schama has aptly noted, "Landscapes are culture before they are nature; constructs of the imagination projected onto wood and water and rock."[20] In the case of the Rhine, nationalism shaped aesthetic experience by transforming the international Rhine into Germany's quintessential river and envisioning the ruins of fortresses left by King Louis XIII's troops in the Thirty Years' War as proof that France had been Germany's "eternal enemy" for centuries. The Rhineland's scenic beauty, Roman and medieval ruins, and political significance also inspired the early nineteenth-century literary and aesthetic movement known as Rhine Romanticism *(Rheinromantik)* that included artists and writers as diverse as Lord Byron, Mary Shelley, Clemens Brentano, Caspar David Friedrich, and Heinrich Heine.[21] English visitors who appreciated the natural contours of the informal eighteenth-century landscape garden portrayed the Rhineland as an open garden designed by God that merged divine nature with the humble efforts of human beings to toil in the valley's rich vineyards and fisheries. Rhine Romantic enthusiasm helped to create Germany's first nature protection reserve in the Rhine Province, the Siebengebirge near Bonn, as well as the country's oldest preservationist organizations.

Alongside this rich natural heritage, however, lay Europe's busiest shipping corridor and its most productive coalfields, which soon transformed the Rhine Province into one of the Continent's most densely populated and industrialized regions. Three key events—the Congress of Vienna's creation of an international commission designed to remove commercial barriers to free trade along the river in 1815, the advent of steamship travel in 1816, and the inauguration of Baden engineer Johann G. Tulla's project to "tame" the meandering Rhine in 1817—transformed the river into an industrial canal shorn of its biological and visual diversity. The end of hundreds of river tolls, the introduction of mechanized transport, the removal of natural impediments such as the fabled Lorelei rocks, and the straightening of the Rhine's bed enabled freighters to move upstream with ease, making Rotterdam at the mouth of the Rhine the world's largest ocean harbor and allowing navigation as far as Basel, Switzerland, by the early twentieth century. Such "improvement" also enabled mining and manufactured products to move downstream and across the globe at an accelerated pace. The Rhine Province encompassed approximately one-third of the Ruhr basin's bituminous coal-mining region as well as the lignite coalfields known as the "Ville" near Krefeld, natural resources that helped to create Europe's densest concentration of iron and steel foundries. Basalt and trachyte mining in the former volcanic hills of the Siebengebirge provided weather-resistant materials for roads, bridges, and other structures. During the second industrial revolution, the Rhineland emerged as the center of Germany's booming chemical-pharmaceutical sector, with firms such as Bayer, BASF, and Hoechst settling along the river's banks to take advantage of freshwater supplies and transportation possibilities.[22]

Natural advantages and industrial technology thus combined to situate the Rhineland as a catalyst for Germany's economic transformation from a largely agrarian society in 1850 into the Continent's leading industrial power on the eve of World War I, but the ecological results were devastating. As Mark Cioc notes in his recent eco-biography of the Rhine: "The river's most celebrated features—its variegated landscape, quirky flow, and treacherous cliffs—were once the stuff of myth and legend. Now the river more resembles a canal— a monotony of barges and ore carriers—than a fabled or mysterious stream; and it flows more like an industrial faucet than a natural river."[23] The process of transforming the Rhine landscape into an industrial center involved bitter clashes between landscape preservationists, on the one hand, and state and commercial interests beholden to the myth of economic progress, on the other. The region thus offers unique insights into how private organizations and state planners tried to mediate between conflicting demands for natural resources and environmental protection.

Though landscape preservationists admired the natural balance and social cohesion of the preindustrial German homeland, they were not agrarian Romantics who paved the ideological path for the emergence of Nazi Blood and Soil. Until recently, many historians viewed the Wilhelmine and Weimar eras' back-to-the-land impulses as reactionary and protofascist, part of the "special path" of German bourgeois culture that shunned cosmopolitan Enlightenment values and Germany's emerging urban-industrial society in favor of *völkisch* myths and rural imagery.[24] In this view, bourgeois elites' aesthetic preference for the supposedly unchanging countryside manifested a deeply conservative, "feudalized" social vision. Borrowed from the aristocracy that the German middle classes had failed to topple in the revolution of 1848, this vision clung to old-regime privilege in the face of new democratic demands from the masses. As more recent scholarship has shown, however, most *Naturschutz* and *Heimatschutz* advocates were urban professionals who saw industrialization as a necessary evil but believed it could be steered along more environmentally sustainable and aesthetically beautiful paths.[25] The cultural historian William Rollins, for example, has demonstrated convincingly that Wilhelmine *Heimatschutz* organizations showed a nuanced understanding of the causes and consequences of environmental degradation in the German countryside, calling for a "thorough-going reform of German land-use practices, including such things as the retention of hedgerows, a commitment to mixed forests, and a halt to excessive stream regulation." What scholars of the 1950s and 1960s viewed as antimodern, *völkisch* longings appear eminently practical given today's ecological concerns; as Rollins has remarked, "If these were irrational little games, it would appear that the standard of what is rational and what is not may need to be reconsidered."[26]

Though Rollins's revisionist work overstates landscape preservationists' commitment to liberal political reform and democratization, his work makes Wilhelmine *Heimatschutz* seem much more mainstream than did previous scholarship, animated by the same bourgeois and paternalist reform impulses as the American Sierra Club and the British National Trust.[27] By creating nature conservation regions and instituting land-use planning measures, preservationists sought to create a landscape that balanced tradition and industrialism; by reshaping the population's aesthetic sensibilities and stimulating *Heimat* feeling, they hoped to forge a more unified nation. Neither goal was in itself reactionary. Indeed, as Thomas Rohkrämer has recently argued, Germany's tradition of cultural criticism from its educated middle classes (or *Bildungsbürgertum*), which disparaged the leveling tendencies of capitalist *Zivilisation* on German *Kultur*, offered a creative response to the social and environmental crises generated by modernity. Bourgeois elites within the landscape preservation movement sought to tame technological development and the ever-increasing rationalization of everyday life, to bring modernizing processes into line with humanitarian principles and naturalistic insights. They sought a "different and better" modernity, not the rejection of modernity altogether.[28]

These scholars' revisions of previous approaches to landscape preservation and middle-class cultural reform have thus opened up new ways of conceptualizing landscape preservation. Their assertion that *Naturschutz* and *Heimatschutz* organizations were actively engaged in shaping modernity, not turning their backs on it, resonates throughout this study. Yet these new interpretations still leave open a crucial question: if landscape preservation and *Heimat* protection were creative, environmentally informed responses to the crises of modernization, why and how did many preservationists become ardent advocates of National Socialism? Landscape preservation leaders were early and enthusiastic supporters of the National Socialist regime. Many of them believed that Blood and Soil signified a commitment to reforming German society and the economy according to environmental precepts and natural laws, and they cheered the Nazis' destruction of liberal individualism in favor of a centralized, organic state. The Nazi movement, in turn, counted several leaders who had environmentalist sympathies, including Agriculture Minister Richard Walther Darré and Forestry Minister Walter von Keudell. In 1935, the Third Reich even passed the world's most comprehensive piece of environmental conservation legislation, known as the Reich Nature Protection Law, which expanded the number of nature protection regions and created stringent new land-use planning regulations.

This right-wing radicalization of environmental politics was a product of a variety of historically specific factors. Among the most significant reasons for radicalization were the militarization of *Heimat* rhetoric in World War I, the increasing reliance of *Heimatschutz* and *Naturschutz* organizations on state patronage in the early Weimar era, and preservationists' sometimes hostile response to mass society and cultural Modernism in the 1920s—which this study analyzes in the following chapters. The Nazification of *Naturschutz* was by no means preordained in the Wilhelmine era; *Heimat* was not, as some scholars have argued, an inherently "ominous utopia," nor did "back to nature" inevitably lead to racist nationalism and social Darwinism.[29] Indeed, only by examining the entire scope of landscape preservation in the early twentieth century can we see the *discontinuities* between regional landscape preservationists' vision of *Heimat* nature and the National Socialist program of Blood and Soil. Their ideological and institutional rift made the National Socialists' "synchronization" *(Gleichschaltung)* of regional environmentalist groups far more uneven, contentious, and unfinished than many scholars of these movements have assumed.[30]

Despite notable achievements such as the Reich Nature Protection Law, the degree of National Socialist commitment to environmental reform remains a highly contentious issue. Adolf Hitler's highly publicized statements about the need to protect the German countryside and Agriculture Minister Darré's support of organic farming experiments have led several historians to speak of a "Green wing" within the National Socialist movement, drawing questionable connections between the environmental dimensions of Blood and Soil and modern Green sensibilities. Describing the Nazi regime's environmentalist commitment, Simon Schama has written that, "arguably, no German government had ever taken the protection of the German forests more seriously than the Third Reich and its Reichsforstminister Göring . . . It is, of course, painful to acknowledge how ecologically conscientious the most barbaric regime in modern history actually was. Exterminating millions of lives was not at all incompatible with passionate protection for millions of trees."[31] In a similar vein, the historian Anna Bramwell described Darré as "Father of the Greens" in a series of polemical books and articles in the mid-1980s.[32] Yet these bold assertions about the extent of Nazi environmental protection and its relationship to modern Green thought have not been followed up by concrete studies of the regime's implementation of the Reich Nature Protection Law at the regional and local levels, even though landscape preservation remained highly decentralized despite the Third Reich's totalitarian aims.

This book examines the goals of Nazi environmental policy, its implementation in the Rhineland and other provinces, and the relationship between regime initiatives and existing *Heimatschutz* and *Naturschutz* efforts. Although the Nazis' effort to conduct their national revolution according to "natural laws" promised a greater role for landscape preservation in the state's cultural politics, the Third Reich systematically subordinated environmental concern to economic recovery and war mobilization, threatening decades of preservation efforts through *Autobahn* construction, rearmament, land reclamation, and dam building. The regime touted the "Aryan" race's will to reshape the landscape and conquer *Lebensraum,* a claim that offered little protection for the natural landscape and threatened preservationists' vision of Germany as a diffuse tapestry of culturally and historically shaped landscapes.

Although this study focuses on the cultural and nationalist significance of German landscape preservation, its implications go beyond the German case to engage broader questions raised by environmental historians about the relationship between environmental perception, political change, and cultural symbols. In the past decade, the so-called wilderness debate has animated American environmental historiography, yet few environmental historians have considered whether the terms of this discussion apply outside the United States. In a recent critique of the American wilderness tradition, the environmental historian William Cronon argued that wilderness advocates such as John Muir and Aldo Leopold created a dichotomy between nature and civilization that placed human beings entirely outside the natural. This dichotomy depicted all human use as abuse, setting too high a standard for what counts as pristine, and encouraging individuals to escape the immediate environmental ramifications of their actions in distant preserves of sublime natural beauty. Cronon called for a new environmental ethic that values "a common middle ground . . . in which all of these things, from the city to the wilderness, can somehow be encompassed in the word 'home.'"[33] Cronon's perspective has triggered enormous controversy within American environmental history and environmentalism, with defenders of wilderness as a pristine site uncontaminated by modern civilization pitted against those welcoming a more human-centered form of environmental perception and stewardship.[34]

The wilderness debate has not unleashed similar controversy among German and European environmental historians. As Mark Cioc noted in a recent review of German environmental history, "the impact of human activity over the past two millenia in Central Europe has been so conspicuous" that German environmental historians have always assumed that the object of their analyses is a cultivated "cultural landscape" rather than nature in itself.[35] As Cioc's review makes clear, German environmental history, or *Umweltgeschichte*, has thus focused largely on the ecological problems unleashed by industrial development and modern technologies—air, water, soil, and noise pollution—as they affect human communities.[36] My analysis of landscape preservation within the *Heimat* tradition bridges the two environmental traditions, offering comparative insights on the evolution of environmental stewardship in these two highly industrialized, consumerist societies. German preservationists' desire to protect the cultural landscapes of *Heimat* is noticeably similar to Cronon's environmental ethic of home, suggesting that American environmental historians interested in alternatives to the wilderness tradition in Western society will benefit from studying Germany's environmental history.

Unlike the American wilderness ethic, an ideal that has valued spaces devoid of human influence, the Germans' concept of *Landschaft* envisioned the ideal environment in a pastoral sense, as a cultivated garden that blends the natural, cultivated, and built environments in an aesthetically harmonious whole.[37] Reinforcing this sense of *Landschaft* as both a cultural and a natural space is the political meaning of the word, which refers to a unit of territorial administration, such as a province or region.[38] The two meanings of the word were often intertwined, so that the visual state of the *Landschaft* was thought to mirror the spiritual condition of the community. The German trajectory of environmental preservation also placed the cultural landscapes of home, not the sublime places of the distant wilderness, at the center of environmental perception and care. German preservationists' attention to place focused on the surrounding vernacular landscape; historic oak trees, nearby waterfalls, even local species of salamanders and turtles were sometimes designated as natural monuments. This attention to one's immediate, familiar surroundings produced a less dichotomous view of nature and culture than did the wilderness ethic; German landscape preservationists valued "second nature" just as highly as the remnants of "first nature." Their vision of the *Heimat* nature as a working landscape rather than a mere refuge from industrial ills, moreover, offered a vision of sustainability over time rather than mere compensation for industrial destruction.

German preservationists' optimistic conception of home as a site of emotional identification and environmental care is undoubtedly appealing, especially in a postmodern world of "expanding horizons and dissolving boundaries."[39] As wilderness loses some of its currency as both a symbolic place and a standard by which to judge human impact on the environment, an analysis of German landscape preservation offers environmental historians the opportunity to explore "home" as a middle ground between nature and civilization. Yet the recovery of this uniquely German environmental tradition must also confront the unsavory political appropriations of *Heimat* in Germany, demonstrating that "home" is an ideologically charged category whose meaning must be interrogated before it is offered as an alternative to the wilderness tradition. Although preservationists viewed their activities as apolitical, protecting a cultural good that transcended the petty squabbling of political parties and interest groups, German landscape preservation was never a neutral instrument of environmental reform. The movement shaped and was in turn shaped by the social values and ideological contradictions of Germany's transient political regimes in the early twentieth century. The result was a tradition of modern environmentalism that included an array of ideological positions—from the conservative paternalism of the Wilhelmine era to the racism of Nazi Blood and Soil ideology— that lay far to the right of the American progressive tradition.

In studying the trajectory of German landscape preservation between 1885 and 1945, we see that historically specific visions of nature and broader power relationships have shaped the goals of environmental reform. Chapter 1 of this volume examines the origins of landscape preservation in the Wilhelmine era (1888–1918) as a response to the environmental impact of and social tensions produced by rapid industrialization in the decades before World War I. In the campaign to protect the Siebengebirge, a scenic chain of hills near Bonn, Rhenish preservationists laid the foundation for the *Naturschutz* and *Heimatschutz* movements' bourgeois, aesthetic, and socially paternalistic approach to environmental reform. By protecting natural monuments and providing healthy recreation areas, preservationists hoped to reintegrate Germans of all political persuasions and social classes into the imagined *Heimat* community. Wilhelmine preservationists thus believed that environmental and moral improvement went hand in hand, with *Heimat* sentiments providing a bulwark against the leveling tendencies of modernity as well as a basis for new forms of environmental stewardship. Chapter 2 investigates the way landscape preservationists renegotiated the relationship between environmental protection, *Heimat,* and modernity in the contentious and often violent debates over German identity that surfaced in the wake of World War I (1918–1923). During the war, nature and *Heimat* protection became enmeshed in national and provincial efforts to secure the homefront in a cultural battle designed to mobilize the population's emotional loyalties. This attempt to use natural symbols to forge a mythic *Heimat* community mobilized against external and internal enemies continued in the Rhenish borderlands well into 1923, when Rhenish separatists, French occupation forces, and hyperinflation called into question Rhinelanders' sense of belonging to the German Reich. Preservationists' faith in the unifying power of nature to shape German character and dissolve political and social differences helped to resolve this cultural crisis, but not without a lingering undercurrent of anxiety about the character and boundaries of Germanness. This psychological unease ultimately made it difficult for preservationists to construct a pluralist vision of homeland that suited the Weimar Republic's liberal and democratic aspirations.

Despite these challenges, preservationists found new ways to articulate a modern vision of landscape protection amid growing economic rationalization, political democratization, and mass consumerism between 1925 and 1932. Chapter 3 shows that the Weimar era's streamlining and corporatist restructuring of industrial production processes encouraged provincial officials and landscape architects to develop parallel discourses about land use. These groups sought to link traditional *Naturschutz* and *Heimatschutz* to landscape conservation, or *Landschaftspflege,* a new, holistic, and functionally driven form of regional land-use planning. Amid lingering fears of worker unrest after the revolution of 1918 and public concern over the "superfluous" younger generation, preservationists referred to nature experiences as the most important "social healing method" in an era of unprecedented social dislocation and political unrest. By the end of the 1920s, preservationists had abandoned nineteenth-century Romanticism in favor of an objective approach that emphasized applied science, not sentiment, to stem Germany's environmental destruction and resolve its social woes.

Chapters 4 and 5 focus on the Nazi era. Chapter 4 examines the *Gleichschaltung* of landscape preservation organizations and the Third Reich's uneven attempt to incorporate *Heimat* and nature protection ideologically and institutionally into its emerging racial state. The synergy between Nazism and *Naturschutz* was based not on antimodern agrarian Romanticism, but rather on a shared belief in the therapeutic power of nature and centralized landscape planning to effect far-reaching social change. Yet there were important differences between preservationists' environmentalism and Nazism's racist conceptions of social reform that caused *Gleichschaltung* to remain uneven. Chapter 5 analyzes the discrepancy between the Third Reich's environmentally friendly image and the massive environmental destruction wrought by Nazi development projects. Rather than protecting the *Heimat* landscape, the regime favored a form of environmental mitigation pioneered by *Autobahn* landscape architects that used ecological restoration to regenerate destroyed natural areas. These so-called landscape advocates touted their efforts as a form of biological restoration, reflecting a faith in applied science that meshed well with the regime's racial-hygienic policies.

The conclusion reviews the key political, cultural, and environmental factors that precipitated the decline of regional landscape preservation in the postwar era and paved the way for the ecologically inclined Green movement to emerge in the 1970s. Though *Heimatschutz* and *Naturschutz* activities continued unabated into the 1950s, Germans faced intractable environmental problems in the postwar era that challenged preservationists' aesthetic approach to environmental reform. Moreover, as Germans sought to overcome the Nazi past by identifying themselves with a "European" community that transcended national borders, *Heimat* rhetoric that described the landscape as a reflection of national character appeared suspect. The new environmental fears and transnational political context made landscape preservationists' focus on visual aesthetics and the emotional appeal of *Heimat* appear outdated. The new environmental problems and the transformation of German political identities paved the way for the popular reception of ecosystem paradigms that superseded the cultural landscape at the center of the German environmental imagination.

# Nature's Homelands: The Origins of Landscape Preservation, 1885–1914

The nature protection movement wants to preserve the richness and
beauty of the nature of our *Heimat,* so that the people can draw from her
joy and instruction.

—KONRAD GUENTHER, *DER NATURSCHUTZ* (1912)

Though nineteenth-century Romanticism revered nature as a source
of divine inspiration and national character, the movement brought
little in the way of concrete nature protection measures. Germany's
natural environment grew in importance as a site of refuge from the
city and inspired artistic and literary works, yet little was done to
maintain its features until late in the century. Technological optimism
predominated in the Kaiserreich (1871–1918); as the noted author
Stefan Zweig once wrote: "This belief in the uninterrupted, inexorable 'progress' truly had the power of a religion; people believed in this
progress more than the Bible, its Gospel appeared irrefutably proven
by the daily new wonders of science and technology."[1] Proof came in
the form of steamships and street cars, electric telegraphs and electric
lighting, artificial dyes and new tonics for minor ailments; change in
itself appeared as an inherent good. During the second industrial revolution, between 1880 and 1914, Germany emerged as the European
continent's premier industrial power, making the decisive transition
from an agrarian and rural society to an industrialized and urbanized
one. By 1907, owing to inner migration, nearly half of the country's
citizens did not live in their place of birth. Though the size of the
country increased by half between 1870 and 1900, cities grew twice
as fast as the population as a whole; a country that was two-thirds rural in 1870 became two-thirds urban by 1900.[2] As the pace of change
accelerated, with new transportation modes making transcontinental

travel easier and novel communication technologies allowing real-time long-distance messages, people's sense of time and space began to collapse. The modern individual without an organic connection to history or place was born. This process also led many to perceive their natural and built environments in new ways. As intellectual historian Thomas Rohkrämer has argued, "Even though humankind had already transformed its environment before, the creation of a 'second nature' achieved a new character. The world has since then become ever more an artifact."[3] The hand of humankind seemed to be everywhere in Europe, making it difficult to locate an authentic natural world that counterbalanced the forces of civilization.

Not all Germans celebrated these changes in their environment. During the 1880s, a growing cadre of individuals within educated middle-class circles began to argue that industrialization and urbanization threatened to wipe out Germany's historic landscapes and to destroy the last remnants of primordial nature existing within the country's borders. These individuals bemoaned the spread into the rural countryside of smoking factories, high-tension power lines, regulated streambeds, and crass billboards, which they argued "disfigured" the national homeland. These nascent environmentalists contended that the country needed a program of state regulations, private initiatives, and public education dedicated to preserving the landscape against the capitalist onslaught in order to protect the values of *Heimat,* or homeland, for future generations. Much of the real work of nature protection and *Heimat* protection began in Germany's provinces, where local groups battled state indifference and entrenched propertied interests to save endangered scenic areas.

One of Germany's first organized landscape protection campaigns—the effort to save the Siebengebirge hill country near Bonn from the mining industry—developed out of preservationists' *Heimat*-centered and aesthetic approach to environmental reform. Rhenish preservationists recast the language of Rhine Romanticism for a late-nineteenth-century urban audience, convincing Prussian state and Rhenish provincial authorities that this natural monument embodied the character and aspirations of the entire people. They asserted that the Siebengebirge deserved protection because, unlike historic buildings or works of art, it emanated an aura of longevity impervious to the flux of historical events, political debates, and social unrest. Nature protection thus served a larger patriotic and socially therapeutic purpose, anchoring the moral geography of *Heimat* and linking individuals' subjective experiences in nature to the larger national community, regardless of class, religion, or regional origin. The rhetoric of nature preservation and the promise to protect the imagined contours of the *Heimat* landscape also articulated bourgeois cultural anxieties about the pace, scope, and effects of modernization, filtering ecological concerns through an aesthetic and nationalist lens. The success of the Siebengebirge campaign made it a model of public-private cooperation in nature protection and nature preservation, influencing the national environmental reform efforts that came on the scene in 1904.

One wing of this national campaign for environmental reform, associated with the Danzig botanist Hugo Conwentz, was known as *Naturdenkmalpflege* (literally, the "care of natural monuments"), which I will refer to as natural monument preservation. Alexander von Humboldt had first used the term *Naturdenkmal* to refer to unusual or historically significant trees.[4] Natural monument preservation was closely associated with historical monument preservation, or *Denkmalpflege,* which protected and restored a broad array of memorials and commemorative sites, including intentionally constructed monuments of battles or famous statesmen; historically significant parts of the built environment, such as buildings, walls, or ruins; and works of art from the past, especially pieces of sculpture and religious relics from the Roman and medieval periods.[5] During the nineteenth century, several German states, including Prussia, Baden, and Bavaria, had established monument preservation offices to inventory and preserve such objects as part of a cultural-political effort to legitimate their monarchies and edify the public.[6] When Conwentz established the Prussian State Office for Natural Monument Preservation (Staatliche Stelle für Naturdenkmalpflege) in 1904, he transferred the nationalist and educational goals of *Denkmalpflege* to the natural environment. The state office sought, with the help of private organizations, to identify and preserve scientifically valuable natural objects, such as rare geological formations, as well as large-scale parcels with characteristic plants and animals, known as nature protection regions.

At about the same time, the Dresden music professor Ernst Rudorff created the German Association for Homeland Protection (Deutscher Bund Heimatschutz, or DBH) to protect Germany's characteristic his-

torical landscapes from further destruction.[7] In contrast to Conwentz's natural monument preservation, which viewed protecting individual landmarks or conservation regions as its key task, the
*Heimatschutz* movement viewed *Naturdenkmalpflege* as only one
facet of a broader program of heritage preservation and environmental reform. In Rudorff's view, *Heimatschutz* encompassed the entire
"physiognomy" of the landscape, including both the natural and the
built environment of each regional or municipality. Within *Heimatschutz* organizations, therefore, protecting meadows and forests went
hand in hand with restoring peasant cottages, researching rural customs, and publishing poetry and stories in regional dialects.[8] The
turn of the nineteenth century thus marked a watershed in Germans'
perception and use of the natural environment. It signaled a shift
away from considering the natural environment solely in terms of
economic development, artistic appreciation, and recreation and toward actively preserving and managing natural features as part of the
country's national heritage.

Central to *Heimatschutz* and *Naturschutz* alike was a belief that
the landscape was both a product and an active shaper of Germans'
unique natural character; German culture, they argued, was "closer
to nature" than that of other European nations. Konrad Guenther's
faith that nature's beauties would bring "joy" and "instruction" to
the people reflected this sentiment. Guenther believed that such experiences would stimulate ordinary Germans' emotional attachment to
the national homeland in a time of rapid economic development, social instability, and political divisiveness. Though both movements
gradually broadened their activities to promote recognizably ecological concerns such as sustainable forestry, habitat protection for endangered species, and wetland conservation, their initial program reflected prevailing bourgeois notions of environmentalism. This form
of environmentalism saw nature protection primarily as a form of
social reform. Conwentz, Rudorff, and Guenther all believed that
there was a causal link between an aesthetically pleasing environment
and an individual's proper moral and physiological development, as
well as a close connection between environmental health, national
character, and social stability. They blamed a variety of social and
political ills—including working-class discontent and the incessant
wrangling between political parties—on Germans' alienation from
the natural landscape, the physical substrate of *Heimat* sentiment.

Landscape preservation thus transformed the idiom of Romantic nature aestheticism to suit the needs of a mass industrial society, providing a bulwark of ideal values in an age of material progress.

Preservationists' message of national renewal based on a return to nature and *Heimat* was shared by a number of other cultural reform, back-to-the-land, and "life reform" *(Lebensreform)* movements that flourished during the Wilhelmine era, the political and cultural period marked by Wilhelm II's ascension to the throne in 1888 and the collapse of the Kaiserreich in 1918. The desire to locate German identity in an organic community of *Heimat* away from the city, for example, found expression in rural preservation organizations such as Heinrich Sohnrey's German Association for the Care of Rural Welfare and *Heimat,* as well as in the *Heimatkunst* movement in literature and art that rejected amoral realism in favor of sentimental motifs unfolding in rural settings. Nature preservationism also resembled the Garden City movement, which sought to plan cities with expansive green spaces, lower population densities, and factories located away from residential areas. In their attempts to promote outdoor recreation as a path to higher forms of spirituality and self-cultivation, *Heimat* enthusiasts also shared ideological affinities with youth hiking organizations such as the *Wandervögel,* founded in 1899, as well as with the growing numbers of vegetarians, nudists, and "natural healing" advocates. Taken as a whole, groups with such neo-Romantic reform tendencies believed that nature offered an authenticity that could not be found in the barrenness of urban life.[9]

Back-to-nature discourses that envisioned nature as a source of healing for industrial society appeared especially urgent to bourgeois observers in the Rhineland during this period. In this region, the rise of new political and social movements, especially political Catholicism and social democracy, appeared to be unraveling the national consensus and enthusiasm that had accompanied the defeat of France and the creation of the Second Empire in 1871. Bismarck's "cultural battle" *(Kulturkampf)* against Catholicism, which the area's Protestant National Liberal Party had supported, had weakened the traditional alliance between liberals and Catholics against Prussian hegemony. Catholics' sense of alienation from Prussia and the national state had fueled the growth of the Center Party, which by 1914 had become the province's largest political party.[10] Bismarck's attempt to destroy the nascent Social Democratic Party (Sozialdemokratische

Partei Deutschlands, or SPD) by outlawing it between 1878 and 1890 had also left a bitter legacy in the province, galvanizing the party's appeal among the Rhineland's industrial workers.[11] In this context, preservationists appealed to nature as a unifier of *Heimat* and *Volk,* one that might integrate disparate social and political factions on the basis of shared homeland sentiment. Far from an "agrarian-romantic" strategy to pacify the masses through preindustrial imagery, however, preservationists' desire to imagine Germany in the natural landscape articulated a form of middle-class paternalism designed to manage industrial and urban modernity through cultural reform, not to reject it altogether. They envisioned an alternative modernity in which landscape sustainability, industrial technology, and *Heimat* sentiment could grow together "organically," ensuring the nation's future through careful cultivation of its natural-historical past.

## Rhine Romanticism and the Revolution in Nature Perception

The Rhineland's cultural landscape became world famous in the early nineteenth century for its historical significance and scenic beauty, inspiring European Romantics to seek out the sublime in the meandering river, the striated cliffs of the Lorelei, the play of light and shadow caused by billowy cloud banks from the North Sea, and the ruins of medieval fortresses and cloisters. Rivers had an important place in the Romantic pantheon, for their ever-changing contours and constant flow of water and energy reminded visitors of nature's ceaseless cycles of life and death. Born in the mountains of Switzerland, each drop of Rhine water crossed an array of natural and human frontiers on its way to the river's delta in the Netherlands, where the waters joined the sea, perhaps to evaporate, mix in the clouds, and fall to earth again as rain. The Rhine had also shaped the many human communities that had occupied its banks, from the ancient Celts who gave the river its original name, *Renos,* to the Romans who brought viticulture to the region more than two thousand years ago, taking advantage of the soils enriched by prehistoric volcanic activity. Long before the advent of modern industry, outcroppings of rock provided an ideal terrain for medieval fortresses from which tolls could be exacted on river traders, and small flat areas along the banks offered just enough room for fishing villages to establish themselves.

Germany's first nature protection efforts emerged as a result of Ro-

mantic fascination with the Drachenfels, a stony precipice south of
Bonn. Named for a legendary dragon that was supposed to have inhabited a cave on the side of the mountain, the area is rich in natural scenery and classical and medieval artifacts, including a breathtak-
ing panorama of the Rhine Valley from its summit, vineyards dating
back to the Roman period, and twelfth-century watchtower ruins.
The Drachenfels is one of the "Seven Mountains" that give the
Siebengebirge region its name. This chain of more than forty hills, the
remnants of volcanoes, is the highest point on the lower Rhine, serving as the gateway to the "Romantic Rhine" Gorge that stretches to
Mainz.[12]

The Siebengebirge's unique combination of natural scenery and ancient human history helped to fuel the Romantic revolution in sensibility. In the late eighteenth and early nineteenth century, English aesthetes, such as the poet Anne Radcliffe, descended upon the Rhine
to find what Radcliffe termed in 1795 its "awful, sublime and picturesque" landscape.[13] That Romantics sought out the painterly qualities of the picturesque Siebengebirge was not surprising, for the
Drachenfels had appeared in the background of devotional imagery
as far back as the twelfth century and was prominent in Dutch and
Flemish landscape paintings and etchings from the seventeenth century onward. A more dramatic symbolism was also present in the
river's ceaseless flow and the ruins that manifested the insignifance of
humankind in the face of divine nature. English aristocrats and upper
bourgeois on their so-called Grand Tour of the Continent soon added
the Rhine to their itinerary. In 1788, the Reverend John Gardnor
completed a series of Rhineland portraits, *Views Taken on or Near
the River Rhine,* which enumerated a compulsory canon of sites for
elite tourists. Many English Romantics proposed that divine forces
had created in the Rhineland those very features they valued in their
own landscape gardens: naturalistic curves, winding paths, indigenous vegetation that spilled out into the countryside, and Gothic
ruins.[14] The taste for picturesque nature, in other words, followed aesthetic shifts in eighteenth-century garden design that favored natural-
ness over the formal rigidity of the French baroque garden.

The Rhine was thus "God's garden," an ever-changing panoply of
natural and historical delights for those with a trained eye. Lord Byron was among the new visitors; he described the region as a "spectacle of the gods" and dedicated the opening lines of his 1816 *Childe*

*Harold's Pilgrimage* to the Drachenfels, writing, "The castled crag of Drachenfels, frowns o'er the wide and winding Rhine."[15] Byron's fascination with the medieval Drachenfels ruins was another important motif in English Romanticism. Unlike Enlightenment intellectuals, who had viewed the Middle Ages as the pinnacle of superstition and barbarism, Romantics rediscovered the period as a repository of heroism, community, and sacredness.[16] Byron's visits soon prompted waves of English and other European tourists to visit the Rhineland, making the region one of the world's first sites for large-scale tourism. Among the Rhineland's hills and valleys, the emerging industrial bourgeoisie could escape the noise, pollution, and social discontent caused by industrialization and cultivate a taste for landscape that distinguished them culturally from their social inferiors.

The advent of standardized travel guides for the region and the introduction of steamship and railway service during the 1820s and 1830s hastened this "discovery" of Rhineland nature. Steamship travel shortened what was once a fourteen-hour trip from Rotterdam to Cologne to just over five hours. In 1840, only thirteen years after regular steamship service was introduced into the region, the *Allgemeine Gasthofzeitung* reported that more than 400,000 passengers had used the new transportation service. The flood of visitors was so overwhelming that the engraver Karl Simrock noted in 1840 that "in all art and book shops . . . picturesque views of the Rhine area . . . can be purchased in such numbers that between Mainz and Cologne hardly a house, hardly a tree can be found which has not set in motion a pen or a gouge."[17] By the mid-1800s, the number of visitors had reached a plateau, and English elites were bemoaning the commercialization of the landscape. Having been discovered by ordinary vacationers, the Rhineland had become a cliché; it no longer tantalized the sophisticated traveler with its sublime aura.

German aesthetes and intellectuals had also helped to produce Rhine Romanticism, or *Rheinromantik*, though their observations of the area often combined aesthetic glorification with attention to the nationalist meaning of natural features. The poets Clemens Brentano and Achim von Arnim, for example, conducted a series of travels along the Rhine in 1802 that inspired their folk song collection *Des Knaben Wunderhorn*, in which they which claimed to have rediscovered the spirit of the Middle Ages embodied in the Rhineland's castle ruins. The Wars of Liberation also led the Heidelberg scholar Joseph

Görres to gather popular legends and myths among Rhineland peasants, whom he presented as the authentic voice of the German *Volk,* as part of the propaganda against Napoleon. Countering French claims to the Rhine as France's natural border, the Bonn professor and nationalist Ernst Moritz Arndt's 1813 *Germany's River but Not Germany's Border* imagined the Rhine flowing through the body of the Fatherland, with *both* banks firmly within the boundaries of the *Heimat.* This rediscovery of Rhenish cultural character later found expression in the writings and speeches of nationalist thinkers such as Johann Gottlieb Fichte and Gottfried Herder, who proposed that peasant cultures and landscapes formed the basis of national identity.[18] Rhineland legends and myths that evoked the region's Germanic character surfaced in popular collections such as Alfred Reumont's *Rhineland Tales and Stories* (1837) and later Wilhelm Ruland's *Rheinsagen* (1894), which would appear in fifty editions by the 1970s. The Rhine and its landscape inspired German literature, music, and poetry, including August Schlegel's popularization of the *Nibelungenlied,* Heinrich Heine's poem *Lorelei* (1824), and Richard Wagner's opera *Das Rheingold* (1876). The popularity of these works was instrumental in constructing the Rhine as the mythical origin of the nation.[19]

Following the Congress of Vienna in 1814 and 1815, both French and German nationalists continued to lay claim to the river, thereby extending the rhetoric of the Rhine as Germany's birthplace far into the nineteenth century. In 1840, for example, French foreign minister Adolf Thiers threatened the Rhine in an attempt to defuse through nationalist enthusiasm his country's discontent with the July Monarchy. The attempt failed, but not before Max Schneckenburger had penned "The Watch on the Rhine" ("Die Wacht am Rhein") and helped put it to music. The song became one of Germany's most popular national anthems; its words would later ring out as young men marched to battle in the Franco-Prussian War of 1870. The adoption of the Rhine as Germany's quintessential national symbol, moreover, transformed the visual import of the historic sites and natural landmarks along its banks, inscribing these features with a new nationalist genealogy. Like many medieval ruins along the Rhine, the watchtower atop the Drachenfels had been destroyed by the French king's troops during the Thirty Years' War. In the wake of Napoleon, German nationalists such as Arndt claimed that such castle ruins symbolized the ancient struggle between French and German "peoples," and that the Prussian victory over Napoleon's armies in 1813 represented a decisive step toward finally vanquishing the threat of Germany's "hereditary enemy." This process gave the Rhine and its medieval ruins an aura of national sacredness, marking Germans' primordial origins and commemorating their continuing struggle against the French.[20]

Because of its fame as a historical and natural landmark, the Drachenfels became the focus of Germany's first nature protection efforts, especially as the area was also a site of key natural resources. Underneath the mountain's surface were valuable deposits of trachyte and basalt, both important construction materials. Quarries had operated there since the Roman period, and builders had even used the stone to construct the Cologne Cathedral. Economic expansion in the Rhineland after the Napoleonic wars rapidly increased the demand for such materials for building and road construction. This led to a clash between mine owners and Romantic nature enthusiasts, because blasting holes in the mountainside was causing the rock layers under the ruins to subside and the ruins themselves to crumble. In 1828 the public outcry among citizens in nearby Cologne and Bonn led the Prussian king Friedrich Wilhelm III to issue ordinances banning mining operations in the area. The king commissioned the partial restoration and preservation of the ruins, and in 1836 the former watchtower and its surrounding landscape on the summit became Germany's first nature park. With its tower and its commanding view of the Rhine and the distant western border, also now restored, the Drachenfels appeared to contemporary observers as a symbolic guardian of the interior against further French aggression.[21]

By preserving the Drachenfels as a natural and historical monument, Friedrich Wilhelm hoped to use *Denkmalpflege* to justify the Hohenzollern monarchy's presence in the region by linking it to a romanticized medieval past and the popular nationalist strivings voiced during the Wars of Liberation. Prussia had annexed the Rhineland in 1815 as a result of the Congress of Vienna, where Metternich had tried to bolster Prussian power by expanding its territory to the French frontier. Though many Rhineland liberals welcomed the end of French hegemony, German nationalism did not necessarily transfer into Prussian enthusiasm. Many saw the Prussian annexation as a betrayal of the liberal-democratic goals espoused during the 1813 campaign, and argued that the Prussian three-class voting system was

*Ruine Drachenfels* by Bernhard H. Hundeshagen, 1842. The Drachenfels was an icon during the heyday of Rhine Romanticism because of its association with the aesthetics of the picturesque, river lore, medieval heroism, and the Wars of Liberation. *Source:* Siebengebirgsmuseum, Heimatverein Siebengebirge e.V., Königswinter, Germany.

an affront to liberal aspirations. Rhineland patriots such as Joseph Görres had deep-seated reservations about "the Lithuanians," as civil servants from Berlin were often called.[22] Cultural patronage was one path to overcoming such political divisions. The Prussian state's efforts to begin the restoration and completion of the Cologne cathedral, as well as its restoration of such Rhineland castles as Lahneck and Stolzenfels, are good examples of how monument preservation helped to naturalize Prussian hegemony.[23]

Prussia's defeat of France in 1870 unleashed a new wave of anti-French nationalism that spurred bombastic monument building to celebrate Germany's victory and national unification. Although Germany was not the only country to construct an array of national monuments in the late nineteenth century, its belated nationhood may have produced an overall greater need for such objects.[24] Not surprisingly, the Rhine Valley provided an important setting for many of these new memorials, such as the *Germania* monument overlooking the village of Rüdesheim (1877–1883) and the Kaiser Wilhelm statue (1897) in Koblenz. The Drachenfels site was among the finalists for the latter monument, though it was eventually erected at the confluence of the Rhine and Mosel Rivers.[25] Such monuments further naturalized conflicts with the French through ethnic myth rather than concrete historical circumstances. The Rhineland was also one of the most important centers of Kaiser Wilhelm II's campaign in the 1890s to promote the Romanesque as the authentic "Germanic" style by restoring medieval churches such as the Aachen and Trier cathedrals and commissioning new buildings with historicist designs modeled on this period.[26] In short, through historical monument preservation, the Hohenzollern monarchy sought to exploit the Rhineland's symbolic capital to imagine the Second Empire as the natural successor to Charlemagne's Holy Roman Empire.

## The Rhineland Environment in the Age of Industrialization

While the Rhine's memorials articulated the monarchy's conservative vision of German character, the area's nature protection efforts began as a middle-class endeavor to broaden popular participation in nation building. In 1869 the Beautification Society for the Siebengebirge (Verschönerungsverein für das Siebengebirge, or VVS), an association composed mainly of urban professionals from nearby Bonn and Cologne, took over control of maintaining the Drachenfels monument from the Prussian state. The VVS embraced a nineteenth-century faith in nature appreciation as an instrument of moral improvement, and undertook a far-reaching campaign to beautify the Siebengebirge and increase visitors' access to the region. The society planted trees and shrubs, picked up trash and debris, created hundreds of kilometers of walking paths and roads, erected hiking shelters, and placed benches and platforms at scenic lookouts.[27] Such efforts were designed to accommodate the Rhineland's foreign visitors as well as urbanites from the surrounding Rhineland and Ruhr regions. Once the Drachenfels became a popular national symbol after the defeat of the French in 1870, the VVS helped to make room for a new wave of visitors by building roads and hotels in the region and even financing the construction of a funicular railway up the side of the mountain that whisked tourists to the Drachenfels summit. From the precipice, visitors enjoyed a panoramic view of the Rhine's left bank; the height enabled them to visualize the distant Eifel hills to the west, the Cologne Cathedral to the north, the Westerwald to the east, and the Rhine islands to the south as elements of Fatherland topography.[28]

By the 1880s, the accelerated industrialization and urbanization associated with the second industrial revolution had begun to take their toll on the Rhineland landscape. The Rhineland was at the center of Germany's rapid late-nineteenth-century economic transformation and population growth. The province's population doubled between 1870 and 1914, rising from approximately 3.6 million to 7.9 million inhabitants, many of whom were immigrants to the Ruhr area from the eastern Polish-speaking provinces of Silesia and West Prussia. By 1875, more than 116 chemical production plants were located in the Rhineland, and the construction of the famous Bayer pharmaceutical works in the town of Henkel, now known as Leverkusen, marked the development of the Cologne-Düsseldorf region as Europe's largest pharmaceutical manufacturing center. The Rhine Province also contained about a third of Germany's most important coal-mining and steel-manufacturing district, the Ruhr industrial complex, within its borders. The use of steam-powered water pumps and the development of the railway network in the region increased coal production from 70,000 metric tons in 1774 to an astounding 115 million in 1913, a 1,600-fold increase.[29] As this area developed, towns such as Duisburg and Essen became some of Germany's most valuable industrial centers. The Rhineland's cities and factories attracted migrants from the province's own rural areas. Declining agricultural prices in outlying districts such as the hilly Eifel on the Belgian border and the Hunsrück on the Rhine's left bank had led to chronic poverty in these regions. Many rural workers left the agrarian life in search of higher wages in nearby cities; others emigrated to the United States, leaving Germany altogether for farmsteads in the Midwest or factory work in Chicago, Milwaukee, and St. Louis. The result was that the Eifel district barely grew in population during this period, despite the overall increase in the province's population.[30]

Nature lovers were especially concerned about the growing sprawl of urban civilization and technology into the rural landscape caused by these socioeconomic changes. Railways connecting the Rhenish cities of Aachen, Bonn, Cologne, and Düsseldorf with other major

European cities, for example, soon created the most dense railway network in the world.[31] Dams, which destroyed wildlife habitat, woodlands, and watersheds, were also increasingly commonplace in the decades before World War I. In 1899, the Ruhr Dam Association was founded to "improve the quantity and quality of water levels on the Ruhr through the construction of dams in the Ruhr's watershed." The first dams were built in the nearby Sauerland between 1901 and 1904; as the Ruhr's water needs grew, so did the number and size of such dams, until nearly all upstream water was captured. Since most German rivers flow north to south, east-west canals were eventually built to link the entire system together: one historian has compared the resulting network of mechanized waterways to an "autobahn of water transportation."[32]

The Rhine itself became more like an organic machine than a natural monument during the nineteenth century, transformed into the river most modified by human hands in the world. The Rhine that early Romantics had experienced contained thousands of islands, uncertain currents, underwater cliffs, acres of wetlands, and abundant salmon and mayfish populations. Then in 1817 the Baden civil engineer Johann Gottfried Tulla, the so-called Tamer of the Wild Rhine, took charge of straightening and diking the river for flood control. Tulla was followed by hydraulic engineers in other riparian states who oversaw the dredging of the channel, the removal of natural barriers, and the construction of ports and bridges for easier two-way shipping. Such "improvements" reconstituted the river as a navigational canal to benefit industrial production, reducing its length between Basel and Mannheim by a staggering 100 kilometers.

This "correction" of the Rhine did indeed make navigation easier, and it decreased the incidence of malaria and typhus along the Rhine's banks, but it also produced a host of other, unintended ecological effects, including the loss of rich alluvial soils that were deposited along the river's banks during periodic floods, a lowering of the region's water table owing to the deeper stream bed cut by the river, an increase in sediments and pollutants in the waterway due to deforestation and erosion, and the destruction of floodplain forests and biotically diverse marshes used as nurseries for fish and bird species. The Rhine also refused to be tamed; preventing floods in upstream cities such as Strasbourg merely displaced the problem to downstream sites such as Koblenz, which were inundated by higher waters and sediment levels.[33]

Some of Germany's most significant ecological degradation during this period occurred in the Ruhr coal-mining region, which was afflicted by water pollution, air pollution, and overdevelopment. To secure water for the Ruhr region's coal mines and factories, German engineers pioneered the practice of siphoning freshwater from the Ruhr River, using the water for manufacturing processes, and returning it, untreated, into tributaries such as the Emscher River. The resulting mass of slow-moving, reeking black sludge in the Emscher prompted one Prussian parliamentarian to call it the "the river of hell."[34] The Rhine also suffered from the dumping of industrial and municipal waste; one parliamentary deputy in 1901 declared the river a "sewer" in which it was no longer possible to bathe and whose flooding posed a risk of infecting drinking water supplies with typhus and cholera bacilli. Even the threat of disease did not lead government to restrict industrial effluents, however. Instead, scientists argued that certain stretches of a river could be sacrificed to industry (the so-called *Opferstrecke*) without damage to the river's entire length.[35]

Air pollution also plagued the Rhineland's environment. In the 1880s, Julius von Schröder and Carl Reuss identified sulphur dioxide from smokestacks and the resultant acid rain as major causes of "forest death," while public health officials recognized the deleterious effect of coal smoke on the human respiratory system. The Ruhr region developed one of the highest concentrations of polluting factories, thanks to the legal criterion of the "district norm." Once an individual town or village welcomed a factory that brought jobs and economic growth, judges and bureaucrats often designated the zone surrounding the manufacturing facility as an industrial region and used that fact as grounds for licensing more industrial facilities in the same area. Just as the "sacrificed stretches" of rivers kept getting longer until they included the Ruhr's entire watershed, so did the patchwork of industrial districts grow in the Ruhr area until air and water pollution constituted the "district norm" for the entire region. In 1915, for example, a judge ruled that a local farmer did not deserve compensation for smoke damage to his orchard because it was "unreasonable" to expect to grow fruit trees in the Ruhr Valley, even though such agricultural practices had been commonplace only fifty years previously. Companies usually responded to lawsuits by building higher chimneys, which merely blew the toxins farther away from their origin, making it more difficult to pinpoint their source and hold a factory owner liable.[36]

Ordinary citizens did not need scientific studies to show that something was terribly amiss in the Ruhr's environment. Hans Klose, who later became a provincial nature protection commissioner in Brandenburg, had spent his childhood in the region and described its transformation in personal terms. In 1890, he noted, "We had a certain right to feel proud of the American-style development of our local *Heimat* and its neighboring area and felt ourselves to be members of a goal-oriented community full of work tenacity and creative zest." Environmental changes occurred stepwise, with rows of houses pushing into fields and wastewater canals crisscrossing the countryside. Gradually, wrote Klose, "after we had taken off our children's shoes," came the realization of a "dreadful tragedy" taking place in the landscape: a "death sentence for the colorful woodlands, followed by the loss of the coming of spring; here *Heimat* nature died without hope."[37] Environmental degradation thus produced not only the death of nature but also a loss of memory, destroying the ties between selfhood and *Heimat* deemed necessary for emotional and physical development.

Individuals' ability to avoid the worst impacts of pollution depended largely on social class. When the steel magnate Alfred Krupp could no longer bear the smoke and noise from his Essen factory, he built a spectacular villa on a hill outside the city with its own private park and transplanted trees. Such permanent refuge was not possible for ordinary laborers and foreign immigrants, however; they had to learn to cope with the existing air, water, and noise of modern Essen. Government officials in the Wilhelmine era were reluctant to intervene legislatively to ameliorate such problems, because it would mean placing restrictions on industries considered vital to the nation's economic growth, political stability, and military superiority.[38] Given such government indifference, it is not surprising that many German workers turned to radical political alternatives; class consciousness was a product of the home environment as much as the factory floor. By 1914 the SPD, whose platform called for the overthrow of capitalism through a workers' revolution, had more than one million members and an electorate in excess of four million, making it the largest socialist party in Europe.[39]

While allowing the state and private firms to sacrifice the Ruhr region to the needs of industry, many middle-class observers hoped that the Rhine Gorge and other scenic areas would remain sanctuaries

Gruss vom Drachenfels

Postcard of the Drachenfels, early 1900s. As the twentieth century began, many middle-class observers thought that the spread of Rhineland kitsch and the increasing numbers of tourists in the Rhine Valley had dimmed the symbolic aura of the Rhine and the Drachenfels. *Source:* Siebengebirgsmuseum, Heimatverein Siebengebirge e.V., Königswinter, Germany.

from the evils of materialism. Yet the tourists and Sunday visitors who came to inundate natural areas on weekends and holidays led to increasing anxiety over the commercialization of the Rhine's Romantic landscapes. Nature preservationists bemoaned the railway lines, billboards, hotels, souvenir shops, "Father Rhine" pubs, and other amenities established to accommodate the growing number of tourists in the region. While these venues were the life's blood of many Rhenish towns, *Heimat* advocates complained that they cheapened nature, debasing its symbolic power and further damaging the natural environment. The future *Heimatschutz* movement founder, Ernst Rudorff, for example, wrote the widely cited 1880 essay "On the Relationship of Modern Life to Nature" to protest the VVS's plan to build the funicular railway up the side of Drachenfels. Rudorff claimed that tourists' sightseeing in the area was merely "barhopping in an altered form," and satirized visitors' consumption of natural scenery. In an outdoor restaurant, he asserted, the waiter might ask if guests preferred their soup first, then the sunset, or the other way around. Rudorff demanded that instead visitors be mindful of the "genuine, living piety for Nature" and not treat it as a mere curiosity or souvenir.[40] As a repository of ideal values, nature was to be strictly separated from commercial impulses. Concerned Rhenish citizens and provincial officials soon echoed Rudorff's concerns, claiming that nature protection, rather than beautification and expanded recreational development, was the key to securing the area's future.

## Saving the Siebengebirge

This aesthetic perception of environmental problems, which focused especially on the loss of outstanding scenery while often neglecting the mounting ecological costs of pollution and hydraulic engineering, was characteristic of bourgeois landscape preservation in the decades before World War I.[41] Despite the massive transformation of the Rhine's entire watershed that occurred during the nineteenth-century industrialization of the river, nature protection campaigns selected sites enshrined in the Romantic pantheon as subjects of concern, as was the case in the campaign to save the Siebengebirge from the mining industry. In the early 1880s, mining operations near the summit of the Ölberg peak in the Siebengebirge opened an enormous gash on the side of the mountain. The scar was so large it was visible to strollers on the Rhine's banks in Bonn and steamship passengers gliding toward the Drachenfels, the gateway to the Rhine Gorge. Mining had resumed in the Siebengebirge with a vengeance in the 1880s, since the construction of modern streets, waterways, and river embankments had led to an unprecedented demand for the weather-resistant basalt found in local mines. While the Drachenfels remained a protected area, the remaining peaks in the Siebengebirge were vulnerable to further incursions, as the mining industry had plans to excavate the stone at several sites in the region.[42]

The Bonn attorney Josef Humbroich, leader of a group of Bonn citizens outraged by this disfigurement *(Verunstaltung)* of the local landscape, first turned to the Hohenzollern crown prince Wilhelm II in 1884 to solicit his help in protecting the area. That appeal failed; the state, he was told, lacked the funds to purchase land parcels in the area. Then, instead of stepping in to aid Humbroich and his followers in their preservation effort, the Rhenish Provincial Association (Provinzialverband) in Düsseldorf enraged the group when it purchased the basalt mines on the nearby Petersberg peak in April 1886.[43] The Provinzialverband hoped to line its own pockets with the profits from the mine. Although the VVS had taken control of the Drachenfels monument in 1869 and had been responsible for efforts to enhance the Siebengebirge's beauty for visitors, it was embroiled in internal disputes at this time that rendered it unable to assist Humbroich in his campaign.[44]

Faced with a complete lack of state and private support, Humbroich founded the Society to Save the Siebengebirge (Verein zur Rettung des Siebengebirges, or VRS) in May of 1886, an organization dedicated to preserving the area from further development. The VRS passed a resolution, signed by key political, educational, and commercial figures in the region, calling on the Provincial Association to stop its mining operations in the area.[45] Focusing on the aesthetic impact of mining, the petition claimed that the "broad, powerful, and magnificent Petersberg" was an essential part of the region's beauty, and that damage to it would ruin the "wonderful and uniquely beautiful panorama of the entire mountainous area from Bonn to Godesburg." Within a few years, the resolution continued, quarry activities would produce so many "deep wounds" in the landscape that it would disfigure the entire series of Rhine-facing hills.[46] Anyone taking a short hike from Bonn to the mountains could already see the results of such activity. "Crippled plum trees" and "thin grass and desolate weeds" showed the futility of planting over the rubble heaps produced by extracting rock; the landscape offered a "sad melancholy" in comparison to the wonderful forests and orchards that once covered the base of the mountains. After a bitter public campaign, provincial officials bowed to popular opinion and sold the Petersberg mine in 1889, stipulating that no future mining operations be conducted there.[47]

VRS members saw themselves as stewards of the province's natural heritage, and in the process of agitating to save the Siebengebirge they helped to nationalize the landscape, transforming the Romantic experience of nature into a celebration of national cohesion.[48] Whereas the 1836 Drachenfels preservation had focused on nature as a scenic frame for the twelfth-century watchtower ruins, the 1886

Siebengebirge campaign proposed that nature itself deserved protection, offering concrete traces of a primordial territoriality that had
existed in the mists of time. To demonstrate the site's national significance, the VRS created an organic history of the nation that anchored German identity in the Siebengebirge's natural and cultural
heritage. The Siebengebirge's defenders noted that the area's basalt
and trachyte were the result of volcanic activity millions of years ago,
with rare species of indigenous plants later inhabiting the rich soil
produced by eruptions. Natural history then became the substrate of
human settlement, and archaeological digs provided evidence of the
Celts, Germanic tribes, and Roman occupiers who had made use of
nature's bounty and formed fishing villages and agricultural communities. The Romans were the first to mine the Drachenfels, and the
vineyards that dotted the region and thrived in its rich volcanic soil
were first planted by those occupiers from southern Europe.[49]

The result was a palimpsest of nature and history, a "unique garden of God" with fertile earth, fruit orchards in the valley, and vineyards clinging precipitously to the sides of mountains. Nowhere else
in Germany, claimed the VRS, could visitors find such diversity in
such a small space; "every minor high point, every pathway brings
constantly new images, never of the same form, each equipped with
its own attraction." The stories and legends about the region, such as
Roland, the knight who had slain the Drachenfels dragon, anchored
the Siebengebirge in popular memory, further bolstering its significance as a national monument. "Thousands upon thousands make
a pilgrimage there every year," noted the VRS, "freed from everyday
trials, to expand their heart and chest, to get new energy and new
spirit for the strains of their daily occupations through fresh hiking
excursions and Rhenish cheerfulness." Nature's beauty was available to all; it required no special education to enjoy a hike along
a Siebengebirge path or to relax on a picnic in one of its meadows.
The region was thus truly an "ideal possession of our people," a
"holy property of the Fatherland" rather than a place of quick profits
for few greedy investors. Having so often been called to defend the
Siebengebirge with their "heart's blood," the people laid claim to the
region as one of the "holiest and dearest possessions of the nation . . .
to be preserved in the magic of its forests and in the undiminished
beauty of its mountains!"[50]

The VRS's depiction of the Siebengebirge as a popular site of national pilgrimage echoed the middle-class belief that nature could heal social divisions. As Germans young and old, elite and poor, male and female experienced the natural landscape, they found a common ground unavailable in the city or any other historic venue; nature subsumed difference in its immediate emotional appeal. Noting the cultural-political significance of nature's social function, the VRS wrote: "Especially in our time, with its sharp social differences, the ideal goods of the nation represent a conciliatory, balancing moment; it would be a sin to rip them out of the heart of the people!"[51] Such nationalist rhetoric emphasized nature protection as a fight to protect ideal values against the leveling forces of materialism and factionalism. The effect of the VRS report was thus to nationalize natural features, creating a portrait of Germany as a nation rooted in the organic world, rather than one produced by contingent political compromises.

The VRS's portrayal of Siebengebirge protection as a patriotic campaign eventually found resonance among Prussian state and Rhineland provincial officials. One of the organization's most effective rhetorical strategies was to portray the Siebengebirge as a "natural monument," on a par with or even more essential than the historic and artistic objects of traditional state *Denkmalpflege*. An 1887 petition to Prussian officials declared that, while "our laws protect old built monuments of historical or artistic value, they should also protect hilltops which through their form and beauty give the landscape a special character, such as the Petersberg and the Ölberg. Monuments of nature deserve as much protection as the monuments of art." In this view, natural monument protection was a logical outgrowth of the state's ideal role as the guarantor of national heritage. The state would lead the people in subsuming materialistic impulses in the name of higher ideals. "Even down-to-earth America," the petition noted, "has declared the Niagara Falls and other regions as national parks and does not allow any industrial exploitation and disfigurement there."[52]

Despite the VRS's success in saving the Petersberg, several sites within the Siebengebirge region remained in jeopardy. The Ölberg was threatened anew, as the mine owner Franz Merkens announced plans to build a railroad to the summit for transporting stone down the mountain. The need for a united front against such destruction soon prompted the VRS to merge with the VVS, creating a new VVS organization dedicated to ending mining operations in the region and securing the natural landscape for future generations.[53] For the first time, nature protection, rather than recreational development, would dominate VVS concerns. Whereas the VVS's 1869 charter had stated that the organization was dedicated to "creating and maintaining roads, riding paths, and footpaths, as well as facilities, that could contribute to the comfort and convenience of the Siebengebirge's visitors," its 1899 statement declared its primary goal to be "the lasting preservation and protection of the Siebengebirge against destruction and damage."[54]

This shift from beautification to preservation brought the VVS new participants and added prestige; by 1902, the organization counted 730 members. Although the VVS included members from as far away as Berlin, most came from nearby cities, such as Bonn and Cologne, as well as communities near the Siebengebirge, such as Königswinter and Honnef. Most VVS members were educated and well-to-do, including civil servants such as university professors and judges, professionals such as lawyers and doctors, and representatives from the commercial, financial, and industrial sectors, such as bankers and factory owners, many of whom carried the honorary title *Kommerzienrat,* conferred by the government only on distinguished businessmen.[55] The society's emphasis on the aesthetic and nationalist meaning of the Siebengebirge's cultural landscape undoubtedly reflected the predominance of classically educated urban elites in the VVS, individuals for whom Romanticism and its glorification of nature represented a distinctively German contribution to world civilization.[56] Yet the VVS did attract members from more modest economic and educational backgrounds, including small business owners, state employees such as teachers and foresters, and a high number of retirees, whose income varied from person to person. The organization had no manual laborers as members, however, and only a small number of women, many of whom had joined in conjunction with their spouse. The VVS nevertheless provided a venue for a broad cross section of the province's middle classes to engage in reformist, civic-minded activities designed to improve the local environment, a far cry from the bourgeois escapism or reactionary "cultural despair" that scholars once used to characterize middle-class *Heimat* activities.[57]

This view of nature protection as a duty for the enlightened state

Photograph of the Drachenfels and Siebengebirge, late nineteenth century. The Siebengebirge was not a wilderness but a cultural landscape of forests, vineyards, and small villages facing "Germany's river," the Rhine. To convince state and provincial governments to protect the area from the mining industry, preservationists argued that the Siebengebirge was a "natural monument" whose scenic beauty appealed to all Germans regardless of political affiliation or social class. *Source:* Archiv des Landschaftsverbandes Rheinland, Kulturabteilung, No. 1487.

convinced the Rhineland's Prussian-appointed head president *(Oberpräsident)* Berthold von Nasse to support VVS efforts, and his vocal backing for the preservation campaign was indeed crucial to its success. In a speech in the presence of Kaiser Wilhelm II, Nasse called for an end to the mining industry's "nature vandalism" in the Siebengebirge, and he admonished Berlin to assist regional officials in preserving the entire area. Such language had an effect. After a survey of the area led by the Prussian Ministry of the Interior, according to one account, "All of the participating officials were of one mind that active assistance needed to be given, if the most beautiful and important points of the Siebengebirge were to be preserved for posterity."[58] As a result of Nasse's mediation, the Prussian Cultural Ministry granted the VVS the right to conduct a series of lotteries to raise funds for purchasing land within the Siebengebirge. Held in 1899 and 1906, the lotteries brought the VVS approximately 2.4 million marks, a crucial sum that allowed the organization to secure the area.[59] With these funds, the VVS was able to purchase a number of key parcels from the mine owners, including the Ölberg summit.

In addition to the right to hold lotteries, the state granted the VVS the right of eminent domain *(Enteignungsrecht)* for any part of the area that "as a consequence of present or expected use might spoil the beauties of the Siebengebirge."[60] Aesthetic ideals thus provided the legal basis for land expropriation; the protection of the "landscape beauties of the Siebengebirge" against disfigurement became the key criterion for determining which parcels of land were threatened and thus subject to eminent domain. By the 1890s, the spread of vacation facilities, such as hotels and weekend cottages, was also of growing concern, and the VVS was permitted to apply dispossession rights to areas that might be developed in this manner. The state did not sanction the use of eminent domain, however, in areas in which "expected uses" did not involve activities that destroyed the area's aesthetic beauty, such as forestry, or where the VVS could convince owners to restrict their use voluntarily.[61] The granting of dispossession rights nonetheless marked a significant step in the evolution of German nature preservation policy, for it asserted the state's right to infringe on private property rights in the name of protecting natural areas.

Prussian officials were not the only government representatives to take an active interest in preserving the Siebengebirge; the Rhineland's own provincial and local authorities stepped in to help secure the area as a nature reserve. In 1899 the VVS received grants of 50,000 marks from the city of Bonn, 100,000 marks from Cologne, and 200,000 marks from the Provincial Association for purchasing or leasing land in the area.[62] These regional and municipal grants reflected the Siebengebirge's growing importance as a regional symbol and a refuge for urban denizens from Bonn and Cologne. Remarkably, some officials even placed nature protection above historic preservation in securing Rhenish identity. The mayor of Cologne, for example, claimed that the Siebengebirge ought to be more cherished than the Cologne cathedral; if the cathedral were to collapse, he noted, it could be rebuilt, whereas the Siebengebirge was irreplaceable.[63] In recognition of the role of state and provincial officials in supporting VVS activities, the organization named several of the region's leaders to its board of directors, including Head President Nasse as the organization's permanent honorary chairman, the mayor of Bonn, the Prussian-appointed Cologne district president *(Regierungspräsident),* the county heads *(Landräte)* from the Bonn and Siegkreis counties where the Siebengebirge is located, and elected representatives of the Provinzialverband, the city of Cologne, and the city of Bonn.[64] This combination of state support and private initiative reflected state authorities' belief that it was most expedient to encourage private organizations' cultural activities through grants and administrative assistance, rather than by taking over their financing and administration directly.

Despite the fact that a combination of Prussian-appointed officials, provincial authorities, and municipal representatives were involved in the Siebengebirge preservation effort, the Rhenish Provincial Association's support proved the most substantial and enduring in the organization's long-term development. The Siebengebirge was an important national symbol, but regional sponsorship ensured that the locale also remained a repository of Rhenish cultural heritage and identity. Provincial officials "could not fail to recognize that, just as the Siebengebirge is a general good of the population in the heart of the province, the Provincial Association has without a doubt an essential interest in preserving [its] landscape beauties." Major newspapers, such as the *Bonner Zeitung (Bonn Newspaper)* and the liberal *Kölnische Zeitung (Cologne Newspaper)* echoed such sentiments, arguing in favor of the plan to preserve the "Rhineland's Pearl" from destruction.[65] Stressing nature protection's ability to overcome social and political differences, the *Kölnische Zeitung*'s editors honored the VVS as "speaker for the Rhenish population of all classes and parties." The Provincial Association chastised the mining industry for its greedy pursuit of financial profits, which had replaced the Siebengebirge's "natural beauties" with "barren cliff surfaces and ugly heaps of rubble."[66] Such rhetorical strategies enabled provincial officials to fashion themselves, not distant Berlin bureaucrats, as the moral guardians of their population's long-term interests. In the years to come, the VVS would receive numerous additional monetary grants from the Provincial Association, making it the major beneficiary of provincial nature protection funds during the early part of this century.

Such provincial cultural patronage had evolved during the course of the nineteenth century along with regional demands for greater autonomy. The VVS received its provincial funds under the conditions specified in the Prussian Endowment Laws from 1873 and 1875, which had granted the Prussian provinces an annual lump sum of money and the right to tax their population for the purposes of managing their internal affairs. The Endowment Laws helped Prussian authorities to streamline their administrative tasks and accommodate regional demands for greater independence from Berlin.[67] This devolution of control onto the Rhine Province had led in the 1880s to the creation of the office of provincial governor *(Landeshauptmann)*, who became the highest elected official in the province; the formation of the Provinzialverband, the official agency of Rhenish self-government in the province; and the creation of the Provincial Committee (Provinzialausschuss), a thirteen-member commission that was charged with carrying out the Provinzialverband's administrative and budgetary tasks. In addition, the Endowment Laws specified that the provincial administrators should take control of a number of activities, including street building and public health administration. The scope of provincial self-administration increased throughout the Wilhelmine and Weimar periods, becoming a cornerstone of Germany's decentralized administrative approach.[68]

One of the areas that fell under provincial control was *Kulturpflege* (the "care of culture"), which included supervision of key cultural institutions, such as universities, theaters, museums, and music societies, as well as *Denkmalpflege* activities. This devolution of administrative and cultural authority onto the province helped to lessen some of the traditional conflicts between Prussia and the Rhineland's liberal and Catholic factions. Provincial control over cultural affairs afforded Rhinelanders the freedom to shape their own sense of regional heritage and culture, yet at the same time ensured their ultimate loyalty to Prussia and the national state.[69] Provincial control nevertheless contributed to a decentralized vision of national culture, one in which regional diversity, rather than central control from Berlin, was seen as the keystone to national character. When the Provincial Committee approved funds for the VVS to protect the Siebengebirge, it recognized that natural monuments provided a bridge between provincial identity and national consciousness, stating that "the diversely formed basalt and trachyte mountains and the lovely valleys attached to them, to which manifold memories from sagas and stories cling, are known to every Rhinelander. The region of the Siebengebirge has become dear to the hearts of the Rhenish as well as German people."[70] Sites such as the Siebengebirge, in other words, offered a popular venue for provincial Rhinelanders to envision their local surroundings embedded within the larger German nation, and for German nationals to recognize regional diversity as the key to national strength. Nature provided a bridge between local, regional, and national conceptions of homeland, even in a province with a traditionally ambivalent relationship to Berlin. This regionalist inflection of national identity reflected the reality of the German Empire, which was a loose federation of regional states whose territorial boundaries and historical referents lay in the Holy Roman Empire, rather than a centralized nation.[71]

While the Siebengebirge's defenders and public officials designated nature protection as a communitarian goal above "material interests," they recognized the economic advantage of nature protection for the area's tourism industry. In 1886 alone, the VRS claimed that eighteen trains and steam ships had stopped daily in Königswinter at the base of the Siebengebirge, along with twenty-six additional trains in Mehlem across the river, bringing thousands of visitors to the region.[72] These visitors had an enormous economic impact on the region; as the VRS's 1886 petition to the Provincial Assembly in Düsseldorf noted: "The Siebengebirge with its wonderful and uniquely beautiful mountaintops draws thousands of foreigners annually into this area of the Rhine, and it is to this tourism that the numerous surrounding localities owe their blossoming prosperity," adding that it was "natural beauty," first and foremost, that attracted the guests to the Siebengebirge.[73] The decisions by the city of Bonn and the Rhenish Provinzialverband to grant funds for securing the Siebengebirge area were also based in part on economic calculations. "It must be expected," noted Rhineland officials, "that the richly endowed Rhine Province, which expects to accrue considerable material advantages from the landscape beauties of the Siebengebirge and through the growth of tourism," should also make sacrifices to protect the area.[74] By comparison, the mining industry employed a "relatively small" number of workers; its pernicious form of "temporary profit" and "overexploitation" (*Raubbau,* literally "activity built upon theft") left a sterile landscape of worthless rubble heaps and gashes in the sides of cliffs, a "wasteland" that could never again be used productively.[75] Aestheticism did not blind nature lovers to economic realities in a capitalist system. Siebengebirge advocates did propose, however, a different calculus of costs and benefits, one that recognized the long-term social cost of industrial exploitation of nonrenewable natural resources.

Despite the VVS's success in galvanizing popular support for Siebengebirge protection, local business and political leaders challenged the organization's claims about the preservation campaign's economic benefits, in an effort to reclaim local autonomy and private property rights. In an October 1900 resolution, the city council in Königswinter asserted that dismantling the mining industry in the area would result in economic disaster for the region. Rejecting the VVS's populist claim that all Rhinelanders were behind the preservation effort, the council argued that ordinary manual workers, "Christian and loyal to the emperor," feared the loss of employment opportunities. The council believed that the region needed sources of income beyond tourism, which was restricted to the summer months. Angry at Prussian authorities for granting the VVS generous financial support and dispossession rights, the council accused the district president in Cologne of a "lack of objectivity and love of the truth" in depicting environmental threats in the area. It was the municipalities, they claimed, not Prussian state leaders, who best understood the region's needs. The council asserted that private ownership, not state control, had made the region great and would remain the key to the area's future. "It is absolutely necessary to present to the public the current conditions in the region clearly and correctly, since on all sides . . . the view has been widespread, that the whole Siebengebirge finds itself in the clutches of people who exploit the realm both above and below with a merciless hand out of monetary interest and are gradually transforming the hills into a heap of rubble." According to the council, this perspective was completely false, as private owners had created magnificent villas that gave the region its notoriety and cared for the long-term economic sustainability of their property through careful land management.[76]

Nothing revealed the gap between urban elites' preservation goals and local ideas of land stewardship more than the groups' conflicting conceptions of landscape beauty. The council noted sarcastically that it did not wish to fault the "sense of beauty" among the "influential gentlemen of the VVS," but that "such points could be debated . . . one can have different opinions about [what constitutes] landscape beauty." The council claimed that the VVS's reports about the destruction of the landscape were exaggerated: "Of the 100,000 visitors to the hills perhaps only 100 have even seen the Ölberg stone quarry."[77] More important, in the council's eyes, the aesthetic views of a few elite gentlemen should not be allowed to override economic development and the state-guaranteed primacy of private property. As one mine owner noted bluntly: "We share the enthusiasm for this charming little piece of German soil, but even more highly do we estimate the idea of *property* and the right to *do with this as we see fit.*"[78]

These debates over the relative value of aesthetics versus economic development soon resulted in lawsuits challenging the VVS in Germany's courts. While the state had allowed the VVS to hold lotteries and had granted the organization funds to purchase or even dispossess land in exceptional cases, the VVS had no secure legal basis for restricting property owners from opening new mines or otherwise economically developing their lands within the Siebengebirge. To stop economic development in the region, nature protectionists relied on an 1899 police ordinance issued by the Cologne district president, that placed stringent restrictions on commercial development in the Siebengebirge region and on land directly across the river. The ordinance forbade the construction of new factories or additions to existing ones, as well as the establishment of stone quarries or brickworks, "which by regular operations are known to cause dangers, disadvantages, or disturbance for the public."[79] The ordinance relied on a broad interpretation of the police's right, established in 1850, to restrict activity "which had to be regulated in the interest of the community and its inhabitants." The ordinance made no mention of authorities' primary concern of protecting the Siebengebirge's scenic beauty, however, because such aesthetic arguments could not withstand legal scrutiny, as an earlier case had shown. In an 1882 decision, the Prussian Upper Administrative Court (Oberverwaltungsgericht) in Berlin had voided a police ordinance that would have prevented the construction of a building blocking residents' views in the Berlin-Kreuzburg neighborhood. Referring to the Prussian General Property Law of 1794, the court stated that the police were allowed to regulate only construction projects that disturbed public order. They could not issue ordinances for general welfare purposes, which is how landscape-aesthetic goals were defined.[80]

The Oberverwaltungsgericht's 1882 decision provided a legal wedge for mine owners to dismantle local ordinances restricting mining operations. The owner of the Petersberg mine was the first to use this decision to challenge the 1899 Cologne district ordinance by announcing the opening of a new mine in the Siebengebirge in 1901. The highest Prussian court, the Kammergericht, decided that the ordinance restricting such a move was indeed invalid, using reasoning similar to that of the Upper Administrative Court in the Kreuzberg case. The Kammergericht stated that the district president was permitted to issue such ordinances only in cases where the "dangers and not merely disadvantages or annoyances for the public . . . were to be averted."[81] The Cologne district president rereleased the Siebengebirge ordinance in May 1902, following the letter of the court's rulings about the scope of its purview by stating that mining constituted a danger to the public. However, when the state tried to prevent the reopening of a mine at Leyberge in 1913 based on this ordinance, the Prussian Upper Administrative Court once again declared the Siebengebirge ordinance invalid. The court noted that the operation of a mine was not a danger to the public, as evidenced by the many mines outside the Siebengebirge that had never required police intervention.[82]

While the Siebengebirge ordinances were successfully challenged in court, the VVS's dispossession rights, granted in 1899, withstood legal challenges. In 1912, the Prussian Commission for Municipal Affairs considered a petition from one mine owner who sought to end or place a time limit on the VVS's right to eminent domain in the Siebengebirge. Angered by the VVS's infringement of his property rights, the owner claimed that the VVS's privilege had not been granted through appropriate legal channels, and that he had never learned why his property had been taken away from him. Although in practice the VVS had used the right to eminent domain sparingly (the society had forced the sale of only two parcels of land, totaling 2.62 hectares, and no dispossession had occurred since 1900), the claimant argued that the VVS's expropriation right functioned as a "never-ending threat, through which property in the Siebengebirge had become insecure" and even unsaleable.[83]

In this case, the Prussian government decided that the VVS could continue to exercise eminent domain until it had secured the necessary parcels for maintaining the Siebengebirge in its "characteristic beauty," which it interpreted as the full 1,100 hectares it had intended to set aside as a reserve in the area. Since it had purchased only 750 hectares, the state reasoned that the VVS could continue to use its dispossession rights, but noted that if an owner agreed to preserve the land in its characteristic beauty, then purchase or dispossession was unnecessary. Confirming the state's commitment to protecting the Siebengebirge's unique character, the committee concluded: "Although it cannot be argued that the possibility of expropriation limits the free disposal of property in many respects, it should not be underestimated that certain obligations to the population as a whole accrue to the owner of a piece of property in a place that is especially beautiful and for which there is barely anything similar to be found in Germany."[84] The commission thus confirmed the state's willingness in certain cases to countenance an infringement on property rights for the sake of nature protection goals.

The use of aesthetic, nationalist, and educational criteria to judge areas deserving of state protection continued in the first half of the twentieth century, a reflection of bourgeois elites' belief in nature's ability to elevate individuals morally and to stimulate their emotional attachments to *Heimat* regardless of their social background. Finding a legal basis for nature protection that would enable the state to restrict private property nonetheless remained a key problem for the *Naturschutz* movement. Despite these challenges, the Siebengebirge preservation campaign met its goals. Mine owners for the most part remained unclear about the legal status of the ban on mining operations, or felt pressured by public opinion to halt their operations. These factors kept the region stable until the bitter disputes of the Weimar era.[85]

## Natural Monuments: Hugo Conwentz and the Science of Nature Protection, 1904–1914

Despite uncertainty about the Siebengebirge protection ordinances, nature protectionists viewed the campaign to save the region as a success and used it as a model for similar state and private efforts in the decades before World War I. A visit to the Siebengebirge in 1898 convinced Breslau schoolteacher Wilhelm Wetekamp that Germany needed nature parks comparable to those established at Yosemite and Yellowstone in the United States.[86] As a member of the Prussian Assembly, Wetekamp called on the state to assist in the "protection of monuments of the developmental history of nature that are indispensable to scientific research and nature study instruction, as well as the declaration of untouched natural areas as state parks similar to the national parks of the United States."[87] Echoing the VVS's conception of state-sponsored nature protection as a guarantor of ideal communitarian values, Wetekamp noted that "none of us could imagine that these type of beauties should be destroyed for such [materialistic] purposes in a civilized state [like Germany]."[88] One of Wetekamp's listeners in the assembly was Friedrich Althoff, the head of the Prussian Cultural Ministry, who responded with enthusiasm to Wetekamp's suggestion and began to investigate the possibility of creating such parks in Germany. Althoff commissioned Hugo Conwentz, the head of the West Prussian Provincial Museum in Danzig, to publish a report outlining the causes of the destruction of natural landmarks and the measures needed to protect them.

The result of Conwentz's three-year effort was *The Endangerment of Natural Monuments and Recommendations for their Preservation*, published in 1904.[89] This report became the cornerstone of Prussian nature preservation policy in the years before World War I. Based on Conwentz's suggestions in the report, Althoff sponsored the creation of the State Office for Natural Monument Preservation in 1906 within the Cultural Ministry. Althoff placed the State Office under Conwentz's leadership; it was first located in Danzig and was moved to Berlin in 1911. Conwentz was a good choice for heading up the new agency. A pragmatic scientist rather than nature romantic or *völkisch* nationalist, Conwentz was willing to work within existing parameters to protect Germany's natural monuments. As one historian has noted, a "sense of exactness and soberness and a certain tendency toward meticulousness characterized him already during his time in primary school and furthered his interest in natural science."[90] Also in 1906, Bavaria established its own State Agency for the Care of Nature, which was followed by the creation of a similar state office in Württemberg.[91] Given Prussia's dominance in the German Empire, the founding of the State Office proved to be a milestone in the country's development of a legal and institutional framework for environmental affairs. The National Socialists transformed this office in 1935 into the Reich Office for Nature Protection, Germany's first national nature protection office, which survived World War II to become the Federal Republic's initial environmental protection agency.[92]

Although Wetekamp saw the American national park system as a model for Germany, Conwentz recognized that large-scale reserves such as Yellowstone were inappropriate, given Germany's size and population density; one park the size of Yellowstone would have encompassed the entire kingdom of Saxony. The Nature Park Society, a private organization founded in Stuttgart in 1900 that counted 14,000 members by 1918, was successful in raising money to secure the first parcels for national parks in the Austrian Alps and the Lüneburger Heath near Hamburg, but such large-scale reserves remained the exception rather than the rule.[93] Conwentz envisioned the State Office as an umbrella agency for a decentralized array of regional and local efforts to secure individual natural objects or smaller conservation regions. He referred to his program as natural monument preservation *(Naturdenkmalpflege)*, whose linguistic affinity with historic monument preservation *(Denkmalpflege)* was a pragmatic attempt to extend the idea of heritage preservation, as well as its cultural-political aim of building national identity, to the natural world. Conwentz distinguished natural monuments as works of creation not influenced by human hands, whereas the traditional historic and artistic objects of *Denkmalpflege* revealed the workings of human artifice. Recognizing that most of the German landscape was not pristine like that of North America, Conwentz made room in his definition of the natural monument for areas where human influences were visible. "Here and there the concept [of natural monument] will need to be somewhat broadened," he wrote, "since completely untouched landscapes, as in other developed countries, hardly exist anymore."[94]

To implement natural monument preservation at the regional and local levels, Conwentz urged Prussia's provinces to form provincial and district nature preservation offices composed of state officials and leading members of private natural history and *Heimat* organizations. The Rhineland's provincial office, the Rhineland Provincial Committee for Natural Monument Preservation, was established in 1906. It included five district committees representing different geographical regions of the province, including the Bergisches Land (the "hilly region" on the Rhine's eastern bank south of Düsseldorf) and the left-bank lower Rhine, as well as offices in Cologne, Koblenz, and Trier. Like the VVS, the Rhineland Provincial Committee included a cross section of Rhineland officials and elites, including the Prussian head president Clemens August von Schorlemer, who replaced Nasse in 1905; the Rhenish provincial governor Ludwig von Renvers; the Bonn art historian Paul Clemen, the provincial conservator of monuments; and the Cologne district president Eduard zur Nedden, who was also commissioner of the Rhenish Association for Monument Preservation and Homeland Protection (Rheinischer Verein für Denkmalpflege und Heimatschutz, or RVDH); as well as university botanists, forestry officials, and mayors of the major cities throughout the region.[95] In addition to the state agency, private organizations such as the Eifelverein, dedicated to hiking and tourist promotion in the remote Eifel region along the Belgian-Luxembourg border, and the Rhineland-Westphalia Natural History Association often received state help for local nature protection efforts. The public-private cooperation first established at the Siebengebirge thus became a model for the state's subsequent nature protection activities.

By the early 1900s, observers began to refer to these combined state and private efforts as a new social movement: the *Naturschutzbewegung* (nature protection movement).[96] The *Naturschutz* campaign drew strength from Germany's existing networks of middle-class hiking, beautification, natural history, and outdoor recreation clubs, which often added nature protection activities to their repertoire of activity areas. New organizations devoted entirely to nature protection also emerged during this period of back-to-nature reform. For example, Lina Hähnle's German League for Bird Protection, founded in 1899, enjoyed rapid success in the Second Empire; its membership rose from 6,100 members in 1902 to 41,233 in 1914.[97] Arguing against the traditional division between "useful" and "harmful" birds, the group encouraged Germans to view both types as part of the overall balance of nature and thus worthy of protection. This effort was among the first to link aesthetic insights with broader ecological understanding. Bird protectionists successfully petitioned the Reich government to pass a law in 1888 that sought to stem the loss of bird diversity by limiting the hunting of targeted species and eliminating hunting methods deemed to be especially cruel. Bird protectionists also pioneered new ways of lobbying for public support, in-

cluding selling postcards and photographs, and showing films. They
instituted practical measures for bolstering bird populations as well.
These measures included establishing copses, building nesting boxes,
establishing winter feeding schedules, calling for an end to the use
of exotic bird feathers in the women's fashion industry, and encouraging rural families to abstain from using songbirds in their cooking,
a practice still common in the late nineteenth century. Unlike the VVS
and other nature protection and *Heimat* protection groups, Hähnle's
leadership enabled women to play a significant role in the organization; they made up 40 percent of the organization's local branch
heads.[98] The nature protection movement could thus muster support
from a variety of sectors in German middle-class society for protecting the flora, fauna, and landscape of the Fatherland.

Reflecting his training as a botanist, Conwentz's 1904 report focused its recommendations on protecting nature for scientific study,
education, and recreation. Science, rather than sentiment, would
guide his efforts at natural monument preservation. Through annual
nature preservation conferences and the office's journal, *Contributions to Natural Monument Preservation,* Conwentz established a
professional forum in which preservationists from across Germany
could coordinate their efforts. Through these venues, a scientific understanding of conservation based on the emerging field of plant geography became increasingly influential within *Naturschutz* circles
in the decade before World War I. Whereas preservationists during
the Siebengebirge campaign had relied primarily on aesthetic, historical, and cultural criteria to argue in favor of protecting the area,
Conwentz tried to establish scientific and presumably objective standards for identifying and preserving natural features. This scientific
perspective was especially evident in the designation of so-called nature protection regions *(Naturschutzgebiete),* such as bogs, moors,
meadows, and forests. Using insights from plant geography,
Conwentz envisioned these areas as characteristic parcels of the vegetation that had once dominated Germany's different regions. Plant geography gave Conwentz's work a holistic focus that was lacking in the
conservation of individual natural forms, and it prepared the way for
broader ecological insights about the relationship between floral or
faunal communities and their external environment.

Plant geography traced its roots to the early nineteenth century,
when the noted German geographer Alexander von Humboldt exam-

ined the way the natural environment shaped the distribution of plants in South America and beyond. Humboldt broke with the natural-historical traditions established by Carolus Linnaeus, who had focused on the taxonomic classification of plants and animals based on similarities and differences in their form and structure. Such an enterprise, Humboldt proposed, could never lead to what he termed *physique générale,* a universal science that he hoped would discern the underlying unity of all of nature. Humboldt proposed that the earth's vegetation formed itself into discrete plant associations, whose distribution was determined by environmental factors such as temperature, rainfall, sunlight, and soil conditions. He viewed these vegetational communities as superspecific, ontological units of study with unique properties akin to individual organisms. In his 1807 essay "The Geography of Plants," Humboldt presented the results of his research on vegetational distribution in South America's Andean cordillera. He correlated plant distribution with the earth's isotherms, areas following lines on a map of the earth that connect the regions having the same annual mean temperature. In this manner, Humboldt grouped all of the earth's vegetation into about fifteen general categories identified by the major plant type in each community: palms, firs, cacti, grasses, and so forth. Humboldt even noted that an individual mountain contained its own patterns of zonation, with lush rain forests flourishing in the damp, sunny, and rich soil areas near the base of the mountain and mosses and lichens in the extreme conditions of the mountain's peak. For Humboldt, the physiognomy of landscape revealed an ideal biological order that undergirded empirical data in a wide range of environments.[99]

Subsequent nineteenth-century biologists and geographers shunned Humboldt's quasi-theological belief that the close relationship between organisms and their environment revealed a divine plan in nature. Yet Humboldt's environmental analyses and holistic focus remained prominent in the work of such botanists as August Grisebach, Andreas Schimper, Joachim Schouw, Eugenius Warming, and Oscar Drude, who continued Humboldt's inquiries into the relationship between vegetational communities and their conditions of life. In his 1872 work *The Vegetation of the Earth,* Grisebach used the term *vegetational formation* to refer to meadows, forests, and moors as phytogeographic associations linked by shared environmental conditions and relationships with one another. In the wake of Charles

Darwin's theory of natural selection, Drude and other plant geographers emphasized the adaptive significance of the vegetational formation, retaining a holistic focus even though Darwinian analysis clearly posited the individual species as the only real unit of biological study.[100]

Despite its relative insignificance within German botanical studies at the university level, plant geography gave Conwentz the scientific basis he needed to establish natural monument preservation on a supposedly objective footing. The theory that plant formations were unified, stable communities uniquely adapted to particular climatic regimes led nature preservationists to advocate setting aside entire representative tracts of Germany's major biogeographical regions, including heaths, bogs, mountain forests, and lake regions. Such thinking guided preservationists' efforts to protect the Lüneburger Heath, for example, which they viewed as an example of the heath formation associated with northern Germany's climate and soils. In those regions where the landscape was damaged by economic activity, plant-geographical ideas were also applied as guidelines for restoration efforts. In the Siebengebirge, the VVS commissioned Bonn University botanists to help restore the areas destroyed by mining. In a protected reserve within the nature park, the group planted or transplanted species that were once "probably native" to the Siebengebirge. In addition, club members maintained in a plot near the town of Bad Honnef specimens of the area's famous orchid varieties, as well as an artificially created marsh for growing bog plants such as ferns and mosses, which they hoped to transplant later into the nature park.[101]

While Conwentz sought to establish scientific criteria for preserving and restoring the landscape, his writings nonetheless filtered environmental concern through a nationalist lens that reinforced the close connection between the natural environment and national character. Conwentz's belief in the importance of preserving or reintroducing Germany's indigenous species, for example, reflected concerns about the porousness of national borders, rather than merely the dictates of environmental factors. In a 1913 letter to the VVS, Conwentz underscored the negative impact of introducing foreign species into the native homeland. "How wrong it is," he noted, quoting one letter, "when the gardener smuggles into stands of trees . . . foreign forms from the Asiatic and American *Heimat* without thinking of the indigenous character of the [German] forest, [or] when he plants between our [own] oaks ash or elm species that do not at all fit the nature of our *Heimat.*"[102] In a similar vein, Conwentz criticized the VVS's practice of using American red oaks in areas of the Siebengebirge designated for commercial forestry. "Although for economic reasons it is only in a few cases possible to preserve the forest in naturally growing stands and [to promote] natural development," Conwentz wrote, "one should nevertheless in general avoid bringing exotic species into the forest as well as into the landscape scenery." While VVS members touted the brilliant fall color and rapid growth of the American red oaks, arguing that they had become "native" through cultivation efforts, Conwentz insisted that the society could achieve similar "picturesque" results using native German hardwoods.[103] Though couched in terms of neutral scientific observations, the preservation of natural monuments mapped national borders onto the physical landscape, shaping the natural world for the purpose of consolidating nationalist feeling.

Though Conwentz envisioned natural monuments as symbols of national pride, natural monument preservation also helped to produce a new sense of environmental stewardship at the regional and local levels. Unlike North American national parks, Germany's natural monuments and nature protection regions remained first and foremost local landmarks, cared for by local clubs and accessible to nearby residents. Rhineland *Heimat* advocates envisioned the region's juniper trees, red deer, extinct volcanic craters, and Rhine tributaries such as the Ahr as fellow members of the homeland, not distant, exotic experiences. They wrote poems to these natural monuments using the familiar second-person *Du,* organized hikes to describe their features to local schoolchildren, and created picturesque etchings that blended bucolic hills and forests with cultivated fields, church steeples, and half-timbered houses.[104]

In contrast to popular obsession with "charismatic megafauna" in the United States and on the African continent, *Heimat* environmentalism found a place for species not usually seen as majestic, beautiful, cute, or cuddly. Nature protectionists in the Rhineland, for example, sounded the alarm over the precipitous decline in the populations of local reptiles and amphibians, creatures that had suffered horribly in modern society's "war of destruction against primordial nature." As one preservationist noted in the pages of Conwentz's *Contributions to Natural Monument Preservation,* these animals were especially sensitive to changes in their habitat, such as the draining of bogs and ponds for agriculture, the straightening of streams for transportation, and the dumping of polluted wastewater. Unlike birds, who could in some cases escape such destruction by flying to a different habitat, reptiles and amphibians "cling to the soil of *Heimat* to a much greater extent, and for them a change in their habitat caused by development means in most cases not the signal to migrate, but rather certain death." The closeness of these animals to the lakes, streams, and soil of the *Heimat* also made them indicator species for wider changes in the landscape's overall ecological health. When turtles' shells wrinkled or peeled away due to habitat loss and pollution, preservationists maintained that it meant a much deeper disturbance in the balance of nature had occurred that would affect animals and humans alike.[105]

To make their case for protecting reptiles and amphibians, preservationists had to overcome individuals' revulsion for such animals, redefining concepts of beauty and value to encompass such creatures within *Heimat* sentiment. Among the animals most favored by nineteenth-century preservationists were birds, which bourgeois Germans admired for their freedom in flight, their cleanliness, and their careful attention to their young. In contrast, many observers found creeping amphibians and slithering reptiles "disgusting"; when touching a frog, children often cried, "How cold and wet!" and they believed erroneously that holding toads caused warts. Learning to recognize these fauna, as well, as members of a *Heimat* community required observers to recognize other types of sensory experiences. One author reminded readers of their childhood joy in collecting newts, salamanders, and tadpoles, or in hearing the "stupendous concert" emitted by frogs in a nearby pond. The author bemoaned his own hometown's decision to fill in a pond, located on the road leading to the town center, which had once supported a lively chorus of bullfrogs and other wildlife. In place of the "stimulating magic" of the old pond he now found the "sterile soil" of park benches and walkways, where sparrows took "baths of dust." Though the townspeople spoke with pride of their new "big city facilities" and the "sanitary value" of the new improvements, the town "was no longer the warm, cozy place I had preserved in my memory." *Heimat* memory could thus at times work to reinforce ecological concern, transforming ordinary animals into symbols of childhood innocence and linking environmental destruction to a loss of identity itself. Far from ignoring "real" environmental problems in favor of Romantic effusion, *Heimat* discourse was capable of fusing subjective nature experiences with a nascent vision of ecological interdependency.[106]

To counter Germans' ignorance about their country's flora and fauna, Conwentz devoted a majority of the State Office's resources to public edification. Reflecting his educated middle-class background, Conwentz attributed the endangerment of natural monuments to the population's "lack of education," rather than to industrial capitalism per se. He recommended that district offices create inventories of endangered natural monuments and raise public awareness about them. He furthermore urged primary schools to pay more attention to Germany's natural treasures in their science curricula, for "knowledge of the homeland and the Fatherland is the most important means to promote love of the Fatherland."[107] And just as bourgeois self-cultivation required the ability to control one's sensual appetite, so too did Conwentz propose that a highly cultured nation must curb its population's materialist impulses in order to attain the ideal goal of long-term environmental stewardship. Bemoaning the visual effects of such materialism among the masses, Conwentz condemned tasteless infractions such as walking paths bordered by makeshift railway tracks, brightly painted signs in scenic areas, and gaudy billboards in the countryside. He also denounced visitors' lack of respect for nature reserves, decrying the disposing of trash in protected woodlands, the plucking of rare flowers for bouquets, and the maiming or killing of small animals.[108] To counteract such actions, Conwentz encouraged outdoor clubs to print guidelines for hikers on postcards, pamphlets, and signs. While such efforts contributed to a heightened sympathy for nature protection, they nonetheless reflected nature preservationists' increasingly ambivalent attitude toward the general public, whose support they needed if they were to realize comprehensive environmental reform.[109]

## Preserving the Landscape's Physiognomy: Ernst Rudorff and the *Heimatschutz* Movement, 1904–1914

Conwentz's concerns about the spread of urban culture into the countryside reflected the growing influence of another wing of the landscape protection movement: the German Association for Homeland Protection. Founded in 1904 by Ernst Rudorff, the DBH dedicated itself to comprehensive landscape protection, including both historic and natural monument preservation, to save what Rudorff termed "the entire physiognomy of the Fatherland, as it has developed in the course of centuries and millennia."[110] Rudorff's focus on the face of the landscape infused the *Heimatschutz* movement with a holistic vision, a sense of moral purposefulness, and a conservative anticapitalism largely absent in Conwentz's more limited program of natural monument preservation. Romantic in temperament and broad-ranging in his abilities, Rudorff was equally adept publishing collections of Chopin's works and studying the plants and animals near his family's estate in lower Saxony.[111] His groundbreaking 1880 essay "On the Relationship of Modern Life to Nature" described for the first time the environmental damage to the German countryside caused by rapid industrialization in the years after national unification. Like Herder and Riehl, Rudorff viewed the landscape as an aesthetic totality that manifested its inhabitants' history, customs, and character and thus deserved protection and care. He once remarked that "in the inner and deep feeling for nature lies the actual roots of Germanic character."[112] Whereas the harmonious preindustrial cultural landscape had balanced human activities with natural processes, Rudorff feared that industrialization had irreparably disrupted this equilibrium. Through tasteless architecture, the straightening of waterways, the ever-expanding railway network, and the creation of tree farms in place of diverse woodlands, the proponents of industrial progress were "doing their best to make the pleasant and variegated countryside into a schematic plan—one that is as bare, clean-shorn and regularly parceled out as possible."[113] In Rudorff's view, this disfigurement of the German landscape reflected the lamentable moral condition of the German people, whose materialism had cut them off from their natural roots in the landscape. Rudorff also linked the aesthetic harmony of the preindustrial landscape to a deeply conservative social vision that feared the leveling tendencies of the liberal era, even arguing that alienation from nature was partially to blame for the "red menace" in Germany's cities.

To counteract these tendencies, Rudorff founded the DBH as a "gathering of all like-minded individuals who are concerned about preserving the German people [*Volkstum*] unweakened and unspoiled, as well as that which is inseparable from this, to protect the German *Heimat* with its monuments and its nature from further denigration. Because here and nowhere else lie the roots of our strength."[114] In the case of *Heimatschutz,* these "like-minded" individuals were from far more elite and educated backgrounds than most members of local *Heimat* and beautification societies and included prominent architects, art historians, lawyers, university professors, civil servants, and natural scientists.[115] Yet the club also attracted members from more modest backgrounds, including teachers and pastors, doctors and health care workers, and artists and journalists, as well as a considerable number of businessmen. Women accounted for only a small proportion of *Heimatschutz* members; many joined alongside a husband or other relative who was already a member. Rudorff's holistic vision of landscape protection led the DBH to endorse a broad range of preservation goals of which *Naturschutz* was only one component. The group pledged to carry out activities that might stop or redirect all forms of landscape disfigurement, including natural and historic preservation, saving the indigenous animal and plant world, and researching and preserving local folk art, morals, festivals, and costumes.[116]

Despite Rudorff's lofty goals and the DBH's high-profile membership, its record of concrete achievements at the national level remained disappointing in the years before 1914 because of the German state's unwillingness to infringe on property rights or economic development in the name of environmental protection. Among the fledgling group's first campaigns was the unsuccessful 1904 push to save the Laufenburg rapids on the upper Rhine in Baden from a hydroelectric dam. According to one DBH pamphlet, the dam promised to destroy a highly scenic series of rapids, "one of the most beautiful landscape scenes in Germany, or indeed the world." The DBH managed to convince such intellectual luminaries as Max Weber, Ernst Tröltsch, and Werner Sombart to support the campaign, arguing that the benefits of hydroelectric power and the lure of jobs at the electric plant did not outweigh the losses to the area's tourist industry.[117] Such advice was ignored, however, and a regional advisory board and then the Baden government approved the dam project in short order and let the rapids be obliterated. Commenting on the environmental significance of this loss, the architect Paul Schultze-Naumburg noted bitterly:

A time will come when it will be recognized that man does not live from horsepower and tools alone . . . because when man has gained every-

thing that can be gained using his technology, he will realize that the resulting easy life on a disfigured Earth is no longer worth living; that we
have torn up everything that our planet has handed to us, that this sub-
versive activity has destroyed [the planet] and thereby ourselves. Every
person should do his part, so that a transformation comes before it is
everywhere and forever too late.[118]

Such rhetoric demonstrated that local preservation battles had global
significance. Only by protecting the natural environment could Germans turn their backs on a merely materialistic culture; real *Heimatschutz* would result only from a fundamental change in cultural
values.

The DBH was also active in rural and town preservation; here the
results were mixed. *Heimatschutz* pressure was instrumental in encouraging Berlin lawmakers to consider broadening Prussia's 1902
Disfigurement Law, which forbade advertisements in picturesque regions such as the Rhine Valley, to include areas that were "scenically
beautiful" rather than "exceptionally scenic," as the law specified.
DBH leaders rightly concluded that such a change in the law would
give communities the power to protect a broader array of historic and
natural monuments and to direct development along more aesthetically pleasing lines, goals that echoed Rudorff's desire to preserve the
land's entire physiognomy. Unfortunately, the revised law, passed in
1907, fell short of their expectations, owing to pressure from property rights advocates who demanded compensation for any infringement on their exploitation of land. The law did enable local authorities to intervene in building decisions that could lead to the "gross
disfigurement" of town streets and squares, and exceptionally scenic
rural areas. *Heimatschutz* members serving on local advisory boards
were thereby able to have some influence on building projects and
historic preservation efforts in their municipalities.[119] Yet the 1907
law did not create new provisions for protecting "merely scenic" portions of the vernacular landscape, leaving numerous landmarks
without regulatory protection. District presidents, moreover, found it
difficult to develop criteria for designating an area "exceptionally scenic" according to the 1902 law's provisions, creating a wedge for
property owners and commercial interests to challenge the law's stat-
utes, as they had done in the case of the Siebengebirge.[120]

Like Conwentz's State Office for Natural Monument Preservation,
the DBH remained a loose amalgam of regional affiliates and local

clubs, each pursuing its own program of heritage preservation. In the Rhineland, the RVDH quickly developed into a semi-official arm of the Rhineland Provincial Administration's cultural affairs division, depending predominantly on administrative grants instead of membership dues or private donations to sustain its preservation mission. This organizational fusion of the RVDH and provincial cultural affairs ensured that the RVDH channeled its preservation and educational activities toward the Provinzialverband's goal of asserting the province's autonomy from Prussia and promoting the Rhine Province's special place within the newly unified German nation.

Securing this special place for the province meant that the Wilhelmine RVDH focused primarily on historic preservation rather than natural landscape protection.[121] The Rhine's former role as the boundary between the Roman Empire and the Germanic tribes had left the Rhineland with the largest share of Germany's archaeological objects and structures dating from classical antiquity, including the famous amphitheater ruins in Xanten and the thermal baths in Trier. RVDH art historians and conservators assisted the province in maintaining these Roman artifacts as well as the province's Romanesque, Gothic, Renaissance, and baroque structures. Provincial officials and the RVDH viewed these ruins as proof that the eighty-year-old Rhine province had had its own "culture" a thousand years before the rest of Germany. The American writer Grant Allen's comment in his 1899 book *The European Tour,* that "the Rhineland alone is the real and original civilized Germany," echoed the sentiments of many Rhinelanders who saw the river as a dividing line between themselves and the "barbarians" to the east.[122] The cultural landscape did, however, lead the RVDH to expand the field of preservation activities to include objects outside the traditional realm of churches, palaces, and bourgeois homesteads. Whereas the Hohenzollern monarchy focused on preserving artifacts of throne and altar, the RVDH saw the *Heimat* landscape as an aesthetic totality in which historic buildings and the natural landscape were part of a coordinated ensemble. The RVDH's attempts to research and preserve folk customs and dialects spurred efforts to preserve the Rhineland's vernacular peasant architecture, including entire rural villages, in the belief that the peasantry best represented the *Kulturlandschaft* ideal of culture and nature coexisting in aesthetic harmony. Many preservationists believed that destroying such architecture would also obliterate the traditional agrarian life that anchored German identity.

## Toward an Alternative Modernity: Industrial Society and Environmental Reform

While *Naturschutz* and *Heimatschutz* groups displayed a deep ambivalence about the environmental, social, and psychological effects of mass society, they were by no means "agrarian-romantics" who were hostile to all forms of technological development or economic progress.[123] Preservationists instead developed a nuanced approach to diagnosing modernity's environmental ills, one that focused predominantly on reshaping cultural values rather than restricting industrial production. Most landscape preservationists did not condemn the process of industrialization itself but believed that state oversight and public education could curtail its most damaging effects. In his 1904 report, for example, Conwentz identified tourism, personal irresponsibility, and a lack of education—not industrial capitalism or business interests—as the critical reasons for environmental destruction. Conwentz listed several economic processes that were especially harmful to maintaining animal and plant habitats, including agricultural reclamation, the destruction of moors for peat exploitation, and the regulation of streams for flood control and power generation. He noted that industrial gases had a detrimental effect on forests and other vegetation, and that industrial pollutants such as lead oxide had destroyed aquatic life in streams. Yet he never once suggested that industrial growth be curtailed in any way, only that certain features "here and there" be set aside as examples of scenic beauty or for scientific interest.[124] Rather than calling on the state to turn back the clock on economic development, Conwentz, like the majority of his contemporaries, considered industrialization and technological development as necessary evils.

Conwentz's conciliatory attitude toward industry also reflected the political realities faced by the State Office for Natural Monument Preservation at the time. Most representatives in the Prussian State Assembly rejected any attempts to infringe on private property ownership for the sake of nature protection; both conservatives and liberals blocked the passage of a 1912 law for the protection of natural monuments.[125] Persons designated as district nature protection commissioners were not considered state employees but served in an honorary capacity. Their main tasks consisted of identifying the natural monuments in their area and entering them into a centralized registry. The State Office also had no legal basis for preventing property owners from developing their land. Provincial and district committee members relied on persuasion to convince property owners to restrict development voluntarily or to request that planning officials consider the need to protect natural monuments in the issuance of building permits. The State Office did not provide funds for purchasing endangered sites, nor did it create rights of eminent domain for securing parcels of land. Conwentz left financial matters and legal issues to local groups, who had to raise the funds and popular support necessary for purchasing or leasing the land to create nature reserves. On the whole, therefore, the establishment of the State Office for Natural Monument Preservation provided neither the regulatory means nor the personnel for creating an extensive network of nature protection reserves.[126]

The *Heimatschutz* movement also moved toward a more conciliatory stance with industry in the decade preceding the First World War. When Paul Schultze-Naumburg became chairman of the DBH in 1904, he abandoned Rudorff's stern antiurbanism, directing *Heimatschutz* organizations to seek out ways to balance technological development with historical tradition and environmental stability. A founding member of the German *Werkbund* and the Secessionist movement, Schultze-Naumburg was well known as a vocal critic of nineteenth-century architectural historicism. He argued that the "Babylonian stylistic confusion" and "decoration insanity" of buildings in the period since unification, which borrowed from classical, Romanesque, Gothic, and baroque motifs, had created an unappealing mélange of styles. Schultze-Naumburg claimed that this eclecticism was unsuitable for a modern age that demanded sleek, tactful, and functional design. Unlike more radical modernists such as Otto Wagner and Paul Behrens, Schultze-Naumburg maintained that architects could achieve these goals while still preserving the historical ambience of a town or the character of a natural landscape. His architectural tastes tended toward the "around 1800" movement, which argued that the clean lines and bourgeois simplicity of the Biedermeier era of design (1815–1848) could serve as a model for contempo-

rary architecture and furniture. Crucial to his reevaluation of Biedermeier style was the belief that such architecture melded seamlessly
into the contours of Germany's landscapes. It was this insight that
gave Schultze-Naumburg interest in the ecological health of the landscape and the possibilities for naturalizing the built environment of
modern life.[127]

Like Rudorff, Schultze-Naumburg's interest in harmonizing the
built and natural environments began in his childhood. He spent long
hours armed with a sketchbook or watercolors, depicting the harmonious balance between historical churches, roads, walls, and houses
and the surrounding hills, orchards, wheat fields, meadows, and
streams of his Thuringian *Heimat*. After studying painting and then
architecture in Karlsruhe, Schultze-Naumburg moved to Munich in
1893, where he quickly joined the emerging Secessionist movement
there, and he continued his ties to the movement when he moved
to Berlin in 1897.[128] Between 1901 and 1917 he published his immensely influential *Cultural Works* series, which pioneered the use of
modern photography and clear, nontechnical language to popularize
*Heimatschutz* ideals among a broader reading public. "The books are
not exclusively directed to those who call themselves 'the educated,'"
he wrote, "but rather it is our hope to win over the entire people, the
lower middle classes, the peasants, the workers, everyone who over
time has been active in transforming the countenance of our land."[129]

The *Cultural Works* volumes covered nearly every detail of architectural, landscape, and urban design, which Schultze-Naumburg referred to collectively as the "environment," or *Umwelt*, a word that
would become common in environmental circles only after World
War II. Using side-by-side photographs of "good" and "bad" design
to popularize *Heimatschutz* aesthetic tastes, Schultze-Naumburg
condemned the "appalling disfigurement of the physiognomy of our
country" that had taken place in the previous fifty years. He set out
with missionary zeal to reform the entire "culture of the visual":
houses, monuments, bridges, streets, forests, machines, and defense
installations. Driven by a nineteenth-century faith in the power of
environmental reform and public education, Schultze-Naumburg believed such photographs demonstrated to all—from the businessman
to the gardener, from the street cleaner to the old woman placing
flowers in her window box—the advantages of *Heimatschutz* principles. In his view, such aesthetic judgments were wholly objective and

accessible to everyone, regardless of class or status. Since all Germans had contributed to shaping the environment, each person needed to participate in setting it on a more beautiful and sustainable footing.[130]

To a far greater extent than Rudorff, Schultze-Naumburg believed that planners and landscape designers could ensure a harmonious balance between industrial technology and the natural environment in the countryside. Just as Biedermeier style provided a blueprint for twentieth-century functional design, he reasoned, pre-1850 manufacturing facilities that were close to the land—windmills, paper mills, mines, artisans' workshops—also offered prototypes for modern factories. He believed it was possible to naturalize new technologies in the landscape; even the railroad, which early observers had often depicted as a steam-spewing monstrosity, was now an "old friend . . . which has captured a place in our emotional life." Schultze-Naumburg proposed that railways had become part of the organic landscape, but that more recent technologies, especially the dams, power lines, and transformers of the hydroelectric industry, disturbed the "changing rhythm" of the countryside.[131] In a similar vein, Schultze-Naumburg proposed that modern city planning had "sacrificed" the cozy squares, irregular streets, and hidden courtyards of older cities to the "Moloch of bureaucratism," the rationalizing tendencies that placed accelerated traffic circulation above the socio-psychological needs of urban dwellers. Cities, too, could be made more organic, by reducing their size and density, by creating extensive and accessible green spaces, and by retaining the irregular contours of the natural topography.[132] Such perspectives were welcome in the heavily industrialized and urbanized Rhineland. Schultze-Naumburg's vision of organic development led to numerous RVDH projects that blended factories and apartment houses into the surrounding landscape and led Cologne city planners to advocate new green spaces and the preservation of medieval squares.[133]

Schultze-Naumburg's view of city and countryside as unified organisms led him to investigate the broader ecological significance of environmental changes. He disparaged foresters who transformed the "holy cathedrals of German freedom" into "conifer factories," noting that the loss of species diversity destroyed the forests' value as animal habitat and left them vulnerable to insect infestation. Schultze-Naumburg also noted that modern farmers' tendency to remove the hedgerows separating their fields destroyed the habitat of birds, who are natural insect eaters, leaving the cultivator no choice but to rely on artificial insecticides. "This is how it goes in most cases," he lamented, "that whenever the terribly clever person takes a small wheel out of the great clockworks . . . [he] . . . does not think that then the entire mechanism comes to a halt."[134] *Heimatschutz* was by no means agrarian-romanticism; instead, advocates argued that proper planning and design could mesh technological development and environmental concerns into an organic whole. Far from being a cultural pessimist, Schultze-Naumburg believed in the possibilities of an alternative modernity in which, as one of his biographers has noted, it was possible "to combine the beauty and idyllic nature of the still preindustrial and still highly cultivated time around 1800 with the prosperity, comfort but also unprecedented growth in power of an industrial society."[135]

Despite Schultze-Naumburg's ability to create a modern vision of landscape planning, both the *Naturschutz* and *Heimatschutz* movements remained unable to articulate a program of environmental reform that appealed to broad sectors of German society. Preservationists continued to view nature as common ground and a site of social reconciliation, yet they tended to see this symbolic power as a way to quell political discontent and stem growing demands for a further democratization of Wilhelmine politics and society. This view grew in its scope and intensity in the years just before World War I, when the Social Democratic Party became the largest party in the Reichstag, the Imperial Parliament. In his widely read treatise *Der Naturschutz* (1912), for example, the noted botanist Konrad Guenther asserted that the goal of the nature protection movement was "to preserve the richness and beauty of the nature of our *Heimat,* so that the people can draw from her joy and instruction." In patriotic language much stronger than that of Conwentz or Rudorff, Guenther described how his own experience of Germany's natural beauty in travels "from the North Sea to the districts of Silesia" had stimulated his emotional attachment to the nation. In Guenther's view, the German *Volk* had a unique and primordial connection to nature, as evidenced by the ancient Germanic tribes' worship of nature, by folk songs that evoked the sounds of local birds, and by towns and places named after plants and animals. Such examples fostered Guenther's belief that "love of nature is the root of love of the Fatherland," and that the "roots of the people's strength" lay in the landscape itself.[136]

In Guenther's view, the destruction of natural features was the result of the alienating effects of a "relentlessly advancing [modern] culture," symbolized by the technologies and intellectually barren enticements of the city. "It has become very quiet in Nature," wrote Guenther, "but the noise of machines and the enjoyments of people ring all the louder." With people seeking leisure-time amusement or killing time in pubs, modern individuals failed to recognize that "true joy" did not come without "understanding" and "work." Though Guenther held scientific understanding to be the best form of nature appreciation, he also spoke of the immediate aesthetic appeal of nature as a remedy to urban superficiality. "Only under green trees and in clear air," he wrote, "is the ordinary man able to gain contentment and joy." Echoing the VVS's earlier emphasis on the egalitarian quality of nature experiences, Guenther stressed that nature offered a more powerful means for stimulating emotional attachments to *Heimat* than such high art forms as painting, music, and poetry. While these cultural productions were reserved for urbanites with leisure time and money, in nature, he said, "there is no difference between the high and the low, the poor and the rich. Nature is the mother to all persons in the same way. She demands no costs, and is available to everyone." More sacred than art itself, he said, "the forest is a cathedral more magnificent than anything that a human hand has ever built."[137]

Given the growing strength of the labor movement and the SPD in 1912, Guenther's populist characterization of nature carried deeper political significance; in his eyes, contact with the landscape could mitigate class strife. In an attempt to discern the reasons for industrial laborers' rejection of the existing system, Guenther portrayed alienation from nature as the root cause of class conflict. "The worker's walk through the park and over the meadows on his way home from the factory," he wrote, "pours into his heart a contentment that he cannot achieve elsewhere."[138] Like many nature preservationists, Guenther viewed urban workers' alienation from the land, which had left them "rootless" and without bonds to community and *Heimat*, as the source of their social unrest. "Modern times have brought a terrible change," he argued: "It is above all industry that draws the *Volk* into the city and alienates them from nature. A large part of the discontent that holds sway among the factory workers can be explained by this change, because while the healthy joys of the forest and field are open to all regardless of their status, the pleasures of the city are for the most part available only for the well-to-do."[139] Guenther contrasted the ugliness of the urban environment and the inequality workers faced in the city with an idealized view of the rural peasantry. He believed that peasants had retained their connections to the landscape's plants and animals, thereby leading a more moral and joyful existence. By experiencing the aesthetic pleasures of nature, workers would see past class differences and find themselves filled with *Heimat* feeling. Nature protection in the Kaiserreich, in this sense, was part of a larger conservative and paternalist social policy, one that sought to reintegrate workers into the fabric of national life through common appreciation of the natural landscape. Yet this project emphasized the lower classes' integration into a national community of sentiment fashioned by elites, not empowerment to participate in fashioning the nation on their own terms.

Not surprisingly, landscape preservationists achieved only limited success in using nature appreciation to woo workers back to the national fold. The aesthetic language of bourgeois landscape appreciation found little resonance among the organized sectors of the working classes. Rather than participate in such bourgeois hiking organizations as the Eifelverein, many Rhenish industrial workers joined the proletarian hiking club the Friends of Nature (Naturfreunde), which had one of its largest affiliates in the Rhineland. Founded by skilled Social Democratic workers in Vienna in 1895, this group spread to Germany and other European countries, gaining more than 10,000 members in Germany and Austria by 1914.[140] The Friends of Nature offered an alternative to middle-class outdoor leisure and nature appreciation. The organization's slogan, Free Mountains, Free World, Free Peoples, contrasted the unencumbered world of nature with the oppressive conditions of urban life under bourgeois capitalism and signaled the club's belief that knowledge of *Heimat* and nature was a stepping stone to political mobilization. Responding to plans by the Rhenish "iron power" August Thyssen to open a new gravel pit near Berlin and destroy cherished hiking areas, the editors of the group's magazine wrote, "It is hardly believable with what impudence capitalism attempts to sink its claws in everywhere."[141] Rather than affirming the classless solidarity of the local *Heimat*, Naturfreunde sought to use "social hiking" as a means to enhance proletarian class-consciousness.

The organized youth movement was also impervious to the *Heimat* message. Nature preservationists worked hard to win young people to their cause, organizing school presentations and public lectures at youth club meetings to popularize environmental protection. They expected a sympathetic audience; after all, *Wandervögel* clubs shared nature preservationists' belief in the spiritual healing powers of nature as well as their critique of urban life and tourism. These clubs affirmed preservationists' belief that a return to the land was a path to social and cultural reform. Yet young people's focus on individual authenticity and self-cultivation clashed with preservationists' attempts to promote group identities based on nation and *Heimat*.[142] *Heimatschutz* lectures were often greeted with "impatience" and youth club members found the self-important "posturing and affectation" common among bourgeois orators tiresome.[143] Young people were willing to support individual nature protection campaigns when their own hiking activities were placed in jeopardy, but few permanent ties developed between middle-class hiking groups and youth organizations.

Guenther's *völkisch* tirades against urban life and his idealization of nature have often been viewed as proof of a growing xenophobia within preservation circles on the eve of World War I, a protofascist tendency that equated the purification of land with the purification of the race. There were voices within the nature preservation movement around 1912 and 1913 that criticized Conwentz's *Naturdenkmalpflege* and sought to shift the movement's goals in more radically nationalist and racist direction. The Association for Nature Protection, founded in 1909, for example, disparaged the older preservation organizations and the State Office for Natural Monument Preservation for their lack of success and limited conception of preservation. The popular children's writer Hermann Löns, a key member of this group, demanded more comprehensive preservation and planning for the entire cultural landscape.[144] Criticizing natural monument preservation for its lack of vision, Löns remarked that "the destruction of nature is working 'broad scale,' nature protection 'on the details.' It is bureaucratically organized, has official recognition, yet has to avoid confrontation because industry, trade, and transportation [interests] have powerful semiofficial and official connections." In Löns's eyes, state nature protection was "insignificant" *(Pritzelkram)* and stood in the way of a more broad-based movement focusing on the landscape as a whole. "The work of natural monument preservation has no meaning for the general population," he concluded. For Löns, the significance of environmental reform was to protect the race; as he remarked: "The nature protection movement has often been thought of as a purely scientific movement. This is, however, not the case; on the contrary, it is a battle for the preservation of the health of the entire population, a battle for the strength of the nation, for the well-being of the race."[145] Such social Darwinist language was a striking departure from earlier *Heimat* rhetoric, which emphasized local civic participation and spiritual well-being, not racial struggle.

Despite Löns's popularity as a writer, his racist conception of *Naturschutz* was never more than an undercurrent within the Wilhelmine landscape preservation movement. It never successfully displaced preservationists' local, cultural, historical, and geographical understandings of *Heimat* and nation. The majority of Wilhelmine preservationists remained traditional conservatives, wedded to the didactic notion that aesthetic training would create better Germans. Guenther, for example, maintained the optimistic faith that education and educational reform would enlighten the population and lead them to take better care of the natural environment. The Kaiserreich's humanistic ideal of *Bildung*, he asserted, was partially to blame for Germans' lack of understanding for nature, because it had created a school system that remained averse to scientific instruction.[146] In a similar vein, Schultze-Naumburg, in the last volume of his *Cultural Works* in 1916, indicated that environmental destruction had slowed since 1900, and that public edification efforts had achieved noticeable results. He remained optimistic about the possibility of environmental reform, remarking that "one may not say that it is merely fate, that it cannot be otherwise. We humans are the ones who have caused the transformation of the earth's surface. It depends on our will to shape it in a different way."[147] Like that of so many preservationists, Schultze-Naumburg's optimism would soon fade. World War I and the Weimar period—a bloody four years of conflict and then continued political turmoil in the early 1920s—helped to recast *Heimat* ideals and nature sentiment along xenophobic and racist lines alien to environmental reformers in the long nineteenth century.

Landscape preservationists have often been overlooked in studies of the formation of German national identity in the Kaiserreich, yet they played an essential role in promoting the idea of landscape as the symbolic and emotional center of Germany's imagined national community. Middle-class preservationists fashioned a narrative of national development that went beyond the medieval past promoted by the Hohenzollern monarchy, locating Germany's origins in a natural world outside the flux of history. Their efforts reflected the Wilhelmine era's search for unifying symbols that stood above political factions. Germany's formal unification had not yet fulfilled early nineteenth-century hopes for a cohesive and stable nation; the newly unified German Reich remained "unfinished" in a number of ways. This unfinished quality was the product of lingering regional and religious fragmentation, as well as the new social and political anxieties produced by mass industrial society. By locating the nation's creative energy in nature, preservationists believed that they had found a way to mitigate the environmental consequences of industrialization and resolve the social tensions of modernity. Nature's accessibility and immediate aesthetic appeal provided a visual and tactile reminder of the nation's perdurability, signifying national solidarity in an era of cultural and social fragmentation.

Landscape preservation during the Kaiserreich was neither agrarian-romantic nor reactionary, as demonstrated by the diversity of political and social goals within the organizations from this period. The Siebengebirge's defenders believed that protecting this natural monument would ensure a recreational resource for the province's industrial workforce and believed that tourism would expand the local economy, not stem its growth. Conwentz's attempt to balance development by setting aside nature reserves and Schultze-Naumburg's faith in organic industrial design were not intended to turn back the clock on economic growth. Both *Naturschutz* and *Heimatschutz,* moreover, also achieved broader ecological insights in the process of agitating for landscape preservation. Though their aesthetic approach to environmental reform overlooked issues such as pollution and urban hygiene, preservationists recognized the interconnection between the landscape and all forms of life, from human communities to the salamanders in local creeks. They also realized that environmental transformations in one area often had rippling and unintended consequences, such as an upsurge in pests as a result of hedgerow destruction or a decline in fish species owing to river regulation. Though preservationists often idealized the period before 1850, they recognized that there was no going back to an agrarian society. Germans had the power to steer technological development along more environmentally sustainable paths that would protect the ecological and sociopsychological foundations of their local world. But they first needed a vision of an alternative modernity in which technological forces would be subsumed under environmental needs and ethical precepts.[148]

Despite their noble goals, nature preservationists could only partially resolve the German Reich's many environmental, political, and social challenges. Germany remained a loose conglomeration of diverse states, provinces, and landscapes, despite preservationists' assertion that local *Heimat* protection was simultaneously a form of national patriotism. The fusion of regional and national identity therefore remained contested. The competing Reich, Prussian, Rhenish, and local definitions of *Heimat* and environmental reform that emerged in the years after World War I called into question any easy connection between local and national homelands. Despite the unifying rhetoric of *Heimat,* moreover, class distinctions continued to permeate the nature preservation movement, as most members remained wary of the "masses" and envisioned themselves as stewards and educators, rather than cocreators, in the project of *Heimat* cultivation. Instead of mobilizing *Heimat* sentiment "from below," landscape preservationists relied on the state to secure their place as regional cultural stewards. As the next chapter shows in greater detail, preservationists' goals evolved in tandem with the state's cultural-political needs; when the state needed *Heimat* sentiments to secure public loyalty and disparage perceived "enemies," preservationists developed a far more rigid and xenophobic vision of nature's homelands.

# CHAPTER TWO

# The Militarization of Nature and Heimat, 1914–1923

> The German landscape in its unending diversity, solemn and yet festive on the North Sea coast, full of magic in the lowlands, lovely and charming in the mid-lying hills and majestically exalted in the high mountains—this German landscape, which in this time of struggle and battle is for us the greatest thing we have to defend . . . says to you [the reader] this is your *Heimat,* this is your Fatherland, this you must protect against enemies and those who begrudge us, for this your sons summon life and blood to protect it for you.
>
> —FRANZ GOERKE, PREFACE TO WILHELM BÖLSCHE'S *DIE DEUTSCHE LANDSCHAFT IN VERGANGENHEIT UND GEGENWART,* 1915

The outbreak of the Great War in 1914 indelibly altered the rhetoric and practice of regional landscape preservation in Germany. To sustain state aggression in an age of total war, Reich, Prussian, and provincial officials called on *Heimatschutz* and *Naturschutz* organizations to bolster civilian morale, mobilizing the home front's so-called "spiritual weapons" *(geistige Waffen)* to help sustain the industrial warfare that was killing millions in Belgium, France, and East Prussia. Landscape preservationists viewed their efforts to assist the state in building *Heimat* sentiment as a logical extension of their previous national idealism, and they embraced their new role with increasing enthusiasm. This new relationship between landscape preservation and state propaganda efforts reshaped the institutional framework and cultural-political meaning of landscape preservation, infusing *Heimat* and nature with novel and sometimes ominous meanings largely absent in the Wilhelmine period. The Great War replaced nineteenth-century Romantic aestheticism with a militarized understanding of *Heimat* and the natural landscape. As Franz Goerke's comment demonstrates, images of Germany's primordial landscape articulated a new kind of patriotism, one that legitimized young men's sacrifices by framing the nation as a timeless, organic entity.

This new patriotism viewed rivers, woodlands, hills, and farmlands as symbols of the inviolate *Heimat,* but it quickly became more aggressive. To create an emotional arsenal against Germany's enemies, landscape preservationists reinterpreted natural monuments as guardians of a Germanic spatial and ethnic identity that was differentiated geographically, culturally, and racially from French and Slavic peoples. Such geographic and ethnic determinism proposed that the German ethnic character emerged organically from the homeland soil. The landscape's aesthetic beauty alone was not what sustained soldiers' battle in the trenches; rather, it was the recognition that landscapes nurtured the biological roots of their *Volk.* Outside the *Heimat,* young men were demonstrating the superiority of German *Kultur* in the devastated meadows and forests of Flanders and northern France. Inside the *Heimat,* an increasingly feminized depiction of *Heimat*'s untouched meadows and meandering streams beckoned for them to return to their homeland, even in death. This sharp division between the masculine war front and the feminine home front called on patriotic Germans to do their part by maintaining vigilance against the enemies, external and internal, that threatened to desecrate the timeless splendor of the *Heimat.*

The war thus provided a discursive wedge for bellicose, *völkisch* rhetoric to insinuate itself into landscape preservationist discourse. This new rhetoric glorified the primordial, biological bond between the German *Volkstum,* a racist-tinged formulation of *Volk,* and its central European homeland, arguing that German ethnic character grew from the soil of the *Heimat.* Had Germany's political and social situation stabilized after its defeat in 1918, such essentialist rhetoric, and the state organs that supported it, might have faded in favor of traditional bourgeois aestheticism and quiet civic reconstruction. Yet in borderland regions such as the Rhineland, the armistice brought no peace, and the mobilization of *Heimat* continued long past 1918. Soon after German representatives signed the Treaty of Versailles, French occupation of the region brought the "enemy" closer than at any point during the war itself, while French propaganda and separatist movements tried to disconnect the province from the Reich. Economic collapse following a general strike in the Ruhr also kept the region in a state of emergency until 1923. Landscape preservationists resharpened their spiritual weapons against the new invaders; *Naturschutz* and *Heimatschutz* publications depicted nature as the organic force that gave meaning to the war experience and that would spearhead Germans' cultural and racial renewal. In this view, *Heimat* landscapes provided a bulwark against "foreign" influences and a force for "rooting" unruly segments of the population to the national soil, a depiction that often overwhelmed older references to nature as an idyllic site for inner contemplation. Such rhetoric also enabled chauvinist rhetorical structures and new forms of geographic and ethnic determinism to shape the meaning of *Heimat* and the agenda of nature protection for years to come. The continued militarization of *Heimat,* moreover, placed landscape preservation in an ambiguous relationship to Germany's new republic. Despite the supposed normalization of everyday life between 1925 and 1929, vigilance about the character and boundaries of *Heimat* created an undercurrent of anxiety in the Weimar preservation movement that made it impossible to articulate an open, inclusive, and pluralist concept of *Heimat* befitting a democratic government.

## Mobilizing the *Heimat* in World War I

The outbreak of World War I in August 1914 engendered cautious optimism among *Heimat* and nature enthusiasts, who greeted the war as an opportunity for Germany to end its growing international isolation and to begin a process of national renewal. In the Rhine Province, the fear that the area would quickly become a battlefield initially halted *Heimat* activities altogether. The Eifelverein, the middle-class hiking organization that promoted tourism in the province's far western Eifel hills, discontinued hiking and trail-marking activities in the vicinity of the Belgian and French borders because of its proximity to the western front.[1] Most organizations assumed that such measures would be temporary and that German victory would bring a rapid end to hostilities. Even though their fears about a Rhenish front did not materialize, preservationist organizations experienced growing organizational and membership problems once they resumed their activities. Because many club members were called for military service or were fully engaged in providing for their family, preservationist organizations experienced steady declines in membership throughout the war period. The Eifelverein reported a drop in its number of local organizations from 132 in 1914 to 102 in 1918, and inflated railway prices and war conditions stemmed the flow of tourists into the area.[2]

Normal patterns of club sociability were also affected; the Rhenish Association for Monument Preservation and Homeland Protection (RVDH), for example, chose not to hold its planned tenth-anniversary celebration because of the war.[3] Such limitations on activities and growth nonetheless appeared minor in light of the patriotic demands of the time.

Rather than viewing the war as a detriment to *Heimat* activities, most preservationist leaders spoke of war as an *opportunity* to realize "ideal" organizational aims stymied by late-Wilhelmine political wrangling and class tensions. Kaiser Wilhelm II's declaration of a *Burgfrieden,* or "fortress truce," in 1914, designed to bring the country's different political parties, social classes, and regional interests together for the duration of the conflict, resonated throughout regional *Heimat* organizations. Groups such as the RVDH claimed that their local attempts to promote homeland awareness had prepared the way for the current flowering of German patriotism. Club members trusted that, in this great patriotic moment, *Heimat* ideals would finally attain the recognition they deserved from state officials and the public at large. The RVDH called on Rhinelanders to put aside the long-standing tensions between the Rhine Province and Prussia in recognition of Prussia's role in uniting Germany and providing a bulwark against the Reich's enemies. RVDH publications claimed that before Prussian annexation in 1815, the Rhineland had remained divided among competing dynasties that lacked awareness of the region's "German" character, enabling the region to fall into the hands of French enemies. "Weak-willed and meekly the population tolerated the occupiers' rule," wrote one RVDH member, "because the feeling for Fatherland and a national sensibility had been whittled away through the narrowness of small state pettiness, because higher goals were missing."[4] In his view, the Prussians, not Napoleon, had first rescued Rhinelanders from this predicament, allowing them to awaken politically and to demand self-determination. Rhenish *Heimat* groups were thus willing to embrace the Prusso-German variants of national memory during wartime, a recognition that state power overrode particularism in securing a German victory. In this context, they hoped that *Heimatschutz* could also shed its reputation for antiquarianism and elitism and be recognized instead as an "immediate duty" and a vital contribution to uniting all factions of the German "people's community" *(Volksgemeinschaft).*[5]

Despite this emphasis on Prussian statism in forging German unity, war imbued local *Heimat* activities with novel meanings and provided broad opportunities for popular participation. The *Gymnasium* teacher Georg Kreuzberg, for example, praised German schoolteachers for conveying a proper "understanding of their time" to pupils and planting within them a "duty-conscious" desire to serve the community during the war.[6] In Kreuzberg's view, their efforts at *Heimat* studies—including local geology, natural history, history, art, and industry—opened up cognitive pathways to national patriotism, for "without the right love of *Heimat* there cannot be the right love of Fatherland," and "one can love only what one knows." Kreuzberg also believed that wartime imbued everyday objects with a sacred quality, making them immediate artifacts for *Heimatschutz* collection. He encouraged teachers to guide students in collecting "witnesses of our great present," such as announcements from military officials, soldiers' letters, war cards, death notices, photographs with *Heimat* significance, or even their own diaries containing details about ordinary townspeople's heroic sacrifices. Such items would give "flesh and life" to existing municipal *Heimat* museums or could form the nucleus of a collection where such a museum did not already exist.

Kreuzberg's vision of the wartime *Heimat* left no room for skepticism about victory, doubts about social cohesion, or despair about wartime violence and deprivation. The artifacts would instead provide material witness "into the distant centuries . . . [of] . . . the iron unity of our people, of the fantastic enthusiasm . . . the willingness to sacrifice among all sectors of society . . . the general will to victory."[7] Local *Heimat* collections thus participated in a new kind of memory work during the war, one that instantaneously converted formerly antiquarian interests into monumental history. This new focus transformed individual experiences into documents of national glory and self-consciously hoped to consolidate the nation's future by providing the *Volksgemeinschaft* with testaments of unity long after the inevitable national triumph.

The growing militarization of *Heimat* sentiment soon reshaped the content and meaning of landscape imagery, giving new life to *Naturschutz* demands for better environmental protection. Using the same marketing strategies that had once attracted tourists to the Rhine Valley, Black Forest, and Harz Mountains, government officials used postcards, etchings, and posters to remind Germans of their duties to the home front. Sketches of sleepy villages surrounded by forests and bucolic farmland admonished Germans to buy war bonds, ration goods, and send letters to their sons at the front.[8] Even ordinary nature study could support the new patriotic enthusiasm. In his 1915 book *The German Landscape in Past and Present,* the noted popular science writer Wilhelm Bölsche described the Eifel as the "Yellowstone Park of our Fatherland," whose nearly "fresh volcanoes ... [and] ... intact lava flows look like they solidified only yesterday," reminding visitors of the geological origins of their homeland. He wrote of how powerful shifts in the earth's crust during the Tertiary Period (approximately five million years earlier) had later created the primordial bed for the Rhine, in which melting ice gradually eroded shale deposits to form a powerful river. According to Bölsche, such pivotal natural-historical events "tell us at every step about the incalculable periods before our time," connecting Germans to a landscape millions of years old.[9] Franz Goerke, head of the Urania popular science society in Berlin and the book's publisher, asserted that such a book should "bring you luminous hours even during these solemn, difficult times, and *Heimat* and love of *Heimat* should ring in your heart." Nature thus connected the nation through time and space, giving individuals the courage to weather the difficulties of the present in the hope of a rapid victory.

As the war dragged on, however, and hope for a quick victory vanished, *Heimat* and nature groups found themselves adapting to the prospects of long-term war by linking themselves more closely to state and provincial political aims. These aims required a mobilization of sentiment, of the spiritual weapons necessary to justify German war aims and boost sagging civilian morale. As Celia Applegate has noted, the conduct of total war required a carefully crafted and increasingly gendered dichotomy between the home front and the war front that juxtaposed bucolic landscapes unsullied by industry or conflict with the violence taking place at the front. Wartime thus intensified the nineteenth century's cult of domesticity by clarifying its opposite; *Heimat* was to function as a site of maternal stability, hometown cohesion, and pastoral beauty that made soldiers' horrifying sacrifices worth the effort.[10] Georg Kreuzberg spoke of the importance of local *Heimat* for the national cause, noting that "the ordinary man of the people, who stands across from the enemy in the trenches, who gladly endures all types of privations and risks his life in heroic fulfillment of his duty, wants to protect his homeland and his family. To him *Heimat* and Fatherland are concepts with the same meaning . . . If our love of Fatherland is to have any content—and it must have this, if it is to retain vitality—it can only gain this through *Heimat*."[11] One Rhenish soldier on the Polish front echoed this conceit, noting that "the *Heimat* lies like a dream far behind us. But how often our thoughts wander from East to West, where . . . wife and child . . . hope for our return." Yet such comforting images of love awaiting him in the Rhenish homeland had to be subordinated to the proud thoughts of a German soldier, who had been called to "serve Germany's honor against a world of enemies, if necessary with his heart's blood."[12] References to the maternal *Heimat* allowed Germans to imagine a sharp division between home front and war front. A Darwinian struggle for existence characterized the fierce battles of the war, while visions of Germany's pastoral natural landscapes, beautiful yet vulnerable, spurred soldiers' fighting spirit and their hope for a safe return home.[13]

The rhetorical division between pastoral *Heimat* and the Darwinian front also found expression in soldiers' everyday experiences in the trenches. As George Mosse showed in his pathbreaking work *Fallen Soldiers,* the war gave a cruel and ironic twist to bourgeois youths' faith that a return to nature elevated the spirit. Young men who had once appreciated the landscape's beauty from railway cars and observation towers now dug into the earth in what many of them viewed as a descent from civilization to barbarism. Engulfed in mud and slime from the rain, fog, and porous soil of northern Europe, soldiers imagined themselves as "swamp beings," experiencing nature in a new and horrifying way that made death and decay a way of life. As Mosse notes, death was ever present, as soldiers used unburied corpses as supports for their guns and as markers to find their way back into the trenches. The surrounding landscape, moreover, "was more suggestive of the moon than the earth, as heavy shelling destroyed not only men but nature, a devastation that would haunt the imagination of those forced to live in the trenches."[14]

Soldiers' diaries and war correspondence repeatedly drew comparisons between natural destruction and the death of soldiers, with both types of devastation manifesting the collapse of nineteenth-century civilization. In their writings they commented on the "murder" of pine forests that fell just as quickly as the men who went over the top into no-man's-land, while the soils of Galicia "drank" more blood than any spot on earth. "Who would want to measure it," asked one war reporter, "and what would the number of the all-powerful crimson streams that have flowed and dried up over there mean, which the earth rescues into her merciful arms, which the all-mighty sun pulls back into its sphere of light?" Commenting on the freshly dug graves that dotted the countryside, the same reporter noted that "the wooden crosses on top of heights and meadows . . . not only cover over the corpses of the fallen men and their pain, but also announce a world of sorrow that the living must bear."[15] Despite the carnage that accompanied total war, such images of nature recovering the blood of soldiers demonstrate that observers often used Romantic nature imagery to make sense of the war. Soldiers' letters repeatedly described the colorful spring flowers blossoming alongside the trenches or larks flying into the air, a hopeful contrast to the grim and increasingly hopeless machinery of death.[16] Some German intellectuals even imagined a new man emerging from the trenches, one whose experience with nature's elemental forces of life and death would create innovative ideals to replace the nineteenth century's outmoded and "mechanistic" vision of reality.

Those who experienced the front were also struck by nature's power to heal itself, as scarlet poppies emblazoned the burned-out landscapes of Flanders and clover covered the scars on the earth's surface. As one British nurse commented, natural recovery seemed to overpower memory. "Nature herself conspires with time to cheat our recollections," she wrote; "grass has grown over the shell holes at Ypres, and the cultivated meadows of industrious peasants have replaced the hut-scarred fields of Etales and Camier where once I nursed the wounded in the great retreat of 1918."[17] Other observers imagined gravesites as gardens, where the planting of corpses collapsed national distinctions in the fields of the dead. "In a field behind the churchyard was a new burial site," wrote one correspondent. "There lay Germans, Austrians, Czechs, and Russians, each buried in their own part, and in my glance over these equally spaced rows, which gave the impression of a bed in a freshly dug garden, the image of death appeared to me in the form of a gardener who had tilled his land in loving orderliness and deliberate preparation for a giant harvest."[18] This image of soldiers' corpses as seeds for the next cycle of natural renewal continued into the postwar era, when cemeteries and memorials turned gravesites into landscape gardens. Such fields of the dead embedded soldiers' bodies in nature's maternal bosom; elsewhere "Germanic" oak trees were used to signify fallen soldiers in "heroes' groves."[19] The belief that corpses became one with the cosmic rhythms of nature gave new meaning to wartime sacrifice. Indeed, many postwar Germans would later believe that just as springtime vegetation could heal the wounds produced by technological warfare, so too could the soil itself rejuvenate Germany and heal her social divisions and political wounds.[20]

Employing *Heimat* motifs about nature's healing powers to understand soldiers' experiences in the trenches thus blurred the boundaries between war front and home front. This dissolution of boundaries also occurred within the home territory, where the conditions of total war led to an unprecedented militarization of civilian life. In 1916, a memorandum from the War Ministry spoke of the need to harness ordinary hiking activities for military purposes: "Hikes, which have belonged for a long time to the most pleasant recreations of German life, deserve to be recognized as a form of healing and should also find use in military preparation plans."[21] Eifelverein leaders responded favorably to this proposal, for it offered a new, patriotic rationale for hiking and outdoor recreation. The club's publication chairman, Michael Zender, wrote that hiking was not merely a matter of "conviviality and enjoyment," but rather followed "higher and more noble goals." The Eifelverein's "carefully executed hiking movement strives for the physical training of the population," he said, while experience with a "magnificent mountainous region awakens the love and joy of *Heimat* nature and of the Fatherland near and far in the widest circles [of society]."[22] Another club leader echoed this view, noting in 1915 that youth hostels were necessary for the "development and strengthening of our people" and emphasized the value of hiking as an instructional tool for furthering "self-confidence, modesty, a steeling of the body, and the strengthening of character."[23]

This militarization of ordinary hiking frowned upon the youth movement's vision of nature as a refuge from bourgeois norms. In 1916, Cologne's mountaineering and hiking association spoke out against the "excess[es] of the contemporary hiking movement," which it referred to as "wild *Wandervögel*." The club chastised "hiking brats" for mistreating natural areas and for their "feminine, often dubious entourage . . . the carnivalesque looking clothing of many male and female hikers, the nerve-racking, overwhelmingly loud twanging on all sorts of musical instruments."[24] The wartime *Heimat* could no longer tolerate young people's use of nature as a refuge or a place in which to cultivate their individuality; it had to subsume such impulses under the state's cultural needs.

Homeland and nature protection groups not only assisted officials in mobilizing sentiment in the trenches and at home but also wielded their spiritual weapons to defend Germany against foreign propaganda. The RVDH depicted the war as the latest confrontation in the age-old conflict between Germans' deeply emotional *Kultur* and the superficial and materialistic *civilisation* of the French. When the French labeled the Germans "barbarians, Huns, and Vandals" for firebombing the Reims cathedral and circulated pamphlets and cards portraying the tragic event, RVDH members helped to downplay the destruction. "The broad masses of the people," noted Friedrich Wilhelm Bredt, "whose immature taste, as seen in the area of postcards, is well known, buy such touched-up pictures and suddenly believe them."[25] The Rhineland's cultural stewards also reminded the population of French atrocities committed in the seventeenth century. Bodo Ebhardt noted that Rhine Valley ruins "teach us what our fate would be if the hordes of our enemy descended upon us again . . . Think on the picturesque image of the Heidelberg castle ruins . . . and let it . . . be a call to hatred, to revenge, and to battle to the bitter end."[26]

Ebhardt's evocation of Rhineland castle ruins to rekindle Rhinelanders' hatred of the "hereditary enemy" reflected a wider tendency in *Heimatschutz* circles to imagine their Rhenish homeland as a sharply bounded and organic entity, rather than a fluid and dynamic zone of cultural contact. Before 1914, the concept of *Heimat* had indistinct contours and multiple emotional referents; the "mental map of *Heimat* consciousness," notes Celia Applegate, "had differentiations but not divisions. Home was not a clearly bounded concept; and even among 'homelands,' things slid into one another." Wilhelm Heinrich Riehl had described Germany as a rainbow in which it was impossible to tell "where the yellow-orange stripe ends and the orange-yellow stripe begins."[27] During the course of the war, in contrast, *Heimatschützer* tried to pinpoint the border between cultural landscapes in exact and "scientific" terms. Ignoring evidence of Norman-French architectural influences in Lorraine, for example, one RVDH architect claimed that differences between the "Roman"-

style stone house and the "Germanic" half-timbered cottages *(Fach-werkhäuser)*, as well as the variations in place names and language use in the region, revealed an "ancient nationality border."[28] The French monarchy's incorporation of the area in the seventeenth century had supposedly disrupted this natural frontier. The author hoped that its rediscovery would guide architectural and, presumably, political reconstruction after the war. This wartime obsession with delineating the spatial perimeters of the homeland, a process that continued well into the Weimar Republic, was an attempt to make the aesthetic concept of *Heimat* more concrete. Preservationists maintained that ethnic groups literally stamped their character onto a particular landscape and were in turn shaped by that same topography, creating an organic whole impervious to ephemeral diplomatic agreements or political decisions. By visualizing the border between nationalities, in other words, the *Heimatschützer* put a material face on the spiritual battle between *Kultur* and *civilisation*.

Constructing *Heimat* as a bounded, organic whole rooted in the landscape required ever sharper differentiation from ethnic Others who did not share Germanic cultural sensibilities. The attempt to demarcate nationality based on visual differences in cultural landscapes also shaped the experiences of soldiers on the eastern front, where Germans needed to maintain the cultural and ethnic boundaries between themselves and the "inferior" Slavs. During his tour of duty in Poland, for example, the Rhenish *Heimat* enthusiast Hugo Otto wrote of learning about the land and people of Poland during his "numerous hikes through his new wartime *Heimat*," which he hoped would later "replace the raw war experience with pleasant memories." Otto's "pleasant memories" nonetheless focused on the "primitive" conditions of Poland, to him a clear sign of the Poles' inability to manage their natural resources properly. Describing the highway from Ostrow to Kalisch, Otto was astounded by the "unregulated" landscape, which to him manifested "the stamp of real Polish economy." His descriptions noted that trees were planted along the sides in disorderly groups in which "stately acacias with their typically beautiful forms . . . [stood alongside] . . . Canadian poplars . . . [and] cherry, apple, and plum trees, often with everything confusingly multicolored and untended." The Poles' inability to bring order to the landscape reinforced German stereotypes about Poles' cultural and racial inferiority. Otto lamented Polish villages' unregulated streams, unsanitary waste disposal, and primitive cottages made of "clay and unbaked bricks" topped by straw roofs. The dwellings, he said, "obviously reflect the poverty of the inhabitants. In such huts only a race of slaves, without culture and full of servile unworthiness, could thrive . . . In Poland everything is in the end Polish, i.e., carelessness and dirt dominate all conditions."[29] By depicting the Polish cultural landscape as impoverished and inferior, Otto justified the war as a "civilizing" mission that would spread German *Kultur* and technical know-how to these areas.

Reconstruction of the eastern borderlands destroyed in the battles with Russian forces at Masurian Lakes and Tannenberg provided the opportunity to create a physical bulwark against such Slavic influences. In 1915, the Prussian State Assembly passed a series of building ordinances directing planners to incorporate "native" medieval styles in new, functional buildings so that they would reinforce the region's "Germanic" character. German Association for Homeland Protection (DBH) members applauded these plans as a triumph of *Heimatschutz* architectural and landscape ideals, a clear sign that the war had confirmed the movement's status.[30] The public would view *Heimatschutz* advocates' "grounded" *(bodenständig)* architectural principles not as the "costly hobby of unworldly aesthetes" but as ideas that combined "utility and beauty."[31] More important, the reconstruction would serve as an architectural barrier against "Eastern" influences. One National Liberal deputy noted that "when one considers that the future East Prussia should be a border marker of German culture against the 'Asiatic' East, then we need to make sure that the outward characteristics of the built environment in towns find consideration here."[32] This conception of "Germanic" reconstruction reflected the militarized rhetoric of war by insisting that landscape and urban design should reflect essential ethnic characteristics. This reification of *Heimat* reflected a new xenophobic and defensive tenor in landscape protection and heritage cultivation, one that continued into the peacetime era of the Weimar Republic.

## Remobilizing the *Heimatfront,* 1918–1923

By 1918, the *Heimat* movement's task of rallying popular support for the war became increasingly futile. The Reich government's mishandling of civilian provisioning, which led to near starvation in many of

Germany's major cities, made a mockery of the inviolate home front. Discontent among manual laborers, soldiers returning from the front, and, especially, working-class women led to a revolution in November 1918 that toppled the Kaiserreich. Deprivation had left its mark on the landscape; Eifelverein leaders noted in 1919, for example, that the Eifel's forests had suffered decimating losses due to the need for wood as heating and building material during the war. "During the war years," noted one publication, "the old trees in our region were heavily cleared due to a great lack of timber. Numerous ancient oaks, beeches, lindens, and nut trees fell to the ax." Club leaders hoped to rally their members and the public to protect the remaining old-growth stands by creating a registry of ancient trees and forests and by declaring them natural monuments. Yet transportation and paper costs, as well as general demoralization, prohibited any immediate progress for such *Naturschutz* projects.[33]

Landscape preservationists hoped for a period of stabilization after the war that would allow them to inventory environmental losses, begin planning for future nature reserves, and undertake restoration efforts. The *Heimat* movement now had a new mission: to spearhead the "inner healing" of German society by rebuilding ties to nature, homeland, and nation.[34] Echoing the feelings of frontline soldiers and *Heimat* clubs during the war years, preservationists touted the healing power of nature as Germans' only hope for national renewal in the face of military defeat and international condemnation. As Hermann Bartmann's 1920 work *Heimat Care, Monument Preservation, and Homeland Protection* noted, "Today on German soil *Heimat* feeling is again stirring everywhere, and care of the *Heimat* has again become a demand of the day." Claiming that *Heimat* feeling was available to all Germans, regardless of status, Bartmann commented that "I have written this book for the life of the *Volk*, to show the way toward the beauty of *Heimat* for all of those who cannot satisfy their spiritual needs with big-city sensations. It is a book of love that promotes love of the *Heimat* soil, the final thing, next to the power of our labor, that has saved us."[35] Another work from 1920 reminded readers of their emotional ties to *Heimat*, "the old trusted nest" they had learned to appreciate in their youth. "Like a true mother," wrote one author, "the old *Heimat* gathers all of her children to her with the same enormous love. Even if status and property, education, and belief divide people so much from one another, in the *Heimat* all are the same; in it they find themselves standing together solidly."[36] Homeland sentiment offered psychological comfort in the wake of military defeat and continued deprivation.

This attention to *Heimat* as a force for building cross-class solidarity took on a problematic cast among more conservative observers, who argued that the people's "uprooting" during the process of industrialization had left the home front vulnerable to a range of ills, from socialist ideas to gross materialism. The nature protectionist Konrad Guenther, for instance, argued shortly after the war that the country's defeat was the result of Germans' not being rooted firmly enough in the soil of *Heimat*. In Guenther's view, the dire postwar situation required that "the ground upon which the people stand can only be the soil of *Heimat*. The more firmly [the people are] rooted, the harder [they are] to uproot . . . People who love their *Heimat* defend it to the extreme and are unconquerable. But what does one love in the homeland? . . . One loves Nature!"[37] Just as the Romantics had used nature to rediscover German national identity during the Napoleonic era, so too would the people use forests, rivers, and moors to rebuild their strength in the 1920s. If Germans did not turn back to nature, Guenther warned, they would become "cultural fertilizer for other nations."[38]

Despite Guenther's admonishment that Germans return to their natural origins, nature protection activities as a whole foundered as political turmoil stymied cultural organizations' attempts to reestablish the old associational networks. As the historian Detlev Peukert aptly noted, the First World War did not really end in the western borderlands in 1918; instead, French occupation, separatist movements, territorial losses, and hyperinflation continued the conflict until 1923.[39] When the French entered the Rhine Province in December 1918 for an anticipated fifteen-year occupation, ordinary Rhinelanders faced the "enemy" more closely than they had during the entire course of the war, and this reignited tensions between the two belligerents. The Treaty of Versailles, which came into effect 10 January 1920, also created profound disillusionment. Many Rhinelanders viewed the loss of the Eupen-Malmedy districts to Belgium and the creation of the Saar protectorate south of the province as egregious violations of the Wilsonian self-determination principles that had guided peacemaking efforts.[40] In this context, the militarist vision of *Heimat* as a sharply demarcated boundary and *Heimat* groups' apprenticeship to the state were reestablished in the postwar era, making it impossible to fully return to the quiet civic engagement of the Wilhelmine era.

The political turmoil caused by the 1918 revolution and continuing left-wing and right-wing violence in Berlin also rekindled anti-Prussian sentiment in the Rhine Province, especially among Catholics in the Center Party, creating popular support for provincial autonomy. Hugo Preuss's 1919 German Constitution upheld the Reich's federalist structure and supported a further decentralization of authority; Article Eighteen even contained language providing a legal pathway, through plebiscites, for further self-determination efforts. Yet the Constitution fell short of disbanding Prussia, which fueled debates about the so-called Rhineland Question. With slogans of "Free from Berlin" and "Berlin is not Germany," the emerging autonomy movement of 1918 and 1919, whose key organs were Center-oriented newspapers such as the Cologne *Volkszeitung* and the Trier *Landeszeitung*, sought the dissolution of Prussia. The autonomists called for the creation of a separate Rhenish federal state, akin to Baden or Bavaria, which would encompass Westphalia. The Rhine Province also included more radical separatist movements, such as Hans Adam Dorten's Rhenish People's Union and Josef Smeet's Rhenish Republican People's Party, which advocated complete separation from the Reich and the creation of a Rhenish Republic.[41]

Though the separatists lacked popular support, autonomist political rhetoric calling for a dissolution of Prussia achieved widespread resonance. Autonomy advocates reminded Catholic Rhinelanders of Bismarck's *Kulturkampf* and the Center Party's underrepresentation, vis-à-vis National Liberals and Conservatives, in provincial administrative positions before 1918. Center Party supporters also opposed the Social Democratic Party's dominance in Berlin, especially the Reich Cultural Ministry's plans to create a sharper division between church and state in cultural affairs, including the control of primary education.[42] With the Center Party as the linchpin of the republic's founding coalition and the dominant party in the Rhenish Provincial Assembly, the autonomists had a number of key sympathizers, including Cologne mayor Konrad Adenauer, to press their claims. Even though the Cultural Ministry backed down on its plan to secularize schools, autonomists remained dissatisfied with the Reich government and gained strength during the early 1920s, becoming one of the many political forces that called into question Rhinelanders' sense of national belonging and undermined the republic's legitimacy in its founding years. The use of *Heimat* rhetoric to bridge national and regional identities was beginning to fray as autonomists demanded greater independence from the Reich.

French occupation forces exacerbated the tensions between province and nation by backing Rhineland separatists. This support for separatism reflected French frustration with the Versailles Treaty's provisions. During the war, French military officials and politicians had proposed extending the French border to the left bank of the Rhine as a key war aim. Even after Alsace and Lorraine had been transferred into French hands as a result of Versailles, French president Raymond Poincaré pushed the British and Americans to allow France to annex the Rhineland, or at the very least to create a separate Rhenish state as a buffer zone between France and Germany. As one member of the right-wing French League of Patriots noted: "It has often been said that the Rhine is the natural border of France. We would like to point out that it is also the legitimate border of France."[43] When the Allies refused to accommodate France's Rhineland aims, the French settled for a demilitarization and fifteen-year occupation of the Rhineland, along with the Saar protectorate, whose fate would be decided by plebiscite. These provisions thus left open the possibility of future border revisions, since they did not guarantee that the Rhineland or the Saar would be reintegrated into the German Reich at a future date.[44]

The French occupation and the contending separatist and autonomist movements challenged Rhinelanders' sense of national belonging and enabled the militarized rhetoric of *Heimat* to carry over into the supposed peacetime of the early republic. State officials and *Heimat* groups were particularly wary of French attempts to mobilize popular opinion in the Rhineland in support of revising the Versailles provisions in France's interests. Under the direction of General Paul Tirard, the leader of the French military administration known as the Haut Commissariat, the French launched a cultural campaign they referred to as "peaceful penetration" *(pénétration pacifique)*.[45] Through concerts, theater, cinema, newspapers, and journals such as *L'Echo du Rhin* and *La Revue Rhenane,* the French portrayed themselves as liberators from Prussian tyranny, rather than conquerors, claiming that Rhineland destiny belonged squarely in the sphere of French *civilisation.*

A belief in "geography as destiny" played a key role in this vision of peaceful penetration, and the French employed the rhetoric of nature and nation for their own ends. French historians, already methodologically more open to blending history and geography, revisited the notion of French revolutionary Georges Danton that the Rhine was the "natural" border of France, being one of the natural frontiers that included the Atlantic, the English Channel, the Alps, the Pyrenees, and the Mediterranean. French propaganda also used racial arguments, claiming that Rhinelanders' biological roots were Gallic and Roman rather than Teutonic.[46] Cardinal Richelieu and King Louis XIV's attempts to annex the area during the seventeenth century, according to French historians, were designed to remedy the mistake made at Verdun in 843, when the Franks divided the Carolingian patrimony into eastern and western kingdoms. The French Revolution and Napoleonic rule had reunited Rhinelanders with their Gallic cousins, bringing them political and economic freedoms that had spurred the region's commercial prosperity. In the French geographic imagination, the Rhine marked the boundary between Occidental culture and the barbaric, "Oriental" Germanic and Slavic races to the East. General Tirard even exempted Rhinelanders from German war guilt by claiming that they had suffered more than one hundred years of Prussian oppression; by joining the French, he said, Rhinelanders could once again participate fully in Western modernity.[47]

The policy of *pénétration pacifique* had little chance of success, mainly because Rhinelanders recognized that France's primary aim was to extract reparations from provincial industries, not to liberate them from the Prussians. French cultural propaganda nonetheless unleashed unprecedented government anxiety, especially among Berlin officials concerned about the Rhine Province's growing separatist tendencies. In rhetoric similar to that of World War I, state officials spoke of the need to recreate the patriotic homeland front by marshaling the forces of German *Kultur* against the hereditary enemy. German historians countered French claims to the Rhineland by focusing on the aggressive consequences of French nationalism and state centralization. France's six-hundred-year history as a unified state had led to destructive expansionist tendencies like those of the Roman Empire. Germany's loss of Alsace and Lorraine and French claims to the Rhine's left bank were seen as the latest installment in France's imperialist drive. Unburdened by the "federalist dispersion of Germany," France had repeatedly achieved hegemony over Europe and would continue to do so if left unchecked.[48]

While France's cultural policy spurred an upsurge in right-wing nationalist and *völkisch* rhetoric in Germany, state officials failed to devise a coordinated response, even a convincing and broadly resonant vision of Germanness, to challenge *pénétration pacifique*.[49] German historians criticized French expansionary zeal but failed to offer a secure and compelling notion of national identity to challenge France's territorial claims. Instead, geographic-determinist myths of a vulnerable *Mitteleuropa* gained increasing cultural resonance among German intellectuals. As the people of the European middle, noted one *Heimatschutz* member, "We are among the nations most strongly influenced by the diverse pressure of ideas from the outside. While in France the idea of national sovereignty was carried upward by the social movement of the Third Estate, the process went much more slowly in Germany because it always had to assimilate so much heterogeneity into itself."[50] With its fluctuating and porous borders, *Mitteleuropa* remained vulnerable and German national consciousness unfinished; maintaining a stable identity would thus require new founding myths and the policing of cultural and geographic boundaries.

Rather than galvanizing a united *Heimatfront,* French policy exploited and deepened the existing divisions within Germany's federalist structure, as Reich, Prussian, and provincial officials created divergent cultural strategies for dealing with the French menace.[51] To coordinate counterpropaganda efforts, Reich statesmen created the organization Care of the Rhenish People (Die Rheinische Volkspflege, or RVP), a front organization for the Reich Center for Homeland Service. Having failed to win the hearts of Alsace and Lorraine residents, the Reich government was determined to create a strong German presence in the Rhineland and eventually to restore full German sovereignty. The Homeland Service established information centers in major cities throughout the region and maintained agents in those cities to disseminate German news, propaganda tracts, posters, and teacher training on the other side of the Rhine. Many of these agents were anti-Catholic and anti–Center Party, and this, along with their being regularly exposed by the French as spies, curtailed their success in the region. The RVP's insistence that Rhineland officials follow a policy of strict noncooperation with the French, even on minor municipal matters, also antagonized local observers. Many Rhinelanders perceived RVP activities as an intrusion on their autonomy and a sign of Berlin's distrust of their region's loyalty to the Reich. One

Rhinelander decried RVP efforts to instruct Rhinelanders in appropriate Germanness, stating that "one should constantly imagine to oneself how [such attitudes] offend the pride and self-worth of Rhinelanders, who were German long before Berlin even remotely existed. It is really high time that it becomes clear to those in Berlin that the Rhinelanders are German through and through." Defending regional autonomy as part of German national tradition, the observer noted that "the fact that a more or less strong federalist movement is making its presence felt does not change this. Federalism is a political view that has nothing to do with treason and un-German conviction."[52] The result of RVP propaganda was thus an "ever deeper embitterment and boundless mistrust against everything that comes from Berlin." In this context, a nationally coordinated response to French cultural penetration became impossible.

The RVP's failure to launch a successful counterattack against French propaganda led Reich and Prussian officials to reorient their strategy toward decentralized cultural politics. The Reich agreed to allocate a certain amount of money annually to the states; the purpose, as the Reich interior minister stated, was "to put the existing clubs and interest groups in the service of German cultural propaganda."[53] This decision reinforced the Wilhelmine pattern of cultural regionalization, as the state shifted the work of *Heimat* defense to existing associational networks.[54] By conducting their cultural politics in this fashion, the Reich and Prussia could count on the Rhenish Provinzialverband to add its own funding and support to *Heimat* activities. More important, these policies led middle-class cultural organizations, including *Heimat* and nature protection groups, to reestablish their institutional and financial ties to the state, reinventing themselves as defenders of *Heimat* rather than mere cultivators of sentiment. State funding aided provincial elites in establishing the prominent but short-lived Rhenish Heimat Association (Rheinischer Heimatbund, or RHB) in 1920. The RHB sought national renewal by galvanizing devotion to German *Kultur*: "The German people stand today on the grave of their outer glory. A people are only destroyed, however, when they have lost the belief in their cultural capability. The German people have not given this up." The association dedicated itself to disseminating the "two-thousand-year-old" cultural achievements of Germans, and especially Rhinelanders, among all sectors of society, including those who "up to now have had no inside participation in German culture," so that they could themselves become "German cultural creators."[55] Embracing Weimar pluralism, the RHB also pledged to recognize diverse cultural expressions rather than favoring a single religious, social, or political worldview.

Echoing postwar faith in the regenerative power of nature, the RHB placed nature protection and landscape design at the center of its vision for cultural reform. Like the *Heimatschutz* movement, the RHB declared that "it is imperative that landscape planning design the people's surroundings in forest and field, village and city in such a way that they become for the *Volk* a true *Heimat*." The RHB viewed nature protection as necessary to create sites of recreation for a population still recovering from wartime deprivation. Through drives and hikes into the countryside, the RHB hoped people would balance cultural enlightenment with physical fitness, for "a healthy spirit can exist only in a healthy body."[56] Nature thus emerged as a leading force within the arsenal of spiritual weapons needed to reinvigorate the *Volk* in the face of political instability, economic decline, and international isolation.

The use of landscape as a tool for rebuilding the *Volk* received scientific support from institutes dedicated to historical geography and regional studies. One scholarly group that enjoyed state and provincial support in the early Weimar years was the Institute for the Regional Historical Study of the Rhineland (Institut für Geschichtliche Landeskunde der Rheinlande), established at Bonn University in 1920.[57] Under the leadership of Hermann Aubin, the institute sought to give regional studies academic legitimacy. Prussian authorities of the Wilhelmine era had favored Heinrich von Treitschke's histories that glorified the role of Prussian militarism and state power in unifying and stabilizing Germany. These authorities had rejected regional histories as particularist and potentially disruptive to the Reich's nationalizing aims. Aubin distinguished the new regional history methodologically from its older forms, which had focused on dynastic-political history and peasant life. Aubin argued that narrowing the focus to a single region enabled the historian to use interdisciplinary perspectives, including insights from economics, linguistics, and geography, to create an objective depiction of an entire "cultural space" *(Kulturraum)*. The concept of the *Kulturraum,* which Aubin developed in his famous 1926 work *Cultural Currents and Cultural Provinces in the Rhineland,* made use of geographer Friedrich Ratzel's "anthropogeography" to analyze regions synchronically as products of such environmental conditions as topography, climate, soil fertility, and natural resources.[58] Aubin's historical-geographical perspective gave the Rhineland a coherent regional identity by showing how riparian geography had shaped the area's transportation, agricultural, and commercial activities. While Aubin insisted on strict standards of objectivity in the institute's work, he nonetheless served state interests by defusing questions about the Rhineland's status within the German Reich. Aubin and his colleagues clearly emphasized the Rhineland's place within a Germanic cultural sphere, rather than a Roman or Gallic one, by demonstrating the myriad commercial and cultural links to the Holy Roman Empire. Anchored in the academic respectability of Bonn University, the Landeskunde Institute provided state authorities with a relatively effective weapon against French propaganda, crucial in the reconciliation of provincial and Reich interests.[59]

Despite the institute's scholarly success in defusing the Rhineland Question, 1923 brought the province's political tensions to an unprecedented crisis and further intensified the defensive rhetoric of *Heimat*. Using a delay in reparations payments as a pretext for strengthening their hold on the area, French and Belgian troops occupied the Ruhr coal-mining and manufacturing region, which lay outside the occupation zone dictated by Versailles, to force shipments of goods and natural resources to the west. To the horror of nature protection groups, the French also stepped up their cutting of forests and hunting of game in the Eifel and Westerwald areas to squeeze additional wealth from the province.[60] The Reich government called on the population to engage in passive resistance to the occupation. Ruhr industrial workers and transportation personnel refused to work, while other citizens boycotted the French-operated trains and mail service. The Rhineland's provincial leaders condemned the occupation as flouting Wilsonian self-determination. In June 1923, the Center Party and the Social Democrats, the two major parties in the Rhineland's Provincial Assembly, issued a joint declaration on the conditions in the area: "In the middle of peacetime a free, defenseless people that calls an ancient culture its own, is being oppressed and deprived. Our defense, passive resistance, is born out of the people and lives in the masses. We Rhinelanders will not lay down these, our only weapons, until justice and freedom are secured for the Rhineland. The Rhineland Question exists [for us politicians], but not for the Rhenish people!"[61]

Passive resistance reinforced the populist basis of homeland defense, uniting workers and the middle classes in a common front against the oppressors. *Heimat* groups in turn evoked homeland rhetoric to muster the population's endurance. One Westphalian journal depicted "love of *Heimat*" as a "sturdy wall against which the arrogance of foreigners will break." Merely retaining the Ruhr's coal deposits was not the aim of building up this love of homeland; rather, "love of *Heimat* must sustain us in the hard days that we spend under the persecution of the foreign occupiers."[62] The use of *Heimat* rhetoric to strengthen workers' nationalist sentiments and to portray the homeland as a vulnerable site needing protection from foreign enemies thus enabled the war's "spiritual weapons" to retain their ideological power far past the armistice of 1918.

*Heimat* sentiment alone could not uphold Rhinelanders through the crisis, however. To support workers during the passive resistance, the Reich government paid out unemployment benefits by expanding Germany's money supply. This action fed the inflationary pressures that first arose during the war. By the summer of 1923, the mark's value sank to an astonishing 4.2 trillion to one dollar. The dire economic situation forced Prime Minister Gustav Stresemann to call off passive resistance in September 1923.[63]

The separatist leaders Hans Dorten, Josef Smeets, and Josef Mathes misjudged Berlin's weakness during the Ruhr crisis and the desperate conditions in the Rhineland in the fall of 1923 as making the region ripe for a political putsch. Separatists occupied the Bonn city hall on 24 October 1923, declaring a Rhenish Republic; this was followed by similar actions in Rhenish cities and towns including Koblenz, Königswinter, Beuel, and Godesberg. General Tirard recognized the republic on Friday, 26 October, but the separatists' lack of popular support was evident, since they required French military backing to remain in power throughout the area. With so little popular support, separatist bands headed to the shelter of the province's most important natural monument—the Siebengebirge—raiding area farmsteads and towns for food, munitions, and other supplies. Nineteenth-century efforts to restore the area's forests now provided shelter for the discredited political radicals. Small "city protection" bands, which soon included members of paramilitary organizations such as the "Steel Helmet" *(Stahlhelm)* veterans, organized to defend individual towns against separatist raids. From 15 to 17 November, separatist bands confronted these armed security squads in the towns of

Himberg, Hövel, and Aegidienberg. The so-called Battle of Aegidien-berg left approximately fourteen separatists dead and nearly fifty others wounded, while Siebengebirge residents reported two deaths. The separatist movement soon collapsed altogether; on 3 Decem-ber the green-white-red flag of the Rhenish Republic was removed from the Bonn city hall, and by 28 December the remaining separatist groups had disbanded.[64] The citizen militias had thus turned to real weapons, rather than spiritual ones, to purge the *Heimat* of those who threatened the region's German character.

The year 1923 represented an utter defeat not only for the separat-ists but also for the entire cultural policy of *pénétration pacifique*. In its aftermath, Rhenish officials and elites repeatedly emphasized that "Rhinelanders are and will remain German" and that "Germany's fate is also our fate. In the Fatherland's time of emergency we want to remain its loyal members . . . A change in our relationship to Prussia and to the Reich can therefore happen only through constitutional means."[65] The separatist defeat did not destroy the autonomist move-ment, but channeled its energies along a constitutional path. Provin-cial leaders remained distant from Berlin in the autumn of 1923 be-cause Stresemann's initial currency reform, creating the reichsmark, had excluded the Rhineland economy, which he contemplated leav-ing to Allied administration. Wilhelm Marx's new cabinet, elected in 1924, abandoned this "ditching policy" that threatened to cut off the Rhine and reintegrated the area into the national economy. Rhinelanders thus enjoyed the benefits of the stable currency and rep-arations table worked out under the Dawes Plan in 1924. On 25 Au-gust 1924 the French withdrew from the Ruhr; the next year Ger-many signed the Treaty of Locarno, in which the German government accepted the border established in 1919 as the legitimate one. The agreement paved the way for Germany's acceptance into the League of Nations in 1926 and for the stepwise demobilization of French and Belgian troops from the Rhineland, culminating in their final with-drawal in June 1930. Allied withdrawal allayed lingering fears of French annexation or an autonomous Rhenish state. The *Heimat*, it appeared, had been saved.

The Rhineland's tumultuous political history between 1914 and 1923 challenged Rhinelanders' sense of national belonging and trans-formed the overall tenor of nature protection and *Heimat* cultivation in the province and beyond. Instead of merely encouraging individu-

Free the Rhine! Cover page of the *Neuwieder Zeitung,* 1 December 1929. French and Belgian occupation of the demilitarized Rhineland continued wartime chauvinism and anxieties about *Heimat* vulnerability long after the end of the war in 1918. According to the Locarno Treaty of 1925, all occupation forces were to evacuate the region by 1930. "The enemy still keeps watch," according to poem, but the river "must remain German like the force of Nature." *Source:* Franz Petri and Georg Droege, *Rheinische Geschichte in drei Bänden* (Düsseldorf: L. Schwann, 1976).

als' emotional attachment to place, *Heimatschutz* and *Naturschutz* leaders joined state officials in transforming landscape preservation into a new spiritual weapon designed to defend the *Heimat* against foreign enemies and internal dissent alike. Moreover, the wartime obsession with demarcating scientifically the borders of the Germanic cultural landscape made natural landmarks into symbolic guardians of an organic cultural and ethnic identity rooted in the soil. These postwar symbols did not entirely replace older Romantic imagery, nor did they exhaust the array of back-to-the-land practices that emerged during the mid- to late 1920s, the heyday of Weimar culture. Landscape preservationists did find new ways to accommodate modernizing tendencies in the 1920s, but they never overcame a lingering fear that their beloved homeland remained under siege—by foreigners, by materialism, by Americanization, by the uneducated masses. The next chapter examines the ways that this siege mentality made it difficult for them to articulate an environmentalist vision that was simultaneously forward looking and democratic in its political content, especially amid the republic's second crisis in the early 1930s.

# CHAPTER THREE

# The Landscape of Modernity in the Weimar Era

> The monuments of art, history, and nature, as well as the landscape, enjoy the protection and care of the state.
>
> —ARTICLE 150 OF THE WEIMAR CONSTITUTION

In 1925, Rhinelanders celebrated their most important *Heimat* festival of the Weimar era: the One-Thousand-Year Anniversary *(Jahrtausendfeier)* of the Rhineland's Incorporation into the German Reich. The theme of commemoration was an unfamiliar historical event—the 925 merging of the Kingdom of Lotharingia (the French called this the Duchy of Lorraine), which had once included the Rhineland territories, with Henry I's East Frankish Kingdom. Henry I later became emperor of the Holy Roman Empire, the "First German Reich"; this gave credence to Rhinelanders' claims that the area had been part of the German political orbit for a thousand years, despite ongoing French claims to the territory.[1]

Festival organizers envisioned the millennial anniversary as a grand celebration of national belonging designed to make "the house on the Rhine resistant against wind and weather for a long period of time" after the trials of 1923.[2] The foundation of *Heimat* feeling was in disrepair but not crumbling; local celebrations flowing with *Glühwein*, song, and goodwill would prepare Rhinelanders to work side-by-side to put the region on a solid footing.[3] The anniversary gala included grand art and cultural exhibitions and opera performances in Cologne and Düsseldorf, wine tasting from area vineyards in Koblenz, sport competitions at the Siebengebirge, and many local celebrations that encouraged conviviality and brought in sorely needed tourist money.[4] Although festival organizers used the event to counter French claims to the region once and for all, the tone of the event was inclusive rather than xenophobic, cheerful rather than belligerent.[5] Festival booklets *(Festbücher)* touted the Rhineland's role as a "transmitter" of cultural values from southern and western Europe into the German heartland of Central Europe. "As an area on the margins [the Rhineland] could only preserve the German culture of its inhabitants as part of a large German state. Belonging to the German Empire has therefore never prevented the acceptance of the good things from outside." Safely ensconced within the German state, the Rhineland could "Germanify" outside currents while retaining its own German character.[6] By linking Rhineland character to the medieval Germanic empire, the millennial celebration anchored the province's roots in Germany, using history to heal the psychological trauma of 1918 and 1923. From this point the Rhineland enjoyed a brief period of relative political calm and economic stability that lasted until the onset of Depression in late 1929.

The festival's visual celebration of the natural landscape as the basis for regional identity signaled a new appreciation of the environment in provincial cultural politics. A key unifying theme at the exhibition was the natural landscape, whose description each visitor encountered in the Cologne exhibit's opening hall. The displays in this hall included maps of local topography, vegetation, and climate, representations of space that identified the environmental variables that all human inhabitants in the Rhineland had lived with, regardless of ethnic, linguistic, or religious origin. The maps were followed by landscape paintings that represented the riparian scenery as both the source of and the inspiration for Rhenish creativity.[7] A growing geographic determinism in Weimar society enabled the Rhineland's provincial elites to argue that nature had forged a cohesive Rhenish character in a region that otherwise enjoyed few shared traditions. As the provincial conservator of monuments, Edmund Renard noted in 1925: "The region of the present-day Rhineland has shown neither a *völkisch* nor economic nor even political coherence . . . But the proud river has always asserted its unifying power as one of the most significant European economic factors and created a more or less unified culture above the unusually strong dispersion of the Middle Ages—a culture in which the character of a borderland is clearly articulated through manifold relationships to neighboring states without suffering losses to its German character."[8] Provincial elites thus rediscovered nature as a symbol of *Heimat* and social integration just as Germany was entering a brief period of political, economic, and social stability between 1925 and 1929, the "golden years" of the Weimar Republic. The Rhine had nourished regional identity in the past, and the river would bring Rhinelanders together once again.

Renard's belief in the unifying effect of nature amid political and social fragmentation articulated a dominant motif of Weimar cultural policy during the golden 1920s. As the Rhenish *Heimatschutz* leader Ernst Tiedge noted in 1925, only the natural landscape could "bring us together again out of the confusion of our present dissolution into countless groups and parties as a unified community of brothers."[9] Though images of Berlin and urban life dominate popular conceptions of Weimar Germany, provincial identities celebrating nature's healing power and the diversity of rural landscapes also flourished during this period. Landscape preservation organizations enjoyed the fruits of this back-to-nature sentiment, achieving a comfortable degree of prestige and state sponsorship by 1929. The Weimar Constitution's recognition of the state's role in caring for the country's natural monuments and landscape was one reflection of this cultural importance.[10] The growth and professionalization of landscape preservation organizations themselves was another reflection of their enhanced significance during the mid- to late 1920s. During this period, nature protection organizations created national and regional associations that bound them together in a common cause: to save Germany's natural heritage from environmental collapse. Institutional growth, in turn, opened up new possibilities for landscape preservationists to lobby for and participate meaningfully in comprehensive environmental protection efforts.

The incorporation of *Naturschutz* into Weimar's progressive vision challenges scholarly interpretations that associate the era's diverse back-to-the-land impulses solely with those right-wing, *völkisch* movements that opposed parliamentary democracy from the start.[11] Though preservationists would later rejoice at Adolf Hitler's accession to power in 1933, their support for Nazism was not a foregone conclusion in 1918. The 1920s and early 1930s undoubtedly witnessed a radicalization and polarization of discourses about the detrimental effects of industrialization and urbanization on German rural traditions and national character. Yet these debates were by no means framed exclusively by *völkisch* writers and jeremiads of cultural despair. Instead, Weimar *Naturschutz* and *Heimatschutz* movements articulated a complex critique of the pace and scope of modernization that does not fit neatly along the traditional political spectrum. Weimar landscape preservationists laid the foundations for a pragmatic approach to environmental protection and a functional interpretation of nature's ecological, political, and social value for a modern industrial society. For preservationists of the mid- to late Weimar period, the landscape of modernity called for accommodating economic conditions rather than confronting them, rationalizing the landscape instead of romanticizing its beauties, and promoting the therapeutic benefits of outdoor experiences rather than seeking sentimental attachment to the landscape. Nature protectionists still saw themselves as battling the cultural forces of materialism, mechanization, and indifference, but they did so with a far more sober and detached perspective than either their Wilhelmine antecedents or their Nazi successors.

The cultural and socioeconomic forces behind this attempt to modernize the discourse and practice of landscape preservation were numerous and multifaceted, but all of them worked to broaden the constituency and outreach efforts of *Naturschutz* groups. Weimar preservationists' call to protect the natural environment achieved greater resonance due to the popularity of geographic explanations of national destiny in this period, particularly the new "science" of geopolitics. Geopoliticians explained the debacle of Germany's defeat in World War I as a failure to recognize the spatial factors—topography, natural resources, population distribution, geographic vulnerabilities—that shaped the destiny of states in the modern era. The geopoliticians viewed space *(Raum)* as a "sculptor of peoples," arguing that mountains, streams, plains, and other natural features were active rather than passive agents in the evolution of history.[12] Although geopoliticians' pronouncements were often vague and contradictory, their belief in geography as destiny resonated with *Heimatschutz* and *Naturschutz* at the regional level, providing new, "scientific" legitimation for the call to protect the natural foundations of nationhood. The desire to locate the nation's strength in the landscape also articulated a powerful desire in postwar society for a return to origins beyond the flux of history that could anchor Germany's rapidly modernizing society.

Landscape preservationists' willingness to compromise with industry and to enjoin economic rather than aesthetic arguments for protecting nature stemmed from the dim economic prognosis of the Weimar era. During the 1920s, the seemingly inexorable economic advance of the Wilhelmine era stalled, prompting most nature preservationists to shed the remaining remnants of their negative stance toward industry and technological development. In this context, preservationists drew from the ideas of the former chairman of the German Association for Homeland Protection (DBH), Paul Schultze-Naumburg, who before World War I had argued that it was possible to reconcile nature and technology through careful planning and naturalistic design. Nature preservationists of the 1920s and early 1930s sought to integrate *Naturschutz,* regional planning, and economic development into the comprehensive form of environmental design known as *Landschaftspflege* (the care of the landscape). *Landschaftspflege,* preservationists promised, would not only harmonize economic development and environmental concerns, but also develop a more efficient and logical use of land and natural resources. *Landschaftspflege* was a conscious attempt to overcome the "false Romanticism" of nineteenth-century bourgeois preservation in favor of a thoroughly anthropocentric and functional approach to nature protection, one that embraced many of the modernizing impulses of Weimar society.

The democratization of German political life and the birth of new forms of leisure were other factors that spurred the transformation of *Naturschutz* in the Weimar era. Wilhelmine nature protection was a largely elite affair, one in which landscape preservationists envisioned themselves as stewards of natural monuments and historic landscapes that needed protection from the materialistic impulses of the uncultivated masses. In the republican era, by contrast, such elitism could lead to political and institutional marginalization. In addition, leisure opportunities and recreational activities heightened the public demand for "nature" and offered a potentially wider constituency for nature protection. Manual workers' hard-won social benefits, such as the eight-hour day and paid vacations, meant that Germans from across the social spectrum had the time off to enjoy outdoor activity, even if it was only a Sunday picnic. Nature became an amenity tied to Weimar's vision of a healthy and modern quality of life, which demanded both greater socioeconomic equality and recreational opportunities for an increasingly mobile and urban society.

Weimar preservationists responded to the rising demands of the new leisure culture by emphasizing the benefits of nature protection for tourism and outdoor recreation. They found new allies among *Lebensreform* advocates, state officials, public health experts, and educational reformers concerned about the "superfluous" younger generation, the numbing effects of economic rationalization on manual workers, and the negative psychological impact of an urban and sexualized culture. These professionals and civil servants believed that experiences in nature could mitigate the detrimental effects of urbanization, family breakdown, and socioeconomic uncertainty on young people and workers. Landscape preservationists embraced this therapeutic language to justify nature protection, arguing that nature had regenerative powers that could heal physiological, social, and psychological ills. The belief that *Naturschutz* offered a form of "social healing" thus furthered the movement's potential significance in a society undergoing a bewildering array of cultural changes in this era of "classical modernity."[13]

Despite the new possibilities for modernizing and popularizing *Naturschutz* ideals, economic conditions, political tensions, and ideological conflicts converged in the early 1930s to unsettle preservationists' attempts to find an institutional home in the Weimar system. As the historian Detlev Peukert has noted, Germans had embarked on their democratic experiment at a time when sharp changes in the country's economic and demographic structure, as well as political conflicts stemming from World War I, made consensus on political reform nearly impossible to achieve.[14] Weimar's pervasive sense of political and economic crisis also made the pace and scope of modernization itself a contentious issue. Since many Germans saw such changes as part of the new republic, rather than as structural changes beyond direct political control, debates over modernization left the political system with a slim group of supporters and a precarious legitimacy that unraveled as the Great Depression deepened in the early 1930s. During the tumultuous *Heimat* emergency that followed, many landscape preservationists returned to the militarized and xenophobic language of World War I to dampen growing political and social unrest. Emphasizing the vulnerability of *Heimat* to the debasing tendencies of "materialism," "internationalism," and "degeneration," preservationists called on the state to help them "root" unruly segments of the population in the national soil, to use landscape protection to create a natural and human bulwark against "foreign" influences that abused the German economy and its natural environment. Many preservationists came to see environmental protection and parliamentary democracy as wholly incompatible, because liberalism could control neither the abuse of nature nor the atomization of the community. They searched for alternatives to the existing political order that could stem the "chaos" of liberalism and bring order to landscape and society alike.

## Landscape Preservation and Provincial *Heimat* Care

With the stabilization of the Weimar economy and politics that began in 1924, landscape preservation entered a period of institutional restructuring and professionalization that made nature protection an important state and private concern. Under the leadership of Walther Schoenichen, the Prussian State Office for Natural Monument Preservation spearheaded efforts to create a nationwide network of nature conservationists. The State Office sponsored numerous national conferences, including its annual Nature Protection Day, which brought preservationists together from throughout Germany to create a national inventory of protected and endangered natural areas, to lobby for a national nature protection law, and to share information on nature conservation techniques. Schoenichen's efforts also led the Prussian cultural, agricultural, and forestry ministries to enact a series of ordinances that restricted development in scenic areas and facilitated the declaration of sensitive areas as protected regions.[15] Private organizations also tried to create stronger institutional ties with one another to enhance their effectiveness in lobbying state officials and creating nature protection regions. Brandenburg Nature Protection Commissioner Hans Klose, for example, created the People's League for Nature Protection in 1922 as an umbrella organization designed to coordinate associations' environmental efforts.[16] By 1930, these combined state and private efforts had helped to establish almost 500 nature protection regions in Germany, with 300 located in Prussia.[17] The Prussian state government also provided new support for *Heimatschutz* organizations at this time, granting the DBH what amounted to one-third to one-half of its income during the course of the 1920s.[18] Private organizations' institutional and financial dependence on the provincial government, a relationship first forged during World War I, thus continued into the Weimar Republic.

Despite these new efforts at the national level, Schoenichen still believed that the provinces, rather than the Reich or Prussia, should manage *Naturschutz* affairs. In contrast to the "overwhelmingly" centralized France, he asserted, German nature protection should be guided by an "emphasis on feeling" in line with the previous regional *Heimat* tradition.[19] After suffering near collapse in 1923, Rhenish landscape preservation organizations gradually recovered members and state support as part of provincial officials' vision of *Heimatpflege,* the care of the *Heimat.* Under the leadership of the Catholic Center Party leader Johannes Horion, who was elected to the Rhine province's governorship in 1922, the Provinzialverband broadened its purview throughout the Weimar period. Regional self-administration blossomed during the Weimar Republic. For the first time, the Provincial Assembly was chosen directly by the people rather than through Prussia's three-class voting system, which in the Wilhelmine era had guaranteed conservative dominance and shut out greater Center and Social Democratic Party representation. Article 72 of the Weimar Constitution, moreover, envisioned new tasks for regional authorities.[20] Horion seized on these new opportunities to strengthen the Rhine Province's regional autonomy vis-à-vis Berlin. He earned a favorable reputation among *Heimatschutz* members as a "father of *Denkmalpflege*" and a proponent of provincial social welfare programs for veterans and young people.[21] As part of the 1925 millennial celebration, Horion showcased these new areas of regional *Heimatpflege* in a comprehensive volume titled *Rhenish Provincial Administration,* which included essays by leading state officials in the areas of medical care, public health administration, road building, historic preservation, and nature protection. Horion saw this expansion as a sign of a more democratic society, arguing that the expansion of provincial *Heimatpflege* had been "called for from the voice of the people and the will of the people" to bolster regional autonomy.[22]

The Center Party's emergence as a key coalition partner in the Reich government and the dominant party in the Rhineland infused Horion's provincial welfare with conservative-religious overtones. One Center Party campaign pamphlet for a 1929 election described the party as the "stronghold of Rhenish character," noting that the connection between German and Rhenish culture was a shared "Christian culture."[23] Catholic elites' depiction of the Rhineland as the cultural axis of Europe posited shared Christian values as the stabilizing force in Central European history. By locating Rhenish identity historically in the empire and geographically with the river, the 1925 millennial observations provided an alternative to Prussian-centered narratives of German national evolution.[24] Horion's vision of regional *Heimatpflege* also embraced Weimar's democratic principles and strove for genuine political plurality.[25] Despite bourgeois fears of the organized labor movement, the province strove to integrate working-class organizations on their own terms. The Provincial Administration's designation of 17,000 reichsmarks for hiking club activities in 1928 included the leftist Friends of Nature alongside Christian hiking groups and such nondenominational clubs as the Eifelverein. Funding decisions were based on length of club-maintained trails and number of members, not ideology.[26]

The expansion of provincial self-administration and Horion's favorable view of *Denkmalpflege* also promised more vigorous attention to nature protection activities. Although conflict between Prussia's Head President Hans Fuchs and Horion erupted in 1925 and 1926 over control of the nature protection office, Horion eventually prevailed and placed the Provincial Committee for Natural Monument Preservation under provincial purview.[27] The Rhine Province's major cultural organ, *Nachrichtenblatt für rheinische Heimatpflege*, devoted a number of issues to nature and landscape protection from the mid-1920s onward, with articles on such topics as bird protection and the merits of ordinances banning billboards in the Rhine Valley.[28] Police ordinances issued by the Prussian Cultural Ministry in 1922 helped to guarantee the status of the province's existing natural monuments, including the Siebengebirge, the Neanderthal (site of the famous 1857 excavations uncovering Neanderthal Man), the Landskron in the Ahr Valley, and the Hildener Heath. Provincial funds also helped to create a number of new nature protection regions, including the Kakus Caves near Eiserfey; the Rodderberg, an extinct volcanic crater; and a juniper tree reserve on the Ahr River.[29] The latter reflected a flourishing interest in regionally indigenous plants, including junipers and hollies, which nature protectionists believed had been widespread when Germanic tribes had inhabited the region.[30] By 1926, the Rhineland boasted more than twenty-six nature protection regions dedicated to protecting a diversity of native flora, fauna, and geology. The Provincial Administration also allocated funds to help support the nature and landscape protection activities of more than thirty private organizations, including the Rhenish

Association for Monument Preservation and Homeland Protection (RVDH); the Eifelverein; the Rhineland-Westphalia Natural History Association; the Association for the Mosel, Hochwald, and Hunsrück; and the Rhenish Nature Watch.[31]

*Heimatschutz* engagement in landscape protection also expanded as a result of Horion's patronage. After the death of its beloved publications leader Friedrich Wilhelm Bredt in 1919 and the hyperinflation of 1923, the province's prominent RVDH had experienced the nadir of its financial and institutional stability. New leadership from chairman Franz Schollen and deputy chairman Edmund Renard, however, helped to link the society more closely to provincial monument protection, and it became one of Germany's premier *Heimatschutz* organizations by the late 1920s. Richard Klapheck, editor of the association's noted journal, infused new life into the publication with articles devoted to modern architecture, Rhine tourism, and industrial design appearing alongside more traditional topics such as *Denkmalpflege* and art conservation.[32] In the landscape protection arena, planners used the touristic appeal of the Romantic Rhine to convince regional officials to restrict the spread of unsightly billboards in the lovely Rhine, Mosel, Ahr, and Lahn river valleys.[33] One *Heimatschutz* member argued that the retention of pristine natural beauty along the Rhine and its tributaries was a "national demand" necessary to attract tourists. He noted that the "difficult economic conditions" forced shops and other commercial enterprises to rely on advertising to attract customers, but said that such a situation nonetheless spoke in favor of stronger measures that maintained the landscape's "purity," so as to "exploit the economic advantages of tourism to the greatest extent possible." Preservationists were willing to accommodate economic needs, but "it can no longer be tolerated," he wrote, "that cigarette placards are pasted onto towering cliff walls and the venerable barn doors of centuries-old half-timber houses."[34]

The rapid electrification of the countryside also created new forms of landscape disfigurement that aroused RVDH ire. The club lobbied unsuccessfully to prevent the stringing of electrical cables across the Rhine at Widdig, Andernach, and St. Goar, where, Edmund Renard complained, the homeland protection concerns "had not even been heard." When plans were announced for a fourth cable at Kaiserswerth, the association elicited support from the Art Academy in Düsseldorf, city leaders in Düsseldorf and Kaiserswerth, and the

Düsseldorf Historical Society to convince the power company to protect natural vistas on the lower Rhine. Greater involvement in such landscape preservation concerns was one factor that helped to boost the RVDH's membership. After a low point of 1,969 members in 1921, the club counted 2,316 members in 1929; even with the deepening economic depression, it still had 2,200 members in 1931, the year of its twenty-fifth anniversary.[35]

Electrification was an example of emerging industrial and government threats to the natural environment in the 1920s. These threats were especially evident in the Rhineland's outlying and economically less-developed areas, such as the Eifel and Hunsrück, which received far greater attention in the 1920s than they had during the nineteenth century. The agrarian Eifel region, which many contemporaries referred to as the "Rhenish Siberia," had lost crucial markets to the West during the war and occupation; stagnating agricultural prices in the 1920s allowed little chance for recovery. Out of sheer desperation, peasants in the region had cut large numbers of trees to sell as lumber or to heat their homes.[36] To assist the area's peasantry, the Prussian Assembly had targeted "Western assistance" funds for the area.[37] These funds were used for infrastructure development, such as an electricity network and new water lines for the area. But they also financed environmentally questionable land reclamation projects, including draining heaths and moors to create new farmland and "improving" waterways by straightening rivers, securing embankments, and building dams. Between 1906 and 1915, the province had spent 1.8 million reichsmarks on stream regulation alone.[38]

Boosters for the Eifel often claimed that tourism was the region's only hope for economic recovery. Eifelverein leaders argued for a coordinated effort among spas, craft shops, and hotel owners to update their facilities and to help the hiking club market the area's natural beauty. Noting that the region faced stiff competition from other tourist destinations, club leaders spoke of the need for "intensive ad propaganda" in major German newspapers near holiday times, describing the region's advantages.[39] The Eifel's "quiet and expansive forests" and proximity to Rhenish, Dutch, and Belgian cities offered urbanites a quick escape from their work lives during weekend excursions and longer vacations. To attract visitors, the Eifelverein also developed the *Eifel Calendar,* featuring Eifel scenery and "folk" wisdom, funded a feature film and radio ads about the region, and sponsored a photography contest for better postcard images. The club created specialty advertisements to promote the area, including a "Summer Refreshment Register" that touted the region's natural wonders and gave detailed information about necessities such as post offices, telegraph and telephone connections, religious services, and doctors. The club also convinced the German Railroad Administration to increase the number of trains into the area on weekends, including Sunday trains that offered one-day, round-trip service.[40] Yet tourism also encouraged urbanites to "love nature to death" by spreading automobiles and weekend houses into the countryside. At the Eifelverein's main meeting in Prümer in 1925, club leaders complained about automobile traffic in the Ahr Valley of such proportions that pedestrians and hikers could not visit the area "without danger to their health and life."[41]

The growing number of environmental problems in the Eifel region convinced the Eifelverein to form subgroups dedicated to nature protection issues. These subgroups attempted to educate the public and to secure private donations and provincial grants for setting aside nature reserves. In 1921, the organization created a Protection Office for the Endangered Forest under the direction of a Bonn University botanist, to stop the "massive cutting of Eifel forests." The Protection Office informed Eifelers about the negative consequences of tree loss, such as topsoil erosion and the sinking of the groundwater level, as well as the inability of desiccated soil to absorb precipitation and prevent flooding.[42] The club also raised money to purchase extensive tracts of forests, meadows, heaths, and rock formations; in this way, the club managed to save the Ahr Valley Landskron, a unique series of basalt formations, from a cable railway. The Eifelverein also developed closer ties to the RVDH by selecting Renard for its board of directors, in the hope that he would assist in preventing the disfigurement of historic rural buildings.[43] Club leader Wilhelm Münker claimed that "our grandfathers would turn over in their graves if they could see what has been done to their tasteful cities and villages through excessive slate roofing, sheet metal, roofing felt, and cement, through brick buildings and half skyscrapers . . . through billboards and electrical lines."[44] Local chapters mobilized to save the Eifel cottages' famous straw roofs and oppose the use of modern materials in historic houses.

The Eifelverein's most important nature protection battle of the

Weimar era concerned the Rheinische-Westfälische Elektrizitätswerk (RWE) utility conglomerate's plans to use the scenic Laacher Lake near Monschau as a water holding facility for electricity production. The RWE hoped to pump 3.5 million cubic meters of Rhine water into the lake each evening; during the day, the water would flow back to the Rhine through turbines that would generate extra electricity for daytime consumption. The lake's level would rise and fall approximately one meter daily. One Andernach professor feared that sand and other sedimentary particles in the Rhine water would accumulate in the relatively pristine Laacher Lake, overloading it with sediment. The preservationist also noted that plants and animals would be endangered by the constant rise and fall of the lake, while the canal leading to and from the Rhine would leave an unsightly fifty-meter scar through the forest hills and cliffs north of Andernach. With the Eifelverein's support, local nature lovers, including priests and monks at the nearby Maria Laach abbey, formed the Association for the Protection of Laacher Lake, which successfully petitioned the province to declare the area a nature protection region in 1926.[45]

Private organizations' energetic engagement in nature and landscape protection efforts reflected a growing awareness of the environmental threats that accompanied Germany's economic recovery. Yet landscape preservation also benefited from the postwar era's emerging belief in the broader symbolic, psychological, and physiological healing power of nature. First articulated in the trenches during the war and then along the home front, this belief in nature's healing capacity became a leitmotif for *Naturschutz* and *Heimatschutz* leaders in the 1920s and a powerful justification for protecting the natural environment. RVDH member Ernst Tiedge set the tone for this new perspective in his landmark 1925 essay, "The Significance of Nature Protection Tasks in Our Time," which offered a passionate plea for nature protection in a country still reeling from the effects of military defeat and economic instability. In Tiedge's view, the war guilt clauses in the Treaty of Versailles were not only a blow to Germany's prestige but also a threat to her natural environment. Germany's territorial and colonial losses, as well as the pressure to pay reparations to the Allied powers, meant that Germans would be forced more than ever before to rely on their own "native soil and its natural resources." Tiedge argued, "We have to build up our industrial and transportation facilities further and further, because only through our work and the export of the fruits of our industry will we be able to pay back the monstrous debts that have been loaded onto us." Tiedge feared that the unjust peace settlement would force the "destruction of all values," especially the bounty of nature itself, which had given Germans' ancestors "the harmony and peacefulness of their existence, their inner strength and their deep love of *Heimat*."[46] Tiedge assessed Germany's postwar difficulties through an environmental lens and expressed the country's underlying vulnerability as a threat to the homeland landscape.

In Tiedge's view, this environmental vulnerability was a result not merely of injustice from Germany's former enemies but also of internal alienation from nature. Like Konrad Guenther and other nature protectionists, Tiedge proposed that Germany's military defeat, as well as her postwar discontent and divisiveness, were the result of citizens whose "roots" were not planted deeply enough in the soil of *Heimat*. "The *Heimat* became for many merely a place to make a living that was quickly and easily exchanged when better earning possibilities tempted," Tiedge wrote. Materialism led to reckless environmental behavior that threatened further to degrade the natural environment in a downward spiral of ecological and spiritual decline. Referring to the environmental catastrophe of the Ruhr coal-mining region, Tiedge wrote that "no lasting achievement and no human sense of responsibility can come from heaps of rubble and dirty water . . . the majesty of the woodlands was burnt up in the smoke clouds of ironworks. The joyful swarms of lively fish suffocated in the stinking wastewater of numerous factories . . . in such surroundings, where there were for miles no forest or meadow, no village or field, the spiritual heritage of our ancestors stultified."[47] In Tiedge's eyes, environmental destruction eroded the very foundations of national character. These foundations were not merely aesthetic or spiritual, but were also ecological. To a far greater extent than preservationists in the Wilhelmine era, Tiedge identified and analyzed the environmental determinants of German society and the ecological ramifications of industrialization and urbanization. "Every living thing has a particular role for the balance of nature," he wrote; "nothing can be removed without punishment. Reproduction and destruction are so exactly coordinated in open nature that each species remains steady in its numbers." This fact gave new urgency to the loss of fish species in the Ruhr, for "every change in these factors leads to varied and often wide-ranging transformation of the realm on which life depends. If this is already the case in the small and completely gradual changes [that occur] in open nature, how much more in the dreadful and radical impacts caused by the hand of man!"[48] Tiedge's essay offered a powerful condemnation of postwar environmental neglect that analyzed both the national and the ecological risks of short-sighted natural resource exploitation.

Despite his bleak assessment of Germany's postwar environmental condition, Tiedge did not indulge in the sense of cultural despair or *völkisch* belligerence that often accompanied nationalist critiques of Versailles and Weimar modernization. "Through pessimism nothing will change," Tiedge proclaimed; "at the very most, that which appears hopeless will often be made hopeless . . . To tackle [the problem] and to build [are necessary], not idle moaning and lamenting."[49] Allied injustice and economic difficulties were not excuses for inaction; if nature provided the basis for national character and ecological sustenance, then environmental protection was the only real pathway out of Germany's spiritual, social, and economic malaise. Germans could not afford to lose one single species or scenic area, he remarked. Nature protection should include "everything that lives and breathes in the nature of *Heimat,*" without reference to usefulness or harmfulness.[50] If small environmental damage could have unforeseen negative consequences, so too could small acts of ecological awareness yield unexpected positive results. Refraining from using native holly for party decorations or refusing to buy women's hats that were decorated with bird feathers could protect native species and improve the environment.

Tiedge proposed that local nature protection offered an arena of positive civic engagement in an otherwise fractured polity. "Here is an area," he wrote, "in which all people's comrades can come together in unanimous, unifying work. The natural image of the *Heimat* earth stands as a calming element of peace above the battle between the parties." Forests, meadows, and waterfalls offered common ground, in contrast to the battle between special interests that many provincial Germans believed dominated the parliamentary realm. "Our people will awake out of their bad dream and heal themselves of their difficult disease," Tiedge noted, "only when we can bind them with the indivisible chain of love that no enemy and no peace treaty can steal . . . All of the efforts [at nature protection] can only be successful when, in spite of all obstacles and resistance, [we] galvanize the entire population in all of its occupational groups and social classes for the protection of indigenous nature. Each person must see this as his citizen duty and personal task."[51] Tiedge's assessment of Germany's postwar environmental needs thus articulated both the anxiety and the promise of postwar environmental reconstruction. In an era of political instability, social unrest, and ethical confusion, Tiedge imagined nature as a shared spiritual topography that muted the wrangling of political parties and social classes. Furthermore, Tiedge's "back-to-nature" vision did not disparage Weimar democracy or urban modernity. Instead, he viewed nature protection activities as steps toward positive environmental reform and democratic engagement in a society in which many Germans felt alienated from the existing political and social system.

## Geography as Destiny: The Rhine as a Sculptor of Life

Tiedge's insights about the relationship between organisms and their environmental surroundings echoed broader tendencies toward holistic biology in the 1920s. Though ecology remained a minor branch of university research in the interwar period and scientists did not use the term *ecosystem* widely until the 1960s, Weimar nature protectionists were already noting that organisms living under similar environmental conditions developed systemic relationships. In the absence of natural catastrophe or human interferences, such systems tended toward stability over time. In a 1930 essay, Schoenichen noted that plant geographers in the decades after 1900 had revolutionized ecological study by shifting their focus away from individual species-environmental interactions and toward what he termed "biosociology." They investigated how environmental conditions such as climate and soil fertility created a distinct ecological niche, or *Lebensraum,* in which a spatially delimited *Lebensgemeinschaft,* or "life community," of flora and fauna could flourish.[52] Nature protectionists promoted their cause among state officials by arguing that nature protection regions offered outdoor laboratories in which to study these relationships, yielding insights for forestry and agriculture that could enhance and sustain crop yields. Schoenichen maintained that only large-scale tracts of characteristic biotic communities such as heaths and moors, rather than isolated natural monuments, could produce the appropriate environmental data. These arguments gave practical legitimacy to holistic perspectives once derided as hopelessly "Romantic"; here, however, aesthetic appreciation retreated behind empirical investigation to justify nature protection in modern society.[53]

In addition to providing outdoor laboratories for botanical investigation, nature protection regions offered insights into the long-term environmental impact of humans on the environment. In his 1920 volume *Heimat Care, Monument Preservation, and Heimat Protection,* Hermann Bartmann provided grim details of the cascading negative consequences of human modifications of the landscape. Bartmann targeted land reclamation as an activity with particularly pernicious effects. By draining wetlands such as swamps and moors or straightening streams and rivers, noted Bartmann, farmers and state officials had destroyed the habitat of countless birds, reptiles, and amphibians while lowering the groundwater table necessary for drinking water and irrigation. To a far greater extent than Wilhelmine preservationists, Bartmann decried the destructive effects of industrial pollution on natural surroundings. "Through the smoke gases of industry," he noted, "the plant world at great distances is damaged, while the animal life in rivers is destroyed by wastewater." Chastising industry for its failure to deal with these consequences, Bartmann asked, "Should not our industry, which has become enormous through the spirit of its innovation . . . also discover the means to lessen the negative effects of its operations?"[54] Like Tiedge, Bartmann argued that populations of predators and prey existed in close harmony with one another. Whenever farmers killed predators that ate insects or other pests, the prey populations would explode, requiring additional methods to kill off the mass of juvenile species. The extinction of any plant or animal, even those deemed "harmful," meant a destruction of nature's overall harmony.[55]

In the Rhineland, the emphasis on holism and ecological interdependency in natural systems led preservationists to imagine the Rhine Valley and its watershed as a vital entity whose natural essence transcended the river's political or aesthetic significance. One museum official described the Rhine's watershed as a "living organism" with "continuously interacting parts. The main river—the Rhine—is the product of meteorological conditions, groundwater flows, and thousands of streams flowing on the surface."[56] Having once sculpted the valley's steep cliffs out of raw slate and granite in its search for the sea, the Rhine's glacial waters had created the living spaces shared by plants, animals, and humans alike. Ecological studies of the Rhine emphasized the diversity of niches produced by the area's multitude of microclimates and the dynamic force of the water itself. Just as the 1925 millennial celebration depicted the Rhine as a crossroads of European culture, so too did some preservationists propose that the Rhine Valley provided a perfect habitat for "exotic" species. Unlike the heaths of northern Germany or the hardwood forests of the Harz Mountains, places where one species dominated the vegetation community, the Rhine River Valley was a diverse and fluctuating mosaic of species and ecological niches. Like the Romans who had used the river as a corridor to extend their empire into German territory, Mediterranean plants and animals had followed the water's course to a "second *Heimat*" in the Rhine, Main, and Mosel river valleys' comparatively warm and damp climates. The Rhineland was thus filled with "cosmopolitans" from southern Europe that could survive in a variety of environments.[57] The natural *Lebensgemeinschaft* of the Rhineland was a dynamic equilibrium between foreign species and northern European natives, an ever-changing whole dependent on conditions of climate, rainfall, and soil.

Rhenish preservationists proposed that the Rhine *Lebensraum* had also sculpted a common culture for the region's human inhabitants, regardless of their original language, ethnicity, or place of origin. The Weimar era witnessed the flourishing of geopolitics—ideas that linked the historical evolution and political development of nations to their environmental conditions. This new social-scientific perspective rediscovered the pre-1914 work of Friedrich Ratzel, who proposed that states, like organisms in the natural world, struggled against other states for natural resources and territory. In the geopolitical view, ordinary features of the landscape, such as mountains, streams, and plains, were not merely a passive setting for the unfolding of human agency but worked actively as "sculptors" of peoples. Though driven by growing populations toward expansion, states also adapted to a particular homeland's soil and climate; their borders were like "membranes" that protected the organism from outside invaders and processed raw materials for nourishment and industry. Geopoliticians envisioned this environmental determinism as a scientific "field guide" for statesmen. They believed that awareness of the state's natural conditions of existence would help officials to identify and realize a nation's destiny.[58]

Geopolitical theories were contradictory and, in the end, more programmatic than prescriptive. These pseudoscientific arguments gained acceptance in postwar Germany because they helped ordinary people to understand Germany's military defeat. Geopoliticians proposed that the nightmare of the two-front war and the British blockade of supplies to the home front had reflected German military planners' inability to grasp the environmental limitations of Germany's vulnerable place in the center of Europe. Geopolitical ideas also fueled nationalists' sense of the injustice of the Versailles Treaty; if borders were indeed "membranes," then they could hardly be arbitrarily redrawn by politicians and diplomats. Geopolitics thus offered a vague yet all-encompassing program of national renewal and a "scientific" explanation for war and defeat beyond the confusing flux of recent historical events. If climate, soil, rivers, and mountains were the true sculptors of peoples, then only a return to these biological foundations and a cultivation of extensive geographic knowledge could renew German society.[59]

While local *Heimat* advocates rarely embraced geopoliticians' social-Darwinist call for territorial expansion, the environmental determinism of geopolitics and its regional variants found ready acceptance among landscape preservationists who advocated better nature and landscape protection measures. Peter Zepp, the leader of the Rhenish-Westphalian Natural History Association, proposed that one could understand the evolution of human settlements in the region as a product of naturally given conditions.[60] Because of its narrow valleys and steep rock faces, the middle Rhine Gorge offered few agricultural possibilities. The majority of original inhabitants had therefore relied on fishing and, later, trade, giving the Rhineland a commercial bourgeoisie long before other areas in Germany. Agricultural fields that did exist focused on viticulture, since the valley's mild climate and volcanic soils made vineyards profitable, a fact that the Roman inhabitants had discovered early on. A network of towns had developed on the narrow bands of land at the base of the precipices and along sheltered stream beds, clinging to the steep hillsides in a form "that resembled mussels."[61] Because of the area's prosperity, Zepp argued, medieval lords had scrambled to establish their dominion and taxation powers over the area, creating the famous "fortress highway" of castles, watchtowers, and toll stations along the Rhine's banks. The Rhineland's characteristic landscape, in Zepp's view, was thus a direct product of the topography itself, which delimited the size and morphology of human communities along the mighty river.

Large-scale exhibitions provided a venue for popularizing this vision of the Rhine as the "designer" *(Gestalter)* of the cultural landscape on its banks. The 1927 Düsseldorf exposition "The Rhine: Its Development and Influence" ("Werden und Wirken") used photographs and models to portray the connection between human history and natural geography in the region. Fair organizers described the "motorlike power of the river for its surroundings and its people" as the "incessant, generative main power" for all life in the region.[62] The Werden und Wirken exhibition noted the Rhine's influence on traditional fisheries and viticulture as well as modern drinking water provision and recreation. In the exhibition program, municipal officials touted the Rhine's self-cleaning capacity. Though modern industry necessitated a growing number of municipal treatment plants, these officials claimed that groundwater that ran parallel to the surface water was naturally filtered by sand and gravel, providing one of the largest and safest drinking water supplies in Germany.[63] Water sports, such as swimming and sailing, which offered the modern individual relaxation from work and urban stress, had existed since the time of Germanic tribes, who had prized "physical exercise" and "efficiency." The river thus provided a direct connection between modern Germans and ancient tribes; it was the spatial continuity that bound human communities past and present into an organic whole.

This postwar longing for natural and ethnic origins made environmental determinism especially popular. In the *Heimat* literature of this time, natural features often appeared as irreducible, vitalist forces that linked humans to the homeland. "Every one of [the Rhine's] inhabitants feels the [river's] secret knowledge," noted the 1927 festival organizers, "its development from its origins, its restless creation and effects from generation to generation." While geographers could document the connections between landscape and culture scientifically, it was Germans' "love" rather than "understanding" of the Rhine that gave the river its extraordinary national purpose. The Rhine was the common denominator among different social groups in the province; class and religion dissolved as communities struggled together to survive in the face of naturally given limits and possibilities. Yet Werden and Wirken organizers had no doubt that the result was a specifically

Germanic landscape; as one remarked, "In spite of the diversity of state forms surrounding [Father Rhine], he created a giant unified Rhine family."[64] Preservationists seized on these arguments about the Rhine's creative powers, arguing that only nature protection could secure the river and its environs from environmental disfigurement and ecological destruction. This would require a just balance between economic needs and the historically and naturally given landscape, a "reconciliation" of aesthetic and ethical precepts, on the one hand, and technological development, on the other.[65]

Despite a growing acceptance that returning to nature could heal postwar German society, landscape preservationists still faced significant limitations to realizing their goals within the Weimar system. In 1926, for example, a broad coalition of preservationists, led by Ernst Tiedge, that included the Ruhr Settlement Association president, the provincial nature preservation commissioner, the provincial conservator of monuments, the RVDH, and dozens of local groups and area newspapers worked together to save Bislicher Island near Xanten from gravel mining.[66] This "island" was a low-lying floodplain where the Rhine had once, in an earlier riverbed, formed a slow-moving oxbow. A rich habitat for waterfowl and other bird species, the area contained the best-preserved examples of lower-Rhine riparian plant communities. It was thus an outstanding remnant of how the Rhine's surroundings had looked before the river was dredged and straightened for modern shipping. In an environmental impact report filed by the Lower Rhine district nature preservation commissioner, Provincial Conservator Renard noted that the landscape formed an important aesthetic complement to Xanten's Roman and medieval cityscape. In terms of economics, Rhenish preservationists claimed that the mine would destroy the area's flourishing tourist industry. The report asserted that gravel mining had become unprofitable thanks to an overabundant supply of such material in the early 1920s, and that the new mine would likely employ only nine to twelve people, owing to the increasing use of machinery in the mining process. The tone of the debate was reasoned and analytical; aesthetics, while still important, took a backseat to ecological and economic justifications for protecting the area. "An objective observation of all the aforementioned reasons," noted the report, "will lead one to recognize [that] protection of this stretch of land against disfigurement . . . is absolutely necessary."[67]

As one of the key advocates for Bislicher Island protection, Tiedge viewed the campaign to save the area as an important example of nature's ability to draw together different factions in a common environmental purpose. A pristine landscape like Bislicher Island, he noted, "can bring us together again out of the confusion of our present dissolution into countless groups and parties as a unified people of brothers."[68] In Tiedge's eyes, mobilizing popular support for environmental protection helped to realize the constitutional goal of protecting natural monuments and to place the interests of the "great whole" above the "special advantages and single interests." Echoing his earlier writings about the civic role of nature protection for postwar Germany, Tiedge hoped that the "public conscience" and the "community of all those who recognize higher values" would prevent the desecration of nature's *Heimat,* "the last priceless good that has been left to us after the lost war."[69] In Tiedge's eyes, protecting Bislicher Island would not only save a valuable natural resource but also enable Rhinelanders and other Germans to articulate and achieve a unified, socially useful goal.

Tiedge's belief that nature might heal Weimar political and social cleavages failed to move Prussian cultural and agricultural officials. In a dramatic blow to the nature preservation movement, Prussian authorities required that a nature protection region could be declared for Bislicher Island only if the gravel company owners agreed to it and were compensated for potential economic losses. The gravel company requested a staggering 300,000 to 400,000 reichsmarks, an amount that neither private groups nor the state could procure. Legal measures were also inadequate to protect the island. Entering the region into the Ruhr Settlement Association's green-space plan could not prevent economic activity in the area, and the 1907 Disfigurement Law did not recognize this swampy area as scenically "exceptional." Nature protectionists complained bitterly that yet another precious nature reserve in their densely industrialized province was being sacrificed to the "idols of Mammon."[70] The Depression eventually saved the region when mining plans were called off because of the collapse of markets. In 1940, under the National Socialist dictatorship, Bislicher Island received state protection.

The failure of the Bislicher Island campaign reminded preservationists of the legal and institutional weaknesses of Weimar landscape preservation. Without a national nature protection law, scenic landmarks and sensitive ecological areas remained vulnerable to development. Even the Siebengebirge region, the crown jewel of Rhenish nature reserves, faced increasing development pressures during the 1920s. Throughout this period, mining companies and unions filed suits in district courts challenging the Cologne district ordinances that forbade quarrying activities on privately held land in the region.[71] In March 1919, frustrated workers from the ceramic and mining industry had met on the "Ölberg and Lohrberg peaks in the area to issue an appeal to state authorities to reopen the mines and create job opportunities in the depressed region. Rejecting the belief of the Beautification Society for the Siebengebirge (VVS) that the local population could live off tourism, the appeal criticized the "rich hedonists" who stayed at local hotels.[72] Mining companies, in turn, in the area demanded compensation for their lost profits, which neither the province nor the VVS could afford to indemnify.[73] One district official noted with regret, "Based on my experiences in the Siebengebirge, all plans for the expansion of *Naturschutz* must be given up . . . so long as a Reich Nature Protection Law with a clear ruling about the [province's] compensation obligations is missing."[74] At their national congresses in 1925, 1927, 1929, and 1931, preservationists called for legislation that would implement Article 150 guaranteeing state protection of landscapes and natural monuments, but they were repeatedly disappointed by government stalling. One speaker at the 1931 meeting asked with exasperation, "How long do the [national] government and the Reichstag intend to stand idle on this matter?"[75] The lack of national legislation threatened regional and local nature protection efforts by failing either to guarantee the state's expropriation rights or to offer financial resources for purchasing sensitive natural areas. More important, it left many preservationists dissatisfied with the republic's constitutional guarantees and democratic processes, which appeared impotent in the face of growing environmental despoilment.

## Naturalizing Modernity: The Birth of *Landschaftspflege*

The difficulties that preservationists encountered in saving individual monuments, as well as their emerging conception of the Rhine Valley as a vast, dynamic organism, resulted in new preservation strategies in the late 1920s that paved the way for modern regional planning. This new strategy, known as *Landschaftspflege,* "the care of the landscape," linked *Naturschutz* to comprehensive regional planning *(Landesplanung)*. Whereas Wilhelmine nature protection had focused largely on setting aside natural monuments, these new preservation practices sought to blend industry and nature harmoniously in the environment while creating a more rational pattern of land use. Nineteenth-century *Heimat* and cultural landscape ideals had always envisioned the German environment as a product of human cultivation, rather than as a pristine wilderness. They nonetheless upheld the preindustrial landscape before 1850 as an aesthetic model and remained averse to the intrusion of modern technologies in the countryside. Regional planning and *Landschaftspflege,* in contrast, embraced technological development in an effort to tame and to naturalize the modernizing impulses of Weimar society. "Regional planning is the ambitious attempt to give the historically formed landscape the stamp of our time," noted one news article on nature protection and planning, "indeed a stamp that is organic, meaningfully organized, and mindful of the great interrelationships." Giving the landscape the "organic" stamp of modernity meant that many areas, including the pastoral countryside, would be "reshaped, divided, and transformed, old connections split up and many beloved views destroyed." Yet in the process, the advocates of *Landschaftspflege* promised, the "arbitrary overexploitation of the nineteenth century" would be replaced with a functionally efficient, "state-supported planned economy in which nature protection efforts would fit in without a second thought."[76]

Many aspects of regional planning and *Landschaftspflege* had been anticipated before World War I in the *Heimatschutz* movement's attention to protecting vernacular landscapes. Paul Schultze-Naumburg, for example, had proposed in the *Cultural Works* series that it was possible to reconcile technology and environmental integrity through structural forms that blended into their natural and historical surroundings. Planners also drew on ideas from the Garden City movement, which had gained in popularity in the decade before World War I but which had usually restricted itself to creating green spaces or protecting natural areas within individual cities, rather than addressing entire regions.[77]

Postwar landscape planning was a far more ambitious and proactive program, born of the statist tendencies inaugurated during World War I. Although German military officials had failed miserably to provide adequately for the civilian population during the war, their efforts at corporatist economic planning and rationing offered new models of state intervention that fueled the demand for better peace-time land use and natural resource administration.[78] One regional planner described the goals of landscape design as both "negative" and "positive." The negative functions of planning included curbing "wild and unorganic" development through the "regulating intervention of public force."[79] In this capacity, planners sought to disperse dense urban populations, to separate residential and commercial spaces, to provide urban populations with recreational areas, to ensure convenient transportation, and to designate the most fertile lands for agriculture. Regional planning thus extended "scientific" urban planning concepts beyond the individual city to encompass land use in large-scale economic and cultural districts. This call to rationalize land use and natural resources took on additional urgency as a result of the Treaty of Versailles. As one planner noted, Germany had lost 14 percent of its territory and 28 percent of its coal deposits. At the same time, he said, population density was increasing in the 1920s; according to his estimate, Germany had overstepped the "carrying capacity" of the land by more than 40 percent. The belief that Germany was a "people without space" sparked further discussion of regional planning as a way to mitigate the free market's chaotic distribution of land and resources.[80] By subjecting land use to scientific scrutiny, Weimar's nascent environmental technocrats attempted to find objective criteria for distributing land and avoiding social conflict.

The positive goal of planning was to stimulate the economy and ensure its long-term growth by rationalizing spatial location and land use. Planners would designate agricultural, industrial, and mining areas based on the fertility of soil, access to transportation, and the availability of raw materials, saving corporations time and money and avoiding waste. Planners also hoped to create more efficient transportation and energy provision routes. In the Prussian Rhine Province, the landscape architect Stephan Praeger assisted in developing a land use map for the entire region, designating the appropriate areas for industrial and commercial operations, traffic corridors, gas and electricity lines, and nature protection regions.[81] Aerial photographs and topographical maps were crucial tools for identifying the optimal locations for houses, factories, shopping districts, farms, and parks; as one planner put it: "A place for everything, but everything in its place."[82]

The shift in preservationist practice toward regional planning also represented a pragmatic adaptation to Weimar's sluggish economy. Whereas Wilhelmine preservationists had decried the economy's unchecked growth, Weimar *Naturschützer* realized that industrial economies were subject to deeper structural crises that made Germany's economic status uncertain.[83] Preservationists were thus cautious in pushing preservationist causes that might appear to serve merely aesthetic needs or hurt the economy. "When protecting individual natural monuments," noted one Rhenish preservationist, "we must carefully weigh whether the preservation's value for the general public is great enough to justify economically limiting measures. In a densely populated country such as Germany, *Naturschutz* may not overlook the economic necessities."[84] Unlike the preservationists of the Wilhelmine era, who had condemned all "materialist" valuations of the landscape, Weimar *Naturschützer* found it necessary to justify nature protection on economic grounds.

The goals of centralized land use planning meshed well with the Taylorist and Fordist economic philosophies of the 1920s, which called on economic managers to "rationalize" labor practices through scientific study of human motion and a more articulated division of labor. By dividing and mapping out the functions of the landscape, many planners hoped to obtain the same efficiency and productivity from the landscape that Henry Ford demanded from the factory floor. They could also count on more efficient laborers as a result of proper design. As one planner noted, landscape planning produced more productive and satisfied manual workers. "The working man stands at the center of economic planning," another planner asserted. This "human factor" should not be seen merely as labor power "that is used and used up," he said, but rather as a "creative power" that stands above purely utilitarian demands.[85] In this vision of nature, green spaces and nature parks enhanced labor capacity over time by providing sites of refuge from urban overstimulation, places where manual workers could relax, unwind, and regenerate. This emphasis on worker productivity and health was also a clear indication that the advocates of landscape planning envisioned a far broader and more ambitious social and political agenda for landscape preservation than the largely aesthetic concerns of prewar natural monument protection.

Landscape preservationists believed that nature protection concerns needed to be a vital component of such regional planning, and they used the term *Landschaftspflege* to refer to the synthesis of planning and environmentalism. The major advocates of *Landschaftspflege* were *Heimatschutz* leaders who saw regional planning as a way to modernize landscape preservation. Landscape architects in particular were among the most vociferous advocates of the planning perspective. Discussions about a Prussian city planning law and concerns about haphazard motorization and electrification gave landscape architects a new identity in Weimar society. Rather than seeing themselves as mere garden architects, they claimed that they were designers of the entire landscape.[86] Landscape architects sponsored the Rhine Province's first training programs for landscape protection and design in 1929 to give local nature protection commissioners, many of whom were teachers and pastors, a more sophisticated understanding of design and land use issues.[87] In the eyes of landscape architects and planners, *Landschaftspflege* was a logical extension of their professional terrain, an attempt to place environmental reform under the trained eye of professionals rather than nature hobbyists.

The willingness of many landscape preservationists to embrace *Landschaftspflege* and planning ideals calls into question their reputation as antimodernists who opposed all aspects of Weimar urban modernity. While Weimar historians have often focused on the sharp opposition between the era's *völkisch* anti-urbanism and its celebrations of city life and sleek technology,[88] *Landschaftspflege* provided an alternative vision of modernity, a middle ground of cautious technological optimism tempered by the desire to protect the aesthetic textures and ecological integrity of the landscape. Several preservationist leaders hoped that the shift toward *Landschaftspflege* would enable the *Heimatschutz* movement to cast off the last remnants of Ernst Rudorff's Romantic nostalgia and gain a new appreciation in the eyes of the public. Hans Schwenkel, the state officer for *Naturschutz* in the state of Württemberg, called for a forward-looking connection between history and modernity in 1930: "to be sure, an important element of *Heimat* preservation is tradition, the cultivation of a sense of history and works handed down to us from the past. But not for its own sake, rather for the power contained in works of the past for people of the present day."[89] Schwenkel claimed that both rural and urban landscapes deserved attention in a program he termed "organic" planning, which would reconnect residential, industrial, and transportation facilities to their natural environs.[90]

In a similar vein, the secretary of the German Association for

Homeland Protection, Werner Lindner, in his 1926 book *Engineering Works and Nature Protection,* called on society members to rethink the movement's earlier anti-industrialism in light of new building technologies that enabled architects to embed factories in the landscape "without damage to landscape beauty or for the native country folk."[91] In Lindner's view, nature protection would serve practical, societal needs, such as public health and recreation, rather than mere Romantic aestheticism. Just as the Wilhelmine *Heimatschutz* had once rejected the eclecticism of nineteenth-century historicist architecture in favor of updated, simplified forms, so too did the movement's Weimar successors ask that regional planners give landscapes as a whole the authentic "stamp" of modern industrial society. According to one 1931 news article, planning would create a "harmony between landscape and industry" that would enable not only *Heimat* friends but also "engineers and technical men" to observe their *Heimat* with a "loving soul."[92] Far from being agrarian romantics, Weimar landscape preservationists sought balance between technological imperatives and environmental integrity.

Whereas Schwenkel and Lindner portrayed *Landschaftspflege* as a strategy for embedding industrial and residential structures in the countryside, other environmental reformers envisioned regional planning as a way to naturalize already degraded industrial environments, such as the Ruhr coal-mining region. In the nineteenth century, nature preservationists had focused their efforts on protecting natural monuments along the Rhine Gorge, such as the Siebengebirge, while abandoning the Ruhr's coal-mining fields as *Opferstrecke,* industrial wastelands "sacrificed" to the needs of industry. During the 1920s, however, the Ruhr became the object of intense environmental concern in an effort to transform the area into a more economically efficient and livable space for its inhabitants. To meet the need for expanding coal deliveries to fulfill the reparations schedule set by the Treaty of Versailles, economic forecasters estimated in 1919 that the region would need to accommodate an additional 150,000 workers; with family members included, they anticipated the total would be approximately 600,000 new residents. This rise in population would put a tremendous strain on the area's housing stock, transportation networks, and recreational areas that only planning ahead might alleviate.[93]

Planners' interest in the area also reflected lingering anxieties about workers' alienation from nature and homeland. Like many middle-class Germans, nature preservationists feared the revolutionary potential of manual laborers in the coal-mining area, many of whom had participated in the political unrest of 1919 and 1920 or were recent Polish-speaking immigrants from East Prussia and Silesia. In the Westphalian *Heimatschutz* organization, members decried immigrants' "coal pot" environment and "cultureless" living quarters, the "sheer brutality of a soil that no longer had anything earthly about it . . . and whose motherly heart had stopped beating ever since the bodies of machines pulsed with their iron rhythm."[94] Preservationists hoped that long-term "Germanic" workers would instruct the newcomers in the ways of *Heimat,* but the Ruhr offered few scenic areas in which to anchor such homeland sentiments. By expanding green spaces and regulating residential development in the Ruhr area, planners hoped to create a more environmentally friendly *Lebensraum* and to plant laborers more firmly in the homeland soil.[95]

In 1920, the Prussian Assembly passed a law creating the Ruhr Settlement Association (Ruhrsiedlungsverband) to coordinate transportation, residential, commercial, industrial, and recreational needs in the Ruhr region, which soon became a model in Germany for supralocal planning. The Settlement Association included representatives from counties, municipalities, labor unions, and trade unions throughout the 4,500-square-kilometer area; it sought to overcome the prewar "municipal political imperialism" caused by eighteen cities' making individual, short-term decisions about land use. The planners' concept of a large-scale, "functionally integrated" spatial plan included establishing interconnected transportation "arteries" and distributing land based on available natural resources and economic demands.[96]

Expanding on Garden City ideas from the turn of the century, Ruhrsiedlungsverband planners envisioned expanding the Ruhr's "lungs" by setting aside or creating green spaces, which they believed provided healthy recreation for manual workers. Using a 1922 tree protection law drafted by the Prussian Welfare Ministry to regulate woodland cutting, the Settlement Association was able to protect approximately 65,000 hectares out of the remaining 72,000 hectares of forest in the district. All told, the association protected 141,000 hectares—or 37 percent of the Ruhr coal-mining region—as green space, despite the influx of new workers during the course of the 1920s.[97] In this way, "the contrast between city and countryside, industry and agriculture, urban economy and agricultural economy [was] subordinated to a structure made up of organically determined functions that all stand in a particular relationship to the overall plan."[98] Organic planning thus promised to transform the Ruhr into a true *Heimat* for its inhabitants.

Planners' vision of saving green fields and making brown fields more efficient included mitigating the adverse ecological effects of industrial activity or even restoring areas degraded by resource extraction or manufacturing. The Ruhr Settlement Association was among the first planning agencies in Germany to consider pollution control in its vision of supralocal environmental organization. During the manufacturing standstill of 1923, many observers had commented on the more salubrious air resulting from the lack of smoke and gaseous effluents. This temporary reprieve from air pollution gave Ruhr inhabitants a taste of a better environment that many hoped could be extended into peacetime. Scientists also decried the widespread effect of airborne toxins such as sulphur dioxide on surrounding vegetation, which had led to "forest death" in vast stretches of the region. To remedy the situation, planners recommended planting trees that were less sensitive to smoke than conifers, such as poplars and moor oaks, though others tried to convince factories to use natural gas or electricity instead of coal as fuel. Though such measures were a far cry from actually restricting industrial emissions or assigning penalties for toxic pollutants, they did indicate a broader understanding of environmental problems that went beyond landscape aesthetics alone.[99]

Despite growing interest in pollution mitigation, however, the Settlement Association's activities still focused predominately on improving the landscape's visual appearance. Planners recommended the retention and reuse of topsoil, for example, to aid natural revegetation along new roads and around buildings.[100] Landscape architects also advocated the creative transformation of abandoned industrial sites such as slag heaps. "From a landscape perspective," noted one article, these sites "were in no way necessarily evil, which one must simply get rid of or hide, but can instead in many cases be put to use as valuable and desirable portions of the overall appearance of the landscape."[101] Landscape designers claimed that the slag piles, once covered with native vegetation, could form natural-looking hills in otherwise flat areas, while abandoned quarries could be transformed into artificial lakes. Pastoral garden landscapes could blossom where industrial ashes once smoldered.

The naturalization of industrial slag heaps as aesthetic elements symbolized landscape planners' conscious distancing from what they termed a "Romantic" approach to the landscape, which they characterized as perpetuating a sharp opposition between the natural and the human realms. One article noted that Ruhr planners set aside forest tracts and open areas not for "natural monument protection" or for "nature-friendly feeling," but as part of the "use of nature" for societal purposes: "It is characteristic of land use planning that the protected, maintained, or built-up green spaces are in no way untouched nature. They are parks, consciously designed landscapes, which are dependent upon and intended for humans and which in the context of the organic integration of an economic region serve particular public health or economic purposes."[102] In its most extreme form, this abandonment of Romantic nature recognized few distinctions between green spaces devoted to anthropocentric needs and nature preserves such as the Siebengebirge or Laacher Lake. "These [preserves] are the foundation," the article continued, "which stand [only] in slight contrast to the artificially created and harvested forests." For planners, such nature preserves were necessary for the scientific study of rare geological formations, the conservation of endangered species, and the provision of recreation areas, but had little intrinsic value. This process drained natural monuments of their aura as sites of aesthetic rapture, divine presence, and self-cultivation. Planners argued that both cultivated green spaces ("secondhand Nature") and nature reserves served functional, societal needs rather than ideal, aesthetic interests. In their eagerness to embrace this modernized outlook, however, few landscape architects, urban designers, or preservationists considered that such a technocratic and anthropocentric view might also undermine their claim that nature served as a font of *Heimat* feeling, individual authenticity, and ecological wisdom in an increasingly urban and mobile society. *Landschaftspflege* was nonetheless a crucial step toward imagining a landscape of modernity that accommodated environmental concerns and *Heimat* identification within a rationalizing framework, even though its advocates accomplished few concrete land use reforms until the Nazi era.

## Nature Protection as "Social Healing": Environmentalism in a Mass Society

Through *Landschaftspflege* and tourism promotion, landscape preservationists had proven themselves adept at accommodating the demands of modern society. Public health, however, provided preservationists with their most important utilitarian justification for *Naturschutz*. During the 1920s, the popular slogan "light, air, and sun" *(Licht, Luft, und Sonne)* drew increasing numbers of Germans into the outdoors to counteract the physiologically and psychologically debilitating aspects of modern urban life. This new ethos found expression in hiking excursions, weekend holidays to the countryside, nudism, rural communes, and other "life reform" activities.[103] As Walther Schoenichen remarked in 1931, "The contact with nature has risen in the last several years to an unprecedented size," indicating that a growing number of Germans recognized the value of the outdoors for quality of life. Weimar society created a new social framework for popular leisure, including the eight-hour workday and paid holidays, which enabled broader sectors of German society to experience the landscape.[104] While the upper middle classes relied increasingly on automobiles for their excursions, urban factory laborers and white-collar workers used the convenient railway connections between Rhenish cities and the Siebengebirge and other major landmarks. Even those workers plagued by unemployment or insufficient wages could join the *Schrebergarten* ("allotment garden") movement and receive a plot of land to till on the outskirts of the city, and the increasing "mechanical reproduction of nature," such as August Sander's famous Siebengebirge photographs, offered an appealing replacement for those who could not experience nature firsthand.[105]

Molding the participants in this new leisure culture into advocates of *Naturschutz*, however, would require a novel style of cultural politics, one that suited an age of democratization and mass culture. Preservationists were accustomed to operating in a shared bourgeois milieu in which behind-the-scenes lobbying often proved far more effective than direct appeals to the public.[106] Yet Weimar environmentalists recognized that their recruitment efforts and public campaigns had to appeal to a much broader constituency than the core of educated elites and state officials who had supported Wilhelmine *Naturschutz* efforts.[107] The Rhineland botanist Peter Zepp argued that "*Naturschutz* must become a 'people's task' [*Volkssache*]," one that planted a "deep respect" for nature in the farthest circles of German society, rather than relying solely on state patronage and police ordinances to protect nature.[108] The potential to transform *Naturschutz* into a "people's task" certainly existed, as many Germans found *Heimat* and back-to-nature ideals comforting antidotes to national political tensions and Weimar's dizzying array of social changes. The *Heimat* and nature protection message nonetheless had to compete for Germans' hearts in a new pluralistic culture that included a number of competitors—from a resurgent proletarian culture to the avant garde, from the new mass consumers to the *völkish* right—making recruitment and advocacy challenging.

This fragmentation of cultural forms and the need to compete for Germans' hearts in the new mass culture unleashed profound anxiety among landscape preservationists about their ability to retain their status as cultural stewards of the *Heimat* landscape. Though Schoenichen applauded the Weimar era's back-to-nature ethos, he also warned that the "great masses" would soon endanger nature if preservationists did not "foster their interaction with nature in the proper way."[109] The ambivalence about the masses and their contact with nature reflected in part preservationists' traditional distaste for the leveling tendencies of democracy and mass culture, yet this ambivalence would take on new, more disciplinary forms in the Weimar period. Preservationists allied themselves with state officials, public health experts, and social workers in creating a social-therapeutic model of *Heimat* cultivation that promoted nature experiences designed to tie potentially unruly segments of the population, particularly industrial workers and young people, to the national landscape.

Bourgeois elites had already come to view these groups as volatile and uncontrollable in the pre–World War I period, but their participation in the popular revolution of 1918 and 1919 that toppled the Kaiserreich transformed fears of the elites into a reform campaign designed to pacify and integrate the masses.[110] Preservationists spoke of contact with nature as a means of relieving these groups' physiological and psychological distress; Schoenichen claimed that *Naturschutz* served the entire people because it was among the most important "social healing methods [*soziale Heilmittel*] of our time."[111] This belief that nature protection was a form of social healing offered a powerful tool for modernizing and broadening the *Naturschutz* message, one that enhanced the Weimar tendency to view the natural environment as an indispensable part of modern living. Like *Landschaftspflege*, it reflected preservationists' shift away from the Wilhelmine era's Romantic concern with the moral cultivation of individuals. Preservationists embraced instead a managerial ethos of social healing that promised a therapeutic resolution of social problems, if only workers and young people would submit to their tutelage in the ways of nature.

To shape popular perceptions and to win new members, the Weimar *Naturschutz* movement embraced a variety of mass media. In the Rhine Province, columns detailing local nature and homeland protection activities appeared regularly in special *Heimat* supplements in area newspapers such as the Center Party–oriented *Kölnische Volkszeitung,* the National Liberal *Kölnische Zeitung,* and the Social Democratic *Rheinische Zeitung.* Nature preservationists also noted that photography and film could be used to capture the public's attention and to document endangered plant and animal species before they died out.[112] The leader of a Berlin school showed his pupils films of the enormous herds of bison in the Bialowies national park on the Polish-Lithuanian border as part of natural history instruction. Hugo Conwentz had commissioned a Berlin filmmaker to document the animals in their natural setting shortly before they were nearly wiped out during the course of the war and German occupation. The school official argued that nature films would enable preservationists to compete with Weimar's new urban entertainments. "With today's 'cinema interest,'" he noted, "such a film is not only the best teaching method but also certainly presents a good way to advertise nature protection affairs."[113] Films were both documentary and evocative, charting the loss of species but also depicting the drama of an "animal tragedy" that young people could transfer into sympathy for protection measures within Germany.

Nature preservationists also advocated establishing closer ties to the *Heimat* museums that were proliferating in Germany's towns and villages during the 1920s. They argued that these museums' natural history collections could be supplemented by information about nature protection measures. Nature preservationists found allies among the members and officials of the Rhine Museum in Koblenz. The Rhine Museum embraced a holistic view of the Rhine River as a "total entity," one that resembled the *Lebensgemeinschaft* principle being articulated in botanical journals. Breaking from the traditional taxonomic approach of natural history museums, the Rhine Museum gave visitors an "overview of the whole," instead of information from isolated scientific disciplines, and taught them about the "great interdependencies" in nature that formed the Rhenish *Heimat.*[114] The ex-

hibition space featured three floors of displays detailing the relationship between natural and cultural history in the region. The first-floor
exhibit, "The Rhine in the Making," depicted the region's topography
during various geological epochs, including the volcanoes that once
dominated the landscape. On the second floor, "The Historical Rhine
Landscape" featured paintings and models of cities, towns, and ships
from the medieval and early modern periods. The third floor was
divided between "The Romantic Rhine," which included paintings,
lithographs, and models of the river during the artistic era between
1790 and 1850, and "The Producing Rhine," which presented modern industrial and commercial activities, particularly shipping, that
made the region one of Germany's economic heartlands. The museum's displays depicted the continuous evolution from a prehistoric
to a preindustrial to a modern cultural landscape. Visitors learned
that Rhenish culture and history were intertwined with the fate of the
river itself.

Such exhibitions offered important venues for reaching a mass audience. In 1931 Schoenichen sponsored a Nature Protection Exhibition in Berlin that gave each province an opportunity to tout its environmental protection achievements.[115] The Rhenish exhibit divided its
displays between a section titled "Natur an sich" ("Nature in Itself"),
including the region's famous geological monuments, mild climate,
and flora and fauna, and a section on the cultural landscape created
by *der Mensch,* the human being. The exhibit organizers painted a far
more grim portrait of human occupation than the Rhine Museum did.
According to the displays, *der Mensch* crowds out nature because
of his "malice, stupidity, and greed"; for this reason, he must protect
nature from himself.[116] In a scene reminiscent of Fritz Lang's film
*Metropolis,* one panel featured Moloch, the god who consumed beleaguered manual workers in the film, as the head of a caravan of
modernist buildings and factories that consumed the province's rural
areas. "In the last fifty years," it noted, "the cities, industry, and transportation in the Rhine Province have devoured more than 120,000
morgens [75,708 acres] of land!" The exhibit also decried the social
effects of environmental destruction. Amid scenes of drunkenness and
prostitution, the following panel noted that "the big-city person easily
loses his relationship to nature and young people are especially apt
to become rootless."

The 1931 exposition showcased green-space development in the

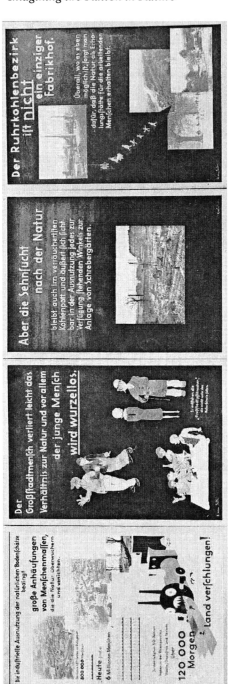

Nature Protection Exhibition, 1931, Berlin. Expositions were an important venue for disseminating nature protection ideas in the mass-media environment of the late Weimar Republic. These panels comment on the social and environmental consequences of overdevelopment, rootlessness, and alienation from nature and illustrate the need for allotment gardens and green-space planning. *Source:* Archiv des Landschaftsverbandes Rheinland, Kulturabteilung, no. 3783.

Ruhr as a way to combat alienation and class tension. *Heimatschutz* groups of the Weimar era argued that the Ruhr's factory workers deserved a better living space, for they had proven their loyalty to the Reich by participating in the general strike to protest French seizures of coal and steel supplies. At the same time, the memory of worker unrest in the revolution of 1918 fueled preservationists' fears that manual laborers remained detached from the *Heimat* landscape. This distance led workers to embrace Marxism's proletarian and materialist ideology rather than the communitarian and idealist sentiments of *Heimat*. The 1931 exhibit thus applauded the *Schreber* garden movement, which encouraged urban denizens to grow their own fruits and vegetables in small gardens on the outskirts of cities, as a useful way to satisfy Ruhr factory workers' continued "yearning for nature." Preservationists also praised the Ruhr Settlement Association for ensuring that the Ruhr region did not become "a single factory yard" through the setting aside of recreational areas. The city of Essen provided another role model for planning; it offered laborers nature education, healthy recreation, and urban "lungs" through its famous bird protection stations and urban forest program.[117]

The 1931 exhibit portrayed natural monuments as the catalysts for social healing in the industrial district, noting that easy access to local nature reserves helped to integrate workers into the fabric of *Heimat*. Hans Klose argued that hiking enabled workers to learn reverence for nature; "proper hiking," he noted, "creates an entryway into nature and culture" and makes people into "members of the *Heimat* community."[118] Through hiking, noted a local outdoor recreation club in the Sauerland, workers could overcome the temptations of dance halls, cinemas, and the "alcohol devil." Landscape vistas would enthuse workers for the "wonders of God's nature" and give them a "completely different morale and mood" when they returned to work the following workday.[119] These therapeutic benefits of nature transformed *Naturschutz* from a bourgeois luxury into a cultural good for the entire people. As one Rhenish official noted, the Siebengebirge might be the only real "mountains" that children from Cologne and lower Rhine industrial districts ever saw; only there could they experience what it was like to romp around under an open sky.[120] Drawing on this populist dimension of nature protection, the 1931 exhibit's last panels featured a map of the Rhine Province's existing nature protection regions and indicated which areas still needed to be set aside, to galvanize popular support for their preservation.

The 1931 exhibition's concerns about industrial workers' lack of rootedness was a familiar theme in preservationist discourse stretching back to the 1890s, but the social-therapeutic model of landscape preservation found new populations to treat in the 1920s. In particular, youths *(die Jugend)* were of vital concern during this period. Preservationists' interest in youths was in part pragmatic; many believed that the movement needed to attract young people to bolster declining membership rolls. But nature protectionists also joined other middle-class reformers in arguing that the state had not done enough to integrate young people back into German society after the trauma of war and military defeat. As the historian Detlev Peukert noted, the "'mystique of youth' was a more pervasive part of public consciousness in the Weimar Republic than it was in other contemporary Western societies or than it had been in other periods of German history."[121] A short-term peak in the birthrate between 1900 and 1910 had created a relatively large group of fifteen- to twenty-five-year-olds by 1925, whose conspicuousness was exacerbated by the loss during the war of so many in the now thirty- to thirty-five-year-old age group. The younger generation was coming of age at a time when economic growth was slow and jobs were scarce, and this fueled their bitterness toward the older generation. Weimar officials were particularly concerned about the many children who had grown up without fathers, a situation many observers believed had loosened the bonds of patriarchal authority and spurred an increase in juvenile delinquency. The "problem of youth" was a key area of provincial concern and intervention. At the primary school level, growing numbers of boys and girls were being expelled from traditional schools because of behavioral problems, while adolescents, demoralized by the lack of job prospects and the breakdown of familial structures after the war, were unable or unwilling to find a place in Rhenish society. *Die Jugend* were also conspicuous as the pioneers of Weimar's new leisure ideals, "Americanized" consumer culture, and alternative *Lebensreform* movements. Despite Weimar's economic constraints, young people enjoyed radio, cinema, dance halls, shopping, and other urban entertainment to a much greater extent than their parents. The older generation often found many of these social changes disconcerting and threatening and feared that young people were particularly susceptible to movies and literature that condoned sexual promiscuity and other "deviant" behavior.

While many boys and girls joined church groups or municipal sports clubs, Weimar youths also developed their own associational networks without adult supervision.[122] After the war, the *Wandervögel* evolved into the more nationalistic *Bündischen*, while socialist youth groups such as the Friends of Nature experienced splits between their Social Democratic mainstream and more radical Communist Party members.[123] Although the workers' youth movement and *Bündisch* groups counted only about 420,000 members, their influence was much greater than their relatively low numbers suggested. Leaders from these two movements played a prominent role in shaping the mystique of youth by disseminating their own publications and recruiting young members from within the education profession. The two groups attracted advocates of educational reform, sexual reform, alternative lifestyles, and avant-garde culture, which heightened fears about the unruly younger generation as a whole.

Young people's visibility in Weimar society and their lack of familial structures prompted on-going debates among state officials and social policy makers about how to solve the perceived "youth problem." Most of this debate focused on educational and welfare policies that would help to socialize the new generation and to facilitate its adoption of traditional moral values. Given their close ties to provincial officialdom and belief in the power of nature to heal society, nature preservationists became active participants in fashioning a provincial youth policy.[124] During the 1920s, hiking and back-to-nature organizations expanded their appeal to adolescents. As the RVDH member K. J. Fassbinder noted in 1927, the Rhine Province's major railway stations were filled on Sunday mornings with "throngs" of young hikers, since "every club and every organization that has anything to do with youth is building hiking groups these days."[125] Like many nature protection advocates, Fassbinder celebrated young people's desire for such "golden freedom" and hoped that such excursions would deepen their love of *Heimat*. Yet getting back to nature could also have unintended effects, and some middle-class observers feared that hiking and youth hostelling were invitations to escape parental and state supervision. Nature, in this view, offered young people a site of unsupervised leisure, which might include premarital sex, alcohol, and gambling, the very sorts of activities preservationists had linked to urban ills. Preservationists complained bitterly about the garbage, noisy parties, and drinking that resulted from group hikes, especially those of the *wilde Cliquen,* the marginal, nonconformist youth groups recruited among the working classes.[126] This ambivalence about young people's back-to-the-land experiences articulated broader anxieties about Weimar society's ability to control and integrate its youth.

Weimar *Naturschützer* recognized the risks of cultivating a back-to-the-land ethic among young people but hoped to bend such impulses toward greater *Heimat* awareness and conservative integration. Many preservationists had been *Wandervögel* members during the Kaiserreich and wanted to reform, rather than outlaw, youth hiking activities. They saw nature experiences as a way to ensure proper psychological and physiological development in a population still reeling from the effects of wartime deprivation.[127] *Heimat* advocates and social workers believed that the sheer lack of nutrition during the Allied blockade had badly damaged school-age children and adolescents; light, air, and sun were thus necessary to recharge their ailing bodies.[128] As one preservationist remarked, "How many rays of sun would be necessary to scare away all the darkness that has bathed the youth of today through war and defeat, to once again brighten up all the physical and emotional gloominess of our times?"[129] Many came to see outdoor experiences as one remedy to the postwar era's widespread pessimism, a beam of hope amid fears of further environmental and social decline.

To accommodate these new social demands, provincial administrators devoted additional funds to renovating, expanding, and maintaining the Rhineland's stock of youth hostels as part of its "care of youth" *(Jugendpflege)* activities. Two hostels, the Hammerstein Castle in Neuwied and the Freusburg Castle on the Sieg River, were designated as central administrative centers. The new hostels helped to allay middle-class fears of wild and unsupervised hiking trips. Social workers and educators envisioned the youth hostel system as a microcosm of a society, founded on careful hygiene, *Heimat* feeling, and closeness to nature. Embracing the Weimar era's emphasis on streamlined efficiency, supervisors at the Stahleck Castle youth hostel touted the "impeccable," sanitary, no-nonsense facilities: clean beds, spotless toilets and showers, and simple but nourishing food.[130] Hostels brought together young people from different social backgrounds—

university students, apprentices, young manual workers, and white-collar clerks—as one *Volk*. The workers would learn from the academics the "spiritual values" and the "effect of art, music, and painting," so that later in life the laborer would remember "not only that which divides but also that which unifies. One can without exaggeration say that life in the youth hostels stems from the striving for a people's community [*Volksgemeinschaft*] and furthers its realization." Wilhelm Münker, secretary of the Reich Association for Youth Hostels, echoed this view when he said he hoped that the registration of communist youth groups to use the national hostel network might have a "decontaminating" effect on disaffected proletarian youth.[131] In the youth hostels, bourgeois preservationists and youth advocates saw the potential for a harmonious society close to nature and steeped in love of the Fatherland. With more than 300,000 overnight guests in 1926 alone, Rhenish youth hostels seemed well on their way to creating a new appreciation for nature among provincial youth.[132]

Provincial officials and nature protection leaders tried to draw adolescents into *Heimatschutz* and *Naturschutz* organizations, to transform the psychological benefits of hiking into a desire to protect the natural world. Landscape preservationists held several conferences that called for greater cooperation between youth groups and nature protection organizations. In 1929, district representatives, mayors, and *Heimat* enthusiasts in the province's Bergisches Land district sponsored the symposium "Heimat, Nature Protection, and Youth." The exhibitions portrayed the local natural and historical monuments young people might encounter on their hiking trips and offered models and drawings of vernacular building styles considered historically significant.[133] The Eifelverein established special youth divisions and activities for the first time in 1920. Local groups were encouraged to establish separate groups for young men between the ages of fourteen and eighteen and to hold *Heimat* evenings for young people that were free from alcohol and tobacco. The Eifelverein pledged to help maintain the region's hostels and issued pamphlets such as the "Ten Commandments for Hikers," which asked visitors to avoid picking flowers, carving on trees, catching small animals, or littering in nature reserves, so that they could be enjoyed by everyone.[134] Preservationists' youth policies thus exemplified a new program of outreach that Walther Schoenichen referred to as "folk-oriented paths of enlightenment and people's instruction," whose goal was to establish a "new culture for dealing with nature."[135] In this new culture, young people would learn to see again the different shades of green in a local park, the minute changes in foliage from day to day, the rare species that might occupy a local stream. The emphasis was on building environmental awareness in a backyard setting, not in a distant national park. Environmental stewardship began at home.

In light of these goals, national preservationist leaders such as Schoenichen allied *Naturschutz* with the *Heimatkunde* educational reform movement in schools to influence young people in the classroom.[136] Teachers and education officials believed that *Heimatkunde,* which linked a child's immediate cultural, social, and natural surroundings to the larger structures of civil society and the state, offered the best vehicle for developing an individual's connection to the nation. The 1920 Reich School Conference issued guidelines on school and *Heimat* that declared: "For cultural, pedagogic, and social reasons, *Heimatkunde* within and outside of the school must be afforded the greatest attention and cultivation." National guidelines developed in 1922 embraced this principle, requiring schools to integrate "*Heimat* schooling techniques," such as "hiking, field trips, teaching outdoors, gardening, and stays in the country."[137]

In the context of such educational proposals, preservationists envisioned another socially therapeutic role for nature protection. As Peter Zepp argued, children's subjective emotional attachments to place provided a vital component of personality development, emotional stability, and social integration. Contact with nature and heritage, he asserted, enabled children to realize that "our ego is deeply anchored in the homeland" and that each individual forms part of a larger "living organism." He noted that "the recognition of these truths is not new . . . but has never developed so much as in the period after the war, when the motto of the new German man became the sought-after pedagogical goal." Zepp recommended that biology and geology instruction include nature protection at all academic levels and called on sport and hiking clubs to include landscape and nature study alongside "muscular achievement."[138] Schoenichen noted that small activities such as maintaining bird feeders or keeping frogs in a classroom terrarium could be used to foster awareness of each species' relationship to broader ecological networks and to help students see that nature did not recognize the categories of useful and harmful animals imposed by human standards. "Within a *Lebensgemeinschaft*,"

Schoenichen wrote, "the balance is disturbed as soon as just one of its members is destroyed."[139] Taking students on a small field trip could show them remnants of Germany's geological past such as the Siebengebirge's volcanic rocks or stands of trees that had been part of Germany's primeval forests. The trips could also point out the horrors of industrialization, including granite mines that destroyed surrounding vegetation and smoke-spewing factories located next to majestic escarpments.[140] The nature of *Heimat* was thus the nucleus from which the individual could move outward into the world without losing sight of the complex interdependencies that bound humans to each other and to nature. Both utopian and disciplinary, the therapeutic vision of nature tried to encourage workers' and young peoples' sense of self while anchoring them in the homeland soil.

## Resentment and Racism

During the 1920s, then, landscape preservationists expanded public outreach efforts in hopes of reforming workers and youths and making nature protection a "people's task." Yet just as environmentalists faced severe legal constraints that challenged their ability to create nature protection regions, so too did they encounter significant limits to local *Heimat* mobilization during the Weimar era that fueled a growing frustration with the republican system. Preservationist clubs were hit hard by the 1923 hyperinflation and found it difficult to regain their institutional momentum even after the economic stabilization of 1924; most groups, in fact, faced stagnating or declining membership levels during the Weimar Republic.[141] The Eifelverein, for example, reported difficulties recruiting and retaining members, despite a host of innovative lecture series, *Heimat* evenings, automobile excursions, and youth programs designed to attract new members. The club's total membership declined slowly during the period of stabilization between 1924 and 1929 and then fell precipitously after the onset of the Depression in 1929. In 1926, the club reported having 145 local branches and 18,500 members; by 1932 this had decreased to 132 local branches and 11,000 members. Eifelverein leaders attributed the club's lackluster recruitment to the continuing "impoverishment of the middle classes." In 1932, the decline in membership forced the club to lower its members' dues from 2 to 1.8 reichsmarks and to rely on loans to carry on with its activities and pay its bills. The club's appeals to youth had also shown little result; by 1931, only five local groups reported having active youth divisions.[142]

Despite substantial outlays of time, energy, and funding, preservationists' efforts to achieve long-lasting ties to the youth movement were also uneven and disappointing. Among bourgeois youth, interest in *Naturschutz* and *Heimatschutz* affairs did grow, as evidenced by an increasing number of articles in youth journals and newspapers dedicated to nature protection. Children and teenagers helped adult preservationists to hang bird nesting boxes, identify rare plant species, and clean up trash along riverbanks. Yet such activities usually occurred at the urging of adults; few young people took the initiative in nature protection activities. Most adolescents became ardent preservationists only when their favorite recreation areas, such as the Lüneburger Heath, were at risk. Not surprisingly, youth groups then quickly became corporative members of the Nature Park Society, which dedicated itself to maintaining a national park in that region.[143] The local *Heimat* significance was nonetheless often lost in such engagement. Young people continued to define themselves against dominant middle-class norms, rather than as members of a *Heimat* community.

Lasting ties were even more difficult to forge with proletarian hikers, for whom concept of "social hiking" provided an alternative model of nature appreciation from that of bourgeois conservation.[144] Like bourgeois youth organizations, working-class recreation clubs strove first and foremost to maintain their members' access to the outdoors. They readily participated in trailblazing and cleanup activities and lobbied the railway system to offer cheaper weekend train fares. Young workers needed such access for relaxation from physically demanding labor and to establish leisure patterns in anticipation of demanding work schedules. For them, nature offered temporary relief from workplace routines and difficult physical labor, not a pathway to patriotic feeling.[145] For example, trade school teachers complained that their apprenticeship students lacked deeper interest in *Heimat* activities and the wonders of nature during school-sponsored hikes. One instructor muttered that on a recent excursion students had stolen his cigarettes and grumbled about boredom; instead of taking interest in the flora and fauna around them, they remained "quarrelsome, impatient, and egotistical."[146]

Proletarian hikers in the Friends of Nature and other socialist-affiliated recreational groups, which reached the height of their popularity under Weimar, had even more important reasons to remain diffident toward bourgeois *Naturschutz:* they believed that only the triumph of socialism, whether through the ballot box or through revolution, could resolve the social and environmental contradictions of capitalism. "Social hikers" placed the blame for environmental despoliation squarely on the shoulders of capitalism, not on a "culture of materialism."[147] In their eyes, only limits on private property, not new cultural values or the piecemeal establishment of nature reserves, could achieve lasting change. Proletarian hikers were also far more attuned to the conditions of rural workers than their bourgeois counterparts. In one illustration from a Socialist Fighting League essay, the authors included a picture of rural laborers gathering hay from the fields. The caption read, "Rural people do not have the time to admire the landscape."[148] Proletarian hikers' recognition of the social foundations of landscape aesthetics drove a troublesome wedge in preservationists' organic vision of the *Heimat* community. Despite preservationists' efforts to promote nature as a symbol above social divisions, nature protection remained a movement of the educated middle classes, rather than the people as a whole, which limited its effectiveness in the democratic political realm.[149]

The cultural and social constraints on preservationists' ability to shape a "new culture of interaction with nature" under conservative middle-class auspices were especially evident during the "*Heimat* emergency" of the late 1920s and early 1930s. During this period, communitarian impulses across Germany dissolved in the face of economic Depression, the government's financial crisis, and antiparliamentary ideologies on both the left and the right that cast doubt on the viability of parliamentary government. Homeland images failed to soothe the sense of crisis at the popular level. One member of a local natural history club commented bitterly in 1932 that the *Naturschützer* had ultimately been unable to convince Germans that nature and *Heimat* offered them a common ground: "Regrettably it appears to be a fact that our people are no longer rooted in nature and pursue places of enjoyment, political battles, and extreme interest-group ideas that bring no advantages for either the spirit or the emotional inner life . . . 'Back to Nature' has been the slogan for a long time and yet our people distance themselves ever more from it."[150] *Heimat* feeling appeared impotent in the face of a national crisis.

As nature preservationists were forced to admit the limited success of *Heimat* ideals in rooting workers and young people and stemming the national emergency, many of them registered their frustration through an increasingly vitriolic critique of the "masses" they had once hoped to win over to the *Naturschutz* cause. One common theme was to decry the insidious spread of mass commercial culture in the natural landscape.[151] Walther Schoenichen inveighed against the "invasion of the masses into nature"—people who damaged trees, defaced cliff sides with graffiti, and dared to play gramophones in the outdoors. He described such actions as the "reflection of a lack of culture, impurity, a fondness for snacks, continuous thoughts of eating and drinking, vanity, [and] the need for admiration."[152] Preservationist discourse of the late 1920s and early 1930s created a sharp moral division between cultured Germans who appreciated the ideal values of *Heimat* and the "uncultured" masses seduced by popular fashions and modernist standardization. Commenting on noisome traffic and outdoor advertisements in the Rhine Valley, the botanist August Reichensperger remarked, "What is left of the German Romanticism of the old Father Rhine? It has fled before leveling, equalization, mechanization, industrialization, regulation, and internationalization. Modern *Sachlichkeit* (functionality) has striven to transform the wreath of vineyard hills and the forest crown of the mountains into uniformlines."[153] By the early 1930s, nature preservationists had become skeptical that the masses would submit to their tutelage in building a new *Heimat* culture that cared for nature.

In targeting "internationalization" and "*Sachlichkeit*" as cultural menaces, preservationists also found themselves embroiled in a broader late-Weimar battle between proponents of a transnational Modernist culture, on the one hand, and conservatives who valued homeland traditions, on the other.[154] Though *Landschaftspflege* had promised to tame the forces of modern technology in the name of both functional efficiency and environmental sustainability, preservationists were less sure that Modernist aesthetic principles or commercial mass culture could be successfully integrated into the *Heimat* vision. While the Depression sharpened the rhetoric on both sides, the terms of the debate reflected a deepening cultural malaise whose momentum continued irrespective of actual economic and environmental conditions. Preservationists echoed right-wing critics who proposed that Germans were under the spell of "foreign" influences whose values were anathema to authentic Teutonic culture. In his 1929 essay "On the Feeling of *Heimat*," the Saxon *Heimatschutz* member Max Kästner-Frankenberg argued that "rootlessness" and "alienation from *Heimat*" were far more insidious problems than Germany's loss of international stature or its economic condition. "Such [problems] are more or less external diseases," he wrote, "that in the short term or long term can be rectified, if only the body of the people [*Volkskörper*] remains healthy." The national body was, however, sick; it "swam and splashed about with apparent joy in a flood of West European and American conceptions that . . . will pull away the mother earth under its feet if it does not become self-conscious."[155] The only way to pull the people back from ethnic oblivion was to re-kindle the feeling of *Heimat*, which for most people, according to Kästner-Frankenberg, remained merely a "flicker" located deep in the "subconscious."

One way to make people aware of such repressed sentiments was to show them an authentically German landscape. As Kästner-Frankenberg explained: "Hold two landscape pictures next to each other, one that is familiar [*heimatliches*] and one foreign, say an Italian or African [landscape] . . . The foreign one, despite its splendor and abundance, leaves you cold [while] the homeland, in spite of its modesty and simplicity, warms your heart because everything it depicts is dear and familiar to you."[156] Contact with native flora and fauna was paramount; while dahlias, gladiolus, giraffes, and zebras might be a "feast for the eyes," the indigenous forget-me-nots, wood anemones, deer, and foxes of German meadows and forests "look at you trustingly like sisters to their brothers." In the crisis of late Weimar, the notion of the native *Heimat* landscape took on an increasingly xenophobic cast as preservationists tried to erect a spiritual bulwark against the imagined onslaught of foreign cultures and leveling modernization.

Kästner-Frankenberg's image of Germany awash in foreign influences was an important right-wing trope of this period, one that resurrected and magnified preservationists' immediate postwar fears of the fluid and unstable boundaries of *Heimat*. Preservationists had never overcome a gnawing fear of Germany's spiritual, territorial, and ecological vulnerability, anxieties they tried to overcome through the ordering principles of regional planning and the promotion of nature's healing powers. In the national crisis of the early 1930s, however, preservationists became less sanguine about their ability to manage the forces of modernization. Cautious optimism faded in favor of *völkisch* rhetoric that depicted mass culture as an alien value system infecting the national organism. Schoenichen warned that Germany's cultural decline and environmental degradation were symptoms of this invasion of foreign elements into the national body: "Our age stands once again under the sign of an appalling tidal wave of foreign cultural influences, a high tide of internationalism, that swells up ever more powerfully and threatens to encrust irretrievably with its sediments everything that is of our own character and primordial. Its water level is highest in the large and industrial cities; but from here it expands in thousands of canals and rivulets over the entire country."[157] Schoenichen's fears of inundation and encrustation recast *Heimat* as vulnerable to insidious outside influences, largely invisible to the eye, which worked slowly to erode national character from within. Such rhetoric recalled wartime depictions of *Heimat:* pastoral and indivisible, on the one hand, but under siege from internal and external enemies, on the other. To combat such vulnerability, preservationists sharpened their spiritual weapons against outsiders who were eroding the national body from within.

The belief that internal illness and a flood of "Western" ideas were to blame for Germans' alienation from nature opened a discursive wedge for racist and eugenicist forms of homeland rhetoric, which supplanted the critique of the masses with a fear of ethnic infiltration and racial pollution. Several leading preservationists shifted the blame for environmental degradation and the negation of *Heimat* ideals from the uncultivated German masses to "foreign races" living within the Reich's borders. In 1930, Paul Schultze-Naumburg, who had become a member of the National Socialist Party in that year, attacked Modernist architecture's geometric shapes and flat roofs as visual signs of "inferior" and nomadic racial elements in the nation, whose dwellings were alien to German architectural and landscape traditions.[158] The Westphalian *Heimatschutz* leader Karl Wagenfeld echoed this sentiment when he condemned German schools for filling children's heads with the "traditions and sagas" of "Kaffirs and Hottentots" rather than the fairy tales, songs, and sagas of Germanic tribes.[159] Wagenfeld insisted that "members of a foreign race" had misused "their rights as guests in Germany," corrupting the people with a "creeping poison" of newspapers, literature, and art. The "foreign penetration" of Polish immigration into the Ruhr region had destroyed its inhabitants' "tribal connection" to the landscape and created a "blood mixture" of the "most varied emotional and physical character."[160] By the late 1920s many preservationists were specifying that "foreign races" were to blame for Germany's environmental degradation and cultural crisis.

Preservationists' focus on pernicious outside influences as an explanation for Germans' alienation from nature gave credence to other forms of racism within the environmental protection movement. This turn toward racialism undoubtedly reflected the growing Nazi presence in late-Weimar political discourse, yet it also articulated the belief of many preservationists that the "natural laws" of race provided a more scientific understanding of society than either environmental or cultural factors.[161] Walther Schoenichen warned in 1926 that a "racial-hygienic collapse" threatened the German people and called on the state to regulate reproduction to prevent "degenerate" elements from reproducing and encourage "racially valuable" women to have more children.[162] Schoenichen's comments reflected a desire to rationalize reproduction, to bring it under the same type of scientific scrutiny and enhanced productivity found in land use planners' drive to make the landscape more economically and environmentally efficient. Though racial hygiene and *Landschaftspflege* shared the same rationalizing impulses, however, they articulated divergent visions of social reform and national regeneration. *Landschaftspflege* advocates still believed that environmental improvement would create more productive, rooted, and politically loyal inhabitants. Racial hygiene, on the other hand, called into question the efficacy of environmental improvement and public education in creating social stability and fortifying German culture. If foreign elements and racial degeneracy were to blame for Germany's environmental ills, then neither contact with nature nor further aesthetic training could redeem many of the country's "uncultured" or prevent further foreign intrusion. Instead, racial-hygienic and eugenic measures that improved the national organism biologically by separating or eliminating "weak" or "foreign" racial elements seemed to offer a more potent solution to the country's economic distress, political instability, and environmental decline.[163]

Despite the increasing racialism of preservationist discourse in the early 1930s, the path from local perceptions of the "*Heimat* emergency" to National Socialism was by no means linear. While Rhenish nature preservationists were clearly frustrated by the late Weimar Republic's economic, parliamentary, and cultural crises, sentiments that left them open to right-wing political alternatives, there were limits to the appeal of racial hygiene at the regional level, especially in the traditionally Catholic and liberal Rhineland. Provincial cultural elites were not uncritical followers of Schultze-Naumburg and Schoenichen; at the local level, regional, aesthetic, and cultural perceptions of *Heimat* competed with racialist understandings of national character. The Rhenish architect and RVDH leader Richard Klapheck, for example, rejected Schultze-Naumburg's blanket condemnation of Modernism. He argued further that the former DBH chairman's affinity for the early-nineteenth-century Biedermeier style in architecture reflected his "Thuringian" upbringing and that this design did not fit the "rhythms of the land" in the Rhine Province.[164] Many provincial leaders also remained suspicious of racial ideas that some labeled "Prussian," code for the extension of centralized power into the provinces.[165] Rhenish preservationist organizations also remained relatively open to diverse members and cultural tendencies. Amid growing anti-Semitism and racist xenophobia, the RVDH published a special issue of its journal in 1931 devoted to Jewish cultural monuments. The articles proposed that legal discrimination and spatial segregation, rather than racial inferiority, explained Jewish artisans' tendency to imitate dominant cultural motifs instead of developing their own characteristic style of art and architecture.[166] Even in the more agrarian and conservative Westphalia, some *Heimatschutz* members had their doubts about the racist direction of much homeland rhetoric. The Westphalian Heimat Association's secretary insisted that "living space [*Lebensraum*] and history" were equally important as fixed racial characteristics in understanding the cultural traits and customs of Ruhr inhabitants.[167] For many preservationists, race remained among the numerous coordinates of *Heimat* identity; it was by no means hegemonic within the preservation movement of the late Weimar period.

The Rhineland's Catholicism was another factor that limited the appeal of racial hygiene. The Rhine Province's *Landeshauptmann* Johannes Horion, who replaced Werner Lindner as DBH secretary in 1931, rejected eugenicists' solutions for "streamlining" Germany's social welfare system out of a Catholic belief in the sanctity of human life. Horion issued a sharply worded rebuttal to Ernst Mann's essay

"The Morality of Power" that appeared in the *Kölnische Volkszeitung* in 1931.[168] Mann had proposed that the state should establish health boards to identify those with incurable or hereditary illnesses and to euthanize them "for the good of all." Horion condemned Mann's essay and other racial improvement ideas as Nietzschean and barbarous. "Which life is 'not worth living' and should be destroyed?" he asked. Commenting on the way political opinion might influence such decisions, Horion remarked: "[After this law's passage], will the life of a National Socialist appear worth living to a Communist and vice versa?" Horion noted that proletarian mothers would suffer under such a system because rich families would be able to care for their sickly or disabled children, while the state would refuse welfare funds for working-class children. "In addition to these cultural and humanitarian reasons," he noted, "we Christians must also consider that God has given us the weak and the suffering" as confirmation of the "highest virtues of Christianity." The Catholic belief structure of many Rhineland elites thus hindered a racialist redefinition of *Heimat* before 1933.

In addition to Catholic disquiet over eugenicists' proposals to end "lives not worth living," most Rhenish preservationists also believed that the Depression, not foreign influences, was the root cause of their movement's limited popular appeal. This tempered their outrage at the masses; most remained confident that education would provide the most important tool for gaining influence once the crisis had passed. In 1931, the botanist August Reichensperger commented, "It is unnecessary to note that the work of the [nature protection] office was strongly influenced in the past years by the [country's] economic condition. In this period of need it is difficult to steer public interest toward questions of natural monument protection."[169] In a similar vein, the Eifelverein called on its members to weather the current storm of economic instability. The 1932 annual report noted that "for now the word is: persevere! Except for the more or less high losses, the condition of the individual local affiliates is in general not completely discouraging. Among many [groups] there has even been a revival of activity and [a] rise in the number of members."[170] While economic need and cultural criticism heightened preservationists' fears about *Heimat* vulnerability, these passages do not indicate a readiness to abandon traditional back-to-nature activities or cultural notions of nationhood in favor of a mythic racial essence. Even at the very end of the republic, nature and *Heimat* had diverse cultural and environmental meanings; only the rise of Nazism would shift regional nature protection decisively in a racist direction.

While the dichotomies between urbanism and agrarian-romanticism have dominated scholarly interpretations of Weimar culture, the landscape preservationists during this period tried to articulate a middle ground between such extremes. *Heimat* and nature protectionists did not reject the republican system from the beginning, nor did they all embrace a *völkisch* nationalism that vilified modern technology, democratization, and mass culture. Instead, most preservationists tried to negotiate and manage modernizing impulses, to create a landscape of modernity that capitalized on the therapeutic value of nature amid growing economic rationalization, expanding political participation, and mass consumerism. Weimar's anemic economy forced preservationists to demonstrate the "material" benefits of nature protection, such as the appeal to tourists, in their pleas for saving scenic landmarks.

The era's streamlining and modernization of economic production processes, moreover, prompted provincial officials and landscape architects to embrace the concepts of *Landschaftspflege* and regional planning, which stressed the virtues of integrating nature protection into a form of state-directed environmental planning that enhanced economic productivity and efficiency. Rather than falling prey to *völkisch* mysticism, a number of preservationists thereby abandoned nineteenth-century Romanticism during the golden 1920s, especially Romantics' division between the profane urban world and quasi-divine natural areas. The functional approach of *Landschaftspflege* stressed the need to design the landscape consciously and to provide modern workers with valuable recreational areas that facilitated productivity and public health. In the Ruhr region, the new planning tendencies resulted in the creation of extensive green spaces and forest protection programs, though on the whole the aims of *Landschaftspflege* and regional planning remained programmatic in the Weimar Republic and resulted in an increasingly technocratic approach to land use planning that accepted the logic of capitalist exploitation instead of offering ecologically sustainable alternatives to it.

Preservationists also realized that Weimar democracy and the spread of mass culture demanded new strategies for building a popular constituency that extended beyond the circle of provincial elites who had dominated Wilhelmine cultural politics. These attempts were uneven. Landscape preservation remained a bastion of the educated middle classes that was socially conservative and paternalistic in outlook. Its approach emphasized using environmental reform to root politically volatile workers and youths into the homeland, encouraging social integration from above rather than democratic participation from those most affected by environmental despoliation. Not surprisingly, preservationists found it increasingly difficult to woo targeted social groups, particularly workers and young people, away from Weimar's expanding urban mass culture and integrate them into a national community of sentiment based on love of nature and *Heimat* identity.

Preservationists' attempt to articulate a middle ground between economic development and environmental protection ultimately foundered due to their lingering anxieties about *Heimat* vulnerability, the inability of the republic to pass a national nature protection law, and the overall political instability and economic crises of the Weimar era. During the war, nature and *Heimat* protection had touted the healing powers of nature and had become enmeshed in national and provincial efforts to mobilize the Rhenish population's emotional loyalties using landscape imagery and *Heimat* sentiment. This militarization of *Heimat* legitimated new discourses and imagery that viewed national and regional landscapes as embodiments of a fixed, distinct Germanic character, with permanent borders, rather than as hybrid cultural landscapes with indistinct contours. These representations of nature reemerged in the political and cultural crisis of 1929 to 1933 to help explain not only economic collapse but also the broader spiritual malaise of the German people who remained alienated from nature and indifferent to *Heimat*. In this context, several preservationist leaders turned toward racial ideas that depicted mass culture and aesthetic Modernism as forms of degeneracy that could be remedied only by racial-biological means rather than strictly environmental ones. Frustrated by the republic's failure to pass a comprehensive nature protection law and fearful of further environmental decline, many preservationists sought alternatives to parliamentary democracy, which appeared unable to control either the abuse of nature or the atomization of the community.

Chapter 4 demonstrates that this new racial determinism and the heightened concern about the vulnerability of *Heimat* meshed well with the Third Reich's appeal to Blood and Soil, yet they never fully superceded the localist traditions of *Heimat* cultivation, even under the Nazi dictatorship. The Nazis hoped for an easy "synchronization," or *Gleichschaltung,* at the regional and local levels, but they too found that there were limits to their ability to recast environmental protection along racist lines.

# CHAPTER FOUR

# From Landscape to Lebensraum: Race and Environment under Nazism

> The German countryside must be preserved under all circumstances, for it is and has forever been the source of strength and greatness for our people.
>
> —ADOLF HITLER

In its 1933 annual report, the Beautification Society for the Siebengebirge described a dramatic change in its members' morale and the mood of the country as a whole. "The year 1933 marked a change in the nation's fortunes," the report noted. "Our people's chancellor Adolf Hitler has led the German people upward out of their hopelessness and doubt . . . and welded them together into a powerful unity and people's community [*Volksgemeinschaft*]." The club's praise for the "people's chancellor" resonated throughout the Rhine Province's major preservationist organizations, outdoor recreation clubs, and provincial nature protection offices, forming a groundswell of support for the new regime. The VVS tied this national rejuvenation to a back-to-the-land ethos sweeping over the people. "Hundreds of thousands of our comrades pour each year into the mountains, whose natural beauties," the report claimed, "purify their souls from the slag of the everyday and steel their bodies for the new battle with life."[1] In a similar vein, the Eifelverein president Karl Leopold Kaufmann wrote that a "synchronization," or *Gleichschaltung,* of his organization was not needed, for the society's hikers and outdoorsmen "already stood behind [the government], since its activities had always demonstrated, even in the worst years of the [French] occupation, true nationalist loyalty."[2]

The National Socialist regime used the term *Gleichschaltung* to refer to the process of bringing German state and civil society into line with Nazi principles, synchronizing all sectors of the country to achieve economic recovery, rearmament, and racial improvement. Government agencies and private organizations would henceforth form a seamless, organic whole dedicated to pursuing the racial will of the German *Volk*. *Gleichschaltung* was the surest sign of the Nazis' totalitarian aim to dismantle the liberal system, yet historians have recently shown that it was not simply a top-down process of political terror and ideological indoctrination. Landscape preservation groups were among the middle-class organizations that acclaimed the Nazi revolution without direct coercion; synchronization occurred rapidly because Nazism expressed these environmentalists' hopes and desires. Preservationists interpreted Nazi appeals to Blood and Soil as an affirmation of the *Heimat* tradition, an updated version of Wilhelm Heinrich Riehl's appeal to *Land und Leute* that recognized landscape protection's role in fortifying German national identity and reestablishing it on a natural basis.[3]

Though Thomas Childers has called the National Socialist German Workers' Party (Nationalsozialistische Deutsche Arbeiterpartei, NSDAP) a "catch-all party of protest,"[4] the environmental discourse of 1933 demonstrates that Nazism exercised a *positive* appeal in middle-class circles that was not motivated solely by political frustration or cultural despair. The Rhineland's preservationists viewed the Nazi regime as a vehicle for reclaiming their own role as stewards of landscape and *Heimat,* a position that Weimar pluralism and economic deprivation had undermined. "So in the future," wrote the VVS, "the publicly beneficial work of the Siebengebirge Society, which serves the entire people, will find its appreciation."[5] Nature preservationists' acclaim for Hitler's regime and their organizations' rapid "self-synchronization" in 1933 and 1934, moreover, belies their postwar claims that *Heimat* activities and local social life provided an "oasis" from Nazi tyranny during the dark days of the Third Reich.[6] They offered their services willingly to secure the National Socialist revolution at the regional and local levels.

This chapter examines the process of *Gleichschaltung* among national and regional preservationist groups during the Third Reich, analyzing both the possibilities and the limits of their ideological and institutional synchronization in the Nazis' racist and militarist state. Beyond the pull of nationalism and anti-Marxism, nature protection and *Heimat* advocates found numerous points of ideological synergy between themselves and the new regime. Preservationists were impressed by the Nazi slogan, "The general good before individual good," which indicated to them the state's willingness to overcome particularism and to undertake national regeneration based on the ideal values of homeland.[7] In preservationists' eyes, the Nazis were not merely changing the form of the state but were sparking a cultural rejuvenation that would overturn Weimar individualism, materialism, and class tensions for the sake of the national community. By 1930, NSDAP cultural theorists such as Alfred Rosenberg and Paul Schultze-Naumburg had incorporated landscape preservationists' critiques of Modernism, consumerism, and urban life into the party's cultural platform. Most important, Nazism promised a forward-looking national revolution that, like the landscape preservation movement itself, looked to an alternative modernity grounded in the eternal laws of nature.[8]

Though preservationists found numerous points of ideological affinity between themselves and the National Socialist regime, their synchronization remained uneven, contested, and incomplete. Preservationist leaders Schultze-Naumburg and Walther Schoenichen were certainly not immune to fascist ideas. Both embraced racist and eugenic ideas and began to recast nature preservation along racist lines even before 1933. Schultze-Naumburg sought to transform the political significance of "cultural landscape," substituting the Nazis' racist vision of German territory as an expanding living space, or *Lebensraum,* for the concept's traditionally aesthetic and regionalist meanings. *Völkisch* themes appeared with increasing frequency in preservationist discourse between 1933 and 1934. Indeed, the VVS's claim in its 1933 annual report that the Siebengebirge's mountains were necessary for "purifying" the soul and preparing comrades' bodies for "battle with life" marked a departure from previous writings, which had focused predominantly on nature as a site of popular recreation and quiet aesthetic appreciation. The rhetoric of purification even went beyond the militarized *Heimat* language of the war and early Weimar period, which had stopped short of seeing landscape solely in social-Darwinist terms or calling for the racial cleansing of nature and nation.

Yet many scholars have too quickly interpreted such discursive congruence as a sign of deep-seated ideological conformity with the Third Reich.[9] By investigating the diffusion, reception, and implementation of Nazi environmental policies at the regional and local levels, this chapter shows that Nazism's institutional "polycracy"—a system of administration based on multiple, overlapping, and competing centers of power rather than streamlined coordination from above—left substantial room for regional autonomy and initiative in environmental affairs before the onset of war in 1939.[10] The National Socialists recognized the need to secure the support of influential middle-class organizations, such as those of preservationists, to consolidate their revolution at the regional and local levels. They relied on *Heimat* language to appear rooted in local associational life and offered tangible benefits, such as cultural patronage, financial support, and new environmental legislation, to solidify their power and legitimacy among *Naturschutz* and *Heimatschutz* groups in the provinces. Preservationists, in turn, saw Nazism as an opportunity to enhance their own prestige and power. They harnessed the language of Blood and Soil proactively to appear politically reliable, to avoid further incursions into their everyday activities, and to achieve long-standing environmental goals. The discourse and practice of landscape preservation thus remained an unstable amalgam of divergent ideological strains at the regional level, with traditional references to protecting the bucolic *Heimat* landscape coexisting uneasily with racist demands for purifying Germany's *Lebensraum* of all traces of "degeneration" and "Jewish" capital. Even within the totalitarian Third Reich, a cultural and institutional space existed for negotiating the terms of environmental discourse, and hence of power itself, between the Nazi regime and influential landscape preservation groups.[11]

## Blood and Soil: The Racialization of Landscape

Soon after the Nazi seizure of power, Hans Klose, the provincial nature protection commissioner in the Prussian province of Brandenburg, announced that "several favorable comments and signs demonstrate that national and socialist Germany is ready to take *Heimatschutz* and *Naturschutz* concerns much more seriously than ever before." Klose proclaimed confidently that "[we preservationists] can trust that the national government led by Reich Chancellor Hitler hears the call of *Heimat* and will know how to place the work of *Heimat-* and *Naturschutz* systematically in the service of German reconstruction."[12] Klose had good reasons to be optimistic about the new regime, as several National Socialist leaders favored nature conservation and environmentally sensitive land-use planning measures. The so-called green wing of the Nazi Party included Agricultural Minister Richard Walther Darré and Hitler's deputy Rudolf Hess, both of whom promoted experiments with biodynamic farming, a forerunner to current organic farming practices.[13] Walter von Keudell, the head of German forestry in the early years of the regime, advocated sustainable *Dauerwald* forestry methods, which rejected traditional clear-cutting and conifer plantations in favor of selectively removing mature trees and maintaining a diverse mix of evergreens and hardwoods.[14] Fritz Todt, the general inspector for German roadways and the chief engineer for the new *Autobahn* system, hired the Munich landscape architect Alwin Seifert to work with engineers to avoid damaging the countryside while building the new highways.[15] On the legal front, Hitler and Heinrich Himmler, both well-known vegetarians, urged Prussian minister-president Hermann Göring to pass a law banning animal vivisection.[16] On 17 August 1933, Göring issued an order stating that thenceforth "vivisection of animals of whatever species is prohibited in all parts of Prussian territory," though in practice anti-Semitic Nazi officials targeted Jewish ritual slaughter as an example of "unnecessarily cruel" animal treatment.[17] Soon thereafter the regime implemented a series of environmental protection measures, including the Animal Protection Law of 24 November 1933; the Law against the Devastation of Forests of January 1934; and the Reich Hunting Law of July 1934, which contained new restrictions on killing wild animals.[18] Preservationists like Klose believed that such high-level support for environmental issues would also result in a favorable climate for the expansion of nature protection and *Landschaftspflege* in the Third Reich.

Klose's comments indicate that preservationists assumed a fundamental affinity between their nature protection agenda and Nazism's appeal to Blood and Soil. Yet few regional environmentalists fully appreciated the separate intellectual trajectory that had drawn Nazi leaders toward back-to-the-land sentiments. Before 1933, Nazi leaders gave few signs of any environmentalist commitment; in fact, the movement's promise to guide German political development and social policy according to so-called natural laws reflected an amalgam of racist and social-Darwinist principles that were anathema to the *Heimat* movement's emphasis on regional identity, landscape aesthetics, and environmental determinism.[19] In *Mein Kampf,* for example, Hitler argued that Germany's national decline could be attributed to its divergence from biological laws governing racial purity and the struggle for survival. "At this point, someone or other may laugh," he wrote, "but this planet once moved through the ether for millions of years without human beings and it can do so again some day if men forget they owe their higher existence, not to the ideas of a few crazy ideologists, but to the knowledge and ruthless application of Nature's stern and rigid laws."[20] The mechanistic nineteenth century, Hitler continued, had neglected these laws in pursuit of industrialization and material progress. "At the end of the last century," he wrote, "the progress of science and technology led liberalism astray by proclaiming man's mastery of nature and announcing that he would soon have dominion over space. But a single storm is enough—and everything collapses like a pack of cards."[21] Rejecting the division between humans and the organic world, Hitler asserted that nature would take vengeance on those moderns who did not heed her ways.

Racism and the expansion of *Lebensraum,* rather than homeland sentiment, lay at the heart of Hitler's naturalistic conception of history and national fate. Hitler viewed the nation as a racial collectivity akin to an organism in the natural world, with the state serving merely as an instrument for the "preservation and advancement of a community of physically and psychically homogeneous creatures."[22] By eliding the Darwinian ontology of "species" with the socially constructed concept of "race," Hitler argued that nature pitted human races in a never-ending struggle for resources and territory parallel to the "struggle of the fittest" in the organic world. Hitler argued that nature dictated that only pure bloodlines could prevail in such struggles, and attributed Germany's postwar political, economic, and cultural dislocations to racial degeneration. To their peril, he maintained, Germans had forgotten nature's stern and uncompromising laws proscribing racial mixing and material support for the weak or infirm. "No more than Nature desires the mating of weaker with stronger individuals," he wrote, "even less does she desire the blending of a higher with a lower race. If she did, her whole work of higher breeding, over perhaps hundreds of thousands of years, might be ruined with one blow." Hitler blamed Germany's racial degeneration on Jews, whom he referred to as "parasites in the body of other peoples." In his view, Jews had infected Europe's "culture bearing" Aryans with liberal and Marxist ideas, materialist philosophies that embraced an instrumentalist creed in which history progressed as a result of domination over nature. "Millions thoughtlessly parrot this Jewish nonsense and end up by really imagining that they themselves represent a kind of conqueror of Nature," he noted, "though in this they dispose of no other weapon than an idea, and at that such a miserable one, that if it were true no world at all would be conceivable."[23] *Mein Kampf* posited nature as both a biological entity and a normative presence, in which racial struggle provided the key to understanding the rise and fall of nations.

Hitler's understanding of natural laws thus had little to do with environmental protection. The few references to the environment in *Mein Kampf* express Hitler's disdain for the modern city, whose unattractive built environment offered the proletariat no sense of place. In his view, such psychological unease drew residents toward liberalism or Marxism and promoted racial degeneration. Hitler argued further that Jewish capital was responsible for the poor urban environment in German cities. "If the fate of Rome should strike Berlin," he remarked, "future generations would some day admire the department stores of a few Jews as the mightiest works of our time and the hotels of a few corporations as the characteristic expression of the culture of our times." To Hitler, Jews were "nomads" who, lacking a *Heimat* of their own, could exist only as parasites within the homelands of other peoples.[24] The chaos of the modern metropolis was the ultimate expression of this nomadism, because its anonymity and transient social relationships enabled "Jewish" ideas to infiltrate and deceive other cultures. The aesthetic decline of cities thus served as another marker of racial and cultural degeneration.

In its virulent anti-Semitism and conception of the nation as a racial entity, *Mein Kampf* contrasted sharply with local *Heimat* cultivation, which even in its most xenophobic form during World War I envisioned German identity arising out of a landscape shaped by geography, ethnicity, culture, and history, rather than race alone. Hitler's text focused exclusively on heredity, not the natural environment, in shaping German character. In his view, races made themselves manifest in their external environment; the city, in this sense, was the expression of Jewish nomadism. In Hitler's eyes, Germany's major environmental problem was the imbalance between its growing population and the limited *Lebensraum* dictated by the Versailles Treaty and the loss of colonies.[25] Hitler maintained that the state's foreign policy "must safeguard the existence on this planet of the race . . . by creating a healthy, viable natural relation between the nation's population and growth on the one hand and the quantity and quality of its soil on the other hand." In Hitler's view, even the country's 1914 frontiers were illegitimate because they neither encompassed all of Europe's ethnic German peoples nor incorporated the vast historical territories of the Germanic tribes that had supposedly once dominated most of Europe. The constant struggle among races for territory, food, and resources meant that political borders, like the state itself, were merely the contingent expression of deeper biological urges toward expansion and conquest.

Hitler's fixation on racial struggle and territorial expansion stood in stark contrast to *Heimat* ideals emphasizing local traditions and environments as the focus of community identity. By 1930, however, new leaders in the Nazi ranks had synthesized environmental concern with the goal of racial improvement, creating a new, more reactionary right-wing environmentalism. One of these men was Richard Walther Darré, the future agricultural minister, who was responsible for popularizing the *Blut und Boden* political slogan and laying the foundations for a Nazified rural land ethic.[26] Before 1928, the NSDAP had drawn its support mainly from the lower middle classes in Germany's small towns and had sought to build its political base among the industrial working classes. After the party's weak electoral results in 1928, Darré convinced Hitler that the peasantry, rather than urban workers, represented an untapped source of support for the party. Darré then joined the NSDAP in 1930 and was instrumental in making agricultural reforms a key part of the party platform, a tactic he hoped would appeal to peasants reeling from Germany's agricultural depression.[27] Darré's strategy paid off, as the NSDAP posted substantial gains among Protestant peasants in northern and eastern Germany. The result was the Nazis' highest electoral showing up to that point; in 1930, they received 18.3 percent of the popular vote.[28]

Darré viewed the peasantry as the backbone of the German nation, arguing that their long-term viability depended on the health of Germany's soil and rural landscape. Big cities were "infertility machines": they siphoned peasants away from rural areas, transforming them into alienated proletarians without organic bonds to the soil and nation and subjecting them to poverty and diseases that lowered the birth rate. Darré envisioned the complete abolishment of industrial society and its replacement with one based on small- and medium-size farms. Only by rooting the peasant back in the soil—that is, by wedding Blood and Soil—could Germany stem the peasantry's flight from the land and reestablish its national strength. To accomplish this task, Darré passed a Hereditary Farm Law, which gave small- and medium-size farmers complete tenure over their land, and created the Reich Food Estate to ensure quality and set prices at the national level.[29]

Darré's misconstrued reputation as "father of the Greens" stems from his advocacy of sustainable farming practices, known as biodynamic agriculture, that brought ecological perspectives to bear on Nazi agricultural policy. Several members of Darré's staff were followers of Rudolf Steiner, the founder of the anthroposophy movement, which called for a new relationship between society and nature. A key *Lebensreform* advocate of the 1920s, Steiner sought to wed Darwinian evolution with vitalist ideas and pantheistic nature worship. Steiner believed that the soil was a living organism, the basis of the earth's cycles of growth and decay. Capitalist agriculture, however, had exhausted the soil's regenerative capacity through intensive exploitation and the use of chemical fertilizers. To replenish the soil, Steiner advocated composting and crop rotation in place of fertilizers, and promoted the use of biological pest controls instead of insecticides. Such biological controls included local birds, which could be sustained by planting shelterbelts between agricultural fields; these belts, in turn, prevented soil erosion.[30] According to historian Anna Bramwell, the anthroposophists also convinced Darré that biodynamic farming would enable Germany to achieve and sustain autarky better than mechanized agriculture. As the "Battle for Production" accelerated in 1936, the anthroposophists mounted a campaign to convince Darré, Rudolf Hess, and Martin Borrmann that biodynamic farming should become part of the National Socialists' Four-Year Plan. They argued that biodynamic farms achieved higher yields while sustaining the landscape's fertility, provided healthier organic food for the population, and cut out the need for foreign-made fertilizers and insecticides. By 1940, they had won Darré over to their cause, and he remained a fervent advocate of biodynamic farming throughout the rest of his life, even though such policies encountered resistance from Göring and were thoroughly discredited after Hess's flight to Britain in 1941.[31]

Though biodynamic agriculture was an ecologically sound approach to German agricultural reform, its "green" elements were tied to a racist social vision that is anathema to present left-wing environmentalism.[32] Like Hitler, Darré appealed to "natural laws" in bemoaning modern society's divergence from racial purity. Darré supported environmentally friendly agriculture to the extent that it secured a healthy peasantry in the countryside; it was not a goal in and of itself. Darré developed his ideas about the relationship between race and landscape as a member of the Nordic Ring, whose members believed that the Nordic races were the progenitors of German culture. Ring members argued that the German peasantry contained the last vestiges of pure Nordic blood in Germany, but that this racial stock was being threatened by modern urbanization that drew farmers away from the countryside. Ring members, too, claimed that race and space were closely intertwined. The Nordic peasants were especially adapted to the soils of northern and central Europe but were ill-equipped to survive in cities, where they faced both "pollution" by foreign races and physical debilitation due to an unsanitary environment. For Darré, Blood and Soil was not merely a political slogan but a program for saving the peasantry from racial extinction and, by extension, avoiding national collapse. Darré's green reforms, on closer analysis, were designed to replenish and propagate the nation's racial stock in rural areas, not to protect the environment as an end in itself.[33]

Despite Darré's emphasis on race over the environment, several leading landscape preservation leaders embraced the idiom of Blood and Soil to articulate their alienation from the Weimar system during its waning years. The most prominent among these was Paul Schultze-Naumburg, former chairman of the German Association for Homeland Protection from 1906 to 1914, who transformed himself during the late Weimar period from an aesthetic reformer to a Nazi Party member and advocate of racial hygiene.[34] As late as 1928, the year in which the third edition of his famous work *The Shaping of the Landscape by Man* appeared, Schultze-Naumburg had remained wedded to an aesthetic approach to landscape preservation and regional planning that criticized careless industrial development and emphasized the role of public education in securing Germany's environmental future.[35] By the late 1920s, however, Schultze-Naumburg had increasingly come to view race as the key to world history. His 1928 work

*Art and Race* proposed that artistic works reflected the innate racial character of their creators. In his view, the proportionality and grace of classical and Renaissance sculptures, frescoes, and paintings were a sign of their creators' Aryan ancestry and racial health, while Modern art's abstract and nonrepresentational style, especially the tortured human images in German expressionism, was a sign of racial degeneracy.[36] In 1930 Schultze-Naumburg completed his dramatic political and intellectual transformation, joining the NSDAP and becoming a leading member of Alfred Rosenberg's Fighting League for German Culture.

The Fighting League enabled right-wing intellectuals to flesh out a Nazi position on cultural issues that were the traditional purview of conservative critics. Schultze-Naumburg's membership in this group helped to legitimize it among German cultural elites and draw many of them closer to Nazism. Having once been in the vanguard of architectural criticism around 1900, Schultze-Naumburg had found himself on the defensive in the 1920s, labeled a conservative by more radical architects such as Walther Gropius and Mies van der Rohe.[37] As part of the Fighting League, frustration over this loss of status poured from Schultze-Naumburg's angry pen as he denounced the un-German character of Modern architecture. Rosenberg and Schultze-Naumburg employed Blood and Soil rhetoric to revive debates about Modern architecture in 1930, long after the issue had died down in the popular press. Their critique of the so-called International style, which appeared regularly in the German media during the early 1930s, at first simply disparaged the Bauhaus school, founded by Gropius, for its severing of German tradition and the impracticality of its flat-roof style in a rainy, northern European climate. As Darré gained influence within the party, however, the racist language of Blood and Soil began to infiltrate Fighting League pronouncements. Echoing Hitler's anti-Semitic references to Jews as parasites on German cultural traditions, for example, Schultze-Naumburg denigrated Modernist structures as "the works of the nomads of the metropolis . . . who have lost the concept of *Heimat*," while the rural folk and vernacular building styles remained *bodenständig*, literally "grounded" in the soil of the homeland.

Retracing the contours of the arguments about race and aesthetics he laid out in *Art and Race*, Schultze-Naumburg depicted the streamlined geometric forms of modern architecture as manifestations of "desert" (that is, Semitic) peoples whose racial substance was alien to north-central Europe. In the 1932 article "The Purpose of Our Cultural Struggle," the NSDAP newspaper *Völkischer Beobachter* described the Bauhaus as a "cathedral of Marxism, a cathedral, however, which damned well looked liked a synagogue. To the 'inspiration' of this 'model school' we owe not least those oriental boxes which we have described before, [and] which are repugnant to good taste." The article decried the "architectural nonsense" that designed housing developments "in the style of prison cells, and perpetrated an asiatic interlude on German soil."[38] Only National Socialism could reverse this cultural putrification: "In the midst of this apparently all-encompassing wave of internationalism," declared one Fighting League manifesto, "the greatest event of our time is the emergence of the primordial deutsch-German [*sic*] values of the soul, the new discovery of the deep rootedness of every culture and of all genuine, legitimate statehood in blood and soil."[39]

Schultze-Naumburg's belief that Modernist architecture mirrored Germany's racial degeneration also informed his analysis of the causes and consequences of landscape disfigurement. This entailed a systematic recasting of the *Kulturlandschaft* ideal—the tradition of Riehl and Rudorff—along the same racial lines that informed his critique of Modern art and Bauhaus architecture. Schultze-Naumburg proposed that racial degeneracy had created unhealthy human beings who were unable to recognize that reckless environmental behavior would destroy the very foundations of life. "The reason for the insipid physiognomy of our common environment," he wrote, "is the excessive reproduction of the noncreative . . . of the half- and quarter-humans . . . who give our time their stamp."[40] Racial character, not history or cultural factors, thus determined the state of the landscape. In his essay "The Creation of the Landscape," which appeared in the *Heimatschutz* movement's "state of the art" compendium of 1930, Schultze-Naumburg pinpointed the racial causes of environmental degradation. He fashioned a new narrative of environmental declension, one in which racial pollution, not industrialization, capitalism, or materialism, lay at the heart of Germany's environmental decline. His narrative began with Germany's preindustrial inhabitants, whom he claimed had created villages in harmony with their surroundings, "a garden on earth" that was a "feast for the eyes," because their Nordic inhabitants were still racially pure. Such communities were still governed by natural laws of selection. With the coming of the modern era, however, Schultze-Naumburg argued that Western culture had entered a "cul-de-sac" in which Darwinian laws no longer operated: "If all the mice who were born remained alive, the world would quickly consist only of mice, who would have to eat themselves up. If all humans who were born could remain living, the free space for living offered by the earth would soon become too small. The horrible and yet essential and charitable law that prevails here is called selection, and its effects are recognizable when the unfit one quickly goes under and the valuable holds its own."[41] Like Hitler, Schultze-Naumburg was concerned not with the ecological effects of overpopulation, but with the propagation of "inferior" races and "diseased" individuals within the national body.

Schultze-Naumburg also proposed that racial decline explained why so few Germans were interested in *Naturschutz* and *Heimatschutz* by the late Weimar years. Though all authentic Germans could trace their biological roots to their primordial homeland in central Europe, their hereditary substance had become contaminated, he believed, rendering them unable to recognize the instinctual links between themselves and their *Lebensraum*. Casting aside his earlier call for social reform, Schultze-Naumburg wrote that he had still been a "child of the nineteenth century" in his earlier *Cultural Works*, in which he proposed that education and environmental improvement might perfect human beings and integrate them into the *Heimat* community.[42] Despite the success of *Cultural Works*, environmental destruction had accelerated after World War I, leading Schultze-Naumburg to abandon the last remnants of his environmentalist faith. In its place, he assumed that eugenics—that is, weeding out undesirable hereditary traits—would improve the environment and rebuild the nation. Hans Schwenkel, provincial nature protection officer from the state of Württemberg, would later solidify this ideological connection between landscape preservation and racial hygiene by referring to *Heimatschutz* as the "eugenics of culture."[43]

Walther Schoenichen, the head of the Prussian State Office for the Protection of Natural Monuments, also racialized the therapeutic language of Weimar preservationist discourse in the late 1920s and moved aggressively to link *Naturschutz* to Nazism after 1933. In his 1926 textbook *Methods and Techniques of Natural History Education,* Schoenichen claimed that "racial-hygienic collapse" threatened to destroy the German people. While the book was designed to instruct teachers in the principles of nature conservation, Schoenichen used the opportunity to call on the state to institute eugenic measures to encourage racially healthy women to have more children and to prohibit the reproduction of "degenerate elements." Schoenichen joined the NSDAP one month after Hitler's seizure of power and soon became head of the *Naturschutz* agency within the newly created Reich Association for *Volkstum* and *Heimat* (Reichsverband für Volkstum und Heimat, or RVH). In a 1933 essay with the ominous title "The German *Volk* Must Be Cleansed—and the German Countryside?," which appeared in the journal *Naturschutz,* Schoenichen praised the regime for cleansing the country of un-German cultural elements and described the importance of environmental purity for racial health. At the RVH's inaugural conference in October 1933, Schoenichen elaborated on these themes, praising the Nazis for winning over Germans' "hearts" from "liberal-Marxist rationalism" and returning the nation to "the ancient strengths of Blood and Soil that offer the source of life for our entire people."[44] Schoenichen asserted that the National Socialists' rebuilding of the nation must "link with the racially unique foundations of that mystical primeval world of feeling, in which all the power of the love of Fatherland, of morality, and any true culture have their roots."[45]

Schoenichen saw a symbiosis between Blood and Soil and believed that environmental affairs would attain new importance in the Third Reich as an instrument of racial hygiene. The "soil of our *Heimat,*" he maintained, was the "field of force from which hardened racial lines emerge in continual rejuvenation for the battle for existence."[46] He argued that national character emerged as geographic features worked to shape and delimit the original racial inheritance. "Even though it cannot be proven with mathematical certainty," Schoenichen wrote, "it is nonetheless undoubtedly true that the spiritual character of the individual German tribes—excluding the original racial inheritance—are determined through the influence of the landscape." Schoenichen thus believed that a "mystical interdependency" existed between "*Heimat* nature and *Volk* soul" that required the state to recognize the importance of the environment in perpetuating racial health.[47] For him, Nazism provided a new and scientific model for understanding the relationship between landscape, race, and nationhood, one that promised an unprecedented role for *Naturschutz* in maintaining public health.

Schoenichen also argued that the pure natural environment found in nature protection regions offered the ideal space in which to stimulate racial consciousness. Germany's nature protection regions would serve an important educational role in the new state by allowing the population to witness firsthand the struggle for existence in the natural world.[48] "Since the German race emerged out of the darkness of prehistory," Schoenichen wrote, "we see it in a struggle with the harsh primordial forest, which covered our land at that time." Schoenichen thus called on Germans to experience "the undisturbed nature of their *Heimat,* as our forefathers centuries before us did. In this sense nature protection regions are placed in the service of the highest task that there is for our *Volk:* in the service of preserving the German people!"[49] Whereas local preservationists focused on cultivating an aesthetic and scientific appreciation of local *Heimat* flora and fauna as a way to develop community attachment, Schoenichen viewed contact with nature as a tool for stimulating "instinctual" loyalties to the racial nation. The Germanic races could feel at home, he argued, only when they maintained contact with their primordial *Lebensraum.* In Schoenichen's view environmental preservation would provide the necessary conditions for creating the racist *Volksgemeinschaft.*

Landscape preservationists thus found numerous points of ideological synergy between themselves and the Nazi movement. Preservationist leaders Schultze-Naumburg and Schoenichen embraced the regime's call to return Germany to its foundations in Blood and Soil, adapting preservation rhetoric to the growing Nazi presence by diagnosing the racial causes of environmental deterioration and emphasizing the necessity of environmental protection to achieve racial hygiene. As they elaborated on the connections between *Naturschutz* and racial improvement, both men displayed a striking willingness to abandon preservationists' traditional belief in regional landscapes and environmental influences as the foundation of national identity. Instead, Schultze-Naumburg and Schoenichen argued that race, rather than geography, offered a scientific basis for determining German character. Regional diversity emerged as the various "tribes" among the Germanic peoples shaped their individual habitats; geography could thus channel, but never override, the genetic inheritance of the *Volk.* In a similar vein, both authors discarded preservationists' earlier belief that environmental improvement and aesthetic reform would enable Germans to found a new people's community rooted in the ideal values of homeland and devoid of class and political tensions. They concluded instead that the "masses" were incapable of being reformed, for racial degeneration—in the form of "hereditary diseases" within the German population and "pollution" from foreign races— underlay Germany's cultural crisis. Environmental degradation, in this view, was merely one manifestation of a deeper, biological malady. As the Hitler Youth handbook stated plainly, "Inheritance is in the long run always victorious over environmental influences."[50]

Given Schultze-Naumburg's and Schoenichen's ready acquiescence in Nazi racial politics, the regime expected a seamless *Gleichschaltung* of nature protection agencies and clubs once it came to power in 1933. Yet the rhetoric of synchronization—particularly the drive to subsume regional *Heimat* activities under the aegis of centralized authority—achieved uneven results. The following sections examine how the process of *Gleichschaltung* affected each of the major landscape preservation agencies in the Rhine Province—state *Naturschutz* offices, the RVDH, and the Eifelverein. Each of these organizations embraced Nazism's statist and functional approach to regional planning, which they viewed as an extension of earlier *Landschaftspflege* efforts to rationalize land use patterns and link nature protection to future-oriented planning. Yet each also found a place for local initiative, accommodating the Nazi regime's imagined community of blood while maintaining its own traditional, spiritual commitment to regional landscapes, the soil of *Heimat,* as the basis for German identity and environmental stewardship.

## The Reich Nature Protection Law and Organic Planning in the Rhineland

In 1935, the National Socialist regime answered nature preservationists' call for state support in protecting the environment by passing the most stringent and comprehensive environmental protection law in the world: the Reich Nature Protection Law (Reichsnaturschutzgesetz, or RNG). This law, which Hans Klose referred to as the "Magna Charta of German Naturschutz," was Germany's first nationwide nature protection law. In theory, the new legislation overrode the country's patchwork of conflicting and ineffectual state, provincial, district, and municipal ordinances. With the support of Walter von Keudell in the Forestry Ministry, Klose helped to draft the law based on models from the Weimar era.[51] Rhineland nature preservationists quickly applauded the new legislation, which they viewed as the fulfillment of a long-cherished hope that had been stymied by Weimar economic limitations and bureaucratic inertia. "When the Reich Nature Protection Law was passed on July 26, 1935," wrote Provincial Cultural Affairs Officer Hans Kornfeld, "it was a load off the minds of nature's friends. Their decades-long efforts had finally found the resonance that raised the care of nature from a hobby to a duty for the entire people."[52] Oskar Karpa, who served as provincial commissioner for nature protection in the Rhine Province between 1933 and 1935, referred to the law in 1936 as "a milestone not only in the development of German *Heimatschutz* ideals, but also in the stepwise realization of the National Socialist cultural program."[53] The RNG thus symbolized the fusion of nature protection ideals with the National Socialists' cultural revolution.

Nature preservationists' support for National Socialism reflected a broader frustration with Weimar's parliamentary system in the early 1930s, a period that witnessed an erosion of support for liberalism and traditional conservatism across the middle ranks of German society. For many Rhineland nature preservationists, the Nazi movement appeared to be the best way out of Weimar's political, social, and cultural morass; by forsaking the republic, they could save the nation. Nazism's anti-Marxism also resonated among the Rhineland's bourgeois preservationist leaders, who feared the "red menace" in the industrial districts of Cologne, Duisburg, and the Ruhr. Nazi leaders' references to *Heimat* as the emotional foundation for the new *Volksgemeinschaft* suggested that the Nazis supported regionalism and tapped into Rhinelanders' provincial distaste for Berlin.[54] At the same time, the Nazis' rhetoric of national unity appealed to diverse sectors of the Rhenish population still beleaguered by the psychological and economic effects of territorial losses stemming from the Versailles settlement, the French occupation, and the separatist legacy that had left lingering doubts in Berlin about Rhinelanders' Germanness. As the VVS remarked in 1933, the Nazis were leading Rhinelanders step-by-step out of their "hopelessness and doubt," reannexing the Saar region in 1935, remilitarizing the Rhineland in 1936, returning the Eupen-Malmedy districts to the Rhine Province after Belgium's defeat in 1939, and stimulating economic growth in the region's sagging coal and steel industries through rearmament orders.[55] Such measures confirmed that "Rhenish fate was German fate," and that the province would play a key role in Germany's national rejuvenation.

The failure of the Weimar Republic to pass a nationwide nature protection law was preservationists' major grievance against the parliamentary system.[56] Echoing Schultze-Naumburg's critique of liberalism, the Düsseldorf *Naturschutz* officer Robert Rein noted, "We Rhinelanders have very often bitterly experienced the lack of a sweeping nature protection law." A paucity of effective legislation had doomed preservationists' efforts to protect areas surrounding the Laacher Lake near Trier and to prevent the building of a hotel on the shore of one of the Eifel region's lakes. During the Weimar era, Rein noted, drafts of a nationwide nature protection law surfaced annually at the national nature protection conference in Berlin, but "just as quickly disappeared into the drawer, because a single draft could not be passed due to the conflict between different interest groups and parties."[57] In contrast, Nazism's adherence to natural laws helped the state to recognize environmental priorities that had been thwarted by democratic negotiation. As Hans Kornfeld remarked, "It was left up to the National Socialist state, which is founded on Blood and Soil, to pass the Reich Nature Protection Law. The 'parliamentary system' had repeatedly endeavored to do this, but the spiritual conditions were missing to make it a reality."[58] The RNG's rapid passage thus confirmed for preservationists the advantages of Nazi authoritarianism over Weimar democracy, consolidating the National Socialists' reputation as defenders of the *Heimat* landscape and ensuring Rhenish preservationists' support early in the regime.

Preservationists were on the whole pleased by the RNG's stringent and uniform standards of environmental protection. The law's provisions went beyond the 1902 and the 1907 Prussian Landscape Disfigurement Laws in several key respects. In sections 18, 21, and 22, the RNG declared nature protection officials' right to dispossess owners of their property, as well as to levy fines or seek prison sentences for those breaking the law.[59] Oskar Karpa viewed these sections as confirmation of the Nazis' commitment to the idea "that the right to private property has validity only insofar as it does not violate the well-being of the general public."[60] Once a site received protected status, property owners or the state needed government permission to alter the landscape. The RNG also expanded the criteria used for designating a site worthy of protection beyond the vague and increasingly outdated aesthetic concept of "exceptionally scenic beauty," a cornerstone of the Disfigurement Laws. Instead, a variety of sites could receive protection under the law, including those with ecologically unique plants and nongame animals; natural monuments and their surroundings; previously established nature protection regions; and "other landscape areas in open nature, whose preservation, because of their rarity, beauty, uniqueness or because of their scientific, *Heimat,* forestry, or hunting significance, lies in the general interest" (section 1).[61] In section 5, the law specified the range of sites in the open landscape that might be protected, a spectrum far greater than in previous legislation, including groves of trees, groups of shrubs, hedgerows, parks, and cemeteries that contributed to the "adornment or to the brightening up of the landscape's image." Section 19 empowered nature protection officials to set aside portions of the land as "landscape protection zones," thus supplementing the traditional focus on natural monuments and nature protection regions with a new category of protection.[62] Rhenish nature preservationists were gladdened by the landscape protection clauses. Since the Rhine Province lacked the stretches of old-growth vegetation cherished by the *Naturdenkmalpflege* tradition, Rhenish preservationists believed that these provisions would help them to protect the vernacular landscape more effectively. As one Rhenish preservationist remarked, the Rhineland, especially the industrialized Ruhr region, contained "the bloodiest wounds of the German landscape," and that every area having even the "stamp of a certain primordialness" was an "inviolable shrine."[63]

The RNG's landscape protection clauses furthered the tendency within *Heimat* discourse to broaden the array of natural monuments and heritage sites available for public recreation, appreciation, and commemoration. "The German government sees as its duty," noted the law's preamble, "to secure for even the poorest people's comrade his share of German natural beauty."[64] Walther Schoenichen saw a close connection between nature protection and Nazi Party organizations such as the German Labor Front (Deutscher Arbeitsfront, or DAF), which sought to beautify industrial facilities and draw ordinary workers into ideologically sound, healthy recreation. Schoenichen proposed that landscape preservationists sought to enhance the "beauty of landscape" in the same way that the DAF's "Beauty of

Labor" *(Schönheit der Arbeit)* programs created hygienic, aesthetically pleasing work environments. Both programs sought to boost worker productivity; as Schoenichen remarked, nature parks should serve as "sites of recreation for our German working people." The RNG would serve as the anchor of this socially therapeutic vision. Schoenichen remarked that the law's sections 5 and 19 offered "a handle for preserving the landscape as a whole in a *Heimat*-like condition, [so that] the German person's emotional life feels at home there and remains grounded."[65] For nature preservationists, newly created nature protection regions served the national interest by ending the people's alienation from nature and binding them to the Fatherland.

Schoenichen's efforts to depict nature protection as a socially therapeutic activity reflected a continuing emphasis in the Third Reich on the scientific and ecological advantages of nature reserves. Holistic plant ecology, known during this period as plant sociology, enjoyed growing state support in the National Socialist era because of its promise to yield new insights for forestry, agriculture, and even social organization. Plant sociologists proposed that plants that shared particular climate and soil conditions, known as a *Lebensgemeinschaft*, would exhibit interdependent, even superorganismic qualities. Nature preservationists noted, for example, that forests composed of diverse species were not only more beautiful but also less susceptible to insect infestation. The ancient trees in nature protection regions, they argued, offered a baseline of ecological health by which to measure the effects of commercial forestry and to guide reforestation efforts in denuded areas. District nature protection officials worked more closely with forestry agents to restore forests and tried to reform farming practices using ecological insights.[66] One such official in the Westphalian town of Minden, for example, complained that a farmer near Bielefeld had cut down a strip of trees serving as a hedgerow. According to an article in the *Rheinische-Westfälische Zeitung*, this farmer did not understand the "biological significance of nature and bird protection. Hedgerows and strips of trees must remain protected not merely for aesthetic reasons, but more importantly as wind and frost protection for the fields and as nesting sites for the natural pest fighters."[67] By emphasizing the role of nature protection in maintaining local soil and climate conditions, the RNG strengthened the practical and scientific arguments for *Naturschutz*.

Holistic ecology also offered insights for reforming human social organization, transforming scientific trends in plant sociology into a justification of fascist hierarchy. Just as so-called plant sociology showed that each forest *Lebensgemeinschaft* was a "closed organism" in intimate connection with its natural environment, so too did spatial planning and regional planning "understand the totality of the *Volk* as a unified organism which has a certain sum of needs and achievements. The landscape belongs to this type of people in the same way that the concept of the woodland organism extends over a particular woodland soil."[68] Such organic language soon found its way into Nazi thinking about the emerging *Volksgemeinschaft,* which emphasized communal good over individual rights. One forester noted in 1938 that "German experience confirms the biological fact that the forest is a complicated community of living beings, in which each tree species is merely a member, no more and no less important for the health of the whole than the other members."[69] The organismic language of community ecology thus served as a scientific justification for Blood and Soil in the Third Reich, transforming nature parks into outdoor laboratories for investigating the optimal environmental conditions for the Germanic race.

Armed with new legislation and ecological knowledge, landscape preservationists set out to create comprehensive landscape plans for Germany's regions, hoping to realize the *Landschaftspflege* ideal first articulated in the Weimar Republic. In the Third Reich, the rhetoric of centralized planning and order became far more reactionary than in the Weimar era; as one Rhenish planner remarked, "The idea of the total state, into which we are growing, is fundamentally related to the way we perceive and want to see space and landscape. The relationships to the landscape have developed beyond specialized knowledge; they want to create the whole."[70] The RNG extended and deepened the practice of *Landschaftspflege* by ensuring nature preservationists an advisory role in projects with major environmental impacts. Section 20 of the RNG required state and local officials to contact nature protection officers before granting permits for development projects that might lead to "significant modifications of the open landscape."[71] Robert Rein predicted that the RNG would augment regional planning efforts by guaranteeing not only that the tourist landmarks of the middle Rhine Gorge would be set aside, but also that the appearance of the landscape as a whole would be maintained. Regional planners within the Rhineland's *Heimatschutz* organization praised the new approach to spatial planning *(Raumordnung)*. They commended the Third Reich as "the first [government] that gave planning, whose end goal must be the reestablishment of an organic relationship between people and space, the political significance that it deserves and raised Reich and regional planning to a priority task for the state."[72]

The need for RNG oversight was particularly acute in the mid-1930s, since the Third Reich had initiated a host of public works projects designed to stimulate the depressed economy and, ultimately, prepare Germany for war. The law anticipated preservationists' role in mitigating the environmental impact of these projects. As one Rhenish observer recalled, "1937 brought a transformation in the economic and financial condition of the Rhine Province. Overnight unemployment disappeared. Ten thousand unemployed from the Ruhr were used for the building of dams, dikes on the lower Rhine, land reclamation projects, water provision facilities, and the like. Rearmament and the building of the *Autobahnen* even resulted in a lack of workers."[73] The regime's plan to secure the German people "on their own soil" would result in unavoidable "interventions in the natural order," noted Hans Kornfeld, but the RNG would nonetheless enable *Naturschutz* authorities "to make sure . . . that these interventions do not entail damage to the healthy and natural."[74] Despite the threat posed to the natural environment, *Heimatschutz* and *Naturschutz* leaders trusted that the government would seek out preservationists as advisors charged with lessening the impact of the regime's projects. The Rhenish landscape architect Rudolf Hoffmann claimed that German landscape protection agencies were being called to participate actively in "the great building design tasks of the new organization of the German *Lebensraum*."[75] Hoffmann envisioned a new spirit of cooperation between industry, developers, and the general public in rationalizing land use. "In the future," continued Hoffmann, "the task of landscape protection will be to admonish and to advise, wherever a lack of understanding for the idealism of National Socialism . . . threatens to inflict damage on the German landscape's appearance." By participating in landscape planning, preservationists would help to create a new harmony between development pressures and ideal interests.

Scholars who have argued that *völkisch* antimodernism fueled nature preservation's synchronization with the Nazi regime have overlooked this crucial reason for preservationists' enthusiasm for the RNG: the opportunity to tie *Landschaftspflege* to future-oriented planning. Klose described the goal of nature protection as a "timely synthesis" between the environment and the economy, while Hans Kornfeld remarked that the new friend of *Heimat* "not only wants to preserve, but also to create." Kornfeld noted that *Heimatschutz* members were being asked to assist in planning the regime's development and transportation projects, so that "all impacts on the natural appearance of the landscape are limited to a minimum, so that the harmony between human works and nature remains protected in the sense of a real culture."[76] According to Schoenichen, the goal of landscape protection, unlike *Naturschutz,* was not a "static holding on to the landscape image as it has been passed down," nor did preservationists strive to hinder or prevent agricultural cultivation or other economic uses. The preservationist "sees his goal accomplished when the landscape has been shaped in such a way that its natural constitution remains its core health" and in its appearance it "corresponds to our *völkischen* culture and can still be a *Heimat* in the highest sense of the word for the people who are bound to it." Finding a balance between economic, transportation, and commercial needs, on the one hand, and nature protection and recreational demands, on the other, meant that preservationists needed to envision the landscape in a holistic fashion, as undergoing a "constant further development and rejuvenation, comparable to a living organism—in which every single member of the landscape has its own function."[77]

Maintaining the landscape's "core health" meant using historic town centers and agrarian landscapes as models, not templates, for fashioning aesthetically balanced, nature-centered, and economically viable communities throughout Germany. The Munich landscape architect Alwin Seifert underscored this modern approach by noting that homeland protectionists' goal was not "to transform Germany into an open-air *Heimat* museum or to stick people of urban origins and urban careers into lederhosen." Rather, the goal of *Heimatschutz* was a blending of tradition and modernity that enabled the individual to feel himself a part of the larger community. "We demand that each new housing development," he remarked, "incorporate elements of the togetherness of the old Germanic village."[78] Preservationists viewed Weimar's political system as the main impediment they had faced in achieving such goals. The liberal system's misguided economic development and desire for short-term profits, noted Rudolf Hoffmann, had led the movement into a constant battle for the preservation of "irreplaceable treasures," resulting in an "ever stronger conservationist and . . . development-hostile attitude." Most preservationists believed that only an authoritarian state could check such materialism and establish viable environmental protection. "It is obvious," noted Schoenichen, "that these questions have become urgent in Germany as well as most other cultured nations in the world—although only in the authoritatively ruled states will the conditions be met that are necessary for truly comprehensive spatial planning."[79] Landscape preservationists thus portrayed the Nazi era as an opportunity to envision an alternative modernity, freed from the irrational chaos of liberalism, which balanced nature and tradition within the contours of an urbanizing, mobile, and increasingly affluent society.

In addition to being Germany's first nationwide nature protection law, the RNG also laid the foundations for a centralized *Naturschutz* bureaucracy. The Nazi regime transformed the Prussian State Office for Natural Monument Preservation into the Reich Office for Nature Protection, removing *Naturschutz* affairs from the Prussian Cultural Ministry and placing them under Hermann Göring's direction in the Forestry Ministry. Based on the Nazi leadership principle, the RNG envisioned a more articulated and hierarchical relationship between the Reich Office and the nature protection offices at the state, provincial, district, and municipal levels. Walther Schoenichen served as the first Reich nature protection officer until 1939, when he was replaced by Hans Klose because of personality conflicts between Schoenichen and forestry officials. The law named the Reich forestry minister, district presidents, state *(Land)* authorities, district officers, and city mayors as the official *Naturschutz* representatives in their areas of jurisdiction. It also created a nature protection council within the Reich Nature Protection Office, which included Reich and party officials such as Darré in the Reich Food Estate and Ley in the DAF, to ensure coordination between the Reich office and other official agencies whose actions might affect the natural environment.[80] In practice, private individuals, especially *Naturschutz* club members from the surrounding area, served as honorary nature protection officers, much as they had in the Weimar era. Nature protection officers' political reliability was subject to greater scrutiny under the Nazi dictatorship, however, and few former Social Democrats remained in their positions after 1933. Despite its limitations, the RNG extended nature protection officers' regulatory powers at all levels of government. It expanded the number of regional and district *Naturschutz* offices and provided them with a high degree of institutional recognition.

The passage of the RNG thus solidified preservationists' support for the Nazi regime. It underscored the affinities between the Third Reich's commitment to restoring Germany on an "organic" basis and preservationists' desire to protect the country's natural landscapes. The RNG meshed well with the Nazi commitment to creating a people's community founded on Blood and Soil, one that rejected liberal individualism and Marxist materialism in favor of a return to timeless virtues dictated by the natural order. Preservationists, in turn, viewed the new law as an affirmation of *Naturschutz* and *Heimatschutz* ideals, an opportunity to overcome the spiritual barrenness and political gridlock of Weimar in favor of the ideal goals of *Heimat*. Given these ideological affinities, the Nazis expected a rapid and seamless *Gleichschaltung* of German *Heimat* traditions and environmental organizations into the emerging *Volksgemeinschaft*.

Yet *Gleichschaltung* remained uneven at both the institutional and the ideological level. The call to centralize and nationalize *Naturschutz* according to Nazi principles faltered, owing to infighting and competition among a maze of state and party institutions. This created a space in which regional authorities could reassert administrative autonomy in *Naturschutz* affairs. In the early years of the Nazi regime, before the RNG's passage, Alfred Rosenberg's Fighting League for German Culture and Werner Haverbeck's Reich Association for *Volkstum* and *Heimat* vied for control of the *Naturschutz* movement. The RVH enjoyed numerous advantages in this struggle; not only was it part of Robert Ley's expanding DAF, but it was also endorsed by Rudolf Hess as the sole organization for *völkisch* cultural activities. Schoenichen and *Heimatschutz* leader Werner Lindner supported the creation of a Nature Protection Division within the RVH, and they played a major role in organizing its first conference in Kassel in October 1933.[81] Regional nature preservation groups favored the RVH, because they believed that Haverbeck's leadership would afford them more regional and local autonomy. Many were dismayed, in fact, by the National Socialists' *lack* of leadership in cultural affairs. Rhenish *Heimatschutz* leader Oskar Karpa left the

Kassel conference with the impression that the RVH suffered from a "complete lack of direction and confusion." He also opposed the organization's separation of *Naturschutz* and *Heimatschutz,* which he felt would splinter regional preservationists' united efforts for comprehensive landscape preservation.[82] This lack of direction and confusion continued into the following years as Rosenberg's Fighting League reconstituted itself as the National Socialist Cultural Association and was absorbed by the DAF in 1934. Haverbeck was later named the head of the Cultural Association and abandoned his ties to the RVH, but soon thereafter the RNG's passage would place *Naturschutz* under Hermann Göring's Reich Forestry Ministry. Clearly, the jumble of agencies characteristic of Nazism's "polycratic" system thwarted bureaucratic streamlining.

The confusion over *Naturschutz* jurisdiction led Göring to bid for control of the movement and its state agencies. Göring's personal intervention assured the Reich Nature Protection Law's rapid passage, and this one-on-one leadership style also informed his maneuvers to establish and control the Reich Nature Protection Office.[83] Because the Prussian Office for Natural Monument Preservation had been part of the Prussian Cultural Ministry, Bernhard Rust, the agency's director, fought hard to retain control over *Naturschutz.*[84] After the RNG's passage in July 1935, however, the more powerful Göring decided that *Naturschutz* should fall under his own purview in the Forestry Ministry. In a brief telephone conversation on 30 April 1935, Göring informed Rust that, as forestry minister, "I already have the forest and the animals, *Naturschutz* fits much better under my jurisdiction than yours . . . Don't you agree?"[85] Personal power, rather than streamlined administrative efficiency, thus won the day.

The institutional *Gleichschaltung* of the *Heimatschutz* movement also faltered due to infighting among Nazi leaders. Despite Schultze-Naumburg's prominence in Rosenberg's Fighting League for German Culture, the DBH and the RVDH affiliated initially with Haverbeck's RVH, but they left this organization in 1934 because of the organization's chaotic structure and the perceived threat to regional autonomy.[86] The Rhenish provincial governor Heinz (Heinrich) Haake, who had become president of the DBH in 1933, announced that the DBH would become a stand-alone organization with a loose affiliation to the German Gemeindetag, an agreement that specified that the Provincial Association in each Prussian province would steer regional

*Heimatschutz* organizations. Haake rationalized the DBH's structure by designating one regional organization in each state, free city, or Prussian province as that area's representative *Heimatschutz* organization and calling on local *Heimat* organizations to become corporative members of the DBH's regional affiliates.[87] While the RNG had envisioned a centralization of landscape preservation tasks at the national level, continuing conflicts over jurisdiction ultimately allowed Haake and other provincial and state officials to chart an independent regionalist course in environmental affairs.

## Synchronizing the Provinces: Heinz Haake and the Nazification of Rhenish Landscape Preservation

With Haake at the helm, Rhenish landscape preservation entered a new phase of activity in which older conceptions of provincial landscape preservation coexisted uneasily with the Nazi regime's racializing tendencies. Haake, who held power from April 1933 until the regime's collapse in 1945, was one of the Third Reich's most important defenders of regional self-administration. The lack of cultural-political direction from Berlin led Haake to reemphasize traditional discourses of regional autonomy as the best solution to executing administrative tasks and building national character. A member of the NSDAP since 1921, Haake belonged to the small band of party leaders known as the "Old Fighters" and had served as one of only seven NSDAP deputies in the Prussian Assembly between 1925 and 1929. His loyalty to Hitler and a strong and unified Reich were therefore unquestioned. Yet he insisted on the need for regional autonomy within the organic state. He proclaimed that "every German has a duty to his more familiar *Heimat,* where he first really experienced things and where he grew up, on a par with his membership in the greater German *Volksgemeinschaft.* The German landscape and the German person are not uniform in their appearance, but rather German life is embodied in a diversity of forms that in their totality represent Germandom."[88]

As president of the Prussian Gemeindetag, an organization representing the interests of provincial governors, Haake defended Wilhelm Heinrich Riehl's belief in the diversity of "land and people" as the basis of German national character. "The region [*Landschaft*] and the sphere of activity from which we come," Haake noted in a 1940 speech before Interior Minister Wilhelm Frick, "are manifold, because the German stream of power luckily has numerous sources. In the diversity of the landscape and its population lies the strongest proof of the necessity of decentralization and self-administration."[89] Despite Nazi attempts at centralization and racialization, Haake's speeches articulated a sense of continuity with an earlier tradition of regional environments as the basis of national character and governmental control. "Regional self-administration has much deeper roots and goals," he noted. "In each German region, be it Silesia, Brandenburg, the provinces on the North Sea and Baltic coasts, or my home province, the Rhineland, a unique character and special strengths and energies are embedded!"[90] Haake argued that each region required a unique administrative style, executed by a "native civil service" with extensive experience in the area. Haake called on Frick to assist provincial governors in defending against forces of administrative atomization in the region. The Rhenish governor bemoaned Nazism's haphazard division of labor, asserting that "the current state must end, where there are always a huge number of offices active in the same area." According to Haake, provincial self-administration helped to rationalize the state's activities, taking care of tasks that "do not belong in the hand of Reich, party, professional, or local self-administration" so that the Reich as a whole could be rendered "bureaucratically streamlined."[91]

Haake included *Heimatschutz* and *Naturschutz* among the tasks necessary for realizing his vision of regional cultural patronage, in which "the cultural landscape is the mirror image of the state, and the state is constructed in a similar fashion upon healthy diversity."[92] The son of a Cologne municipal architect, Haake had been an avid reader of his father's Rhenish history books and was a staunch defender of local history. He viewed the Rhineland as the key to German destiny, referring to the province as "the site of [Germany's] greatest political experiences, the stronghold of German economy, science, culture, and art."[93] The area's cultural superiority flowed from the beauty of the landscape itself. "The Rhine is, as it were, the absolute symbol of Rhenish life," he wrote. "It embodies the past, present, and future of the people. With all of its vessels it fertilizes the surrounding land with its mountains, valleys, forests, and fields and thereby becomes the dynamic power that fills the working life. It is no wonder that this land, so distinguished by nature, became early on the site of the highest culture and art."[94] Echoing the aesthetic perspective of the region's cultural elites, Haake's promise to build up regional cultural affairs evoked a rhetorical and institutional continuity with previous *Heimat* traditions, thus facilitating the middle-class organization's incorporation into the regime.

Haake's emphasis on the organic region as the basis for state building and cultural promotion led to growing provincial support for *Naturschutz* and *Heimatschutz* activities. Between 1933 and 1937, Haake more than doubled the province's funding for cultural affairs, from 500,000 reichsmarks in 1933 to 1,250,000 reichsmarks in 1937, with a sizable increase for *Naturschutz* affairs. In 1934, for example, *Naturschutz* offices reported receiving approximately 6,800 reichsmarks, with 4,000 coming from the provincial administration and 1,800 from the Rhenish *Oberpräsident*.[95] In 1937, in contrast, the provincial administration reported granting approximately 26,500 reichsmarks for *Naturschutz*. This included funds for a new limnology research center in Krefeld, 4,500 reichsmarks for the Rhineland-Westphalia Natural History Association, and 2,000 reichsmarks for a new provincial journal, *Rhenish Friend of Nature,* which showcased the province's achievements in nature protection and nature study.[96] Provincial funding not only helped state nature protection offices but also provided continuous support for organizations such as the VVS and the Eifelverein, and this bolstered their nature protection engagement. Haake named Hubert Iven, the noted naturalist and former district nature protection officer in Cologne, to become the head of the Rhine Province's nature protection office.[97]

Although the Rhineland's nature protection offices remained honorary posts rather than true civil-service positions, the province took steps to enhance the status of nature protection officers. The province published administrative guidelines for district *Naturschutz* officers, outlining their responsibilities and providing directions for executing the RNG's provisions, and created a series of courses that provided professional training in landscape planning.[98] Under the provisions of the new law, Rhenish nature protection officials were to ensure the protected status of several existing nature protection regions, including the Siebengebirge, the Rodderberg, the Wahner Heath, and the Urfelder Heath, as well as new ones, such as Bislicher Island, by registering them in the so-called Reich Nature Protection Book.[99] Preservationists noted that the law's broader preservation criteria also allowed them to protect a number of unique natural monuments. For example, the law would now cover the geological "erratics" *(Findlinge)*, remnants of the Ice Age glaciers that once covered the region and were unique to the Rhineland. These "witnesses" of the area's unique volcanic past, which Germanic tribes had supposedly used as sites for sacrificial rites, were not impressive enough to be called natural monuments under the old system. To protect them, preservationists had often had to rely on the goodwill of landowners or to declare the area surrounding them as a nature protection region. Under the new regulations, erratics could now be protected.[100]

Haake's reorganization of German *Heimatschutz* also transformed the prominent RVDH into Germany's flagship *Heimatschutz* organization. Beyond mere financial support, Haake gave the RVDH a renewed sense of purpose, a faith that its members could regain their status as stewards of regional *Kultur*. "We are building . . . our organization outward into a useful instrument of regional *Kulturpflege*," noted Haake in 1936. "On this point my interests as provincial governor of the Rhine Province and chairman of the Rhenish Association for Monument Preservation and Homeland Protection are closely linked . . . the [RVDH] will be in the future the decisive authority for *Heimatpflege* in the Rhine Province." Haake also praised RVDH members as connoisseurs of culture, for having countered "loud modernity" and "limitless individualism," and for having prevented a complete "leveling of taste" during the dark days of liberalism.[101] "We are not false Romantics, as we are all too often apt to be called," Haake remarked, "but rather present-minded carriers of a *völkisch* culture that is aware of the heritage of its fathers."[102] Haake argued that Rhine Romanticism was part of this modern, organic reconstruction, rather than merely nostalgic fancy. He wrote that "the oft-mentioned Rhine Romanticism should not be understood as sentimental effusion. It is the outflow of a deep understanding of the dynamic powers of the homeland soil and of history. The true Rhine Romanticism saw in ruins memorable witnesses of a great Fatherland history. Feeling and knowledge are paired within it and teach [us] how to understand truth with the heart."[103] Haake proclaimed the authenticity, dynamism, and relevance of *Heimatschutz* ideals, promising these organizations a key role in revitalizing cultural affairs at both the regional and national levels. Like nature protection officers, *Heimatschutz* members were especially eager to participate in spatial planning and

shed once and for all their reputation as enemies of economic and social progress.

To integrate *Heimatschutz* into regional planning, Haake established the Rhenish Society for Regional Planning, the regional affiliate
of the Reich Office for Spatial Planning (Reichstelle für Raumordnung),
in 1936.[104] Under Haake's direction, the Rhenish Society for Regional
Planning (Rheinische Landesplanungsgemeinschaft) implemented the
Nazi drive toward functionally efficient spatial planning by promoting economic growth, improving the province's infrastructure, ratio-
nally distributing the Rhineland's natural resources, and expanding
the province's stock of public housing. Such measures included many
projects that were detrimental to nature protection, including agricultural land reclamation, street building, dam construction, and suburban expansion.[105] Yet Haake viewed careful regional planning as an
extension of the regime's commitment to preserving Germany's landscape. Spatial planning, he remarked, "is concerned with a social demand, that is creatively based and precisely therefore [reflects] the
harmony with Nature." Calling on the RVDH to work closely with
the Rhenish Society for Regional Planning, Haake charged the RVDH
with helping to create a comprehensive regional plan for the Rhine
Province.[106] Whereas earlier provincial planning efforts had centered
on "defending against damages left behind by the liberal period,"
noted a 1936 issue of *Die Rheinprovinz,* the Nazi regime demanded a
"creative new ordering of the entire space."[107] The new organic landscape would be both functional and beautiful, attuned to aesthetic
needs and the health of the population.

Cologne *Heimatschutz* member Wilhelm Schürmann argued that
"careful planning of land use and economic development" would involve a partition of land into separate zones for residential, transportation, commercial, and industrial uses. Planning would also ensure
that the regime's deurbanization schemes would not result in careless
rural development.[108] In the early years of the regime, Nazi urban theorists such as Gottfried Freder had argued that the regime could heal
the "cancer of modernity" by dispersing urban populations into the
hinterland, distributing them into small- and medium-size garden cities that maintained their communal character. Freder believed that
small-town living would stem the population's alienation from the
land, thus binding them more closely to the Fatherland.[109] Schürmann
warned, however, that maintaining a balance between urban and open

space required that new housing settlements should not "reach long arms out into the landscape," but rather should grow organically from existing town centers. This would also facilitate electricity and gas provision, shorter streets, faster police response, and efficient municipal administration.[110] Density, rather than dispersion, became a hallmark of organic regional planning.

Rhenish preservationists were most concerned about over-development in the Rhine Valley, the province's cultural heartland. Though they recognized that the Rhineland was a cultivated landscape rather than a wilderness in the American sense, *Naturschutz* advocates believed that the relationship between humans and their environment had remained harmonious in the region until the last quarter of the nineteenth century. Since that time the river valley had been undergoing continuous degradation. As Hans Kornfeld argued in his 1936 essay "Hopes for the Protection of the Rhine Landscape," the liberal period had allowed individuals to "stamp . . . their untrammeled personality" on the landscape. The result was that "with a raw hand the epidermis of the majestic landscape was gradually wounded."[111] Many wounds from this time remained visible, including factories that destroyed pleasant views of the river islands from steamships, gaudy hotels that upset the holistic view of the landscape, and oil slicks from ships that polluted fish habitat and caused unsightly marks on the river's surface. Kornfeld claimed that the flat, barren agricultural fields crisscrossed by high-tension wires, which were commonplace in the Rhine region, resembled an "American petroleum field" rather than an authentic German *Heimat*.[112] Korneld called on the government, municipalities, and private owners to design a plan for the entire area bordering the river and to enter the region into the Reich Nature Protection Book.

The economic prosperity of the mid-1930s had also brought a new set of challenges for regional planners, as more and more Rhinelanders used automobiles and built weekend houses, consuming the natural landscape in ways unthinkable during the Weimar years. Nature advocates complained that both suburbanization and touristic commercialization threatened to transform "the proud river, the symbol of German freedom," into a materialistic wasteland.[113] Schürmann noted that the spread of automobiles had enabled many Rhinelanders to reside a considerable distance outside urban centers such as Cologne and Düsseldorf. They tended to live in isolation from their neighbors rather than in closed settlements; the result was "chains" of single homes in rows along the river's banks or creeping up the hillsides. Schürmann maintained that such scattered development was destroying the pleasing transition between villages and open landscape that made river travel so enjoyable.[114] Schürmann also noted that Rhinelanders' desire to "capture" the beautiful landscape had multiplied the number of weekend houses in the Rhine Valley. Hikers who enjoyed the scenic vistas far from the city wanted to retain their piece of "untouched" nature by building a small cottage on the site. Schürmann was not willing to condemn such developments outright. He believed they stemmed from a desire to lead a "healthy" life that was "close to nature," but he called on Rhinelanders to build their weekend houses hidden from view, such as behind hilltops, rather than facing the valley. Other Rhineland preservationists were more forceful in their criticism of tourism. They complained about the mushrooming numbers of hotels, souvenir shops, billboards, and coffee shops in the Rhine Valley that "robbed . . . almost every mountain and every castle of their peacefulness, [and that] degenerated almost every visited town into a veritable fairground."[115] With approximately 87,688 visitors to the Siebengebirge alone in 1935, the Rhineland was awash in visitors that the region could no longer accommodate.[116] Preservationists hoped that the RNG and other land-use laws would enable provincial officials to contain these new threats to the environment engendered by the recent prosperity made possible by the new regime.

To stem such threats to the region, local preservationists evoked the RNG's *Landschaftspflege* provisions, spurring plans for designating the entire middle Rhine Gorge from Mainz to Cologne as a landscape protection zone. Oskar Karpa was one of the first preservationists to call for such a plan. In 1936, he organized a conference in which he expressed the hope that "in the future Rhine Valley, not everyone will be able to erect his 'villa' on a favorite spot, that the bank areas will not be bared of every tree and bush, that factory and hotel palaces will not take away the view of gentle slopes and precipitously colossal cliffs on the riverbanks." By applying the RNG in a proper fashion, he said, Rhinelanders could fashion an organic regional topography in which "the villages that turn their barren gables toward the river . . . [will] gradually receive a more friendly face that fits in harmoniously with the total picture of our marvelous Rhine landscape

Ungeordnete bauliche Entwicklung einer Ortschaft am Rhein.

Baulich klar voneinander getrennte Dörfer am Flußufer.

Organic town growth. (top) "Disorderly development of a town along the Rhine." (bottom) "Spatially discrete villages on the riverbank." *Source:* W. Schürmann, "Siedlung und Landesplanung," *Zeitschrift des rheinischen Vereins für Denkmalpflege und Heimatschutz* 30, no. 2 (1937): 35–36.

through careful plantings that gently cover all ugliness."[117] Haake soon followed Karpa's lead; in 1937 he called for a "Rhine protection action" that resulted in a series of excursions along the river in 1937 and 1938 to discuss environmental issues facing the region. The boat trips assembled more than 300 invited participants, including leading representatives from the agricultural and transportation ministries; nationally recognized nature protection advocates, such as Hans Klose and Walther Schoenichen; and regional and local nature protection officials. The discussions during these trips focused primarily on the aesthetic damage to the Rhine Valley caused by road and railway construction, agricultural reclamation, factory construction, and excessive tourism along the river's banks. In a more ecological vein, several participants also bemoaned pollutants such as phenol and untreated municipal wastewater, which were destroying the Rhine's fisheries and making the river unsafe for bathing. By the end of the first trip, ministers had committed themselves to some environmentally friendly actions, with the railway and river navigational administration promising to "green" features in the landscape by hiding embankments, track areas, and electric line easements behind plantings of poplar trees and bushes.[118] Such rapid progress confirmed for many regional environmentalists the efficiency of an authoritarian government in managing environmental affairs. As Schoenichen noted, "This Rhineland trip is a significant recognition of the idea of landscape protection; it is at the same time an impressive manifestation of the will to act."[119]

The result of these trips was a comprehensive landscape protection ordinance for the middle Rhine Gorge that portrayed the Rhine as a "natural monument of the first order, the glorious site of the greatest of German history and *völkischen* experience, the life vessel of German culture, art, and economy." Stressing the need for both organic planning and environmental restoration, the ordinance called for the "energetic rebuilding of the Rhine landscape according to its own law."[120] While the plan allowed most existing economic practices to continue in the area undisturbed, it forbade any modifications of the landscape within the protection zone that would disfigure the landscape's appearance or detract from the enjoyment of nature. The plan also restricted commercial and industrial development to a select number of areas and directed local officials to consult nature protection authorities before allowing new transportation corridors or other major developments. In consultation with the provincial conservator, planners directed that buildings use only white, red, green, and blue paint, to harmonize colors throughout the region. Billboards, which *Heimatschutz* members had long condemned as eyesores of commercial culture, were completely forbidden outside of cities and 10,000 that were deemed particularly ugly were also removed from cities along the Rhine's banks.[121] Most important, the plan specified that materials "rooted in the soil" *(bodenständig)* be used for new buildings and asserted that only "native" plants could be planted, except in a few select forests and gardens.[122] The project was conceptually bold for its time and considered a model of landscape planning in Germany, yet it was never fully realized because of the outbreak of the war in 1939.[123]

Both the *Naturschutz* and *Heimatschutz* movements thus made significant progress during the Third Reich in protecting portions of the natural environment and developing plans for more sustainable growth. As a local figure who shared preservationists' regional patriotism and *Heimat* ideals, Heinz Haake represented both the links with previous cultural stewardship and the new possibilities offered by the National Socialist regime. Despite the elements of continuity in Haake's administration of cultural affairs, however, there were numerous signs that *Heimat* cultivation under the Third Reich would be far from business as usual, as Haake sought to bring preservation more closely into alignment with the regime's wider political and social goals. Under Haake's direction, local Nazis scrutinized the political records of all provincial nature protection officers and club leaders to make sure they were not tainted by former links to the Social Democratic or Communist parties and pushed to "Aryanize" the RVDH and other groups by specifying that only "pure-blooded Aryans" could be members of such organizations.[124] Nazification meant the dissolution of the proletarian Friends of Nature, one of the Rhineland's largest youth organizations, because of its ties to the working-class movement. Friends of Nature leaders protested that their organization was "apolitical," existing only to spread awareness of nature's beauties, to advocate for *Naturschutz,* and to promote the health of young people. Leaders even claimed that the organization stood for the entire *Volk* and nation, despite its proletarian membership. Their pleas were to no avail; on 29 March 1933, the Nazi regime dissolved the Friends of Nature nationwide on the basis of anti-Marxist emergency decrees, hoping to channel its young members into party-controlled organizations such as the Hitler Youth.[125]

Haake's Nazification policies paralleled regional historians' and geographers' attempts to colonize the Rhineland's cultural imagination with racist meanings. Haake equated provincial *Heimatpflege,* the "care of *Heimat,*" with the more racist term *Volkstumspflege,* whose goal was the preservation of the Rhineland's "ethnic uniqueness" within the racial body.[126] In this view, the Rhineland's cultural landscape manifested the activities of its former Germanic tribes, branches of the once-proud Nordic races. "The real Rhine Romanticism," claimed Haake, "was always more than a sentimental, literary occurrence; it was the artistic glorification of the great heritage of our race."[127] In a similar vein, regional geographers abandoned the environmental determinism that had guided Hermann Aubin's regional historical institute in Bonn since the early 1920s in favor of racialized understandings of landscape. In his 1940 essay "The Rhenish Cultural Landscape," the geographer Friedrich Metz argued that the unity of the Rhineland's distinctive landscape depended not on geographic features but on the racial character of the inhabitants who had shaped the area. Metz wrote that "we associate the notion of Rhenish nature with a picture of an especially mild climate, an especially blue sky, a special movement of the wind and clouds."[128] Yet such features were in fact transient and varied across the province; blood was the only factor that truly unified Rhinelanders across time and space. "The Rhenish cultural landscape is formed in the last analysis by Germanic, German people," he wrote, "and reflects their spirit, cast of mind, and creative powers. Here the common characteristics [of blood] appear more strongly than the differences, which necessarily would result from the varied geographic conditions, natural provisions, and historical depths of individual portions."[129] Race, rather than geographic factors, determined the character of Rhenish identity and the course of the region's history.

The Nazification of landscape also gave new meaning to ecological concepts of native species, community, and interdependency. Landscape architects in the Third Reich insisted on the need to use only indigenous species in their designs, arguing that the Germanic race felt most at home among similarly "native" species. The Bavarian *Heimatschutz* landscape designer Alwin Seifert, for example, argued that nineteenth-century industrialization had broken the connection between "tribe and living space." The point of landscape design, in his view, was to recapture the essence of the ancient Nordic landscape by planting native "German *Volk* trees" such as lindens and oaks, while avoiding foreign species such as blue spruces and acacias.[130] Nature protectionists followed in this vein by emphasizing their commitment to preserving native species, to defending *German* nature rather than environments across the globe. One preservationist claimed that the RNG's provisions were designed to "protect the pattern of native nature, not the creations artificially brought here from other countries," while the Düsseldorf *Naturschutz* commissioner Rein spoke out against the "introduction of foreign wild species, which blend a foreign, disconcerting hue into the overall appearance of the German animal world."[131] *Heimatschutz* advocates could thus assist the regime in expunging traces of liberal decay; Schwenkel asserted that the movement would aid the regime in its battle against "incompetence, capitalist thinking, and all Jewish-American relicts of a bygone era."[132] Local preservationists' focus on protecting unspoiled nature acquired ominous new meaning in the Third Reich, meshing well with the Nazis' fears of "foreign" races in the national body.

The Nazi desire to create healthy environments for perpetuating and rooting the race also shaped the province's efforts at city planning and the provision of public housing. Haake viewed urban renewal as a process of "purification," and helped the DBH organize a touring exhibition, known as "The Beautiful City: Its Regeneration and Design," that showcased native, organic architectural styles that suited the natural environment. These *Heimat*-sensitive designs, Haake claimed, would "exterminate the traces of decay, the manifestations of an evil past," thus regenerating the city as a healthy and organic *Lebensraum*.[133] In a similar vein, a 1937 article in the RVDH journal entitled "*Heimat* and Housing" proposed that "the highest goal of housing is the rooting of the person with the *Heimat* soil." The author, Berlin architect Friedrich Schmidt, criticized Weimar's Modernist housing settlements for increasing workers' alienation from nature. Instead of providing a real "home," embedded in landscape and tradition, Bauhaus settlements remained a "soulless outer shell." Though Bauhaus architects had brought light and air to working-class dwellings, Modernist architecture's abstract and geometric forms were not *bodenständig;* they could "just as likely stand . . . in Russia or Spain" as in Germany.[134] Once a worker lost his connection to *Heimat,* Schmidt continued, he would flee into pubs, cinemas, or other "sites of enjoyment," or, worse, become susceptible to Marxism, "an enemy of the *Volksgemeinschaft.*"

Whereas Modernism increased workers' alienation from nature, *Heimatschutz* architects hoped to use housing design and individual ownership to give workers a sense of place that would bind them to

the community. Schmidt thus applauded Nazi efforts to build semide-
tached, folk-style cottages with gardens for workers in place of the
Modernist complexes of the 1920s.[135] In such areas, he noted, skillful
architects were attempting to protect natural scenery and incorporate
it into their designs, such as stands of trees, streams, or terrain contours. Workers would feel comfortable and healthy in such surroundings, binding them to the home and the family and strengthening their
love of *Heimat* and Fatherland. "There is scarcely anything more necessary than strengthening the love of *Heimat* through settlement,
through rooting in the soil, through activities on the land, through
creation òf ownership."[136] Such rooting of wage-earning proletarians
appeared particularly imperative in the Rhineland, one of the nation's
strategic borderlands. *Heimatschutz* members pointed to recent
events in the Saar region, which a 1936 plebiscite reunited with the
German Reich, as evidence of the political significance of environmental design. "The political-demographic significance of binding
German blood to German soil," noted Günther Wohlers, "ought not
to be seen as an idle theory in the Reich's Westmark." Wohlers
claimed that the "rooting" of workers in the "inherited soil" had prevented the emergence of a landless proletariat in the Saar region, providing a "powerful bulwark against international ideas" and a clear
demonstration of the need for a "firmly fit-together human wall."[137]

Binding workers to the soil was only one goal of Nazi housing;
another was providing a healthy environment to boost the birthrate
among "hereditarily sound" comrades. The Rhenish Homestead Association, with the assistance of the Rhenish Society for Regional
Planning and the DAF, sponsored the construction of numerous public housing complexes in *völkisch* styles. The Homestead Association
specified that only workers of a "healthy tribe" could occupy the
rental units or purchase the semirural cottages created through public
funds. Architects asserted that the housing complexes' healthy open
spaces and large gardens, which facilitated access to light, air, and
sun, would encourage workers to produce large families of
"hereditarily healthy" children.[138] Such spatial eugenics went hand in
hand with ever-widening plans to exclude "foreigners," those carrying "hereditary diseases," or those deemed "racially unfit" from these
suburban village settlements. The province also created a network
of rural asylums for reconditioning "Aryan asocials," such as juvenile delinquents, before they could be reintegrated into the

*Volksgemeinschaft*. Under Haake's leadership, landscape planning tied itself explicitly to the regime's pronatalist and xenophobic tendencies. This form of biopolitics subordinated environmental planning to the Nazi regime's racist and eugenic vision of national reconstruction.[139]

## Reclaiming the Moral Geography of *Heimat:* On the Limits of *Gleichschaltung*

The growing Nazification of *Naturschutz* and *Heimatschutz* provides strong evidence of preservationists' integration into the Third Reich's racist, authoritarian state. Haake's tenure brought regional organizations closer to the regime's core values, yet the anchoring of nature preservation in provincial cultural affairs also had an opposite effect: it provided an institutional *and* ideological buffer zone between localist understandings of *Heimat* and the national regime's Blood and Soil policies. This buffer zone enabled Rhenish preservationists to promote local aesthetic and *Heimat* ideals, rather than racial ones, in many of their *Naturschutz* and planning policies. A closer look at the dissemination of Nazism's Blood and Soil approach to environmentalism at the provincial level reveals notable fissures within the façade of top-down ideological conformity in which older traditions of environmentalism coexisted uneasily with the new emphasis on race.[140]

Given the growing influence of "biological" racism in Nazi cultural policies, for example, the RNG itself was surprisingly free of references to race or blood as bases for the new law. Klose's preamble to the Reich Nature Protection Law remained close to traditional *Naturschutz* rhetoric by emphasizing that environmental problems often resulted from "economic necessity," and it underscored the state's role in remedying the "spiritual as well as economic damages of such a transformation of Germany's landscape."[141] In a similar vein, the Westphalian nature protection officer Wilhelm Lienenkämper noted in his 1934 article "The German and His Landscape" that "just as race and family researchers see 'Blood' as their area of activity, so too would we [*Naturschutz* advocates] not want to neglect reconnecting the old relationship to the 'Soil.'"[142] Lienenkämper's emphasis on the importance of *both* Blood and Soil reflected preservationists' belief that *Heimat* feeling was the result of a variety of factors—historical, cultural, environmental—that could not be subsumed under a generalized racial identity. When Klose replaced Schoenichen as the head of the Reich Office for Nature Protection in 1939, a move that regional preservationists welcomed, the strident *völkisch* rhetoric of 1933 and 1934 died down.[143] Instead, journals such as the *Rhenish Friend of Nature,* which was founded in 1938, emphasized local, "apolitical" themes such as describing area plant and animal species, reporting details on new nature protection ordinances, and announcing nature club meetings.[144] Rather than embracing Schoenichen's ranting about racial degeneration as the cause of environmental degradation, most regional preservationists directed their ire at traditional enemies: Rhineland tourists and the spirit of materialism. Preservationists actively read their own regionalist and environmental meanings into Nazism's ambiguous and fractured discourse of Blood and Soil.

Unlike Schultze-Naumburg, most *Heimatschützer* continued to believe that Germany's national woes stemmed from cultural factors such as liberal individualism rather than pinpointing racial decline as the culprit. In his 1936 essay "Hopes for the Preservation of the Rhine Landscape," Hans Kornfeld referred to this onslaught as "the sins of an unholy time, that believed it had solved all of the lingering problems with the free expression of personality." In his view, the Rhine landscape's disfigurement, manifested in the "wounds" that marred its appearance, was the result of impiety unleashed by economic greed. "Rather than feeling himself to be a member of the landscape," wrote Kornfeld, "man felt himself to be ruler, and strove to give [the landscape] the stamp of his unencumbered individualism."[145] Returning to the Romantic legacy favored by Germany's educated middle classes, Kornfeld held that those who viewed the world with a "Goethe-esque eye" were still able to distinguish the landscape's divine blessings from the "traces of *Zivilisation,*" to see the Rhine as a majestic symbol rather than a mere "traffic corridor." For Kornfeld, therefore, the older *Bildungsbürgertum* model of aesthetic cultivation provided the pathway to reestablishing harmony between the broader landscape and the community, a perspective largely impervious to racializing tendencies.

Many regional *Heimatschutz* members maintained their belief that environmental improvement, rather than racial purification, offered Germans the opportunity to reject their wicked past and embrace the moral lessons of *Heimat.* Kornfeld exclaimed, "Nature is not some department store in which goods are being sold! It is for us still holy, it is the site of inner contemplation, where we obtain the power to master life."[146] Kornfeld specified that the goal of protecting natural and cultural monuments was to preserve the Rhineland's unique regional character, but he left out the next step: building the racial nation. "Man and landscape have to be one; man is a member of the landscape and as such inseparable from the whole that we call the Rhenish *Heimat* . . . whatever one does [to nature], one does to all of us." Not all regional preservationists followed Schultze-Naumburg in abandoning a nineteenth-century faith in public education and environmental improvement as pathways to social reform.[147]

While *Naturschutz* and *Heimatschutz* organizations articulated an uneasy compromise between racial and aesthetic understandings of homeland, other back-to-the-land groups tried to circumvent Nazi directives altogether. Such was the case in the Eifelverein, the Rhineland's largest bourgeois hiking club. Hiking activities fell under increasing scrutiny during the National Socialist period, because the regime viewed popular recreation as an instrument of mass political indoctrination and as a vehicle for enhancing the population's physical fitness. Like the province's preservation groups, the Eifelverein embraced "self-synchronization" in 1933 and 1934, based on the assumption that Nazism and the older moral geography of *Heimat* were one and the same. Chairman Walter Kaufmann proclaimed that the society would "gladly place its entire work in the service of *Volk, Heimat,* and borderland" in a cooperative effort with the national government.[148] Haake, in turn, praised the organization using a traditional concept of *Heimat* cultivation, noting in a 1938 speech that "*Heimat,* hiking, and homesickness [*Heimweh*] are holy, eternal, and therefore untranslatable words in the German vocabulary. All great Germans hiked, in order to find the basis for their own life's work in the sum of rich life experiences." Hiking, according to Haake, was not merely a sport but a venue for patriotism and moral refinement, allowing Germans to imbibe their natural surroundings and carry *Heimat* within them as the "everlasting legacy of time and eternity."[149] Hiking and nature experience also helped Germans to transcend social divisions; by getting out of the city and experiencing nature together, Germans could overcome "class differences that are hostile to the *Volk.*" Haake also praised Kaufmann for having maintained a "faithful watch on the Reich's western border" during the 1920s, saying that this had "continually awakened the sentiment and understanding for *Heimat* in the heart of the population."[150] Haake

thus underscored the synergy between hiking, local nature appreciation, and the emerging *Volksgemeinschaft*.

Haake's patronage strengthened the Eifelverein's semipublic functions in regional cultural affairs and tourism promotion. Whereas
provincial funds for hiking had dried up in the early 1930s, Haake
provided the Eifelverein with increased and stable annual grants.[151]
Haake helped the club to purchase the entire Genoveva Castle in the
town of Mayen, which allowed the Eifelverein to transform its small
*Heimat* museum and library at the site into a regional museum for the
entire Eifel area, with forty-three halls that "let the great *völkischen*
and historical questions of the Eifel land speak to visitors in an exemplary and lively museum form." The museum was a great success, log-
ging its 100,000th visitor in 1937. Club leaders were also proud of
their new overnight hostel in Blankenheim, which was designed to
serve as a convivial rest stop for hikers and tourists. The hostel provided the organization with conference and meeting space, and also
served as a home base for hiking clubs throughout the Rhineland.
Eifelverein leaders described the hostel in lofty terms as the "spiritual
center of German hiking in the Eifel borderland," a model of
"*bodenständig* culture."[152] New hostels and museums also increased
the Eifel's attractiveness as a tourist destination. The organization reported that there were twice as many foreign tourists to the Eifel in
1936 as in 1934; the total number of visitors increased from 1.13 million in 1935 to 1.16 million in 1936. Nazi patronage thus increased
the Eifel's cultural infrastructure and confirmed club members' belief
that the regime supported local boosterism and *Heimat* activities.

The Eifelverein's more visible presence in regional cultural affairs
led to a steady increase in new members between 1933 and 1939.[153] A
1935 news article portrayed the Eifelverein as "filled by new and fresh
life," finally able to reverse the annual declines in membership that
had plagued the group since 1925. Club leaders noted that the club
had established 24 new local groups over the past year and had recruited 2,000 new members, bringing its total number of affiliates to
157 and total number of members to 12,500.[154] At the Eifelverein's
fiftieth-anniversary celebration in Kyllburg in 1938, the new chairman Josef Schramm reported that the total number of clubs had risen
to 162 and the membership had increased to 14,400.[155] The club
also measured its success by increases in the total kilometers of trails
available to hikers. Schramm reported at the 1938 anniversary cele-

bration that the Eifelverein maintained almost 2,000 kilometers of hiking trails, which linked all of the area's major scenic and geologically unique sites. The club was especially proud of the newly constructed Heinrich Haake trail. The path led from the lower Rhine to Düren; future plans called for an extension to the Saar region, thus providing a north-south axis through the entire province.[156]

The Eifelverein's enhanced financial position and status bolstered club members' support for Nazism and gave the organization a sense of participation in the new regime. Despite Haake's promise to maintain the club's emphasis on local hiking and *Heimat* identity, however, Eifelverein members, like their counterparts in the *Heimatschutz* and *Naturschutz* organizations, learned quickly that Nazi *Gleichschaltung* entailed new institutional and ideological arrangements that challenged local initiative and autonomy. Under the leadership principle, for example, club members no longer elected their directors; existing commissioners appointed them instead. At annual meetings, members merely reported commission activities rather than debating major issues.[157] The club also underwent more direct scrutiny than either the provincial *Naturschutz* offices or the RVDH. Because local hiking activities overlapped with the NSDAP's own recreational programs, the regime restricted the Eifelverein's range of activities and its recruitment efforts. The Nazis removed tourism promotion from local hands by setting up national tourist associations that advertised Germany's attractions. To minimize competition with NSDAP organizations, the Nazis also forbade the Eifelverein from recruiting new members outside the Eifel region itself, except in those areas, such as Berlin, where local branches already existed.[158]

Nazi Party organizations also competed with the organization in attracting young people to outdoor activities. Because the Eifelverein was forbidden to recruit outside the immediate region, club leaders had hoped that new young members would make up for any potential decrease.[159] Yet the Eifelverein found that Hitler Youth and the DAF's Strength through Joy programs not only used the Rhineland's youth hostels more frequently than the Eifelverein but also were far more effective in mobilizing their young members and linking their goals explicitly to the regime's ideology. The Reich Association for Youth Hostels leader expressed the Nazis' vision of hiking and youth policy: "Youth who get to know the Fatherland, such as our young men and women on their trips," he noted, "will be the best guarantee and the most courageous fighters for Germany and National Socialism during times of need."[160] Rather than seeing it as a way to direct young people's attention to the beauty of their local *Heimat,* the Nazis viewed hiking as a further step toward militarizing German society.

Nazi Party organizations' competition with the Eifelverein for young members reflected the National Socialists' broader strategy for recreational activities: to build racial awareness and physical vigor through outdoor activities. Whereas nature protectionists believed that hiking promoted psychological well-being and relaxation, the Nazis considered it to be a form of "physical training" necessary for militarizing the national body. To link hiking organizations more closely to these goals, the Nazis incorporated them into national organizations that focused on hiking as a sport rather than a form of nature contemplation. The Nazis established a Reich Association for German Alpine and Hiking Clubs and placed it under the direction of the Reich Association for Physical Exercise (Reichsverband für Leibesübung, hereafter RfL), rather than making it part of cultural or nature protection affairs. The RfL established hiking excursion quotas for each hiking club, depending on its size, to ensure that the organizations incorporated exercise into their activities. The RfL also directed clubs to recognize their members' sporting achievements. Eifelverein members achieving 100 hikes received a walking stick badge, and those with 250 hikes received a silver ring for their stick; at 500 hikes, club leaders gave members a special honor ceremony.[161]

The RfL worked assiduously to promote hiking as a national sport, at the expense of its local *Heimat* significance. Nazi district leaders demanded that all regional hiking organizations participate in a national "Day of German Hiking" on each Ascension holiday.[162] At the 1937 meeting of the Reich Association for Alpine and Hiking Clubs, which took place in the Eifel village of Mayen, the Rhine Province's head president Josef Terboven called on hiking groups to support the regime's construction of a giant 1,200-kilometer hiking trail across the middle of Germany. Stretching from Saarbrücken in the west to St. Annaberg in Upper Silesia in the east, the trail was marked by signs with a blue cross on a white background. Terboven touted the project as important not only for hiking but for the "entire *Heimat* and *Volkstum* history of the Fatherland." The regime opened the new trail with great fanfare, including a parade of thousands of local hiking clubs flying their own flags behind the swastika of the

Third Reich.[163] The trail thus symbolized growing national integration at the expense of local diversity.

The majority of Eifelverein members opposed the club's inclusion in the RfL and appealed to the Reich Association for Alpine and Hiking Clubs to remain an independent organization.[164] One club member in Westphalia claimed that the Eifelverein's inclusion in the RfL could be "scarcely justified" in light of the club's "development and unique character." The same member also opposed the organization's growing emphasis on fitness: "We do not consider hiking to be a sporting activity. We reject competition and performance-oriented hiking. Through hiking, we want to bring about spiritual as well as physical training. Family hikes should receive particular attention."[165] These Eifelverein members recognized that the regime's policies posed a threat to their organization's traditional goals.

Despite Nazi efforts to redirect hiking activities toward racist goals, the history of the Eifelverein under the Third Reich was not merely one of cooptation or Nazification. Though club members proudly changed their traditional "Mit Waldheil" greeting to "Mit Waldheil und Heil Hitler," such superficial acts of ideological assent took place alongside ordinary local activities, such as trail marking, hut repair, and forest protection. Members still enjoyed traditional folk songs, dancing, and conversation at local *Heimat* evenings.[166] In their literature for new members and recruits, Eifelverein members continued to speak of hiking's aesthetic and recreational advantages for families, not for training the *völkisch* body. Hiking excursions remained focused on local scenery and landmarks. The cover of the 1936 *Eifel Calendar (Eifel-Kalendar)* displayed Eifel youth with swastikas embroidered on their backpacks, yet at the end of the trail stood a cross on a rock outcropping, a sign of outward assent to the regime and inward devotion to local scenery and Catholic religiosity. Nazism had legitimacy only so long as the regime seemed to further or at least tolerate these local meanings. Even the 1937 German Hiking Day in Mayen became an occasion for celebrating regional identity and local culture; its program included exhibits of Eifel art, industry, and handicrafts. On Sunday morning, participants attended a Catholic mass, took bus trips to local castles, and listened to a concert in the evening.[167] Eifel identity and sociability thus remained vibrant despite growing regimentation, filtering the capillary mechanisms of Nazification through the local idiom of *Heimat*.

Eifelverein hiking group on the Mosenberg in the Wittlich District, 1936. Young hikers within the Eifelverein readily adopted the Nazi swastika to express *Heimat* solidarity. The result, however, was an uneasy amalgam of traditional religious devotion, regional sentiment, and conformity to Nazi principles. *Source: Eifel-Kalendar 1936.*

One sign of the Eifelverein's attempts to shield *Heimat* activities from Nazification was the club's resistance to government efforts to transform the popular annual *Eifel Calendar* into an organ for Nazi ideology. The Nazis reviewed the content of *Heimat* publications through the party's Inspection Commission (Prüfungskommission) for the Support of National Socialist Writing.[168] Before 1939, the commission's inspectors found no reason to ban the innocuous *Eifel Calendar,* whose essays focused on topics such as local nature and historic preservation efforts, agricultural information for farmers, regional landscape art exhibitions, and Eifel fairy tales. As Eifelverein chairman Kaufmann wrote in 1937: "[The *Eifel Calendar*] is a *Heimat* book whose contents are geared strongly toward the history, culture, and economy of the Eifel, and which of course also prudently incorporates and treats the great questions of public life within the limits of its original goal."[169] Club members assumed that *Heimat* activities were fully in line with the Nazis' nationalist revolution.

In its 1939 inspection, however, the commission urged the club to include a favorable discussion of Nazi foreign policy. Party censors stated that most of the contributions to the *Eifel Calendar* were acceptable, but claimed that "in general the compilation for the final issue needs an article that deals with the immediate political questions of our time. A year in review is especially necessary that comprehensively acknowledges the great events of 1938 and 1939."[170] Club leaders were frustrated by the inspection process, which they saw as unnecessary for an organization that had already pledged itself to the regime. Eifelverein leaders complained not only about the fifteen-reichsmark fee they were forced to pay the commission for its decision but also that the commission was out of touch with the local patriotism of *Heimat* activities. Kaufmann implored provincial cultural affairs officer Kornfeld to impress upon the regime the need "to preserve the [*Eifel Calendar's*] character as a *Heimat* publication that does not overlook contemporary events, particularly those in the cultural realm, but leaves the political-propagandistic side to the appropriate district or other political publications."[171] For Kaufmann, national events, foreign policy, and political propaganda had their place in German life but remained anathema to the apolitical and communitarian spirit of *Heimat*. Though his remarks appear naïve given the circumstances of the time, they underscore the fact that *Gleichschaltung* had failed to Nazify completely the cultural meaning of *Heimat* within local clubs and organizations.

The Eifelverein's perception that regional identity remained the basis of German character also meant that Nazi racism found little resonance within the organization. While tourist guidebooks referred to Rhinelanders' "cheerfulness and joy of life" as "one of the most precious gifts of the blood," racial character never took precedence in their pages over culture, religion, or especially the *Heimat* landscape itself as the main coordinates of Rhenish identity.[172] The 1936 *Eifel Calendar* described the club's purpose: "Through perseverance it is necessary to build a new *Volk*, to create a *Volk* that loves Nature as the mother of humans' power, a *Volk* that with its whole heart is attached to the land from which it comes and that it helps to design."[173] The Nazis' ideal community of Blood never superseded Eifelers' devotion to the Soil of *Heimat* as the locus of their collective identity. Instead, club members' vision of the cultural landscape as the product of mutual interaction between culture and geography remained intact.

The perseverance of local identity found its most ample expression during the Second World War. The outbreak of conflict in 1939 initially posed a direct and grave threat to Eifelverein activities. Club members were concerned about the Eifel region's vulnerability on the western front; the organization's leaders canceled the 1940 Hiking Day and halted hiking excursions near the border. The construction of the West Wall, a concrete fortification consisting of bunkers and artillery installations, interfered with borderland hiking activities. One club member lamented that the "building of the West Wall has had a detrimental effect on hiking activities, since the many military installations and new streets have changed the landscape considerably."[174] Conscription and war casualties led to a decline in club membership and an inability to continue basic organizational functions, such as maintaining trails. Of the 154 organizations that submitted documentation for the organization's 1940 annual report, most reported significant declines in membership. Membership in the Bonn group fell from 662 to 560, in the Cologne area from 767 to 706.[175] The organization as a whole suffered a decline in membership: from a peak of 14,800 members in 1938, the Eifelverein had only 13,000 in 1941.[176]

After the initial standstill in club activities during the early months of the war, Eifelverein leaders welcomed the return of calm to their borderland and urged members to take up their hiking activities again. Club member and Westphalian nature protection commissioner Wilhelm Münker proclaimed that "the war is no reason not to hike. Therefore out into the fresh air!"[177] The club resumed publication of its *Eifel Yearbook* and *Eifel Calendar,* as well as other *Heimat* publications. Although they were increasingly urged to help mobilize Rhinelanders' support for the war, Eifelverein members reaffirmed instead the importance of local *Heimat.* While area hikers would need to stay in the immediate vicinity during wartime, noted another Eifelverein member, "this was not necessarily a bad thing, because it was certainly worthwhile to wander through the immediate surroundings more often." Instead of seeking out experiences in distant lands, many "comrades" were becoming familiar with the details of their immediate surroundings, where they were "astonished by the many beauties and quiet secrets of nature and the landscape that had remained hidden in their nearby *Heimat,* only because no one until then looked for them or perhaps even guessed [that they existed] here . . . The war therefore has its good side in this respect."[178] Even the Nazis' racist war could be perceived through a provincial lens. Rather than affirming expansionism, club members viewed the conflict as an opportunity to revisit the Eifel's local landscapes, to deepen their emotional ties to the familiar *Heimat* while they hoped for a speedy victory.

The process of *Gleichschaltung* at the regional and local levels situated *Naturschutz* and *Heimatschutz* in an ambiguous position that paralleled the larger contradictions of Nazi cultural policy. The attempt to incorporate these organizations into the Third Reich's cultural apparatus demonstrates that the terms of Blood and Soil rhetoric, as well as the place of environmental protection within the regime, were not fixed but open to multiple forms of appropriation and interpretation. Through their embracing of a racialized vision of landscape, national preservation leaders such as Paul Schultze-Naumburg and Walther Schoenichen opened the pathway toward greater cooperation between Nazism and nature protection before the regime came to power. Yet after 1933, when the regime's totalitarian impulses aimed to subsume nature protection within a racist, social Darwinist vision of nature, many regional preservationists carved out a space for Heimat provincialism and traditional environmental conservation within the interstices of Nazism's disciplinary mechanisms. This space was neither fully autonomous, untouched by Nazification, nor was it fully ensconced within the Third Reich's ideological apparatus. Instead, preservationists created a tenuous, hybrid discourse that spoke of traditional aestheticism while embracing modern spatial planning, and glorified the precepts of race while pointing to the local natural environment as the true ground of German identity.

This hybrid position was the result of political expediency in the early years of the regime. Preservationists saw the Nazi revolution as an opportunity to implement nationwide nature protection legislation and to reestablish themselves as cultural stewards of regional *Heimat,* both of which had been denied to them in Weimar's contentious democratic system. Only an authoritarian state, they believed, could realize the movement's environmental goals. Nazi cultural leaders, in turn, embraced *Heimat* rhetoric and environmental protection to achieve a critical legitimation and acceptance that anchored their party in the provinces. In the Rhineland, Heinz Haake's tenure as provincial governor reinvigorated *Naturschutz* and *Heimatschutz* with new financial resources and the promise of participation in regional planning. Such planning would balance environmental concerns with a forward-looking program of "organic" economic development. Yet Haake also expected nature and homeland protection groups to serve the regime's larger ideological aims. By recasting landscape planning as a tool for protecting *Lebensraum,* he hoped to purify the racial habitat, boost birthrates, and root the population in the soil. Haake's leadership thus provided a conduit for linking *Heimat* activities more closely to the regime's core values of economic performance, racial improvement, and militarist expansion. The process of *Gleichschaltung*—synchronization—was a two-way process, one that combined the Nazis' top-down need for legitimation with preservationists' bottom-up desire to protect the landscape and secure their place in regional cultural affairs. Though *Gleichschaltung* was uneven in its effects, the localist and environmentalist character of *Heimatschutz* was slowly being eroded from within even before the outbreak of war in 1939.

The following chapter analyzes the key factors—particularly war preparation and the rise of new technocratic landscape planners—that accelerated the erosion of regional autonomy. Rather than fulfilling its early promise to protect the nation's natural heritage, the need to create jobs and to plan for military conquest led the Nazi regime to embark on land reclamation and infrastructure modernization campaigns that threatened the German environment far more than liberal capitalism had in the Weimar years. The participation of landscape architects on the regime's massive *Autobahn* construction project, in particular, helped to redefine what counted as a "natural" landscape and challenged preservationists' local autonomy and initiative. These political imperatives and shifting power relationships undercut the tenuous alliance between Nazism and *Naturschutz,* provoking landscape preservationists' frustration and despair in the waning years of the Third Reich.

# CHAPTER FIVE

# Constructing Nature in the Third Reich

Landscape is the trustworthy living space that surrounds us from horizon to horizon, it is the ever-present piece of nurturing Mother Nature, who can either bless us or curse us, depending on how we treat her.

—ALWIN SEIFERT, *IM ZEITALTER DES LEBENDIGEN: NATUR—HEIMAT—TECHNIK*

In the years immediately preceding the Second World War, German landscape preservationists believed that they were living in a golden age of environmental concern.[1] The Reich Nature Protection Law of 1935 had established more than 800 nature protection regions, covering almost 3,000 square kilometers, and 50,000 natural monuments by 1940. In 1944 there were more than 1,100 county and 68 district nature protection offices.[2] The RNG had also created a new role for preservationists in planning and designing the nation's future landscapes. It specified that local *Naturschutz* officers be consulted for all projects involving a "significant modification" of the landscape. Rhineland preservationists, like compatriot regional groups throughout Germany, were wary of the regime's centralizing tendencies, yet their vision of *Heimat,* anchored in both local organizations and the provincial administration, remained vital and intact. Regional landscape preservation had, it seemed, achieved a privileged niche in the Nazi dictatorship's cultural apparatus, wielding state support to overcome Weimar liberalism's "materialist" waste of land and resources while maintaining the prerogatives of provincial *Heimat* stewardship.

In their zeal to affirm the Third Reich's environmental achievements, Rhenish preservationists largely overlooked the critical rhetorical and institutional differences between Nazism's racist and expansionist Blood and Soil policies and their own cultural and regionalist visions of homeland. Their failure to understand these ideological differences left them unprepared for the regime's accelerating assault on the natural environment in the name of job creation, *völkisch* integration, and war mobilization. Preservationists who had looked to the National Socialists to curb the environmental abuses of Weimar's market economy soon found the new state to be a far greater menace to landscape preservation than private industry. With the initiation of its Four-Year Plan in 1936, the Nazi regime commenced a massive public works and land reclamation campaign designed to boost Germany's economy and to prepare for war, a program that had catastrophic effects on local preservation efforts and the natural environment. Nazi Party leaders and military planners either failed to notify local officials about building projects or ignored their recommendations for minimizing the environmental impact of such practices, effectively stifling their voice within the regime's spatial planning agencies.

The divergent rhetorical constructions of nature within the Nazi and *Naturschutz* movements resulted in acrimonious debates over the physical construction of the environment, as evidenced by differing conceptions of land-use planning, resource use, and technological development. The Third Reich's fluid and multicentered power structure had enabled middle-class landscape preservation organizations to fashion a provincial vision of the "people's community" in the early years of the regime. Yet this same polycratic structure also facilitated the rise of new party and state organizations that challenged local authority over environmental affairs. The most significant members of the rival planning groups were the so-called landscape advocates *(Landschaftsanwälte)* of the Reich *Autobahn* project. Under the direction of Fritz Todt, the general inspector for German roadways and chief engineer on the *Autobahn* project, the Munich landscape architect Alwin Seifert assembled a cadre of expert landscape designers to restore naturalistic environments in areas affected by the new highways. Contemporary propaganda referred to the landscape advocates as experts who would fuse nature and technology by embedding the new roadways in the landscape; even today, many observers praise Seifert's work as a model of environmentally sensitive planning.[3] Whereas many scholars have assumed that Seifert drew on traditional *Heimatschutz* principles in formulating his vision of roadside gardens, his landscape aesthetic signaled a departure from existing landscape preservation practices. The landscape advocates promised not merely to avoid treasured natural monuments but to restore land-scapes destroyed by *Autobahn* construction or past environmental abuses. This restorationist claim meshed well with the Nazi regime's public works campaign and its racial ideology, rendering regional *Naturschutz* increasingly ineffective.

## The Mobilization of *Lebensraum*

The Nazi regime made no secret of its intention to sponsor large-scale public works projects and to modernize Germany's infrastructure in an effort to pull the country out of its economic depression. Preservationists accepted the dominant view that drastic measures were necessary to renew the country's economic vitality. Walther Schoenichen, the head of the Reich Office for Nature Protection and a Nazi Party member since 1933, commented that after "a period of unsurpassed economic mismanagement," the new government would create "healthy [economic] conditions."[4] Schoenichen nonetheless believed that the RNG, alongside other animal and forestry protection laws, provided a regulatory framework in which preservationists could counteract the most damaging aspects of this building campaign. "During the all-out attack on undisturbed nature," he remarked, "at least some of the most significant parcels can [one hopes] be successfully maintained."[5] Like the vast majority of private and state *Naturschützer,* Schoenichen assumed that centralized state regulation, even that of a dictatorship, was an improvement over the age of liberal individualism in environmental affairs.

Despite the RNG's formal guarantee of environmental review for all building projects, however, nature preservationists soon found themselves unable to expand the number of nature protection regions in tandem with the regime's rapid transformation of the natural environment.[6] The large number of nature protection regions created during the Nazi era, for example, reflected in many cases a more careful registration of existing reserves rather than a significant expansion over the Weimar years.[7] There were also few institutional differences between the former Prussian State Office for Natural Monument Preservation and the Nazi state's Reich Office for Nature Protection. Next to Director Schoenichen there were only four scientific assistants in the Reich Office, while at the local level nature protection remained in the hands of unpaid regional volunteers or retired civil servants who, as forest historian Heinrich Rubner has remarked, had to "battle against economic interests and planning bureaucrats often without [even] a typewriter."[8] The plans to protect symbolically important areas such as the middle Rhine Gorge also masked deeper weaknesses in the RNG that made it impossible for nature preservationists to realize their larger goals within the Nazi system. The law contained important exemptions for military installations and "vitally important economic concerns," which left sensitive regions open to exploitation. Only on rare occasions, therefore, did preservationists actually invoke the law's dispossession rights to claim additional nature preserves or to force private owners to recognize their authority in land use matters.[9] They relied instead on the same tactics used in the Wilhelmine and Weimar eras: personal persuasion and behind-the-scenes lobbying.

The RNG's weaknesses at the national level were even more pronounced in the regions, where nature protection commissioners lacked the political clout necessary to implement the law's provisions effectively. A community schoolteacher, Wilhelm Lienenkämper, nature protection commissioner in the Westphalian district of Arnsberg, described local officials' plight in a surprisingly pointed critique of the regime's environmental record. According to Lienenkämper, "The Reich Nature Protection Law lays most of the burden of work on the shoulders of the district commissioners. It sees such work as a side occupation, as an honorary post. Whoever takes his role seriously and perceives it as an affair of the heart is not in a position, despite his best efforts, to carry out the spirit and letter of the law alongside his main career [*Brotberuf*]."[10] Lienenkämper complained bitterly about the regime's lack of public outreach support for nature preservation. "The NSDAP supports its propaganda and administrative work through a broadly conceived and well-designed office apparatus, so that ideas and policy announcements are made generally available to all people's comrades within a few days. Yet still not every German is familiar with the word '*Naturschutz*.' The state builds an administrative division for often the most profane things on this earth."[11] Most important, regional nature protection officials lacked sufficient funds to carry out their tasks, in comparison to the enormous government outlays for infrastructure projects and rearmament. "There is no money available!" complained Lienenkämper. "Adolf Hitler's highways [and] the construction of monumental buildings are representative works of National Socialism, for whose construction money is readily available. The preservation of the actual remaining traces of primordial Germany [*Urdeutschland*] through the Reich Nature Protection Law is an equally important task that cannot be carried out without enough money." With such a lack of resources and power, local *Naturschutz* activities remained limited to traditional tasks that had little widespread impact: creating inventories of ecologically valuable sites, researching local natural monuments, or holding lectures about environmental protection. Without additional support, Lienekämper warned, "In the year 2000 Germany will consist of only residential developments, transportation routes, and cultivated steppe land!"[12] Clearly the RNG had not established the regulatory controls for which nature preservationists had hoped.

The Rhineland's natural monuments also suffered a barrage of new threats and abuses in the Third Reich that sharpened the divisions between representatives of Nazi organizations and landscape preservation groups. In the Cologne suburb of Brühl, for example, Nazi youth leaders submitted plans for converting a portion of a local nature protection region into a playground and exercise area. The preserve lay adjacent to the baroque palace built by the famous eighteenth-century Cologne bishop Clements August; it was formerly a hunting reserve and was later converted into a landscape garden. The Nazi plans drew howls of protest from nature protection, bird protection, hunting, and outdoor recreation clubs in the area, who feared the destruction of the town's most famous natural monument and a loss of nesting sites for local songbird species. The Nazi response to these protests was typical of the era: "youth fitness," rather than the protection of animal habitat, was a far more important goal for the *völkisch* regime.[13] In other districts of the province, nature protection officials complained bitterly to party leaders that Sturmabteilung (SA) battalions were using sensitive nature protection regions for marching drills or shooting practice, in complete disregard for the areas' protected status. In one incident, SA members jeered the local forest overseer who tried to stop their activities, calling him a "communist."[14]

Urban planners also found it impossible to keep pace with the rapid urbanization that accompanied the regime's pro-growth and rearmament policies. *Heimatschutz* leaders, for example, bemoaned the loss of historic buildings in Nazi urban renewal projects, which one historian has described as "a veritable blitzkrieg of destruction and construction" in city centers.[15] Labor shortages and the promise of high wages in the Rhine-Ruhr industrial corridor brought a flood of small-town and rural immigrants into the region's major cities, which taxed the province's housing and public services. The influx of new residents spelled a complete reversal of the Nazis' once vaunted efforts to disperse urban populations into suburban garden cities.[16] To ameliorate the housing shortage, the regime fell back on the Weimar practice of constructing rows of apartment houses within or just outside city limits, although these featured superficial decorative changes such as steep tile roofs and peasant murals, rather than the flat roofs and irregular geometric fenestration of the Bauhaus developments.

Rural areas also suffered a "blitzkrieg" of development. Robert Ley's German Labor Front (DAF) sponsored make-work programs such as the Reich Labor Service, whose rural modernization projects spread modern technology into rural landscapes rather than maintaining their unique preindustrial qualities. In the remote Eifel, on the Rhine Province's westernmost border, the Labor Service constructed numerous dams, most of which had been planned during the Weimar era but left unfinished due to the Depression. The concrete structures provided electricity to rural residents and attracted tourists to the newly created reservoirs and lakes, but preservationists complained that they did little to maintain the agrarian ambiance of the surrounding landscape. More ominously, the Labor Service helped to construct the West Wall, the concrete line of fortifications stretching through the Ardennes along the Belgian and French borders.[17] Although the project brought an end to the area's chronic unemployment, the wall's construction entailed a militarization of local life and spurred fears of an impending war. Barbed wire and restricted-access zones soon became as familiar in the local landscape as castle ruins and forests.[18]

The DAF also employed thousands of workers on rural land reclamation programs that created new farmsteads in an effort to boost Germany's domestic food production. These programs included a number of traditional beautification measures, such as cleaning up fields, replanting trees in denuded areas, or painting dilapidated historic houses. Yet the DAF employed many environmentally questionable methods in its quest to create arable land, such as draining marshy areas, securing embankments, straightening streams, and building dams and dikes.[19] Nature preservationists bemoaned the destruction of swamps and marshes, which the Labor Service deemed "wastelands," because these parcels of land provided vital habitat for birds and small mammals. Regional *Naturschützer* also argued that the new dams created stagnant waters that were intolerable for local fish species, which were accustomed to migrating through swiftly moving stream and river currents.[20] Karl Oberkirch, the nature protection commissioner for the Ruhr Settlement Association, warned that land reclamation projects were upsetting the entire "household of nature" by changing local climate conditions, lowering the groundwater table, and desiccating the soil.[21]

Despite preservationists' concerns, the National Socialists accelerated their land reclamation efforts in 1936 as part of the Four-Year Plan, a program designed to gear up the German economy for war. Hitler placed Hermann Göring in charge of the plan; the sad irony here was that Göring was also the Reich forestry minister and, by extension, head of the Reich Office for Nature Protection. Göring called on Walther Darré's Agricultural Ministry to limit the country's dependence on foreign raw materials and foodstuffs, which led to an expanded land reclamation effort referred to as "inner colonization." The drive toward autarky included swamp drainage and dam construction; planners forecast the conversion of more than two million hectares of "wasteland" into arable farms by 1940.[22] Yet Göring viewed Darré, a supporter of biodynamic farming techniques, as too soft for the task at hand. In 1942, Hitler replaced Darré with Herbert Backe, a representative on the Four-Year Plan Council and a supporter of traditional monocultural farming and the intensive use of synthetic fertilizers, which Germany's chemical industry was glad to provide.[23] The state's militarization of resources also put an end to forestry official Walter von Keudell's experiments in sustainable *(Dauerwald)* forestry. A 1937 decree from Göring made clear the primacy of economic use over selective cutting: "The purpose and goal of the forest's structural development is not a natural [*naturgemäss*] forest, but rather a natural economic forest [*naturgemässe Wirtschaftswald*] . . . The purpose and goal of forestry is, in the last analysis, the fulfillment of those demands that have arisen as part of national resource utilization needs."[24] Göring called for increasing timber cutting rates in 1937 and 1938 by 50 to 60 percent above normal.[25] Like Darré, Keudell found his environmentalist sympathies incompatible with wartime goals; in 1939 he was replaced by Lutz Heck, who was more willing to support high-volume forestry.[26]

Inner colonization caused great consternation in nature protection circles. At the first Reich Nature Protection Conference in 1937, Klose announced to the assembled nature protection officials: "There is no one in this room who will not shudder with horror at the thought of the incessant water drainage processes being conducted by agricultural cultivators and the Labor Service, which in many places have already gone too far. In just a few years [such actions] will almost completely disfigure [the landscape] and thereby take away these natural resources from the Fatherland."[27] In this climate of war preparation, nature protectionists found that their desire to compensate for military use through wetland rehydration or the retention of natural curves in waterways fell increasingly on unsympathetic ears. As one planning official put it, the opposition of "petty nature protectionists" who might want to "stand in the way" of land development needed to be overcome as soon as possible, since "it is better for us and guarantees peace much more when the world knows that in case of war we can nourish ourselves rather than take nature protection to an extreme."[28] Having little power, and fearful of appearing not to stand patriotically behind the regime, nature preservationists made protecting individual nature reserves, rather than the comprehensive *Landschaftspflege* promised by the RNG, their top priority. Klose noted that nature protectionists would not object when losses were unavoidable for economic reasons, but he sought to set aside scientifically valuable and irreplaceable reserves, which he referred to as "economically bearable and for the most part spatially insignificant 'enclaves of the cultural landscape.'"[29] In the face of the Third Reich's Battle for Production, nature protectionists saw their plans for comprehensive organic planning dissolve before their eyes.

With the onset of war in 1939, the regime's need for military installations and its thirst for raw materials threatened Germany's remaining natural monuments and protected regions. Military planners viewed open landscapes through a wartime lens: the Wahner Heath near Cologne, for example, was used as a shooting and drill range, while the Haard Forest in the Ruhr region hid antiaircraft artillery.[30] In November 1939, the district nature protection officer and mayor of Bonn pleaded in vain with the local antiaircraft division not to fell a nearby acacia grove that had been designated a natural monument. Citing the RNG, local friends of nature claimed the trees as a first-order *Naturdenkmal*, saying they served as both unique ecological specimens and as a site of memory in numerous "*Heimat* stories about the city of Bonn."[31] Yet homeland narratives that linked trees to municipal identity had dwindling significance in the expansionist Third Reich. Even Germany's one official national park, the Lüneburger Heath near Hamburg, was not safe from military planners. From 1936 to 1941, the regime considered plans for the area that included aircraft landing strips, experimental petroleum drilling fields, and hospitals for victims of air strikes. In its mobilization of German living space for economic recovery and war preparation, the Nazi state proved itself to be a far greater enemy of nature protection than private industry.

## Organic Roadways: Synthesizing Nature and Technology on the *Autobahn*

While the Third Reich had promised to honor the landscape as a source of German strength, its public works schemes and war mobilization plans clearly assumed priority over environmental protection. The National Socialists pursued numerous projects that transformed Germany's *Lebensraum,* but none was more highly publicized and controversial than the *Reichsautobahn* system. Built in a massive wave of construction between 1933 and 1940, the *Autobahn* network included nearly 3,700 kilometers of concrete highways by 1939, leading one Nazi journalist to hail the regime for opening up the greatest epoch of road building in all of history.[32] The *Autobahn* was the most potent symbol of the Nazi regime's aggressive embrace of modernity, a concrete monument portrayed as fusing engineering technology and aesthetically pleasing design. Contemporaries often referred to the highways as "Hitler's roadways," yet the *Autobahn* was not the Führer's innovation but a legacy of Weimar transportation planning. The National Socialists adapted road-building plans first introduced by a lobby of car drivers and chambers of commerce but repeatedly voted down by the Weimar Reichstag. The Rhineland had played a key role in this initial highway planning; the province laid Germany's first stretch of *Autobahn* in the Cologne-Bonn corridor in 1932, though this twenty-kilometer stretched served as a local connector, not for long-distance travel.[33] Economic depression, however, had stalled the republic's plans to extend the road network further. The Nazis were quick to view rapid highway construction as a unique propaganda opportunity, contrasting their "will to construct" with Weimar's inept political gridlock and economic decline.

In authorizing the project, the regime pursued a two-pronged strategy of economic recovery. First, Nazi leaders hoped to stimulate demand for German-produced automobiles, an industry that had not kept pace with that of other industrialized nations. In terms of private ownership of cars, Germany lagged behind the United States, France, and Britain; in fact, West Germany did not reach America's 1920s level of motorization until the 1960s.[34] Second, the regime hoped to provide jobs for millions of unemployed manual workers, both skilled and unskilled, and thereby make good on its promise to rescue the country from economic depression. The Reich touted its success on both counts: by 1936, the sale of German-made cars was five times its 1933 level and a large portion of the country's six million unemployed laborers had found work on the *Reichsautobahn* project, though in reality terrible work conditions and low wages made it increasingly difficult to attract workers to the project.[35] *Autobahn* construction served important symbolic ends as well. Glossy photo collections documented the lives of formerly unemployed workers, including carpenters, concrete finishers, and stonemasons, who had found work as *Autobahn* laborers. The Nazis claimed that the *Autobahn* had liberated such workers from Marxism's "materialist" philosophy by engaging them in a cooperative enterprise that benefited the entire *Volksgemeinschaft*. Though historians have questioned whether the *Reichsautobahn* played a significant role in Germany's economic recovery owing to its high costs, the roads were indisputably an effective propaganda tool.[36] The National Socialists cleverly used the *Autobahn* as the most important example of how they were rescuing Germany from the Depression, providing both jobs and an appealing vision of individual mobility for all Germans along sleek, modern highways. In their eyes the *Autobahn* spurred economic recovery and symbolized a new era of national unity without class distinctions.

The environmental impact of the *Reichsautobahn*'s 3,700 kilometers of concrete was considerable throughout Germany, yet nowhere was it more visible than in the highly industrialized and urbanized Rhine Province. There, *Autobahn* construction created a dense network of highways connecting industrial areas, such as the Ruhr steel-manufacturing and the Cologne-Leverkusen chemical-production areas, with economic centers in Berlin, Hamburg, and Frankfurt.[37] Despite its environmental impacts, the *Autobahn* was touted by the regime as a model of environmentally sensitive planning that fused technology with the "great laws of nature;"[38] Hitler himself directed

*Autobahn* construction near Cologne. Despite propaganda touting the landscape-friendly *Autobahn*, road construction, as shown here between Cologne and Wuppertal, caused massive environmental upheaval in the Rhenish countryside. *Source:* Archiv des Landschaftverbandes Rheinland, Bild 25.

engineers to ensure that "these roads leave no scar on nature's countenance."[39] Preservationist leaders such as Paul Schultze-Naumburg applauded the *Reichsautobahn* for considering the "rhythm of the landscape" and for using designs that promised not merely to "conform, but also sometimes to improve" the landscape.[40] The striking visual effect of the *Autobahnen* "embedded" *(eingegliedert)* in the German countryside, reproduced in countless brochures, tourist guides, articles, and photographic collections, served as another powerful tool of propaganda. This imagery enabled domestic and foreign observers alike to envision the environmental benefits of state control and to affirm Germany's triumph over liberalism's profligate waste of land and resources.

Fritz Todt, the civil engineer who spearheaded the *Reichsautobahn* project, proclaimed that *Autobahn* engineers embraced a distinctive form of "German Technology" *(Deutsche Technik),* a so-called third way, that rescued technology from the soulless materialism of both capitalism and Marxism as well as from the false dichotomy between "nature" and "culture."[41] Todt called on roadway engineers to work "with nature, rather than against nature," balancing technical considerations of road design with aesthetic insights that blended the highways harmoniously into the countryside.[42] Indeed, Todt viewed the *Autobahn* system as an improvement on nature; in his view, the roadways' innovative curving lines, the use of indigenous construction materials, and the efforts to revegetate the median strips and roadsides "make a road as a totality into an artwork that brings the environment joy through its intrinsic beauty and harmony with the environment."[43] The Nazi era thus disseminated the new vision of technology that had remained inchoate in the late Weimar era's debates on aesthetics and modernization. In this view, engineers were designers, or *Gestalter,* rather than mere technicians, who were able to mesh their craft with an artistic feeling for nature.[44]

Todt commissioned the Munich landscape architect Alwin Seifert to assist the engineers in achieving this fusion of nature and technology. In 1934 Seifert brought together a cadre of fifteen expert consultants, the *Landschaftsanwälte,* to serve as advisers on the project. Each landscape advocate was assigned to a specific construction district and was charged to work alongside street engineers in choosing routes and implementing environmental damage mitigation measures. The landscape advocates were professional garden and landscape architects rather than nature protection commissioners; most advocates had developed their affinity for nature in the Wilhelmine and Weimar youth movements and maintained close ties to *Heimatschutz* organizations.[45] Seifert selected men whose vision of landscape preservation extended beyond traditional garden design to encompass a bold vision of large-scale regional development and social reform. In a 1934 essay, Seifert wrote that "in less than three years a new sensibility has come to the fore, which is through and through National Socialist and places the whole over the part, the landscape over technology, the people over the driver, community spirit over individualism." This new spirit, Seifert asserted, recognized "exclusively technical perspectives" in construction that value "the measurable and the countable" as only one part of the equation. The other part was a keen awareness of technology's impact on the landscape. Seifert maintained that "technical work" was complete only "when it in each and every way becomes a harmonious part of the landscape into which it is placed."[46] Achieving this harmony would require both technical mastery of the "measurable" and an intuitive feeling for beauty in the landscape, a reconciliation of the mechanistic and the idealistic that characterized the discourse of German technology as a whole.

The *Reichsautobahn* served as an ideal test case for this comprehensive vision of road design. Seifert called on the landscape advocates to embed the roadways so seamlessly into the surrounding environment that they became "organic members of the landscape."[47] The landscape advocates also claimed they could return the disturbed landscapes along the roadway to a more natural, organic state. This entailed not merely avoiding sensitive areas or replanting roadway margins, but also undertaking large-scale ecological restoration of environmentally affected areas. Seifert described the landscape advocates as individuals who understood "the language of nature" who synthesized technical training, ecological knowledge, and aesthetic feeling. The landscape advocates could thus assist the regime in sustaining or even restoring the country's *Lebensraum* through professional expertise and technocratic oversight.[48]

Scholars continue to debate the ecological significance of the landscape advocates' efforts on the *Autobahn*. Several historians have argued that they achieved at most a naturalistic effect, but no lasting ecological benefit, and that cost considerations, inadequate pay, uncertain status, and mounting tensions between Seifert and Todt limited the landscape advocates' effectiveness.[49] Others have maintained that the *Reichsautobahn* project achieved an unprecedented degree of ecological harmony with the landscape. These scholars have argued that historians need to reconsider the *Autobahn* landscape protection program as an example of positive environmental reform in its own right, rather than a simple reflection of Nazi directives or ideology.[50] Given the Third Reich's and especially the *Reichsautobahn*'s reputation as environmentally friendly, further discussion of the project's ecological impact is important for evaluating the regime's environmental record.

Yet viewing Seifert's efforts solely in light of modern ecological concerns can easily overlook the cultural and ideological significance of his appeal to nature restoration. His claim to privileged scientific knowledge played a key role in elevating the landscape advocates above rival environmental authorities, especially regional nature protectionists, within the power struggles that pervaded institutional life in the Third Reich. Not surprisingly, Seifert's program of environmental reform encountered substantial resistance at the regional and local levels. Rather than greeting the landscape advocates as agents of environmental reform, many regional landscape preservationists saw them as intruders who had little concern for the natural and cultural textures of the regional homeland. Seifert's faith in technological development and the possibilities of ecological restoration clashed with Rhenish preservationists' devotion to the local *Kulturlandschaft*, revealing sharp differences over the meaning of nature and *Heimat* as well as the priorities of landscape preservation. At the heart of the controversy was not the environment alone but the Rhine Province's cultural and territorial identity within the Third Reich.

## Healing the Wounds of Modernity: Alwin Seifert's Vision of Landscape Restoration

Rhenish preservationists only gradually came to see the *Reichsautobahn* as a pernicious threat to the province's natural environment. In the early years of the Third Reich, in fact, the Nazi promise to preserve natural landscapes during *Autobahn* construction and the appointment of Seifert as chief landscape advocate allayed preservationists' concerns about the project. Walther Schoenichen promised that the National Socialists had overcome the liberal era's insensitivity to the environment, stating that the regime had taken "all possible consideration of our homeland values" while planning the *Autobahnen*.[51] Many regional preservationists also agreed with Schoenichen's view that the *Autobahn* network was necessary for leading Germany out of its economic depression and providing a transportation infrastructure that would ensure the country's long-term economic competitiveness. They remained confident that the RNG's Section 5 regional planning provisions would guarantee them a role in planning routes that would avoid or minimize impacts on the natural environment.[52]

The original plans for the *Reichsautobahn* envisioned close cooperation between roadway engineers and landscape advocates, on the one hand, and various regional constituencies, including *Naturschutz* and *Heimatschutz* representatives, provincial street planners, local party officials, and industry leaders, on the other.[53] The landscape advocates' promise to respect regional diversity also encouraged preservationists to view the project in a positive light. According to one article, the landscape advocates understood that "the *völkisch* differences of our regions stem from the character of the individual landscapes— Tirolers, Westphalians, Rhinelanders—they became as they are from the ever-present effects of the landscapes."[54] Seifert himself was a prominent Bavarian *Heimatschützer,* which bolstered his claim that a healthy and beautiful landscape was necessary for keeping the local population strong and rooted in the homeland. "We have to care for a healthy landscape," stated a contemporary article on planning, "that is also a life provider and homeland to the generations after us."[55] The landscape advocates thus appeared to support preservationists' traditional focus on regional concerns.

Rhenish preservationists were also cautiously optimistic that the *Autobahnen* would help to disperse urban populations away from city centers and slow down, or even reverse, Germany's inexorable transformation into an industrial state. Having not yet experienced the problems associated with automobile usage and suburban sprawl, preservationists argued that the new highways would help to relieve congestion along regional roads and city streets and make longer distance travel from suburban garden towns feasible and inexpensive.[56] Furthermore, historic preservationists hoped that the *Autobahnen* would divert traffic away from centuries-old medieval town and city centers, obviating the need for widening streets and destroying cultural monuments. Regional preservationists and planners were thus not necessarily averse to the promise of fast and efficient rural transportation.

Preservationists also trusted that Alwin Seifert himself would serve as a staunch defender of nature protection ideals within Nazi inner circles. When he had first learned of the regime's plans, Seifert had echoed homeland advocates' apprehensions about the *Autobahn* project, describing the *Reichsautobahn* network as "at first thought a horror to any friend of nature."[57] Seifert portrayed himself in his 1962 autobiography, *A Life for the Landscape,* as a heroic figure who had battled the regime to save the environment from destruction. Despite its tendency to overplay Seifert's distance from the Nazi regime and its policies, *A Life for the Landscape* offers an important glimpse into the evolving relationship between Seifert, the *Heimatschutz* movement, and the National Socialist authorities. In this account, Seifert traced his devotion to the landscape to the outdoor experiences of his youth, which provided another point of contact for bourgeois preservationists. Like the majority of *Naturschutz* and *Heimatschutz* members' accounts of their childhood, Seifert's text associates an emerging environmental consciousness with personal memory and a sense of place. He describes spending many hours as a child observing the plant life of his Bavarian *Heimat,* with taxonomy and natural history serving as vehicles for imagining the contours of homeland. "In the first three years of high school *(Gymnasium),*" he writes, "I acquired an almost complete knowledge of the indigenous landscape and its vegetation, [knowledge] which would later be the basis for embedding the *Reichsautobahn* in the landscape."[58]

Seifert claimed that anger over environmental destruction, such as the damning and straightening of the Isar River, had led him to develop an alternative value system from that of his parents. Like many *Heimatschutz* and *Naturschutz* advocates, Seifert spent his adolescence in the *Wandervögel* movement, a "rebellion of youth with their own healthy values against the well-fed life of a beer-drinking and cigarette-smoking bourgeoisie." The young hikers renounced the "soft" life and refused the "accoutrements of 'society,' of fine hotels and Wagner operas [in favor of] the rediscovered folk song."[59] Of crucial importance to the *Wandervögel* movement was the discovery of "the authentic" *(das Echte)* in Germany's rural towns and vernacular landscapes, far away from Florence, Rome, and other famous sites frequented by the middle classes. Seifert thus shared the youth experiences of many *Naturschutz* members and, like them, developed in his adulthood a highly personalized critique of bourgeois *Zivilisation.* He viewed the rationalized landscapes of modernity as symptoms of a cultural malaise of greed and materialism. The familiar nature of *Heimat,* in contrast, not only provided a refuge from the city but also offered the individual a place for moral development outside the materialist nexus of industrial capitalism.

Seifert's professional background made him an ideal candidate for realizing the *Heimatschutz* movement's landscape-aesthetic goals. Trained as an architect at Munich's well-respected Technical University, Seifert embraced the *Heimatschutz* conviction that historic models and naturalistic forms were cost effective and functional rather than outdated and superfluous. Seifert synthesized architectural training with botanical knowledge, and could package his appeal to landscape reform in technical and functional terms familiar to engineers. Seifert also maintained links to *Heimatschutz* organizations throughout the early years of the regime. He unveiled his plans for *Autobahn* landscape design at a DBH conference in 1933 and was a regular contributor to national and regional *Heimatschutz* journals. Seifert also shared the movement's distinctive moral fervency and bourgeois reformism in his insistence that landscape preservation served higher, ideal goals that distinguished it from one-sided political engagement or mundane material concerns. Signaling his debt to the educated middle classes' embrace of Romanticism and *Bildung,* Seifert described Goethe as "the best defender of my way of making myself unpopular." Like Goethe, Seifert asserted that "anyone who feels within himself that he can have a positive impact must be a pest. He cannot wait until he is called; he does not obey when he is sent away; he must be what Homer praised about heroes: he must be like a fly that, when brushed away, lands on people again from the other side."[60] Seifert thus shared the social, cultural, and political values of Germany's homeland and landscape defenders, which led preservationists to trust in his leadership and the regime's *Autobahn* plans.

Seifert also adapted numerous aesthetic principles for street design from *Heimatschutz* leaders such as Paul Schultze-Naumburg and Werner Lindner, linking his work closely to homeland traditions of environmental reform. Like these landscape theorists, Seifert depicted the pre-1850 landscape as an aesthetic ideal for modern street builders to imitate. In his view, one could read the "character of the soul" and "tribal uniqueness" of an area's inhabitants by looking at its streets; beauty could be found wherever roadways were "technically perfect for their time, when technical necessity, technical ability, and artistic feeling for the spirit and law of the landscape are brought together in dynamic unison." In practice, this taming of technology through a feeling for the landscape meant incorporating design features that enhanced the naturalistic effect of the highways and their surroundings, ensuring that roads did not stand out as "foreign bodies" in the textures of their environment.[61] Seifert insisted, for example, that *Autobahn* bridges be made of irregularly shaped local stones rather than poured concrete. He also demanded that gas stations at rest stops use vernacular *Heimat* styles and made sure that no billboards appeared along the highways to disfigure the landscape. On the routes along the Rhine's banks, this new roadway aesthetic encouraged road builders to bring back old milestones that had been replaced by modern mileage markers and to create rest stops offering scenic views of the river.[62]

Seifert's most important design innovations came from applying *Heimatschutz* ideas of naturalistic form and functionality to the street layout, the form of the street bed, and the plantings alongside the roadways. German roadways, including the first stretch of *Autobahn* between Cologne and Bonn, were traditionally built along straight lines. If a simple straight line connecting two areas was not possible owing to difficult terrain or other intervening features, highway engineers used "zigzags" to reorient the roadway's path. In contrast to these methods, Seifert encouraged roadway engineers to build curving roads that followed the natural contours of the landscape, rather than imposing a grid on it. As Seifert put it, "the straight line does not stem from nature."[63] Streets with long, straight avenues or curves of a completely uniform radius were products of a nineteenth-century "bureaucratic" mentality. The mark of a living entity was rhythm, a swinging from "one pole to the other," rather than proceeding straight ahead. Seifert also proposed that making streets that lay closer to nature through "swinging curves" and that followed the contours of the natural environment created more beautiful roadways and was more economical. Following nature's rhythms required less technical intervention, shallower excavations, lower embankments, and less movement of the soil. "That which is closer to nature," Seifert wrote, "is always the most technically complete and, in the long term, is the single economical [solution]." Curving lines, moreover, sustained regional character, since "the swinging is different in Holstein than in Hessen, different in Thuringia than in Württemberg."[64] Like *Heimatschutz* leaders before him, Seifert believed that attention to beauty, form, and regional diversity were completely compatible with the functionality and cost advantages demanded by modernity.

Seifert also proposed that the raised highway beds traditionally used by architects and engineers created an unnecessary separation between the roads and their surrounding environment. Nineteenth-century regional roads had been modeled on railway lines, with raised beds and ditches on the sides, elevating them above the vegetation. Seifert reproached engineers for crafting their blueprints for highways

The curving lines of the German *Autobahn*. Alwin Seifert, the chief "landscape advocate" of the *Autobahn*, celebrated the safety advantages and naturalistic aesthetic of the new roads' "swinging curves" (top), in comparison with the "deadly image" of the straightaway built between Cologne and Bonn in 1932 (bottom). *Source:* Alwin Seifert, *Ein Leben für die Landschaft* (Düsseldorf: Eugen Diederichs, 1962), 17.

in design studios, using rulers and compasses, rather than in the outdoors. Removed from the natural irregularity and diversity of the countryside, engineers expected the landscape to conform to their drawing boards. By contrast, Seifert found ways to accentuate a highway's closeness to the surrounding landscape by doing away with embankments and laying the roadway flush with the surrounding terrain.[65] He believed that modern highways and the automobile were both technologically superior to nineteenth-century mass transportation, and closer to nature, and he wanted a design that enhanced diversity rather than standardization.

Seifert also used safety considerations to justify curving lines and changing scenery, further appealing to engineers' bottom-line mentality. Weimar highway planners had anticipated the need for visual stimulation on modern highways by integrating natural features to achieve aesthetic effects. The original *Autobahn* plans had viewed natural landmarks in terms of isolated monuments, much as Haussmann's Parisian boulevards focused on large buildings, impressive cathedrals, and war memorials to orient that city's road network. Drivers traveling south on the Cologne-Bonn *Autobahn,* for example, had a view of the Siebengebirge in the distance on a clear day. Seifert believed, however, that straight lines fixed on distant landmarks were inappropriate for long-distance driving, in which drivers ran the risk of being lulled to sleep by the soporific effects of endless straightaways and fixed sight lines. "The straight line is by no means the shortest connection between two places; it is too strongly burdened with the danger that . . . [the driver] . . . never even makes it because he crashes along the way."[66]

According to Seifert, the *Autobahn*'s curves and its integration into its environment helped drivers to stay alert by prodding them to pay attention to changing roadway conditions and dynamic surrounding scenery. "It is necessary to create stimulation," Seifert wrote in 1962, "which is more effective and lasting than coffee or cola. This stimulation cannot be a single tree or even a beautifully set group [of trees]; it can only come from the diversity of the ever-changing landscape itself."[67] Such landscape diversity came from retaining as much of the natural landscape as possible along the highways, or restoring greenery where the removal of vegetation was unavoidable. Technicians of the old school, Seifert complained, viewed arboreal stands merely as "decoration." He compared planting symmetrical rows of hedges along the Cologne-Bonn highway to beautifying the façade of a factory: the outside was pleasing in appearance while the inner workings remained dedicated to mechanization.[68] Seifert claimed that there were twice as many accidents on the 1932 Cologne-Bonn *Autobahn* as elsewhere on the Rhineland's new curving highways, which bolstered his belief in the practical efficacy of his aesthetic proposals. Although General Inspector Todt had originally opposed costly outlays for curving highways, the arguments based on driver safety, as well as the cost savings involved in having roadways go around natural obstacles such as mountains and cliffs, eventually won him over to Seifert's cause.[69]

The historian Jeffrey Herf has described the peculiar combination of the *Autobahn*'s homage to modern technology and concern for naturalist aesthetics as an example of the Third Reich's "reactionary modernist" tendencies. In Herf's now classic formulation, the *Autobahn* symbolized the Nazi regime's proclivity for fusing Weimar technological optimism with a reactionary, agrarian-romantic appeal to the *Volk*.[70] In Herf's view, this fusion enabled the regime to overcome Weimar-era debates over modernization by integrating technology, traditionally a sign of progressive Enlightenment culture, with a reactionary *völkisch* agenda based on racial myth. Most historians now view the reactionary modern concept as too monocausal; Nazism's multiple centers of power made such a coherent worldview impossible to articulate.[71] Herf's assumption that Seifert's landscape design reflected a backward-looking glorification of agrarian life also deserves further scrutiny. Seifert's vision of landscape design was neither reactionary nor Romantic in a nineteenth-century sense. Instead, it was a carefully articulated synthesis of modernist design and social integration concerns suited to an age of personal mobility and growing leisure opportunities. By constructing the *Reichsautobahn*, the regime helped to realize an unfulfilled promise from the Weimar era: to create a culture of leisure that crossed class barriers. *Autobahn* planners, like American parkway designers of the 1930s, viewed cars first and foremost as tourist vehicles, as signs of Germany's growing affluence and the expansion of leisure activities to broader sections of society after the Depression.[72]

Seifert's roadway aesthetics served the broader cultural-political purpose of knitting the country together geographically and psychologically, rendering its historical and natural treasures accessible to the entire *Volk*. In conjunction with its unrealized plans for the mass production of affordable *Volkswagen,*[73] the regime envisioned the *Autobahnen* as pathways that would open up Germany's historical, cultural, and natural wonders to all Germans, regardless of income. Indeed, cars allowed ordinary Germans to reach remote landscapes and sites of national heritage that were once accessible only to middle-class Germans with the appropriate income, leisure time, and "taste" to appreciate them. Nazi tourism promotion thus proffered an urbanized view of nature that would make the nation's symbolic capital, embedded in scenic landscapes, available to all Germans. The Nazis hoped that members of the *Volk* would use the highways to visit Germany's cultural and natural sites, thereby strengthening both their emotional ties to the Fatherland and their racial consciousness.[74] The transportation network would facilitate a geographic *Gleichschaltung* to complement the regime's efforts to achieve ideological indoctrination and institutional conformity.

The cultural-political role of the *Autobahn* in forging national unity and racial identity was reflected in routing decisions and highway designs that emphasized the visual consumption of landscape over purely technical or utilitarian considerations. The *Autobahn* planners took great pains to enhance drivers' access to and visual appreciation of the surrounding cultural landscape. Rather than merely linking vital urban and economic regions, *Autobahn* corridors connected important historical and cultural sites in a pleasing aesthetic whole. One scholar has compared the effect of the *Autobahnen* to landscape gardens, in which meandering pathways reveal everchanging scenery and highlight the most dramatic views.[75] Rather than whisking drivers on a straight line through the forest and leaving their sight focused on the gap at the other end, Seifert promoted curves as a way to "enclose" the automobile within the trees, prolonging the illusion of being "back-to-nature." Through curving lines, he said, the driver "experienced the landscape, became part of its rhythms . . . It is not possible to exult [in nature] on a street that is straight-lined and simply draws one toward the endless horizon."[76]

Engineers designed the highways to give drivers the best possible views of placid lakes, mountain peaks, and historic ruins, and placed rest stops at all outstanding scenic points. Enhancing a view could even override safety concerns; drivers of large trailer trucks in the Bavarian Alps, for example, often found it difficult to negotiate the steep grades used to improve the view.[77] Seifert also believed that the *Autobahnen* would enhance drivers' visual pleasure by linking together discrete natural scenes, such as forested hills or rolling meadows, into an aesthetic whole. He writes: "The [roadways'] secret, however, is the constant change from small to large spaces, from broad open areas to enclosed passageways. Along the newly built *Autobahn* the land was torn open; it was now necessary to close it back up, to allow whatever comes out of the landscape to run across the *Autobahn,* to make the simple passage through forests into real gates."[78] Proper design thus improved on nature by synthesizing its beauties into an open-air work of art for the pleasure of modern automobile tourists. Far from reactionary modernism, Nazi roadway design packaged the natural environment according to urban leisure priorities and nationalist integration needs.

Seifert's broader environmental agenda also calls into question the reactionary modern paradigm, for back-to-nature concerns once dismissed as ill-conceived agrarian-romanticism appear today strikingly prescient, given the current understanding of the ecosystem. Seifert's conception of *Landschaftspflege* went far beyond traditional aesthetic, historic, or touristic concerns to include measures that sustained the working landscape's biological health over time. He envisioned National Socialist Germany entering a new "Age of the Living" that would eventually expunge all traces of the materialism and mechanistic thinking that was first born in the Renaissance and achieved its most extreme form in the nineteenth century. The mistake of modern technology, noted Seifert, was to see nature merely as "an accidental collection of things" rather than as a "closed, living organism, in which every single minute part is determined by every other part and every change in one part affects all the rest."[79] A small change in the groundwater level due to reclamation, for example, unleashed unexpected damage such as the death of meadows and trees on the surface. "Nature's revenge for destroying her balance," according to Seifert, "comes slowly but surely."[80] By recognizing the earth's systems as a living superorganism, Germans could evade such ecological catastrophes. Their new Age of the Living would create an organic modernity that subsumed traditional dichotomies, such as nature versus culture or the individual versus the state, under a "biological" worldview.

Like Darré and Hess, Seifert and many of the other landscape advocates embraced Rudolf Steiner's anthroposophy movement and its focus on the soil as the basis for environmental vitality. "Mother earth is not simply that heavy mass that one needs to shovel away . . . [it] is a living organism, a living entity of a higher order that nature has created out of living things and with the help of living things over millennia and provides us today with the basis of our entire existence."[81] Seifert believed that soil fertility depended on maintaining the diversity of organisms living within it, such as worms, insects, insect larvae, fungi, and bacteria. Organismic diversity, in turn, depended on a rich array of native grasses and shrubs. "In its complete abundance this soil life weaves itself only among the roots of those grasses, herbs, shrubs, and trees that are native to that soil and have helped to create it."[82] Fertile soil also provided the basis for native trees, such as oaks and lindens, to reestablish themselves through a process of ecological succession. The total amount of such rich soil "capital" was fixed and irreplaceable; a key duty of environmental planners was to sustain its fertility over time.

Given the soil's importance for landscape health and regeneration, Seifert devised a number of methods he hoped would preserve or replenish it during *Autobahn* construction. Seifert asked engineers to replace topsoil excavated during road construction and encouraged them to compost rather than dispose of accumulated leaves, grasses, and twigs. When trees were cut for the roadway, Seifert encouraged engineers to remove the topsoil before grinding the stumps, thereby rescuing valuable soil that otherwise would be wasted under concrete. Seifert also discouraged landscape advocates from using commercial grass seed when reseeding disturbed areas. Instead, Seifert advised them to use a blend of native grasses and herbs, which he claimed mimicked a natural meadow and provided the basis for further rejuvenation. Seifert believed that his soil preservation and replanting measures obviated the need for artificial fertilizers and insecticides, providing instead a rich organic basis for growth and enabling natural insect predators to establish a habitat for themselves.[83]

The landscape advocates went beyond mere aesthetic replanting in areas disturbed by roadway construction. They envisioned instead a rudimentary form of ecological restoration in which mixed stands of native vegetation would grow in imitation of natural conditions. Seifert looked here to the sustainable forestry practices of *Dauerwald* for models. Prussian foresters sympathetic to these practices had taught Seifert about the importance of native hedgerows in preventing soil erosion and sustaining landscape fertility. These foresters also argued that forests composed of mixed native hardwood such as oak and beech, along with fast-growing species such as pine and spruce, created a more robust organism and a longer-term timber supply than traditional forestry. Seifert used these insights when he called on the landscape advocates to preserve or reestablish native *(bodenständig)* flora in their replanting efforts alongside roadways or in median strips. Seifert argued that such plants not only belonged by nature to the *Heimat* but also were hardier and more economical than traditional garden species. Such techniques generated an environment that was both aesthetically pleasing and closer to nature.[84]

To determine which plants were *bodenständig*, Seifert relied on the latest research in the science of plant ecology. During the early 1930s, Seifert had learned of Hannover botanist Reinhold Tüxen's research on floristic communities. Tüxen's work had transformed German ecological study in the 1930s in much the same way that Frederic Clements's research on the Great Plains had established a new foundation for botanical study in America.[85] Like German plant geographers such as August Grisebach and Oscar Drude, Tüxen argued that the earth's vegetation formed itself naturally into discrete "plant societies," climax vegetation communities based on regional environmental conditions, especially soil and climate. Left undisturbed, such plant societies would exist in a state of near-constant equilibrium with their environment for millennia.[86] To a much greater extent than nineteenth-century theorists, Tüxen's "plant sociology" attributed superorganismic qualities to vegetation communities, postulating that there was functional interdependency between the different species in each plant society. Communities, rather than individuals alone, engaged in a struggle for existence. "What is originally native in a landscape," Seifert wrote, "is thanks to millennia-long natural selection of what is best adapted."[87] Even Germany's human-created "anthropocentric climax," Tüxen argued, still contained semiwild patches of climax vegetation such as the Lüneburger Heath or the alpine forests of the Bavarian mountains.

In Seifert's view, Tüxen's work in plant ecology promised to revolutionize *Landschaftspflege,* for it would guide the landscape advocates in determining on an exact scientific basis not only which areas should be preserved but also which vegetation types should be used to restore the landscape to a natural state. "Here and today begins a new epoch of world history," exclaimed Seifert at one meeting of landscape advocates in Bavaria, "and you can say that you were there!"[88] In Germany's revolutionary Age of the Living, decisions on major building projects would be rendered only after a careful investigation of the climax vegetation normally found in the area's plant communities in the absence of human intervention.[89] Tüxen's work thus legitimated the landscape advocates' claim to applied biology, for it provided blueprints for returning the landscape to a state dictated by nature rather than by humankind.

Seifert was especially enthusiastic about the possibility of using Tüxen's work to regenerate natural environments in places that had been disturbed by *Autobahn* construction or other past uses. "In the large building projects that demand his participation," Seifert wrote, "the landscape designer uses his knowledge of plant ecology to strengthen the landscape's character and, where [this character] has been suppressed or diluted, to re-create it."[90] To protect areas of deep-forest trees exposed to sunlight and wind by *Autobahn* construction, for example, Seifert had workers plant a "coat" of fast-growing conifers and shrubs around their perimeter or paint their trunks with a paste made of loam and cow manure to shield them from desiccation and trunk damage.[91] This technique enabled the trees and light-sensitive understory vegetation to reestablish themselves and kept them from succumbing to rapid-growing, sunlight-resistant species. The process of protecting or restoring native stands of trees also depended on an appropriate aesthetic sensibility. According to the Rhenish landscape advocate Reinhold Hoemann, the landscape designer needed to feel an emotional connection to the land, to "keep his eyes and heart open, so that he sees what the actual surroundings are showing or indicating to him, [so] that with his sense of empathy the new plantings consistently match up with what is naturally given."[92] Hoemann called on his fellow landscape advocates to shape the ever-changing contours of the cultural landscape into a more naturalistic and "Germanic" form whose beauty and health contrasted with the "purely materialist" landscapes of the past.

Landscape advocates were so enthralled by the new theories of plant sociology that they envisioned applying its principles to environmental reform beyond the *Reichsautobahn*. They were confident that similar ecological restoration could transform a heavily degraded industrial environment into a true *Heimat* for its inhabitants, letting gardens blossom where industrial waste had once denuded the landscape. In his 1962 autobiography, Seifert boasted about the achievements of landscape advocate Guido Erxleben, who Seifert claimed had transformed areas laid to waste by mining into pastoral landscape gardens through revegetation and terrain formation. According to Seifert, Erxleben had created a new environment out of "rubble and cinders, out of still-burning slag heaps."[93] Emphasizing the socially hygienic and popular dimensions of the restored ecological areas, Seifert asserted that the new landscape was more dear to Ruhr inhabitants than to the more affluent automobile drivers on the highway. "When this *Autobahn* was opened," exclaimed Seifert, "the rest stops were occupied by miners' families from Saturday afternoon to Sunday evening, because there the most beautiful grass in the whole Ruhrgebiet could be found! They lay in it and looked down without envy at the drivers, who had to remain on the concrete on the other side."[94] Whether workers preferred lying on the grass to owning a car is questionable, but the statement does show that Siefert and the landscape advocates envisioned the *Reichsautobahn* as the first step in a national environmental reform effort led by a new generation of landscape designers and architects. The hallmark of their approach was a belief that large-scale restoration, rather than mere protection of designated sites, offered an unprecedented opportunity to reconcile environmental concern and modern technological development. Using the *Autobahn* as their model, landscape planners would not only create new, more healthy and balanced landscapes but also heal the wounds of past environmental abuse, transforming industrial wastelands and barren agricultural landscapes into more organic and "healthy" ones.

Seifert also shared biodynamic farmers' critique of capitalist land-use practices, arguing that the liberal era had bequeathed to Germany a "sick" and mechanized agricultural landscape that needed drastic reform to sustain its productivity. Seifert noted with alarm that German harvests had not increased in forty years, despite expansion and intensive use of the land placed under cultivation. In northeastern Germany, he maintained, loam had been washed out of the soil and hilltops had become sandy, while the steady rise in the use of chemical insecticides and fertilizers had merely increased the number of pests and the infertility of the soil. He also warned of a growing water deficit, caused by the diking and draining of wetlands and a lowering of the groundwater table, that threatened to turn the German woodlands into an arid, treeless plain. Deforestation and the loss of stream-

and riverbank vegetation exacerbated this problem, since trees and other plants normally acted as natural sponges to absorb precipitation and keep it from flowing directly into waterways. Seifert also warned that newly developed synthetic insecticides and rodenticides killed both predator and prey, leaving fields vulnerable to cyclical infestation in the absence of natural predators.[95]

To stem this accelerating ecological decline, Seifert supported biodynamic farmers' efforts to rid the German countryside of artificial fertilizers and insecticides. He advocated composting organic waste to enrich the soil and establishing hedgerows as habitats for pest-eating birds and animals. Like Schultze-Naumburg before him, Seifert saw many ecological benefits to hedgerows. These rows of trees and shrubs that grow along streams, paths, and at the edges of fields help to protect agricultural fields against wind and to retain water so as to prevent both desiccation and flooding. They also provide habitats for natural insect and rodent predators, such as hedgehogs and weasels that prey on mice, falcons and buzzards that eat moles, and songbirds that consume insects. For Seifert, long-term economic well-being and ecological sustainability were two sides of the same coin, rather than in conflict with one another.

Seifert also openly criticized the German Labor Front's work service programs and the Reich Food Estate's "inner colonization" program to meliorate agricultural land and straighten waterways to prevent flooding. In his essay "The Steppification of Germany" ("Die Versteppung Deutschlands"), Seifert argued that these measures were decimating Germany's groundwater table, creating conditions akin to those that led to the American Dust Bowl. Seifert warned that shortsighted government programs threatened to create the same problems in authoritarian Germany as in America, where capitalist indifference and "big Jewish finance" had created an environmental catastrophe that displaced thousands of rural farmers. In his view, water engineers, unlike *Autobahn* planners and foresters, had not yet returned to the "ancestral wisdom" that recognized water as a living force rather than a mere physical fluid. These engineers believed that laboratory scrutiny and mathematical formulas would enable them to manipulate water at will. Through dredging, straightening, narrowing, and denuding riverbeds, hydraulic engineers had created a "machine landscape" with unforeseen ecological consequences. Narrowing fluvial movement had not only made flooding more severe but also cut deeper river beds, lowered the groundwater table, and prevented the recharging of underground water supplies that normally occurred through minor floods. The result was a "suicidal steppification" of Germany's soil that threatened to destroy the "life balance of the [entire] Central European space."[96]

Seifert's public presentation and subsequent publication of "The Steppification of Germany" caused a huge stir within the Nazi bureaucracy; Ley, Backe, and Darré accused Seifert of endangering the Battle for Production.[97] Such incidents later provided Seifert with psychological tools for heroically distancing himself from the regime; in his autobiography, Seifert claimed that from 1936 into 1942 there was "scarcely any other people's comrade . . . so embattled, hated, in writing so tossed about, accused of paganism as well as urban sentimentality foreign to farmers, as I [was at that time]."[98] Yet government officials did finally come around to Seifert's way of thinking. For a short time in 1939, Seifert convinced Hitler to put a stop to further land reclamation efforts until their effects could be better studied, and by the early 1940s many touted the benefits of hedgerows for wind protection.[99]

Seifert's apologetic autobiography not surprisingly says little about the connection between his vision of environmental reform and the Nazi regime's broader ideological currents, but even a cursory glance at his essays from the 1940s reveals his affinity for fascist and racist understandings of landscape and national identity. His warnings about the steppification of Germany, the potential transformation of the "rich and diverse German landscape" into something resembling the "desolate Russian or American steppes" spoke of the need for a "third way" between communism and capitalism. Akin to *Deutsche Technik,* this third way would subsume technological development under the needs of the *Volk.* The National Socialist revolution, he asserted, would help to realize the third way, since it "is nothing less than the final confrontation between an exhausted Western and Bolshevist materialism that adores the measurable and the countable, on the one side, and on the other side a worldview based on simple truths such as soul, belief, honor, *Heimat,* and nature."[100]

Seifert's warnings about the potential steppification of Germany caused by land reclamation and other environmental abuses also depended for their rhetorical power on the denigration of "racially inferior" landscapes. Many Germans associated the steppes with the perceived barbarism of Slavic peoples and their "Asiatic" roots; fears of *Versteppung* thus fueled anxieties that Germany itself was being transformed into an inferior Eastern landscape. Seifert proposed that the frontiers of Germanic settlement east of the Elba River had traditionally ended where the trees and bushes gave way to treeless plains: "In the East, approximately where the green of the palace estates stopped and where no tree stood in the villages, that is also the border of the German race; there begin the steppes, there begins Asia. The German must have forest, where he can be happy, not pine forests or acres of rod-thin trees, but rather a [real] forest, rich, diverse, green forest." Whereas the Slav was a "man of the [bare] steppes," Germans needed to leave at least thin strips of trees along waterways, paths, the edges of fields, and terraces in order to feel at home. Seifert believed that the continued existence of the German people, and thereby "Aryan humanity" itself, depended on halting the process of steppification, rejecting the mechanistic past, and restoring the healthy cultural landscape that had once flourished in preindustrial Central Europe.[101]

Such arguments reflected Seifert's conviction that race and ethnicity were as important as topography and ecology in shaping the cultural landscape. In a 1937 *Heimatschutz* article, for example, Seifert criticized Modern architecture's loss of a Germanic "tribal reflection" *(Stammesgesicht)*; the best architecture, he noted, displayed a clear connection between the "tribe and its *Lebensraum.*"[102] In advocating the retention of hedgerows in the countryside, moreover, Seifert claimed that Germanic peoples as far back as the eleventh century had first shaped the hedgerow landscape *(Heckenlandschaft)* that once covered West and Central Europe. Such tribes had possessed ecological "wisdom" versus scientific "knowledge"; these preindustrial peasants had instinctively known how to ensure the land's long-term fertility. Seifert's ideal landscape—filled with a network of hedgerows, blessed with orchards, meadows, and pastures, and dotted with quiet dairy farms and unspoiled small villages—embodied not merely aesthetic harmony but also racial health. It was "a Germanic cultural landscape in its highest perfection," a "monument to the race" that had endured for centuries, replenishing the people's character and ensuring their vitality.[103]

The racist tone of this language of steppification reflected Seifert's growing interest in another branch of biological studies: racial science. Seifert had first encountered hereditary studies at his Bavarian *Gymnasium*. In his autobiography, he describes his encounter with these new "exact sciences" as critical to his future activities. Seifert befriended scientists who had pioneered heredity studies and racial hygiene and considered these disciplines value-neutral branches of biological science. Combined with his aptitude for mathematics, chemistry, and technology, Seifert saw himself "well prepared for the full mechanistic worldview of Darwin and Ernst Häckel."[104] While Seifert later distanced himself from this "mechanistic" worldview in favor of intuitive and holistic understanding, he, like Paul Schultze-Naumburg, never disavowed racial science.

Seifert's bias against using "foreign" species of plants along the *Autobahn* reinforced this racialized view of landscape. Just as the National Socialists inveighed against the "poisonous" effects of "non-Aryan" races within the national community, Seifert argued that "foreign species or races" that tried to blend in with native vegetation would in the long run be "overtaken" by the *bodenständig* plant community.[105] The landscape advocates' insistence on using native plants for environmental damage mitigation was in his eyes merely hastening a "natural" process of ecological succession. The goal was nothing less than "to transform the landscape into our *Lebensraum*," as German ancestors had once instinctively been able to do.[106] In Seifert's eyes, the Age of the Living called for a return to natural principles guiding both human populations and ecological systems; racial fitness and environmental health, like Blood and Soil, were two sides of a social policy that was "close to nature."

## An Insignificant Landscape: Regional Critiques of the *Autobahn*

From a twenty-first-century perspective, Seifert's restoration efforts and environmental concepts seem to anticipate contemporary ecological discourses of holism and interdependency. For this reason, several scholars credit him with having laid the framework for future environmental reform in Germany.[107] Given Seifert's reputation as an environmental reformer, one might expect regional *Heimatschutz* and *Naturschutz* societies to have enthusiastically embraced his new Age of the Living, working actively to assist him and the landscape advocates in nature conservation and environmental planning. Yet the opposite occurred. By the late 1930s, many regional preservationist leaders had become trenchant critics of Seifert and the entire *Reichsautobahn* apparatus. Conflicts quickly emerged between the landscape advocates and regional nature protection commissioners over the location and environmental effects of the highways. Despite the Reich Nature Protection Law's provisions guaranteeing nature protection commissioners a role in overseeing major construction projects, regional and local officials found themselves systematically closed out of *Autobahn* landscape deliberations. Seifert and the other landscape advocates routinely failed to consult or ignored the wishes of regional *Naturschutz* commissioners regarding roadway design, which left these officials unable to halt or mitigate the environmental consequences of the project. In 1942, for example, Karl Oberkirch, the district nature protection officer for the Ruhr Settlement Association, criticized the *Reichsautobahn*'s plans to construct a highway in the Ewald-König Ludwig corridor near Essen, because it would destroy valuable woodlands. In a memorandum to the Settlement Association president, Oberkirch complained that the landscape advocates had violated the RNG by failing to notify him in time about the proposed construction. He was thus left unable to judge whether more environmentally sensitive possibilities existed, "since in the present case, as so often, I was not included [in the planning], but [instead] I am supposed to agree to a *fait accompli*."[108] Oberkirch angrily refused to concern himself any further with a "case that was handled in contradiction to the Reich Nature Protection Law" and said he hoped that the landscape advocates would at least call for the smallest possible "tearing up" of the forest.[109]

The landscape advocates' failure to consult *Naturschutz* authorities was not merely a bureaucratic oversight but was part of a systematic attempt to expand their power over national environmental affairs beyond the *Autobahn* project and into areas traditionally under regional nature protectionists' purview. Guido Erxleben, for example, argued that regional preservationists' criteria for planning were merely "aesthetic" and that they lacked the appropriate experience and competency in landscape design. In association with several other landscape advocates, Erxleben encouraged Nazi officials to establish a separate Reich Office for Landscape Design to consolidate planning tasks under their own bureaucratic direction.[110] In 1942, the Rhenish landscape advocate Reinhold Hoemann issued a series of municipal planning guidelines independently of provincial nature protection commissioners. The guidelines were designed to assist communities in restoring soil and plant life, implementing water-quality and waste-disposal measures, and creating ample green spaces. Hoemann anticipated that cities and towns would use the guidelines for the "great planning projects that will take place after the war on an unprecedented scale."[111] Clearly, the landscape advocates anticipated that their own centralized bureaucracy, not that of the *Naturschützer,* would inherit *Landschaftspflege* authority after the inevitable German triumph.

The landscape advocates' critique of regional preservationists' supposedly moribund aestheticism reflected a growing gap between the two groups of environmental reformers under the Nazi regime, a debate over professional competency fueled by the pervasive infighting among institutional actors in the Third Reich. While Seifert drew on *Heimatschutz* traditions in his early work, his growing faith in ecological restoration had led him to part ways with landscape preservationists' goals during the course of the 1930s. At an October 1933 meeting of Werner Haverbeck's Reich Association for *Volkstum* and *Heimat,* Seifert decried *Heimatschutz* and *Naturschutz* members' "mere lamenting" and the fact that they "only complained about what had been lost in the past and [feared] that it would rapidly also happen to the rest [of Germany's natural areas]. As a natural optimist, I could not reconcile myself to such a gloomy outcome."[112] Rather than mourning the loss of natural monuments, Seifert portrayed landscape restoration as the key to a more hopeful and modern approach to environmental planning. By the end of the 1933 conference, he noted, he had resolved "to throw his life in a different direction" from traditional landscape preservation. Seifert argued that *Naturschutz* and *Heimatschutz* belonged to the former mechanistic age; they were concepts that helped to stem environmental destruction in a culture in which "nearly every person went out to smash nature and *Heimat* to pieces." In the new epoch of environmental concern, in which each person would strive "to create an authentic German landscape and thereby an eternal *Heimat* of the Germans, one scarcely needs to talk of *Heimat-* and *Naturschutz* anymore." Instead it was far more important to preserve the landscape in its "full productive power and beauty," embracing a "living development of our *Lebensraum* with the technology of our time."[113] By dedicating himself to seeking state assistance for restoring landscape diversity, native vegetation, and indigenous habitat along streets, railways, canals, and rivers, Seifert would strive for a "rejuvenation" of Germany's entire environment. In his desire to rescue "degenerate" landscapes through applied ecology, Seifert hoped to use landscape restoration to break with the *Heimatschutz* tradition.

Not surprisingly, Rhenish nature protectionists responded bitterly to the landscape advocates' claims that they lacked experience in environmental planning. Oberkirch noted that the Rhineland and Saxony had the longest traditions of *Landschaftspflege* in Germany, and that Rhenish regional nature protection authorities had taken part in hundreds of planning decisions concerning the area's "constantly changing *Kulturlandschaft*" since the mid-1920s.[114] The extensive green spaces in the Ruhr coal-mining region, only one of the many positive environmental achievements of the Weimar Republic, were the result of such planning. Nature protectionists' criteria for planning, Oberkirch continued, extended far beyond aesthetic values, encompassing the full range of "scientific, forest-biological, sociological, forest-economical, soil-scientific, geographic, climatological, water-economic, *Heimat*-oriented, landscape-aesthetic, and literary" factors.[115] Oberkirch accused the landscape advocates of lacking detailed knowledge of local *Heimat* vegetation, a necessary prerequisite for proper landscape design at the regional level.

Oberkirch's frustration with the landscape advocates signaled nature preservationists' growing alienation from Seifert and from the regime's technocratic spatial planning apparatus as a whole. He recognized that it was a struggle for power that guided landscape advocates' treatment of regional preservationists, rather than mere questions of professional competency or scientific knowledge: "In this jointly unjust and mistaken portrayal of *Naturschutz*, its tasks and effectiveness, I now see an intentionally planned defamation of *Naturschutz* in order to replace it with another organization . . . [even though] . . . its work has been in effect only since 1935, that is, for perhaps three years."[116] Another preservationist questioned Seifert's neutrality in assessing environmental impacts, accusing him of operating according to the motto, "whomsoever's bread I eat, that's whose song I sing."[117] Nazism's fluid power structure had encouraged the landscape advocates to challenge regional preservationists' institutional authority over provincial environmental affairs. With their knowledge of plant ecology and support from the powerful Fritz Todt, the landscape advocates represented themselves as modern designers who were better equipped than nature protectionists to restore and sustain Germany's living space in the long term.[118]

The differences between the landscape advocates' restorationist approach and Rhenish *Heimat* groups' preservationist approach to *Landschaftspflege* led to numerous conflicts, but none was more acrimonious than the debates that surfaced over the fate of the Rhineland's most cherished natural monument, the Siebengebirge. The controversy between the two groups erupted in 1939 over the appropriate location for a bridge that was to connect the highways running along the right and left banks of the Rhine River near Bonn, as well as an additional stretch of road linking the Rhineland highway to the Cologne-Frankfurt *Autobahn* that lay further to the east.[119] The Rhineland's provincial nature protection officials and private organizations, as well as Hans Klose, the head of the Reich Nature Protection Office, favored erecting the bridge north of Bonn, where it would connect to the existing Cologne-Bonn *Autobahn* and avoid the Siebengebirge region altogether.[120] Seifert, however, favored a southern location for the bridge, immediately at the foot of the Siebengebirge, with the proposed eastward link to the Cologne-Frankfurt *Autobahn* running directly through the protection area itself.[121]

Seifert was well informed about Rhinelanders' concerns about aesthetic damage and increased auto traffic in the Siebengebirge, but he chose to dismiss them. His arguments in favor of the southern option for the *Autobahn* spoke of "strategic [military] necessity," but his primary focus was on the aesthetic concerns of automobile drivers. Seifert lamented that the northern route passed through an "insignificant" landscape of agricultural land and meadows, whereas the southern route would offer drivers spectacular views of the Rhine silhouetted by the seven peaks of the Siebengebirge.[122] Providing such vistas, however, would require massive technical measures that were wholly unnecessary in the northern route, including concrete pylons to support the roadway as it wound along steep cliffsides and through precarious mountain ravines. In a clear rejection of earlier discourses describing the Siebengebirge as a hallowed natural monument, Seifert argued that the roadway and bridge he proposed would enhance rather than degrade the region's environmental beauty.

Seifert's justification for the southern route rested not only on strategic and aesthetic concerns, but also on a systematic attempt to belittle the area's natural worth. Here the divergence between climax ecological models and cultural landscape ideals was manifest. Seifert wrote: "Against this [southern] route some have objected that it would cut across a nature protection region. Here it should be emphasized that the case of the Siebengebirge does not concern a nature protection region in the usual sense of the word, where a primordial landscape [*Urlandschaft*] is meant, but rather a recreational area that is in every respect a man-made landscape [*Kulturlandschaft*], and in which even the essence of the forests has been falsified by the introduction of conifers foreign to the landscape."[123] Seifert's claim that the Siebengebirge was not natural and therefore did not deserve protected status rested on his belief that it lacked stands of native hardwood vegetation. According to this model, the region's climax community should have consisted primarily of mixed hardwood species, such as oaks, birches, and lindens, rather than fast-growing pines and spruces. Rejecting regional preservationists' pleas to bypass the region, Seifert asserted that in a landscape so "falsified" by human activity a modern highway would not be a "foreign body," especially when blended into the landscape by a "master hand."[124]

Seifert believed that the landscape advocates could quickly remedy environmental damage through landscape restoration techniques. "Since the mountain slopes are covered only with low-quality forests," he noted, "it will not be difficult with good terrain formation and the proper treatment of topsoil to reforest the new embankments, which will cover them over in ten to fifteen years with scrub forest."[125] In the case of the Siebengebirge, in other words, Seifert employed scientific and "ecological" language to *deny* the need for nature protection. This discourse denigrated existing cultural landscapes, which Seifert viewed as degenerate legacies of liberal mismanagement, in favor of an abstract model of climax vegetation that had not existed in the Rhineland, indeed in all of Europe, for millennia.

Rhineland preservationists were outraged by Seifert's environmental assessment of the area. VVS leader Eduard von Gartzen complained that Seifert and the landscape advocates were willing to dismiss more than one hundred years of state and private efforts to protect and restore the Siebengebirge "with a wave of the hand."[126] Gartzen decried the potential setback to the "pathbreaking and exemplary activities of the Siebengebirge organization for *Naturschutz* in our *Heimat* and for future efforts of the same type not only in Germany, but in all of Europe." Herbert Iven, the Rhineland's provincial nature protection officer, also disparaged Seifert's report as "superficial and inaccurate." Iven argued that all sides in the province had agreed that the northern route was best because it preserved the Rhine landscape. "Of all times, now, in a period of high standing for the *Heimatschutz* movement," he lamented, "we learn the grotesque fact that the most precious section of the Rhineland should be divided and cut up, that the river at its most sensitive point should be sealed off, just to create a few more dynamic kilometers for the auto driver."[127] Clearly, Iven believed that Seifert's report was a betrayal of the regime's environmental goals. As one *Heimatschutz* member noted cynically, "as a result of landscape design, Seifert does not see the landscape itself any more."[128]

Rhenish preservationists' response to Seifert's report signaled a resurgence of an older, local view of landscape in which *Heimat* memory and identity were as important as ecological values in setting preservationist priorities. Having experienced the regime's bureaucratic assault on the German *Lebensraum,* regional *Naturschützer* tried to reclaim the moral geography of *Heimat* on their own terms, emphasizing the undeveloped cultural landscape as the font of German identity. In a challenge to Seifert's claim that only remnants of climax vegetation deserved protected status, Gartzen noted that the RNG's Section 5 protected a variety of scenic landscape sites and that "the Siebengebirge's beauties have been praised so often and for so long in both words and pictures that there is nothing more here to be said."[129] Gartzen also disputed Seifert's description of the Siebengebirge as a "falsified" landscape. Since the late nineteenth century, the VVS had been replacing conifers with hardwoods on the society's managed lands, so that 75 percent of the replanted tree stands consisted of hardwoods. Rather than fixing objective criteria for defining the Siebengebirge's status, Seifert's report unleashed a new phase of competing national and regional interpretations of *Heimat* and nature.

Provincial Nature Protection Commissioner Iven also responded to Seifert's challenge. In defending the Siebengebirge as a site worthy of protection, Iven praised the area's ecological and geological significance, including unique volcanic remnants from its Devonian past as well as several rare species of falcons, butterflies, and orchids. Yet Iven's understanding of the Siebengebirge's importance extended beyond natural history to include the site's significance as the province's cultural heartland. "The entire Romanticism of the Rhine," he wrote to Klose, "achieves its most ample expression in the Siebengebirge. The ring of folk tales and legends that have emerged here are enormous in number and colorful."[130] Iven cited the Drachenfels as the inspiration for countless popular poems and legends, as well the key symbol of Napoleon's expulsion from the Rhineland and the birth of German nationalism. In his letter he expressed the multifaceted view of *Naturschutz* and landscape preservation that had characterized regional *Heimatpflege* since the Wilhelmine era. Less concerned about protecting wilderness areas or climax vegetation, which were practically nonexistent in Germany, especially in the highly urbanized Rhineland, Rhenish preservationists sought instead to preserve landscape sites based on a combination of aesthetic, scientific, cultural, and recreational criteria. Iven asserted that "the Siebengebirge counts in the fullest sense of the word as a nature protection region and as a homeland overflowing with beauty, whose territory it is our most holy duty to protect undiminished. The successful battle over this jewel of the Rhine has been going on for more than 100 years and our nature protection offices and *Heimat* organizations are in unison with [provincial] authorities; they will not give up even one foot of what has already been achieved."[131] The Siebengebirge thus remained for Rhinelanders a vessel of collective memory and a site of emotional identification with the Rhineland *Heimat,* a symbol of the Rhineland's distinctive regional character and its important role within the German Empire as a whole.

Iven's references to "cutting up" the Rhine for the pleasure of drivers also reflected preservationists' growing fear that automobile traffic, a by-product of the regime's expansion of tourism and leisure opportunities, threatened to denude Germany's natural and scenic areas.[132] The Rhineland had already witnessed a wave of construction to accommodate the Labor Front's Strength through Joy (Kraft durch Freude, or KdF) excursions and weekend automobile trips.[133] In 1936, the regime constructed a new hotel on the summit of the Drachenfels for visitors in the Siebengebirge, which regional newspapers touted as a "beautiful, functional and more spacious building" on top of the "most visited mountain in Europe."[134] The *Reichsautobahn* bridge seemed an unnecessary step toward further landscape exploitation. Iven noted that the Rhine's banks were already filled with cars from the province's urban areas; additional visitors would only overtax the area's roads, paths, and parking facilities. Gartzen seconded this view. "The further opening up of the small nature protection region to mass tourism through the planned connection between the right- and left-bank *Autobahnen*," he noted, "would mean the destruction of the last great lungs for Rhenish workers' recreation."[135]

Rhenish nature preservationists feared not only automobile tourism's physical threat to their environment, but also the symbolic menace it posed to the spiritual meanings they attached to the experience of nature. Of foremost concern was tourism's commercialization of natural sites. In stern tones reminiscent of the late Weimar era, Oberkirch warned his fellow preservationists about a new wave of "the Bismarck tower disease," by which he meant a rash of observation towers and the related kiosks, billboards, pubs, and souvenir shops that sold nature to the masses.[136] The Westphalian nature protection commissioner Wilhelm Lienenkämper likewise warned that "whoever views *Volkstum* and *Heimat* only as attractions, with the solitary goal of tourist speculation, prostitutes their beauties."[137] By putting a price on nature, such practices transformed natural monuments from sites of patriotic pilgrimage into cheap commodities unworthy of veneration. One newspaper article criticized developers' plans to build a series of weekend houses in a valley adjacent to the Siebengebirge. The owners of such cottages, the article asserted, mistakenly "believe they can quiet their yearning for nature by purchasing a weekend house."[138] While the *Reichsautobahn* brought Germany's natural areas unprecedented popularity and brought tourist money into surrounding villages and towns, preservationists detected an acceleration of tendencies reminiscent of the despised Weimar Republic: the devaluation of the outdoors from a cherished object of nationalist devotion to a banal souvenir sold in gift shops.

Even though the Siebengebirge bridge was never built, owing to the accelerating war efforts of 1940 and 1941, the battle over the Siebengebirge exemplifies the widening ideological gap that separated preservationists from landscape advocates by 1939.[139] The landscape advocates largely ignored Rhenish and other regional *Heimat* advocates' traditional goal of preserving their distinctive *Kulturlandschaft*, choosing instead to transform artificial "cultural" landscapes into more "natural" ones. At stake here was not "modern" ecological restoration versus outdated *Heimat* Romanticism; rather, the contest over what constituted a natural landscape reflected institutional struggles between regional *Naturschutz* officials and the landscape advocates over a place in the Nazi cultural apparatus.

In the scramble for competency and power that characterized the Nazis' polycratic regime as a whole, the landscape advocates were gaining ground on the *Naturschützer*. In 1944, for example, Seifert was named the Reich landscape advocate for water and energy, which expanded his authority over natural resource conservation. *Autobahn* expansion and ecological restoration meshed nicely with the regime's long-term strategy for reconstituting both the physical and the symbolic meanings of landscape. In bypassing regional concerns, the Seifert group advanced the cause of *Gleichschaltung* by overcoming regional fragmentation through centralized power. Regional *Naturschutz* was indeed marginal in a road system designed to link the far-flung corners of the German Empire into an organic whole. The landscape advocates' belief that they could recreate natural landscapes through applied science also had obvious advantages for a regime engaged in a massive program of infrastructural development and modernization. Seifert's comment that a "master hand" could blend the *Autobahn* into the Siebengebirge environment reflected this faith that centralized planning and knowledge of plant sociology, rather than sensitivity to regional concerns, would remedy any damage caused by road construction. Rather than confronting the regime with hard choices about avoiding conservation areas or even with the need to abandon certain public works projects altogether, the landscape advocates promised instead to heal the wounds caused by National Socialist modernization and militarization.

The landscape advocates' desire to heal the environment provides another perspective on their relative success as environmental planners vis-à-vis regional preservationists. Nazi officials favored landscape restoration over traditional preservation because it dovetailed with the regime's racialist understanding of landscape and advanced its goal of overcoming the "biological decline" of the Weimar era. As the battle over the Siebengebirge and the uneven *Gleichschaltung* of *Naturschutz* and *Heimatschutz* in the early years of the regime had demonstrated, regional preservationists consistently equivocated on this point. When asked to embrace fully the regime's racialized view of landscape, nature protection commissioners such as Iven and Oberkirch preferred to see race as one factor among many—historical, cultural, geographical, ecological, and religious—that gave the cultural landscape its environmental and symbolic meaning.

The landscape advocates, in contrast, viewed themselves as technicians of the sick landscape, who, like the Third Reich's racial scientists, public health experts, and medical doctors, promised to heal the nation's biological foundations. They believed that the German *Lebensraum,* like the German *Volk,* needed to be brought more closely in line with natural laws to sustain itself over time. Just as Nazi experts designated certain ethnic or social groups as inferior or hereditarily ill, in need of purification, or, if necessary, elimination, so did Seifert and the landscape advocates view certain cultural landscapes as unnatural and degenerate, in need of both aesthetic reconfiguration and biological revitalization. The racial nation required both a "healthy" and a beautiful landscape, one that would link modern Germans to their biological origins in nature. In the case of the Siebengebirge, Seifert's claim that "landscape-foreign" conifers had diluted the region's purity worked rhetorically to render this landscape as "degenerate," in need of the landscape advocates' "master hand" and biological knowledge. Depicting conifers as "foreign bodies" in the landscape reflected a long tradition of viewing hardwoods, especially oaks, as symbols of an authentic Germanic landscape.[140] Regional landscape preservation thus fell victim to the Nazi era's polycratic power struggles, as landscape advocates were far more effective in tying landscape design and environmental planning to racial myth, a move that would have eventually erased provincial identity within a new empire of Blood and Soil.

Seifert's racialist perspective also found resonance in wartime landscape planning that sought to transform occupied Poland into a *Lebensraum* fit for Aryan settlement. When Germany invaded Poland in 1939, Seifert proposed that hedgerows would help to "Germanify" the area, transforming it into a *Lebensraum* suitable for Aryan settlers and a *Heimat* that would bind the new farmers to the soil. "Every village must be embedded in a grove of fruit trees and lindens," Seifert wrote. "Every stream, every river, and every man-made ditch" had to have meadows, ash trees, and poplars along its banks. Such measures would not only beautify the area but also gradually make the climate moister and offer shelter for predators that would

keep in check harmful insects and vermin that might otherwise destroy newly planted crops. Within fifty years, he asserted, the landscape would achieve outward beauty, health, and productivity, external signs of an "inner biological, technical and agricultural perfection
. . . Who will doubt that this is the greatest glory that our generation
can acquire?"[141]

Seifert's proposal to use landscape restoration to prepare the
East for Aryan settlement echoed sentiments among rival landscape
architects within Heinrich Himmler's Reich Commission for the
Strengthening of the German Race (Reichskommissariat für die
Festigung deutschen Volkstums, or RKFDV), a group charged with
the resettlement of ethnic Germans in conquered territories of Poland.[142] Led by the noted landscape architect Konrad Meyer, RKFDV
designers used the supposed "depravity" of the Polish plains to legitimate German conquest and the introduction of superior "Aryan"
land management techniques.[143] As one landscape architect remarked
in 1941,

> The landscape is always a form, an expression and a characteristic of the
> people living within it. It can be the gentle countenance of its soul and
> spirit, just as it can be the grimace of its soullessness or of a human and
> spiritual depravity. In any case, it is the distinctive mark of that which a
> race feels, thinks, creates, and does . . . Therefore, the Germans' land-
> scapes differ in all ways from those of the Poles and the Russians—just
> as do the peoples themselves. The murders and cruelties of the Eastern
> races are engraved, razor-sharp, into the grimaces of their native land-
> scapes.[144]

This view of "grimaces" on the physiognomy of Eastern landscapes
justified the Nazi belief that the agrarian and economically disadvan-
taged landscapes of the annexed areas were signs of their inhabitants' racial inferiority. This view conveniently left out Prussia's role in
shaping the Silesian countryside and industrial manufacturing areas.
Seifert himself described Poles and Russians as racial groups incapable of proper land-use management and referred to the degraded state
of Polish towns as justification for the invasion and transformation
of those areas. In a similar vein, RKFDV planners argued that it was
not enough "to settle the German race in [the occupied East] . . . and
to remove foreign races. These landscape spaces must receive comprehensive planning appropriate to our character, so that the Germanic

peoples feel at home and are ready to become settled and to defend their new *Heimat*."[145] In this new creation of a Germanic peasantry in the East, noted Seifert, "the difference between the [so-called] achievements of democracy and the work of National Socialism will be shown."[146]

Nazi theoreticians argued that Aryans' closeness to nature made them uniquely suited to achieving this organic harmony between modern technology and landscape integrity. The landscape architect Heinrich Wiepking-Jürgensmann described Germans' "love for plants and the landscape" and their affinity for a "harmonic landscape" as a result of "biological laws innate in our being."[147] Racial purification and efforts to build racial consciousness would awaken these instinctual urges among Germans, improving the overall environment and ensuring social stability. As one 1937 Cologne newspaper article remarked, "The ruination [of nature] would be impossible" if a sense of responsibility toward the landscape "lived in everyone's blood." In the ideal future proposed by National Socialism, noted the article, "the race would not allow that even one tree be unnecessarily and thoughtlessly sacrificed during land cultivation, land reclamation, or street building."[148] Racial ideology enabled Nazi planners to reconcile the theoretical tensions between industrial growth and environmental protection by positing a uniquely "Aryan" ability to sustain the land's appearance and overall productivity.

Nazi planners viewed the *Autobahn* project as the most important manifestation of this racial inheritance. By embedding the roadways in the landscape, the landscape advocates not only reconciled Romantic nature appreciation and Enlightenment technology but also demonstrated Aryans' "instincts" as caretakers of their living space. On the one hand, Todt saw the *Autobahnen* as symbols of Aryan achievement and the new racial empire, a functional and aesthetic masterpiece. "Roads have been the expression of a race's culture and living standards," he noted. "Only the best roads have lasting value, and only such roads deserve to be seen as the historical and cultural creations of a great empire."[149] On the other hand, Seifert believed that the application of ecological models would enable landscape architects to restore the primordial *Lebensraum* of Germany, the unique habitat in which the race was formed and from which it drew its strength. Replanting natural ecological communities, wielding German technical know-how, would help to rejuvenate the Germanic landscape, and sustain the racial body within its natural environment.

The result of landscape advocates' efforts would be a vast garden supporting a technologically advanced yet close-to-nature population. This new *Lebensraum* would not only root the population biologically to its territory but also ensure its emotional loyalty, economic performance, and, most important, healthy reproduction. Reinhold Hoemann remarked that the landscape advocate's task was to ensure that the new "paths" that the Nazi regime "carved" into the cultural landscape remained "German" and "native." Modern landscapes should still carry the "unique imprint of their local homeland, so that the built environment, the organic world, and the homeland-loyal person who belongs there create an organism of peaceful, quiet harmony."[150] Children should be encouraged to plant trees, Hoemann added, so that plants and humans could grow together, bound to the homeland as one living community.[151] Human races, like the plant species found in nature, flourished in particular biotopes.

The social and political dimensions of Hoemann's program conformed to Nazism's evolving vision of the *Volksgemeinschaft* as a biological community "bound to nature" and "loyal to *Heimat.*" Hoemann argued that the purpose of *Landschaftspflege* was to "re-awaken in the people of today the same deep feelings of homeland loyalty and responsibility that already influenced our forebears, and which should also accompany us and our followers as an inalienable good."[152] Proper landscape planning, in other words, would sustain Blood and Soil across time and space. The landscape advocates' efforts to restore the German *Lebensraum* using applied plant ecology complemented the Nazis' attempts to improve the nation's biological fitness through racial hygiene and eugenics. Just as Nazi racial policies promised to restore and perpetuate Germany's "natural" Aryan stock, so did the landscape advocates pledge to re-create and maintain Germany's "primordial" habitat, the "source of power for the people."

The increasing intensity of the landscape advocates' racist claim to environmental authority articulated their own frustration as they encountered major obstacles amid the shifting terrain of Nazi power. The landscape advocates' professional status within the road-building hierarchy remained uncertain, and there was constant pressure to lower their wages. Due to a shortage of skilled engineers during the Third Reich, Todt had recruited many of his road builders from the German railway system; these technicians, trained to find the most cost effective and efficient pathway from point *A* to point *B*, had little sympathy for the landscape advocate's vision of curving, landscape-friendly roadways. The road engineers often bypassed landscape advocates in the decision-making chain regarding roadway environmental mitigation, in much the same way that the landscape advocates ignored local *Naturschützer*. In many cases, *Reichsautobahn* engineers contacted the landscape advocate responsible for a certain region only after plans were laid and the machines had been sent out to begin building the roadways.[153]

General Inspector Todt himself remained an uncertain ally. While he embraced the principles of *Deutsche Technik*, Todt remained skeptical about Seifert's efforts to apply plant sociology to roadway landscaping. His concept of landscape aesthetics, moreover, emphasized the visual consumption of nature and the dynamic experience of the driver far more than ecological restoration. Because of skyrocketing costs of the *Autobahn*, Todt continually admonished the landscape advocates to limit their use of roadside plantings; one historian has estimated that the regime spent only 0.09 percent of its overall costs for the *Autobahn* on landscape concerns.[154]

The Nazi regime's militarization of nature further undercut Seifert's aims. To meet the harvesting targets of Göring's Four-Year Plan, landscape designers on the *Autobahn* were often forced to plant fast-growing conifer farms behind a façade of mixed hardwood trees. With the outbreak of war in 1939, construction on the *Autobahn* came to a virtual standstill as Todt's engineers focused on erecting defensive installations rather than vulnerable roadways. Roadside plantings were often simply abandoned and restoration sites were left unfinished. After the war, street planners distanced themselves from the *Autobahn*'s naturalistic landscape design features owing to their association with the Nazi regime, favoring instead the functional geometry of Germany's post-1945 interstate systems.[155] Even Seifert's promise to heal the environment and bolster racial fitness could not, in the end, overcome the cold-hearted economic calculus used to mobilize the country for war. As the German literary historian Colin Riordan has noted in a survey of German Green ideas, environmental advocates "could not resolve the irreconcilable contradictions which the power imperatives of Hitler's policies demanded. *Blut und Boden* required not only an intimate bond with nature, but also more *Lebensraum* within which to practice that bond. The land could only be required by war, and wars could only be fought with the support of capitalist financiers and renewed heavy industrial output."[156]

Preservationists sustained their vision of the Third Reich as a golden age of nature protection in the early years of the regime through the belief that benevolent state power had finally overcome liberalism's profligate environmental destruction. Rhenish preservationists' early enthusiasm for the regime reflected a perceived synergy between their traditional conservative views and the goals of the new regime, a shared desire to return Germany to values rooted in *Heimat* and landscape. The affirmation of these elite organizations, in turn, gave the Third Reich added legitimacy at the local and regional levels. Yet regional preservationists had misread the NSDAP's rapid passage of the RNG and its rhetoric of *Heimat, Volk*, and nature as confirmation of traditional landscape values. Far from signaling the regime's abiding commitment to *Naturschutz*, the regime's highly publicized landscape protection measures, particularly the RNG, were weak and ineffective. The regime's support for massive land reclamation and building projects, particularly the *Autobahn* system led to questionable environmental consequences and did not take into account the concerns of regional preservation groups.

The public works projects and military buildup that fueled Germany's economic recovery transformed the Nazi dictatorship into a far more destructive and insurmountable menace to environmental protection than the private industrialists or materialist "masses" of the Wilhelmine and Weimar eras. Local *Naturschutz* concerns were of marginal importance to a regime committed to the relentless militarization of space, resources, and populations in preparation for war and territorial expansion. In this context, landscape preservationists feebly clung to the RNG's regional planning provisions to legitimate their role as advisers on construction and reclamation projects while Germany's environmental destruction continued apace. Yet preservationists soon found even this authority challenged as new environmental experts, particularly the landscape advocates of the *Au-*

*tobahn* project, formulated a new discourse of ecological restoration that rendered traditional landscape preservation obsolete in the eyes of the regime.

The debates between Rhenish preservationists and the *Autobahn* planners also call into question those interpretations that portray Nazi-era environmental policy in terms of reactionary modernism or, alternatively, as a precursor to modern Green movements. Both concepts assume that Nazi environmental policy sought merely to reconcile the progressive advance of technology with Romantic values. The reactionary modernism paradigm postulates that the objects of reconciliation were technology and the mystical *Volk,* while the concept of the Green Nazis claims the regime tried to mesh modern development with ecological holism. Reactionary modernism opened up important questions about the peculiar blend of Nazi modernism and homage to the countryside, yet this nostalgia was hardly antimodern. Instead, the *Autobahn*'s promise of personal mobility and carefree leisure used the visual consumption of landscape to break down class barriers and integrate the nation. Those who believe that the *Autobahn* planners' use of climax environmental models provided a Green alternative to industrial exploitation, on the other hand, have rarely investigated regional *Naturschutz* and *Heimatschutz* responses to the project. As the debates over *Autobahn* planning in the Siebengebirge demonstrate, many planners who embraced ecological criteria were hardly nostalgic about the traditional countryside. Instead, planners wielded ecological discourse to legitimate a transformation rather than a preservation of cultural landscapes in order to justify the technological development and the restoration of such spaces to a more "natural" state. Spatial planning and ecological restoration were also integral to the regime's racist and imperialist goals; measures designed to protect German Soil cannot be divorced from the regime's desire to restore Aryan Blood. Like other cultural discourses, environmental ideas are deeply embedded in their political and cultural contexts. They are never neutral guidelines for environmental reform.

Though the landscape advocates and other environmental planners of the Third Reich never realized their environmental goals, owing to the war and Germany's defeat, their synthesis of environmental planning and racial hygiene did create a new sense of time and space that went far beyond nineteenth-century dichotomies of progress and tradition. This synthesis suggests another limitation to characterizing the Third Reich's environmental planning as reactionary modern. In place of what Walter Benjamin deemed modernity's "homogeneous, empty time," the Nazis used organic metaphors of *Ewigkeit*, or eternity, to recapture what Benjamin termed "Messianic" time, a simultaneity of past and future in an instantaneous present.[157] The Nazis grounded their belief in racial character on supposedly objective laws of the natural world; Germans past, present, and future were thus eternally connected by blood. Though Germany's primordial landscape was gone forever, ecological restoration and spatial planning held out the promise that the natural balance in the contemporary cultural landscape could be restored. By preventing landscape deterioration through careful planning and restoration, the German nation would endure forever; both *Volk* and *Landschaft,* Blood and Soil, would renew themselves in a never-ending cycle of birth, growth, death, and rebirth. As the poet Karl Broeger remarked: "Nothing can take away our love and faith in our land. We are sent to preserve and shape it. Should we die, it is the duty of our heirs to preserve and shape it. Germany will not die."[158] Blood and Soil interacted symbiotically to create a closed organic cycle that would replace the relentless linearity of nineteenth-century progress. By returning to their primordial *Lebensraum,* the *Volk* would perpetuate the thousand-year Reich and live, perhaps, forever.

# Conclusion

In July 1946, the British author Stephen Spender embarked on a tour of occupied Germany that began in the Rhineland. He wrote down his impressions in what he termed a "Travel Book of a conventional kind," but the scene he encountered was anything but ordinary. Whereas the Rhine Province's easy access to Western Europe once invited British elites to explore the middle Rhine Gorge on their continental Grand Tour, between 1940 and 1945 its location had left the region vulnerable to massive Allied bombing attacks. One scholar has estimated that 10,000 to 23,000 tons of bombs were dropped on the city of Cologne, leaving approximately 24.1 million square meters of rubble in their wake.[1] Other Rhenish urban areas suffered even worse damage: in the Eifel, the city of Jülich was 97 percent destroyed in World War II, while nearly 99 percent of nearby Düren was obliterated. The loss of civilian lives was also catastrophic. In Essen, the population dropped from 680,000 in 1939 to about 300,000 in 1945; in Cologne, only about 20,000 inhabitants remained in the former metropolis of 770,000. To depict this devastation, Spender's account subverted the time-honored conventions of Rhine Romanticism that once glorified the area's picturesque cities and sublime beauty. Cologne, the Rhineland's hub and site of a magnificent cathedral, had become a "putrescent corpse city" where the gouges left by war would never heal. "The ruin of the city is reflected in the internal ruin of its inhabitants," Spender wrote, "who, instead of being lives that can form a scar over the city's wounds, are parasites sucking at a dead car-cass, digging among the ruins for hidden food, doing business at their black market near the cathedral—the commerce of destruction in-stead of production." The Rhine had a "frightening grandeur" where "girders of [its] bridges plunged diagonally into the black waters . . . frothing into swirling white around them."[2]

The war had also transformed the area around Bonn into a night-marish and forbidding landscape. Spender found shards of Nazi slo-gans, such as "Victory or Siberia" and "The Day of Revenge Will Come," among the ruins of the once bucolic university town, the seat of Rhenish learning and a center of German humanism. In place of docks ferrying visitors into the Rhine Gorge, he noted that "beer gar-dens, hotels and great houses were smashed to pieces. In a space amongst the ruins which formed a protected nest, there was a burnt-out German tank. Scattered all around, its ammunition lay on the ground—shells the shape of Rhine-wine bottles, still partly enclosed in their careful packings of straw and fibre." It seemed that the day of revenge had arrived, its wrath symbolized by swarms of insects feed-ing on and breeding within the stinking piles of garbage among the city's ruins. Returning from a sunset stroll along the Rhine, Spender encountered flies that "lay like a thick bank of London pea soup fog on either side of the river. They swarmed into my eyes, nostrils and hair, dissolving into a thick green splodge of slime when I tried to brush them off."[3] Instead of offering comfort and orientation among the postwar chaos, nature appeared as a malevolent force exacerbat-ing Germans' suffering for the sins of the Nazi regime.

Spender's inversion of Rhine Romanticism and its glorification of landscape was a prelude to a broader repudiation of German Roman-tic nationalism that occurred after World War II. Both European and American historians presented Germany as the Other, in contrast to Western democracy and modernization; Germans had rejected En-lightenment liberalism in favor of a Romantic irrationalism that had culminated in the Third Reich. One might expect that *Heimat* would be discredited in this new ideological climate. The historian Arne Andersen, for example, has argued that discourses of *Heimat* and na-ture became suspect in the postwar era, "so completely defamed," he writes, "that it was scarcely possible to refer to them in political discussion."[4] Yet amid the devastation in Spender's account, we also find traces of a *Heimat* sentiment and regionalist loyalty that enabled landscape preservation and other forms of bourgeois cultural engagement to reestablish themselves quickly in the postwar years. Although a complete investigation of postwar *Naturschutz* and *Heimatschutz* revival lies beyond the scope of this study, its roots were already visible in 1946. Photographs of Hitler had disappeared from Rhinelanders' homes, but popular *Heimat* imagery—much of it produced and purchased during the Third Reich itself—anchored domestic life before and after the war. Spender argued that German sentimentality had increased in tandem with the country's increasing brutality. "Other observers bear me out when I say that I have never seen even in Germany so many sentimental pictures and books and poems as are to be seen to-day in German houses requisitioned by the British and left by their owners," Spender writes. "So many pictures of babies and butterflies and flowers, so many gleaming mountain peaks and sunsets, so many mothers and peasants and cottages and hearthsides, so many tears about home, so much commonplace about father, mother, God and beauty."[5] These banal images of nature and home reveal a substrate of *Heimat* sentiment that had not vanished with the Nazi defeat. Having once been pinned, with Germans' hopes, on the National Socialist regime, these sentiments lay waiting for political change and new leadership that would again give them purpose and meaning.

Alongside the province's material rebuilding, Rhenish cultural leaders were already at work reconstructing the fragments of Rhenish feeling into a revitalized regional identity. Fear and rejection of Nazism's rabid nationalism in no way threatened Rhenish elites' faith in a healthy and untainted *regionalist* vision of *Heimat* to provide solace and guidance during reconstruction. Rhenish intellectuals told Spender that Nazism had never completely colonized Rhinelanders' regionalist and Catholic loyalties. In an attempt to win British favor, one group emphasized that Rhinelanders shared British citizens' hatred of Prussia and its militarist capital, Berlin. Many believed that Germans and the British should be united against a far greater enemy than fascist Germany—the Soviet Union—which threatened to occupy the whole of Europe. The former Cologne mayor Konrad Adenauer, moreover, claimed that Germany's spiritual reawakening was far more important than its material reconstruction. While the Nazis had "laid German culture just as flat as the ruins of the Rhineland and the Ruhr," Adenauer said, he believed that there was a hunger and thirst for spiritual values in Germany that would lead the country's reintegration into Europe's shared Christian culture.[6] By 1946, Rhenish leaders had begun fashioning the contours of a reinvigorated *Heimat* identity—regionalist and European, Christian and anticommunist—that provided an alternative to national memories tainted by the Nazi experience.[7]

Rhenish landscape preservationists also reconfigured the environmental dimensions of *Heimat* after 1945 in response to dire warnings about ecological destruction, the political democratization of West Germany, and the attempt to articulate a transnational, European identity in the wake of World War II. The nature protection bureaucracy established during the Nazi era remained intact under Hans Klose's leadership in the immediate postwar years; the 1935 Reich Nature Protection Law, in fact, stayed in force until 1958. *Naturschutz* organizations of the 1950s and 1960s doubled the number of nature reserves that had existed in 1945 and drew attention to the dark side of the "economic miracle" by vigorously condemning plans for new hydroelectric dams, *Autobahn* extensions, and river canalization. Yet Germans faced new, intractable environmental problems after 1945, such as atomic fallout and pesticide pollution, that challenged the aims and effectiveness of traditional landscape preservation. These new environmental toxins—distant in origin and potentially catastrophic in their effects—demanded novel forms of scientific investigation, environmental awareness, regulatory oversight, and popular participation that went beyond mere visual enhancement, natural monument protection, or green-space planning. While many nature protectionists initially welcomed atomic energy as a way to avoid the need for additional hydroelectric power stations, for example, a new generation of apocalyptic environmental writers and activists, such as Bodo Manstein, Günther Schwab, Reinhard Demoll, and Erich Hornsmann, drew the public's attention to the long-term ecological and public health effects of radioactive fallout, hydraulic engineering, resource depletion, and skyrocketing global population growth. A year after its U.S. debut in 1962, Rachel Carson's book *Silent Spring* was translated into German and quickly became a best-seller that heightened fears about the insidious long-term effects of DDT and other pesticides. Freed from the censorship of the Nazi era, the West German media, including *Der Spiegel*, *Die Zeit,* even the sensationalist *Bildzeitung,* galvanized public awareness about air, water, and noise pollution. By the mid-1950s, the formation of citizen initiatives that used mass demonstrations, lawsuits, and press conferences to halt road building, nuclear proliferation, clear-cutting, and air pollution signaled a growing turn toward grassroots environmental activism. This citizen involvement nurtured the relationship between environmentalism and the democratic public sphere in West German society; a spate of new laws regulating air pollution, land use, and water contamination between 1957 and 1968 reflected the growing strength of popular environmentalism in the postwar decades.[8]

In the Rhineland, these new ecological and political concerns came together in the efforts to clean up the Rhine River in the 1950s and 1960s. The Rhine had earned the name "Sewer of Europe" because of the many organic wastes and toxins that spewed forth from the chemical, pharmaceutical, and mining industries along its banks.[9] The Alliance for the Protection of German Waters, one of the many new environmental organizations that emerged after 1945, noted that more than 100 human-induced fish kills had occurred along the Rhine and its tributaries between 1940 and 1952.[10] In one incident, regional newspapers described in lurid detail the swollen cadavers of salmon, whitefish, and barbell that washed up along a twenty-kilometer stretch of the Ahr River, a scenic tributary near Bonn.[11] The cause: a highly concentrated, toxic brew of sodium cyanide released from a coal purification plant, made even deadlier by trace amounts of naturally occurring ammonia in the river water. Local government officials and citizen groups lobbied the federal government to take action to prevent such catastrophes; in 1957, the German Bundestag passed a comprehensive water management law that helped to curtail some, but certainly not all, point-source river pollution. The ecological concerns and antinuclear protests that galvanized the emerging Green movement of the 1970s were thus part of a renewed environmental concern that had previously peaked in the 1950s and 1960s. Though Green political theory represented a historically unique combination of ecocentrism and New Left social concerns, the movement still drew on existing institutional networks, an informed citizenry, and a long tradition of environmental concern in German culture.[12]

Nature protection organizations that had existed before 1945 grew in size and strength during the 1950s and 1960s as a result of these growing ecological concerns, while new groups formed to respond to specific environmental assaults. Many *Naturschützer* continued to believe that comprehensive land use planning would enable state officials and environmental professionals to lessen the most serious social and ecological consequences of the postwar economic boom. Yet traditional nature and *Heimat* protection were in general slow to respond to the challenges posed by postwar environmental problems such as those of the Rhine watershed. At stake in the Rhine's decline was not merely visual disharmony but human survival: the contamination of an entire watershed serving the drinking water and industrial needs of millions of people. The complexity of the problem was embodied in the term *Umwelt*, or environment, a word commonly used in environmental discourse by the mid-1960s. Unlike concepts of landscape or nature, *Umwelt* drew attention to the unseen public health dangers of the technologically rationalized lifeworld and the complex, interdependent networks that bound human communities and natural ecosystems to the earth's global life-support systems. Though preservationists could argue that *Naturschutz* conserved valuable habitat for birds and other species and helped to heal some of the "diseases of civilization" that accompanied the nation's economic recovery, such a limited form of landscape protection seemed inadequate for the Herculean task of cleaning up the Rhine. Preservationists achieved some success in depicting *Heimat* as the basis for broader ecological awareness and human survival; as one Rhenish preservationist noted in 1960, "The work of *Naturschutz* is aimed more generally today at the undamaged preservation of the bases of our existence, namely water, soil, and climate."[13] Yet landscape preservationists' traditional focus on the nationalist significance of landscape, visual aesthetics, and *Heimat* sentiment appeared outdated in light of continuing *Umwelt* destruction. By the early 1970s, *Umweltschutz*, or environmental protection, had replaced *Naturschutz* at the center of the German environmental imagination.[14]

Since the Rhine's ecological problems were international in scope (its watershed included parts of six European countries), postwar environmentalism also demanded that West Germans move beyond *Heimat* localism to stem the Rhine's ecological decline. In 1950, Germany, France, the Netherlands, and Switzerland formed the International Commission for the Protection of the Rhine against Pollution, to create common standards for measuring the Rhine's pollutant levels, identify the source of its pollutants, and begin the process of limiting those effluents. While efforts to limit toxins such as chloride salts and organic wastes were largely unsuccessful until the 1970s owing to infighting among the member states, the commission did provide a framework for understanding ecological problems as transcending national boundaries. In this context, the conception of the Rhine as "Germany's river, but not Germany's border," a theme that French occupation and Nazi xenophobia had resuscitated during the 1920s and 1930s, declined in favor of seeing the Rhine as a *European* river and a symbol of supranational cooperation after the devastation of World War II. The International Commission took its cue from Charles de Gaulle's November 1945 statement about the Rhine: "Yesterday still a line of battle, tomorrow the bond of union."[15] The Rhine's environmental management and the construction of a European identity transformed nationalist understandings of the Rhineland as a geographic and racial borderland into a zone of international, ecological cooperation.

This postwar reinvention of an untainted Rhenish regionalism and the creation of a European identity for the Rhine and its surroundings should come as no surprise in light of the political adaptability and cultural malleability of *Heimat* and landscape preservationism presented in this study. In an effort to win state and public support for protecting the landscape's biological and cultural diversity from capitalist exploitation, state rationalization, and public indifference, nature preservationists had tuned their rhetoric to the prevailing political, cultural, and social contexts throughout the period between 1885 and 1945. In the Kaiserreich, preservationists touted the social benefits of Romantic aesthetic appreciation and natural historical study, arguments that resonated among state officials and bourgeois elites looking for a counterweight to modern "materialism" and unifying symbols for a newly unified though socially fragmented nation. In the Weimar years, nature protection advocates found that public health and economic justifications carried more weight than aesthetic or nationalist arguments in the broadened public sphere. In the process of rhetorical adaptation, nature preservationists' concept of environmental reform—indeed the meaning of "nature" itself—underwent radical transformations. Wilhelmine *Naturschützer* invested nature with a sacred aura and sought to shield its "monuments" from economic development. Weimar preservationists were willing to subsume preservation to the modernizing and functional needs of regional planning. Nature, in this view, could encompass a range of spaces with varying degrees of authenticity; the most important criteria for setting aside green spaces were public health needs and social integration, not aesthetic appreciation.

Just as preservationists adapted their rhetoric and practices to Germany's shifting political climate, so too did their activities reveal a diverse array of attitudes toward modernity that cannot be captured under the rubrics of agrarian romanticism or cultural despair. In each of the periods in this study, preservationists tried to shape the contours of modernization through environmental reform, but this did not imply a wholesale rejection of urban modernity. During the Wilhelmine period, the preservation movement's efforts to set aside natural monuments in no way challenged either the perceived necessity or the inevitability of industrialization. Instead, these efforts offered compensation for industrialism's negative effects and provided sites of refuge from urban ills. This selective accommodation of modernity was even more pronounced in the Weimar period, when *Landschaftspflege* advocates tried to design environmentally suitable structures, integrate nature protection and regional planning, and steer the spatial development of commercial, industrial, residential, and recreational facilities in an organic fashion. Weimar preservationists also participated in shaping German modernity by promoting nature protection amid growing economic rationalization, political democratization, and mass consumerism between 1925 and 1932. The Weimar era's streamlining of economic production processes, for example, found expression in parallel discourses about land use that stressed the virtues of state-directed environmental planning to enhance economic productivity and efficiency. The functional approach of *Landschaftspflege* stressed the need to design the landscape consciously and to provide modern workers with valuable recreational areas that facilitated their productivity and maintained their health. Amid lingering fears of worker unrest after the revolution of 1918 and public concern over the "superfluous" younger generation, preservationists stressed the therapeutic and pacifying effect of nature. They referred to it as the most important "social healing method" in an era of unprecedented social dislocation and political unrest. By the end of the 1920s, preservationists had abandoned nineteenth-century Romanticism in favor of an objective approach that emphasized applied science, not sentiment, in solving Germany's environmental destruction and social woes. It was precisely this modern, therapeutic approach to landscape planning, not agrarian-romanticism, that drew preservationists toward the Nazi movement.

Regional preservationists' paternalist vision of environmental reform saw nature protection as a pathway to social cohesion, linking them closely to the integrative functions of provincial cultural affairs. They believed that nature offered a common ground above class tensions, religious differences, and political wrangling. Yet the movement was not inherently authoritarian and protofascist. While preservationists retained a deep ambivalence and mistrust of the "masses," their organizations offered a broad spectrum of Rhinelanders from the middle and lower-middle classes the opportunity to participate in shaping the province's landscape and envisioning new forms of environmental stewardship in the midst of rapid industrialization. Regional identity also provided a major limitation to an authoritarian nationalization of the landscape's cultural meaning. Throughout the years between 1885 and 1945, regional conceptions of *Heimat* landmarks often clashed with the central government's vision of a unified national culture. The nineteenth-century tensions between the aristocratic-Protestant Prussian monarchy and the predominantly Catholic and liberal Rhineland found expression in differing conceptions of landscape.[16] While Berlin saw the Rhine as a marker of monarchical, anti-French nationalism, the Rhineland's provincial officials and organizations viewed the river as the symbolic heart of a distinct Rhenish identity and used that symbolism to demand greater autonomy for the province in managing its internal affairs.[17] In 1923, Rhenish separatists tried to transform such autonomist sentiments into popular support for a Rhineland Republic, using the well-known Siebengebirge nature park as a refuge and last stand in their fight against "Prussian" tyranny. Although most Rhenish preservationists remained enthusiastic national patriots, they maintained that Germany's essence lay in its diverse mosaic of cultural landscapes, rather than in top-down standardization from Berlin.

Regionalism also set important limits on the National Socialists' political instrumentalization of landscape preservation. The National Socialist regime initially offered nature preservationists unprecedented prestige and institutional support. Though few preservationists joined the party before 1933, most of them willingly embraced the regime thereafter and worked to realize the Nazis' "idealist" goal of establishing a people's community in touch with its "natural" roots. For preservationists, Nazism offered a way to put an end to a decade of liberal mismanagement of both the environment and the unwieldy masses that had been seduced by urban entertainment and crass materialism. Moreover, despite pressures to link *Naturschutz* more closely to the regime's centralizing and racial policies, the *Gleichschaltung* of nature protection remained institutionally and ideologically uneven, owing to infighting among competing party and state cultural authorities. This left room for nature preservationists to maintain their movement's ties to the regional *Heimat* and a cultural-geographic, rather than strictly racial, sense of Germanness. The result was an unstable blend of racial, cultural, historical, and regional understandings of landscape at the provincial level that was neither wholly Nazified nor completely autonomous. Interpretations that have viewed the *Naturschutz* movement as a mere ideological forerunner to Nazism have often overlooked this dynamic interaction between landscape preservationists and the regime that deflected the totalitarian drive toward *Gleichschaltung*.

The National Socialists did not turn out to be the environmental defenders heralded by the Reich Nature Protection Law of 1935 and repeated in more recent literature on the "green" Nazis. Experiments with alternative agriculture and forestry quickly ended as the regime geared up for war in 1936. Landscape preservationists watched in horror as the regime undermined decades of conservation efforts by draining swamps for farmland, cutting forests to build apartment complexes, and using sensitive nature preserves for troop drills and shooting practice. The regime maintained a commitment to reconciling nature and technology in high-profile projects such as the *Reichsautobahn*, but nature protection commissioners were routinely ignored in the deliberations regarding the location and design of those roadways. Despite their commitment to landscape planning, moreover, landscape preservationists were not equipped to complete with rival environmental authorities, especially Alwin Seifert's landscape advocates on the *Reichsautobahn* project and Konrad Meyer's RKFDV planners in occupied Poland, who promoted large-scale restoration of landscapes damaged or destroyed by the Nazis' militarization of nature. Victims of the polycratic struggle for power in the Third Reich, *Naturschutz* advocates found solace in regional *Heimat* identity and local sociability, but remained politically and socially marginal. They had hoped that government control would end liberalism's arbitrary and haphazard use of natural resources but soon learned that the state, especially the National Socialists' militarist dictatorship, could act as a far more effective agent of environmental destruction than private industry.

While this study challenges historical models that view *Naturschutz* as agarian-romantic or protofascist, there remain a number of crucial questions in the history of German landscape preservation that deserve further investigation. A more thorough comparison of Rhenish *Naturschutz* with other regional movements, for example, would help to determine if the area's relative openness to modernizing tendencies was unique within Germany. In less urbanized areas such as Westphalia and Lower Saxony, for example, scholars have found a more pronounced emphasis on peasant culture and a more ready embrace of racial notions of nationhood within those area's *Naturschutz* and *Heimatschutz* movements, rather than a gradual infusion of racist language as a result of defeat in other cultural arenas, as happened in the Rhine Province.[18] This may reflect the agrarian economy and the more homogeneous cultural heritage in these areas, which contrast with the Rhineland's industrial character and culturally hybrid borderlands.

National comparisons that place German developments within the broader history of Western environmentalism and environmental history also deserve further attention. As recent research on American wilderness protection and British nature conservation have shown, upper-middle-class elites in those countries also viewed nature preservation and outdoor experiences as ways to reinvigorate national character amid social dislocation, urbanization, and political conflict. Even the racializing tendencies within German nature protection of the late 1920s and 1930s were not wholly unique; a willingness to abandon the nineteenth-century faith in environmental improvement and turn toward a eugenicist understanding of cultural and social problems appears to have been widespread in Western societies of the interwar period. Far from expressing a uniquely German culture of despair, landscape preservation tried to come to grips with social tensions and environmental transformations common to all Western industrial societies of the late nineteenth and early twentieth centuries.[19]

The United States offers fruitful points of comparison. Wilhelmine preservationists saw America's Yellowstone Park as a model of enlightened nature protection, yet they quickly recognized the impossibility of establishing large-scale nature reserves in Germany's much-developed landscape. The cultural-landscape tradition that emerged in Germany instead sought to protect the regional, vernacular landscapes that were the basis of *Heimat* and, in some cases, furthered a more local ethic of environmental stewardship that valued backyard urban environments as much as distant nature reserves. The Third Reich's technocratic land-use, development, and planning policies also show striking parallels to American conservation efforts in the 1930s that need further investigation. Just as *Autobahn* planners believed they could mesh technology and nature in the open landscapes, American engineers sought to embed roadways in the landscape in major projects such as the Mount Vernon Memorial Highway. American and German projects were also both motivated by nationalist concerns about urbanites' alienation from nature. Yet how did Nazi racism recast concerns about balancing nature and technology or reuniting Germans and their landscape? Such comparisons will highlight more conclusively what German preservationists perceived as the key features of their landscapes—what made them the basis of home. In addition, they will enable scholars to determine if changes in German preservation practices stemmed from political and social developments unique to that country or were part of broader transformations within Western environmental practice as a whole. What is clear, however, is that German environmentalism has had a variety of cultural meanings and political implications that complicate progressivist accounts of the rise of ecological consciousness in modern industrial societies. Levels of environmental degradation rarely correspond directly to ecological awareness; instead, political actors and social groups envision nature and imagine community through competing nationalist, regionalist, social-class, and other ideological lenses. In Germany, this process has resulted in environmental reform agendas that span the political spectrum from left to right. There is no ahistorical ecological consciousness that transcends human constructions of nature.

# Abbreviations

| | |
|---|---|
| ALVR | Archiv des Landschaftsverbandes Rheinland |
| ALVW | Archiv des Landschaftsverbandes Westfalen |
| BAK | Bundesarchiv Koblenz |
| DAF | Deutsche Arbeitsfront |
| DBH | Deutscher Bund Heimatschutz |
| *EVB* | *Eifelvereinsblatt* |
| KdF | Kraft durch Freude |
| *MRVDH* | *Mitteilungen des Rheinischen Vereins für Denkmalpflege und Heimatschutz* |
| NSDAP | Nationalsozialistische Deutsche Arbeiterpartei |
| RfL | Reichsverband für Leibesübung |
| RHB | Rheinischer Heimatbund |
| RKFDV | Reichskomissariat für die Festigung Deutschen Volkstums |
| RNG | Reichsnaturschutzgesetz |
| RVDH | Rheinischer Verein für Denkmalpflege und Heimatschutz |
| RVH | Reichsverband für Volkstum und Heimat |
| RVP | Rheinische Volkspflege |
| SPD | Sozialdemokratische Partei Deutschlands |
| VRS | Verein zur Rettung des Siebengebirges |
| VVS | Verschönerungsverein für das Siebengebirge |
| *ZRVDH* | *Zeitschrift des Rheinischen Vereins für Denkmalpflege und Heimatschutz* |

# Notes

## Introduction

1. Stephen Spender, *European Witness* (New York: Reynal and Hitchcock, 1946), 7.
2. Ibid., 7–8.
3. The exact size of the nature preservation movement is difficult to estimate, because the movement encompassed a vast array of organizations, many of which were local in character. One scholar has estimated that the *Heimatschutz* associations, one of the movements examined in this study, encompassed 30,000 dues-paying members on the eve of World War I. See William Rollins, *A Greener Vision of Home: Cultural Politics and Environmental Reform in the German Heimatschutz Movement* (Ann Arbor: University of Michigan Press, 1997), 3. In this study I use the term "landscape preservation" to refer to the entire array of *Naturschutz, Heimatschutz,* and related environmental protection activities at the regional and local levels. Though the two movements had different conceptions of environmental reform, they both emphasized the nationalist meaning of nature protection and often cooperated at the local level to halt the environmental damage caused by industrialization.
4. The first generation of works on the history of *Naturschutz* and *Heimatschutz,* written by former nature conservation officials, focused on the formation of state bureaucracies dedicated to nature conservation, nature protection, and landscape preservation, without a critical analysis of the relationship between environmentalism and broader political, social, and cultural changes. These works include Walther Schoenichen, *Naturschutz—Heimatschutz: Ihre Begründung durch Ernst Rudorff, Hugo Conwentz und ihre Verläufer* (Stuttgart: Wissenschaftliche Verlagsge-

sellschaft, 1954), Hans Klose, *Fünfzig Jahre staatlicher Naturschutz: Ein Rückblick auf den Weg der deutschen Naturschutzbewegung* (Giessen: Brühlscher Verlag, 1957), and Walter Mrass, *Die Organisation des staatlichen Naturschutzes und der Landschaftspflege im deutschen Reich und der Bundesrepublik Deutschland seit 1935* (Stuttgart: Verlag Eugen Ulmer, 1969). The rise of the Green Party in Germany, however, has stimulated in recent decades new interest in the history of German environmentalism, correcting what the historian Ulrich Linse once referred to as the pervasive "ahistoricism of ecological thought" in Germany. Recent works that survey German nature conservation, landscape preservation, or environmentalism in a broad-ranging manner include Rollins, *A Greener Vision of Home;* Klaus-Georg Wey, *Umweltpolitik in Deutschland: Kurze Geschichte des Umweltschutzes in Deutschland seit 1900* (Opladen: Westdeutscher, 1982); Ulrich Linse, *Ökopax und Anarchie: Eine Geschichte der ökologischen Bewegungen in Deutschland* (Stuttgart: DTV, 1986); Alfred Barthelmess, *Landschaft, Lebensraum des Menschen: Probleme von Landschaftsschutz und Landschaftspflege geschichtlich dargestellt und dokumentiert* (Freiburg: Karl Albers, 1988); Jost Hermand, *Grüne Utopien in Deutschland: Zur Geschichte des ökologischen Bewusstseins* (Frankfurt: Fischer, 1991), and *Mit den Bäumen sterben die Menschen: zur Kulturgeschichte der Ökologie* (Cologne: Böhlau, 1993); Raymond Dominick, *The Environmental Movement in Germany: Prophets and Pioneers, 1871–1971* (Bloomington: Indiana University Press, 1992); Andreas Knaut, *Zurück zur Natur! Die Wurzeln der Ökologiebewegung* (Greven: Kilda-Verlag, 1993); Michael Wettengel, "Staat und Naturschutz, 1906–1945: Zur Geschichte der Staatlichen Stelle für Naturdenkmalpflege in Preussen und der Reichstelle für Naturschutz," *Historische Zeitschrift* 257, no. 2 (October 1993): 355–399.

5. On the burden of history in the German environmental movement, see Hermann Bausinger, "Zwischen Grün und Braun: Volkstumsideologie und Heimatpflege nach dem Ersten Weltkrieg," in *Religions- und Geistesgeschichte der Weimarer Republik,* ed. Hubert Cancik (Düsseldorf: Patmos, 1982), 215–229; Colin Riordan, "Green Ideas in Germany: A Historical Survey," in *Green Thought in German Culture: Historical and Contemporary Perspectives,* ed. Riordan (Cardiff: University of Wales Press, 1997), 3. On the influence of right-wing nationalism on German environmental thought, see Burkhardt Riechers, "Nature Protection during National Socialism," *Historical Social Research* 21, no. 3 (1996): 34–56; Jonathan Olsen, *Nature und Nationalism: Right-Wing Ecology and the Politics of Identity in Contemporary Germany* (New York: St. Martin's Press, 1999), 53–84.

6. The reference here is to Eugen Weber's classic *Peasants into Frenchmen: The Modernization of Rural France* (Stanford: Stanford University Press, 1976). Useful works that analyze the symbolic construction of nationhood

in Germany and beyond include Benedict Anderson, *Imagined Communities: Reflections on the Origins and Spread of Nationalism,* rev. ed. (London: Verso, 1991); Harold James, *A German Identity: 1770 to the Present Day* (London: Phoenix, 1991); John Gillis, ed., *Commemorations: The Politics of National Identity* (Princeton: Princeton University Press, 1994); Charlotte Tacke, *Denkmal im sozialen Raum: Nationale Symbole in Deutschland und Frankreich im neunzehnten Jahrhundert* (Göttingen: Vandenhoeck and Ruprecht, 1995); Rudy Koshar, *Germany's Transient Pasts: Preservation and National Memory in the Twentieth Century* (Chapel Hill: University of North Carolina Press, 1998); Anthony D. Smith, *Nationalism: Theory, Ideology, History* (Cambridge: Polity Press, 2001).
7. Eric Hobsbawm, *The Invention of Tradition* (Cambridge: Cambridge University Press, 1983).
8. Anthony D. Smith, *The Ethnic Origins of Nations* (Oxford: Oxford University Press, 1986), 188. Other works that discuss the relationship between landscape and national identity include Roderick Nash, *Wilderness and the American Mind,* 3rd ed. (New Haven: Yale University Press, 1982); Kenneth Olwig, *Nature's Ideological Landscape* (London: George Allen and Unwin, 1984); Bernd Weyergraf, *Die Deutschen und ihr Wald,* Exhibition of the Akademie der Künste, 20 September to 15 November 1987 (Berlin: Die Akademie, 1987); Denis Cosgrove and Stephen Daniels, eds., *The Iconography of Landscape: Essays on the Symbolic Representation, Design and Use of Past Environments* (Cambridge: Cambridge University Press, 1988); Stephen Daniels, *Fields of Vision: Landscape Imagery and National Identity in England and the United States* (Cambridge: Polity Press, 1993); Simon Schama, *Landscape and Memory* (New York: Alfred A. Knopf, 1995); Wendy Joy Darby, *Landscape and Identity: Geographies of Nation and Class in England* (Oxford: Berg, 2000); Kenneth Olwig, *Nature and the Body Politic: From Britain's Renaissance to America's New World* (Madison: University of Wisconsin Press, 2002).
9. The literature on *Heimat* in German culture is extensive and cannot be cited here in its entirety. Useful works that detail its political history and cultural significance include Celia Applegate, *A Nation of Provincials: The German Idea of Heimat* (Berkeley: University of California Press, 1990), and Alon Confino, *The Nation as a Local Metaphor: Württemberg, Imperial Germany, and National Memory* (Chapel Hill: University of North Carolina Press, 1997). Other important works include Mack Walker, *German Home Towns: Community, State and General Estate, 1648–1871* (Ithaca: Cornell University Press, 1971); Hermann Bausinger, *Heimat und Identität: Probleme regionaler Kultur* (Neumünster: Karl Wachholtz, 1979); Ina-Marie Greverus, *Auf der Such nach Heimat* (Munich: C. H. Beck, 1979); Rüdiger Gorner, *Heimat im Wort: Die Problematik eines Begriffs im neunzehnten und zwanzigsten Jahrhundert* (Munich: Ludicium, 1991); Jost Hermand and James Steakley, eds., *Heimat, Nation, Fatherland: The German Sense*

*of Belonging* (New York: D. Lang, 1996); Elizabeth Boa and Rachel Pal-frey-Man, *Heimat—A German Dream: Regional Loyalties and National Identity in German Culture, 1890–1990* (Oxford: Oxford University Press, 2000).

10. See Wilhelm Heinrich Riehl, *Die Naturgeschichte des Volkes als Grundlage einer deutschen Social-Politik,* vol. 1: *Land und Leute,* 5th ed. (Stuttgart: J. G. Cotta, 1861). On Riehl and regional identity, see Applegate, *A Nation of Provincials,* 34–41, and Jasper von Altenbockum, *Wilhelm Heinrich Riehl 1823–1897: Sozialwissenschaft zwischen Kulturgeschichte und Ethnographie* (Cologne: Böhlau, 1994).

11. On the contrast between the French Enlightenment's constitutional conception of the nation and German Romantics' organic vision of nationhood, see Olsen, *Nature and Nationalism,* 57–61; Rogers Brubaker, *Citizenship and Nationhood in France and Germany* (Cambridge, Mass.: Harvard University Press, 1992); Elie Kedourie, *Nationalism,* 4th ed. (Oxford: Blackwell, 1993); Liah Greenfeld, *Nationalism: Five Roads to Modernity* (Cambridge, Mass.: Harvard University Press, 1992).

12. On Riehl's sociology of habitat, see Schama, *Landscape and Memory,* 113.

13. Riehl, *A Natural History of the German People,* ed. and trans. David Diephouse (Lewiston, N.Y.: Edwin Mellen Press, 1990), 49.

14. Applegate, *Nation of Provincials,* 4.

15. On turn-of-the-century *völkisch* ideas of *Heimat* and nature, see Jost Hermand, *Old Dreams of a New Reich: Volkish Utopias and National Socialism,* trans. Paul Levesque (Bloomington: Indiana University Press, 1992), and Joachim Wolschke-Bulmahn, "Findlinge, Landschaftsgestaltung, und die völkische Suche nach nationaler Identität im frühen zwanzigsten Jahrhundert," in *Gartenkultur und Nationale Identität: Strategien Nationaler und Regionaler Identitätsstiftung in der Deutschen Gartenkultur,* ed. Gert Gröning and Uwe Schneider (Worms: Wernersche, 2001), 76–85.

16. On provincialism and German national identity, see Applegate, *Nation of Provincials;* Confino, *Nation as a Local Metaphor;* Karl Ditt, "Die Deutsche Heimatbewegung 1871–1945," in *Heimat: Analysen, Themen, Perspektiven,* ed. Bundeszentrale für Politsche Bildung (Ulm: Franz Spiegel Buch, 1990), 133–154.

17. Alon Confino, "The Nation as a Local Metaphor: Heimat, National Memory, and the German Empire, 1871–1918," *History and Memory* 5, no. 1 (Spring/Summer 1993): 42–86, here 54–59.

18. On local sociability as civic engagement, see Applegate, *Nation of Provincials,* 60–62, and Rudy Koshar, *Social Life, Local Politics, and Nazism: Marburg 1880–1935* (Chapel Hill: University of North Carolina Press, 1986), 4–8.

19. On the Rhine's political history, see Helmut Mathy, "Der 'Heilige Strom': Politische und geistesgeschichtliche Voraussetzungen der Rheinromantik," *Beiträge zur Rheinkunde* 36 (1984): 3–21; Hans Boldt, "Deutschlands

hochschlagende Pulsader—Zur politischen Funktion des Rheins im Laufe der Geschichte," and Torsten Mick and Michael Tretter, "Der Rhein und Europa," in *Der Rhein: Mythos und Realität eines europäischen Stromes,* ed. Hans Boldt (Cologne: Rheinland, 1988), 27–46; Horst-Johs Tümmers, *Der Rhein: Ein europäischer Fluss und seine Geschichte* (Munich: C. H. Beck, 1994); Hans M. Schmidt, Friedemann Malsch, and Frank van de Schoor, eds., *Der Rhein: Ein europäischer Strom in Kunst und Kultur des zwanzigsten Jahrhunderts* (Cologne: Wienand, 1995); Lucien Febvre, *Der Rhein und seine Geschichte,* trans. Peter Schöttler (Frankfurt: Campus, 1995).

20. Schama, *Landscape and Memory,* 61.

21. On Rhine Romanticism, see Mathy, "Der 'Heilige Strom'"; Gisela Fleckstein, "Warum ist es am Rhein so schön? Aspekte der Rheinromantik von etwa 1800 bis zur Gegenwart," and Angelika Riemann, "Rheinlust und Reisefieber" in Boldt, ed., *Der Rhein,* 189–222; Heinz Stephan, *Die Enstehung der Rheinromantik* (Cologne: Rheinland, 1922); Horst-Johs Tümmers, *Rheinromantik: Romantik und Reisen am Rhein* (Cologne: Greven Verlag, 1968).

22. On the Rhine's industrialization and economic significance, see Dietmar Petzina, "Industrie und Verkehr am Rhein," and Manfred Köhler and Reinhard Manter, "Maschinen und Medaillen, Stechuhren und Streikplakat," in Boldt, ed. *Der Rhein,* 47–82; Mark Cioc, *The Rhine: An Eco-Biography, 1815–2000* (Seattle: University of Washington Press, 2002).

23. Cioc, *The Rhine: An Ecobiography,* 10.

24. The best examples of works emphasizing the reactionary and proto-fascist dimensions of neo-Romantic naturalism are George Mosse, *The Crisis of German Ideology: Intellectual Origins of the Third Reich* (New York: Grosset and Dunlap, 1964), and Klaus Bergmann, *Agrarromantik und Grossstadtfeindschaft* (Meisenheim am Glan: Anton Hain, 1970). Other useful works in this vein include Gert Gröning and Joachim Wolschke-Bulmahn, *Die Liebe zur Landschaft,* vol. 1: *Natur in Bewegung* (Munich: Minerva, 1986); Rolf-Peter Sieferle, *Fortschrittsfeinde? Opposition gegen Technik und Industrie von der Romantik bis zur Gegenwart* (Munich: C. H. Beck, 1984); Klaus Eder, "The Rise of Counter-Cultural Movements against Modernity: Nature as a New Field of Class Struggle," *Theory, Culture, and Society* 7 (1990): 21–47; Joachim Wolschke-Bulmahn, *Auf der Suche nach Arkadien: Zu landschaftsidealen und Formen der Naturaneignung in der Jugendbewegung und ihrer Bedeutung für die Landespflege* (Munich: Minerva, 1990); Werner Hartung, *Konservative Zivilisationskritik und regionale Identität: Am Beispiel der nieder-sächsischen Heimatbewegung 1895 bis 1919* (Hannover: Hahn'sche Buchhandlung, 1991).

25. Among the most useful works challenging the notion that preservationists were inherently antimodern or reactionary are Linse, *Ökopax und Anarchie,* which argues that environmental ideas influenced the work-

ing-class and anarcho-commune movements as well as forward-looking bourgeois conservationists; Rollins, *A Greener Vision of Home;* Knaut, *Zurück zur Natur!;* Karl Ditt, *Raum und Volkstum: Die Kulturpolitik des Provinzialverbandes Westfalen, 1923–1945* (Münster: Aschendorffsche, 1988); and John Williams, "'The Chords of the German Soul Are Tuned to Nature': The Movement to Preserve the Natural *Heimat* from the *Kaiserreich* to the Third Reich," *Central European History* 29, no. 3 (1996): 339–384.

26. Rollins, *A Greener Vision of Home,* 5, 18.

27. On the relationship between bourgeois nature ideals, middle-class critique of modernity, and social paternalism, see Edeltraud Klueting, ed., *Antimodernismus und Reform: Zur Geschichte der deutschen Heimatbewegung* (Darmstadt: Wissenschaftliche Buchgesellschaft, 1991); Rüdiger vom Bruch, ed., *Weder Kommunismus noch Kapitalismus: Bürgerliche Sozialreform in Deutschland vom Vormärz bis zur Ära Adenauer* (Munich: C. H. Beck, 1985); Orvar Löfgren, "Natur, Tiere und Moral: Zur Entwicklung der bürgerlichen Naturauffassung," in *Volkskultur in der Moderne: Probleme und Perspektiven empirischer Kulturforschungen,* ed. Utz Jeggle (Reinbeck bei Hamburg: Rowohlt, 1986), 122–144; Wilfried Lipp, *Natur— Geschichte—Denkmal: Zur Enstehung des Denkmalbewusstseins der bürgerlichen Gesellschaft* (Frankfurt: Campus, 1987). On German environmentalism from a comparative perspective, see Raymond Dominick, "The Roots of the Green Movement in the United States and West Germany," *Environmental Review* 12, no. 3 (Fall 1988): 1–30; Christoph Spehr, *Die Jagd nach Natur: Zur historischen Entwicklung des gesellschaftlichen Naturverhältnisses in den U.S.A., Deutschland, Grossbritannien und Italien am Beispiel von Wildnutzung, Artenschutz und Jagd* (Frankfurt: IKO, 1994); Karl Ditt, "Nature Conservation in England and Germany 1900–70: Forerunner of Environmental Protection?" *Contemporary European History* 5, no. 1 (1996): 1–28; Karla Schultz and Kenneth S. Calhoon, eds., *The Idea of the Forest: German and American Perspectives on the Culture and Politics of Trees* (New York: Peter Lang, 1996).

28. See Thomas Rohkrämer, *Eine andere Moderne? Zivilisationskritik, Natur und Technik in Deutschland, 1880–1933* (Paderborn: Schöningh, 1999).

29. See David Morley and Kevin Robins, "No Place like *Heimat:* Images of Home(land) in European Culture," *New Perspectives* 12 (Winter 1990): 1–23.

30. For an overview of the institutional *Gleichschaltung* of landscape preservation groups, see Wettengel, "Staat und Naturschutz," 379–380; Raymond Dominick, "The Nazis and the Nature Conservationists," *Historian* 49 (1987): 508–538; and Dominick, *Environmental Movement in Germany,* 85–106. See also Ditt, *Raum und Volkstum,* 151–161; Winfried Speitkamp, "Denkmalpflege und Heimatschutz in Deutschland zwischen Kulturkritik und Nationalsozialismus," *Archiv für Kulturgeschichte* 70 (1988): 149–193.

31. Schama, *Landscape and Memory,* 119.
32. See Anna Bramwell, "Ricardo Walther Darré: Was This Man 'Father of the Greens'?" *History Today* 34 (September 1984): 7–13, and *Blood and Soil: Richard Walther Darré and Hitler's Green Party* (London: Kensal Press, 1985).
33. William Cronon, "The Trouble with Wilderness, or Getting Back to the Wrong Nature," in *Uncommon Ground: Rethinking the Human Place in Nature* (New York: W. W. Norton, 1996), 69–90, here 89.
34. J. Baird Callicott and Michael P. Nelson, eds., *The Great Wilderness Debate* (Athens: University of Georgia Press, 1998).
35. Mark Cioc, "The Impact of the Coal Age on the German Environment: A Review of the Historical Literature," *Environment and History* 4, no. 1 (1998): 105–124, here 106.
36. On the historiography of *Umweltgeschichte* and its focus on industrial pollution and natural resource depletion, see Franz-Josef Brüggemeier and Thomas Rommelspacher, eds., *Besiegte Natur: Geschichte der Umwelt im neunzehnten und zwanzigsten Jahrhundert,* 2nd ed. (Munich: C. H. Beck, 1989); Arne Andersen et al., eds., *Historische Umweltschutzforschung: Wissenschaftliche Neuorientierung—aktuelle Fragestellungen* (Bergisch Gladbach: Thomas-Morus-Akademie Bensberg, 1992); Werner Abelshauser, ed., *Umweltgeschichte: Umweltverträgliches Wirtschaften in historischer Perspektive* (Göttingen: Vanderhoeck and Ruprecht, 1994); Günter Bayerl and Norman Fuchsloch, eds., *Umweltgeschichte—Methoden, Themen, Potentiale: Tagung des Hamburger Arbeitskreises für Umweltgeschichte, Hamburg 1994* (Münster: Waxmann, 1996); Ernst Bruckmüller and Verena Winiwarter, *Umweltgeschichte: Zum historischen Verhältnis von Gesellschaft und Natur* (Vienna: öbv and hpt, 2000).
37. For a good recent review of literature on *Landschaft* and its environmental significance, see Norbert Fischer, "Der neue Blick auf die Landschaft: Die Geschichte der Landschaft im Schnittpunkt von Sozial-, Geistes- und Umweltgeschichte," *Archiv für Sozialgeschichte* 36 (1996): 434–442, and Schama, *Landscape and Memory,* 6–18. I have also found the following works helpful in understanding the aesthetic, cultural, and political significance of landscape: Cosgrove and Daniels, eds., *The Iconography of Landscape;* Ulrich Eisel, "Die schöne Landschaft als kritische Utopie oder als konservatives Relikt: Über die Kristallisation gegnerischer politischer Philosophien im Symbol 'Landschaft,'" *Soziale Welt* 33, no. 2 (1982): 157–168; Manfred Smuda, ed., *Landschaft* (Frankfurt am Main: Suhrkamp, 1986); Nicholas Green, *The Spectacle of Nature: Landscape and Bourgeois Culture in Nineteenth-Century France* (Manchester: Manchester University Press, 1990); Gerhard Böhme, *Natürlich Natur: Über Natur im Zeitalter ihrer technischen Reproduzierbarkeit* (Frankfurt am Main: Suhrkamp, 1992); Trevor J. Barnes and James Duncan, *Writing Worlds: Discourse, Text and Metaphor in the Representation of the Landscape* (London:

Routledge, 1992); Anne Spirn, *The Language of Landscape* (New Haven: Yale University Press, 1998); W. J. T. Mitchell, *Landscape and Power,* 2nd ed. (Chicago: University of Chicago Press, 2002).

38. Schama, *Landscape and Memory,* 10; Olwig, *Nature's Ideological Landscape,* 1–10.

39. Morley and Robins, "No Place like *Heimat,*" 2.

## 1 Nature's Homelands

1. Stefan Zweig, *Welt von Gestern: Erinnerungen eines Europäers,* 16. Cited in Thomas Rohkrämer, *Eine andere Moderne? Zivilisationskritik, Natur und Technik in Deutschland, 1880–1933* (Paderborn: Schöningh, 1999), 52.

2. Rohkrämer, *Andere Moderne?* See also Raymond Dominick, *The Environmental Movement in Germany: Prophets and Pioneers, 1871–1971* (Bloomington: Indiana University Press, 1992), 17.

3. Rohkrämer, *Andere Moderne?,* 38.

4. On the history of *Naturdenkmalpflege* see Michael Wettengel, "Staat und Naturschutz, 1906–1945: Zur Geschichte der Staatlichen Stelle für Naturdenkmalpflege in Preussen und der Reichstelle für Naturschutz," *Historische Zeitschrift* 257, no. 2 (October 1993): 355–399, here 357–363, and Andreas Knaut, "Die Anfänge des staalichen Naturschutzes: Die frühe regierungsamtliche Organisation des Natur- und Landschaftsschutzes in Preussen, Bayern und Württemberg," in *Umweltgeschichte: Umwelträgliches Wirtschaften in historischen Perspektive: Acht Beiträge,* ed. Werner Abelshauser (Göttingen: Vanderhoeck and Ruprecht, 1994).

5. On the term *Denkmal* and *Denkmalpflege* efforts, see Thomas Nipperdey, "Nationalidee und Nationaldenkmal in Deutschland im neunzehnten Jahrhundert," in *Gesellschaft, Kultur, Theorie: Gesammelte Aufsätze zur neueren Geschichte* (Göttingen: Vanderhoeck and Ruprecht, 1976), 133–173; Wilfried Lipp, *Natur—Geschichte—Denkmal: Zur Enstehung des Denkmalbewusstseins der bürgerlichen Gesellschaft* (Frankfurt: Campus, 1987); Charlotte Tacke, *Denkmal im sozialen Raum: Nationale Symbole in Deutschland und Frankreich im neunzehten Jahrhundert* (Göttingen: Vanderhoeck and Ruprecht, 1995); Rudy Koshar, *Germany's Transient Pasts: Preservation and National Memory in the Twentieth Century* (Chapel Hill: University of North Carolina Press, 1998).

6. Koshar, *Germany's Transient Pasts,* 29–31.

7. Andreas Knaut, *Zurück zur Natur! Die Wurzeln der Ökologiebewegung,* supplement 1 to *Jahrbuch für Naturschutz und Landschaftspflege,* ed. Arbeitsgemeinschaft beruflicher und ehrenamtlicher Naturschutz e.V. (Greven: Kilda-Verlag, 1993), 65–205.

8. For Rudorff's views, see Ernst Rudorff, *Heimatschutz* (Berlin-Lichtfelde: Hugo Bermühler, 1926). On Rudorff and the *Heimatschutz* movement, see

Knaut, *Zurück zur Natur!* and Andreas Knaut, "Ernst Rudorff und die Anfänge der deutschen Heimatbewegung," in *Antimodernismus und Reform: Zur Geschichte der deutschen Heimatbewegung,* ed. Edeltraud Klueting (Darmstadt: Wissenschaftliche Buchgesellschaft, 1991), 20–49; William Rollins, *A Greener Vision of Home: Cultural Politics and Environmental Reform in the German Heimatschutz Movement* (Ann Arbor: University of Michigan Press, 1997).

9. On the *Lebensreform* movement, see Wolfgang Krabbe, *Gesellschaftsveränderung durch Lebensreform: Strukturdenkmale einer sozialreformerischen Bewegung in Deutschland der Industrialisierungsperiode* (Göttingen: Vanderhoeck and Ruprecht, 1974); Ulrich Linse, *Zurück, o Mensch, zur Mutter Erde: Landkommunen in Deutschland 1890–1933* (Munich: DTV, 1983); Christoph Conti, *Abschied vom Bürgertum: Alternative Bewegungen in Deutschland von 1890 bis heute* (Reinbek bei Hamburg: Rowohlt, 1984); Michael Andritzky and Thomas Rautenberg, eds., *Wir sind nackt und nennen uns Du. Von Lichtfreuden und Sonnenkämpfern: Eine Geschichte der Freikörperkultur* (Giessen: Anabas, 1989); Diethart Krebs and Jürgen Reulecke, eds., *Handbuch der deutschen Reformbewegungen 1880–1933* (Wuppertal: Peter Hammer, 1998). On Sohnrey, see Knaut, "Die Anfänge staatlicher Naturschutz," 38–39. A good study of *Heimatkunst* is Karlheinz Rossbacher, *Heimatkunstbewegung und Heimatroman: Zu einer Literatursoziologie der Jahrhundertwende* (Stuttgart: Ernst Klett, 1975). On the German Garden City movement, see Kristina Hartmann, *Müncher Gartenstadtbewegung und deutsche Gartenstadtbewegung: Kulturpolitik und Gesellschaft* (Munich: Heinz Moos, 1976).

10. On political Catholicism in the Rhineland, see Dieter Kastner and Vera Torunsky, *Kleine rheinische Geschichte 1815–1986* (Cologne: Rheinland-Verlag, 1987), 31–34; Horst Lademacher, "Die nördlichen Rheinlande von der Rheinprovinz bis zur Bildung des Landschaftsverbandes Rheinland," in *Rheinische Geschichte,* vol. 2: *Neuzeit,* ed. Franz Petri und Georg Droege (Düsseldorf: Schwann, 1976), 604–616.

11. On Rhenish social democracy, see Kastner and Torunsky, *Kleine rheinische Geschichte,* 34–36; Lademacher, "Die nördlichen Rheinlande," 617–632. Cologne was an important center for social democracy, as was the Bergish industrial region with its Protestant skilled-worker base in towns such as Elberfeld, Barmen, Solingen, and Remscheid. The three-tiered election system hindered SPD electoral growth in the Prussian assembly and in municipal governments before 1918.

12. On the history and natural historical significance of the Siebengebirge, see Josef Ruland, *Echo tönt von sieben Bergen: Das Siebengebirge—ein Intermezzo europäischer Geistesgeschichte in Dichtung und Prosa* (Boppard am Rhein: Harald Boldt Verlag, 1970); Herbert Offner, ed., *Naturpark, Naturschutzgebiet Siebengebirge* (Bonn: C. Brandt, 1971); Elmar Heinen,

"Naturschutzgebiet Siebengebirge gestern—heute—morgen," *Rheinische Heimatpflege,* 27 (1990): 112–121; Frieder Berres and Christian Kiess, *Siebengebirge: Naturpark—Orte—Sehenswertes,* 2nd ed., ed. Heimatverein Siebengebirge (Siegburg: Rheinlandia Verlag, 1994).

13. Michael Schmidt, "The Rhine in Its Perception from the Age of Romanticism to the Present Day," in *The Rhine Valley: Urban, Harbour and Industrial Development and Environmental Problems,* ed. Heinz Heineberg, Norbert de Lange, and Alois Mayr (Leipzig: Institut für Länderkunde, 1996): 127–146, here 127.

14. On Rhine Romanticism, see Horst-Johs Tümmers, *Rheinromantik: Romantik und Reisen am Rhein* (Cologne: Greven Verlag, 1968); Helmut Mathy, "Der 'Heilige Strom': Politische und geistesgeschichtliche Voraussetzungen der Rheinromantik," *Beiträge zur Rheinkunde* 36 (1984): 3–21; Gisela Fleckstein, "Warum ist es am Rhein so schön? Aspekte der Rheinromantik von etwa 1800 bis zur Gegenwart," and Angelika Riemann, "Rheinlust und Reisefieber," in *Der Rhein: Mythos und Realität eines europäischen Stromes,* ed. Hans Boldt (Cologne: Rheinland, 1988), 189–222; Mark Cioc, *The Rhine: An Ecobiography, 1815–2000* (Seattle: University of Washington Press, 2002), 7–10.

15. Schmidt, "The Rhine in Its Perception," 127.

16. Schama, *Landscape and Memory* (New York: Alfred A. Knopf, 1995), 103.

17. Cited in Schmidt, "The Rhine in Its Perception," 136.

18. See Joseph von Görres, *Volks- und Meisterlieder aus den Handschriften der Heidelberger Bibliothek* (Frankfurt am Main, 1817; repr., Hildesheim: G. Olms, 1967); Ernst Moritz Arndt, *Der Rhein Teutschlands Strom aber nicht Teutschlands Gränze* (Bonn: Lpz. Rein, 1813); Johann Gottlieb Fichte, *Addresses to the German Nation,* trans. by R. F. Jones and G. H. Turnbull (Westport, Conn.: Greenwood Press, 1979). For a discussion of German Romanticism and the formation of national identity, see Bernd Fischer, *Das Eigene und das Eigentliche—Klopstock, Herder, Fichte, Kleist: Episoden aus der Konstruktionsgeschichte nationaler Intentionalitäten* (Berlin: Erich Schmidt, 1995).

19. Gisela Fleckenstein, "Warum ist es am Rhein so schön?"; Mathy, "Der 'Heilige Strom,'" 5–11.

20. See Ernst Moritz Arndt, *Reisen durch einen Theil Teutschlands, Ungarns, Italiens und Frankreichs in den Jahren 1798 und 1799* (Leipzig: H. Gräff, 1804); Ruland, *Echo Tönt von Sieben Bergen,* 63–68.

21. On the Drachenfels and the 1828 preservation campaign, see Mathy, "Der 'Heilige Strom,'" 10–15, and Theo Hardenberg, "Der Drachenfels: Seine 'Conservation vermittelst Expropriation,'" *Rheinische Heimatpflege* 4 (October–December 1968): 274–310.

22. See Joseph Görres, *In Sachen der Rheinprovinzen: Und in eigener Angelegenheit* (Stuttgart: J. B. Metzler, 1822); Kastner and Torunsky, *Kleine rheinische Geschichte,* 11–24; Tümmers, *Rheinromantik,* 57. On tensions

between the Rhine Province and Prussia in the Vormärz (1815–1848) and Revolution of 1848 periods, see Jonathan Sperber, *Rhineland Radicals: The Democratic Movement and the Revolution of 1848–1849* (Princeton: Princeton University Press, 1991), 3–52.

23. On castle restoration, see Godehard Hoffmann, *Rheinische Romanik im neunzehnten Jahrhundert: Denkmalpflege in der preussischen Rheinprovinz* (Cologne: J. P. Bachem, 1995); Robert Taylor, *The Castles of the Rhine: Recreating the Middle Ages in Modern Germany* (Waterloo, Ont.: Wilfrid Laurier University Press, 1998).

24. Koshar, *Germany's Transient Pasts,* 32.

25. See Archiv des Landschaftsverbandes Rheinland (hereafter ALVR), Kulturabteilung 1504.

26. On Rhineland monuments and *Denkmalpflege,* see Hoffmann, *Rheinische Romanik;* Koshar, *Germany's Transient Pasts;* Dorothee Lange and Gabriele Lohberg, "Denkmale und Denkmalschutz am Rhein im neunzehnten und zwanzigsten Jahrhundert," in *Der Rhein,* ed. Boldt, 171–187.

27. *Verschönerungsverein für das Siebengebirge, Honnef und Obercassel,* vol. 1 (Bonn: Universitäts-Buchdruckerei von Carl Georg, 1885), 1–32; Winfried Biesing, *Drachenfelser Chronik: Geschichte eines Berges, seiner Burg und seiner Burggrafen* (Cologne: Rheinland, 1980), 211–220.

28. On the cultural politics of the view, see Joachim Kleinmanns, *Rheinische Aussichtstürme im neunzehnten und zwanzigsten Jahrhundert* (Meinerzhagen: E. Groll, 1985), and Kleinmanns, *Schau ins Land: Aussichtstürme* (Marburg: Jonas, 1999).

29. Cioc, *The Rhine: An Ecobiography,* 82–84, 116–117.

30. Kastner and Torunsky, *Kleine rheinische Geschichte,* 37–46. See also Jürgen Reulecke, "The Ruhr: Centralization versus Decentralization in a Region of Cities," in *Metropolis: 1890–1940,* ed. Anthony Sutcliffe (London: Mansell, 1984), 381.

31. Kastner and Torunsky, *Kleine rheinische Geschichte,* 45.

32. Mark Cioc, "The Impact of the Coal Age on the German Environment: A Review of the Historical Literature," *Environment and History* 4, no. 1 (1998): 105–124, here 112; Cioc, *The Rhine: An Ecobiography,* 92–93.

33. See Cioc, *The Rhine: An Ecobiography,* 47–75, 145–171; Dominick, *The Environmental Movement in Germany,* 37; Christoph Bernhardt, "The Correction of the Upper Rhine in the Nineteenth Century: Modernizing Society and State by Large-Scale Water Engineering," 183–202, and Dieter Schott, "Remodeling 'Father Rhine': The Case of Mannheim 1825–1914," 203–226, in *Water, Culture, and Politics in Germany and the American West,* ed. Susan C. Anderson and Bruce H. Tabb (New York: Peter Lang, 2001).

34. Recent works that contain useful information on Rhine-Ruhr environmental problems include Cioc, *The Rhine: An Ecobiography,* 77–143, and "Impact of the Coal Age," 109–112; Franz-Josef Brüggemeier and Thomas

Rommelspacher, eds., *Blauer Himmel über der Ruhr: Geschichte der Umwelt im Ruhrgebiet 1840–1990* (Essen: Klartext, 1992); Ralf Henneking, *Chemische Industrie und Umwelt: Konflikte um Umweltbelastungen durch die chemische Industrie am Beispiel der schwerchemischen, Farben- und Düngemittel-industrie der Rheinprovinz (ca. 1800–1914)* (Stuttgart: F. Steiner, 1994); Ulrike Gilhaus, *"Schmerzenskinder der Industrie": Umweltverschmutzung, Umweltpolitik und sozialer Protest im Industriezeitalter in Westfalen, 1845–1914* (Paderborn: F. Schöningh, 1995); Jürgen Büschenfeld, *Flüsse und Kloaken: Umweltfragen im Zeitalter der Industrialisierung, 1870–1918* (Stuttgart: Klett-Cotta, 1997).

35. Dominick, *The Environmental Movement in Germany*, 13; Cioc, "Impact of the Coal Age," 111–112.

36. On this case, see Cioc, "Impact of the Coal Age," 115. For additional information on air pollution in the region, see Franz-Josef Brüggemeier, *Das unendliche Meer der Lüfte: Luftverschmutzung, Industrialisierung, und Risikodebatten im neunzehnten Jahrhundert* (Essen: Klartext, 1996).

37. Hans Klose, "Die Wandlung des westfälischen Industriegebietes," in *Naturdenkmäler: Vorträge und Aufsätze,* vol. 2, ed. Staatliche Stelle für Naturdenkmalpflege (Berlin: Gebrüder Borntraeger, 1919), 7.

38. Klose, "Die Wandlung des westfälischen Industriegebietes," 108, 113–115.

39. On the SPD's size and ideology, see Dick Geary, *European Labor Politics from 1900 to the Depression* (Atlantic Highlands, N.J.: Humanities Press, 1991), 9. Raymond Dominick has argued that the SPD brought such industrial pollution problems to public attention on a much larger scale than did the bourgeois parties. See Dominick, *Environmental Movement in Germany*, 62–64.

40. Rudorff's views on the Siebengebirge are described in Dominick, *Environmental Movement in Germany*, 26–27.

41. See Arne Andersen, "Heimatschutz: Die bürgerliche Naturschutzbewegung," in *Besiegte Natur,* ed. Brüggemeier and Rommelspacher, 143–158.

42. Heinen, "Naturschutzgebiet Siebengebirge," 112.

43. The Provinzialverband was the official organ of Rhenish self-government in the province, one of twelve *Provinzialverbände* in Prussia situated between the Prussian state and the municipalities. Rhenish officialdom at this time consisted of both Prussian-appointed statesmen and provincial officials who were elected through Prussia's three-tier voting system, which apportioned votes based on property taxes, meaning that the wealthy few (usually large landowners) who paid the top third of property taxes in their constituency commanded one-third of the votes in the electoral college for the Prussian parliament; the next group paying the middle third of property taxes (a somewhat larger minority) controlled the next third of the votes; while the vast majority of people who owned next to nothing and paid minimal property tax were able to cast only the last third of the votes. This system skewed

representation in favor of the aristocracy even as their economic power was declining in imperial Germany. This voting system was swept away with the collapse of the Kaiserreich in 1918. The Prussian-appointed officials, whom I refer to as the state, were the provincial head president *(Oberpräsident)*, district governors for Cologne, Trier, Koblenz, Düsseldorf, and Aachen *(Regierungspräsidenten)*, and the county representatives, known as *Landräte.* Elected officials included the provincial governor, known as the *Landeshauptmann;* the Provinzialverband, elected by the Rhineland's municipal and county leaders; and the Provinzialausschuss, a thirteen-member commission led by a chairman that was charged with carrying out the Provinzialverband's administrative and budgetary tasks.

44. On Humbroich's efforts, see Hardenberg, "Der Drachenfels," 309–310; Berres and Kiess, *Siebengebirge,* 15.

45. Verein zur Rettung des Siebengebirges (VRS), *Zur Rettung des Siebengebirges: Eine Rechtfertigungsschrift* (Bonn: Verlag von A. Henrh, 1887).

46. VRS, *Zur Rettung des Siebengebirges* (Bonn: Verlag von A. Henrh, 1886), 7–8.

47. *Verschönerungsverein für das Siebengebirge, Honnef und Obercassel,* vol. 2: *1885–1895* (Honnef: Buchdruckerei der "Honnefer Volkszeitung," Karl Weber, 1895), 12–15.

48. On the historicization of natural features in nationalist mythology, see Anthony Smith, *The Ethnic Origins of Nations* (Oxford: Oxford University Press, 1986), 183–190.

49. VRS, *Zur Rettung des Siebengebirges* (1886), 4–5.

50. Ibid.

51. Ibid., 5.

52. *Verschönerungsverein für das Siebengebirge, Honnef und Obercassel,* 2: 18–19.

53. On the refounding of the VVS, see Berres and Kiess, *Siebengebirge,* 15; Heinen, "Naturschutzgebiet Siebengebirge," 113; and Cologne Regierungsassessor Reeder, "Das Naturschutzgebiet Siebengebirge," 11 November 1927, ALVR 3733.

54. Kiess and Berres, *Siebengebirge,* 15; "Satzungen des Verschönerungsvereins für das Siebengebirge," 13 April 1899, ALVR 3733.

55. See VVS, *Geschäftsbericht für das Jahr 1902* and Verzeichnis der Mitglieder 1905, ALVR 3733.

56. Rollins, *Greener Vision of Home,* 5, 36, 159–161.

57. On fin-de-siècle cultural despair, see George Mosse, *The Crisis of German Ideology: Intellectual Origins of the Third Reich* (New York: Grosset and Dunlap, 1964), and Fritz Stern, *The Politics of Cultural Despair: A Study in the Rise of the Germanic Ideology* (New York: Anchor, 1965).

58. Reeder, "Naturschutzgebiet Siebengebirge," 11–12.

59. Ibid., 12; Berres and Kiess, *Siebengebirge,* 15; Heinen, "Naturschutzgebiet Siebengebirge," 113.

60. Memorandum of the Ministerium des Innern, 27 February 1899, ALVR

280 · Notes to Pages 42–45

3733; *34. Petitions-Bericht der Gemeindekommission,* 14 January 1913, 3, Bundesarchiv Koblenz (hereafter BAK), vol. 245, no. 185, fol. 225.

61. *34. Petitions-Bericht der Gemeindekommission,* 14 January 1913, 3–4.

62. *Bericht und Antrag des Provinzialausschusses,* Drucksachen No. 13, 28 November 1898, ALVR 3733; Reeder reports the amounts as somewhat higher in "Naturschutzgebiet Siebengebirge," 12: 160,000 marks and 320,000 marks, respectively.

63. Reeder, "Naturschutzgebiet Siebengebirge," 12.

64. In 1905 the Prussian officials were Dr. Steinmeister, Graf Galen, and Freiherr von Dalwigk zu Lichtenfels. The elected Rhenish provincial officials were Landeshauptmann von Renvers, Cologne mayor Becker, and Beigeordneter Bottler, respectively. See VVS, 1905 Verzeichnis der Mitglieder, ALVR 3733.

65. "Die Erhaltung des Siebengebirges," *Kölnische Zeitung,* 11 March 1898; "Zur Geschichte der Bemühungen um die Erschliessung und Erhaltung des Siebengebirges," *Bonner Zeitung,* 25 March 1898?

66. "Die Erhaltung des Siebengebirges," *Kölnische Zeitung,* 1–3.

67. On provincial self-administration, see Horst Lademacher, *Von den Provinzialständen zum Landschaftsverband: Zur Geschichte der landschaftlichen Selbstverwaltung der Rheinlande* (Cologne: Rheinland, 1973), 7–67; Johannes Horion, *Die Rheinische Provinzialverwaltung: Ihre Entwicklung und Ihr heutiger Stand* (Düsseldorf: L. Schwann, 1925); and Johannes Horion, *Probleme der Reichsreform,* vol. 7, in *Schriften der Volkswirtschaftlichen Vereinigung im rheinisch-westfälischen Industriegebeit* (Jena: Verlag von Gustav Fischer, 1931). My analysis of the Provinzialverband and the institutional framework for Rhineland preservation policy is based on files from the cultural affairs division of the Rhenish Landschaftsverband, the successor to the Provinzialverband in the state of North Rhine-Westphalia.

68. Lademacher, *Von den Provinzialständen zum Landschaftsverband,* 64–78; Hans-Joachim Behr, "Die preussische Provinzialverbände: Verfassung, Aufgaben, Leistung," in *Selbstverwaltung und Herrschaftsordnung: Bilanz und Perspektiven landschaftlicher Selbstverwaltung in Westfalen,* ed. Karl Teppe (Münster: Aschendorffsche, 1987), 11–44; Karl Ditt, *Raum und Volkstum: Die Kulturpolitik des Provinzialverbandes Westfalen, 1923–1945* (Münster: Aschendorffsche, 1988), 13–25.

69. Ditt, *Raum und Volkstum,* 13–17.

70. *Bericht und Antrag des Provinzialausschusses,* 28 November 1898, 1–2.

71. On regionalism and national identity, see Celia Applegate, *A Nation of Provincials: The German Idea of Heimat* (Berkeley: University of California Press, 1990), and Alon Confino, *The Nation as a Local Metaphor: Württemberg, Imperial Germany, and National Memory* (Chapel Hill: University of North Carolina Press, 1997).

72. VRS, *Zur Rettung des Siebenebirges* (1886), 5–6.

73. Ibid., 6.

74. *Bericht und Antrag des Provinzialausschusses,* 28 November 1898, 2; Notes from Bonn Assembly Meeting, 1898 (?), ALVR 3733.
75. VRS, *Zur Rettung des Siebengebirges* (1886), 6.
76. *Zur Siebengebirgsfrage: Offene Antwort an den Vorstand des VVS* (Cologne: Kölner Verlags-Anstalt, 1901), 7–15, 46.
77. Ibid., 6, 19–20.
78. Alfred Barthelmess, *Landschaft, Lebensraum des Menschen: Probleme von Landschaftsschutz und Landschaftspflege geschichtlich dargestellt und dokumentiert* (Freiburg: Karl Alber, 1988), 133. Cited in Rollins, *Greener Vision of Home,* 51; emphasis in the original.
79. Heinen, "Naturschutzgebiet Siebengebirge," 114.
80. Ibid., 114–115.
81. Reeder, "Naturschutzgebiet Siebengebirge," 13–14. On the 1901 District Court decision, see *Entscheidungen des königlich Preussischen Oberverwaltungsgerichts,* vol. 21 (Berlin: Carl Heymanns, 1903), 324–328.
82. Reeder, "Naturschutzgebiet Siebengebirge," 13–14.
83. *34. Petitions-Bericht der Gemeindekommission,* 14 January 1913, 2, fol. 224.
84. Ibid., 5, fol. 226.
85. Reeder, "Naturschutzgebiet Siebengebirge." By 1927 the money raised through lotteries and grants totaled 2,960,000 marks. The VVS purchased and administed 792 hectares of land and roads in the Siebengebirge directly, while the park's boundaries, which included leased lands and owners whose activities did not disturb the area's scenic beauty, extended to 4,200 hectares.
86. My account of the founding of the State Office for Natural Monument Preservation is based on the following sources: Wettengel, "Staat und Naturschutz," 363–372; Dominick, *The Environmental Movement in Germany,* 51; Josef Zimmermann, "Die Entwicklung des Naturschutzes, insbesondere in den rheinischen Gebieten, und Gedanken über eine allgemeine Geschichte des Naturschutzes," *Eifeljahrbuch* (1995): 39–40. On Wetekamp's efforts, see Konrad Ott et al., "Über die Anfänge des Naturschutzgedankens in Deutschland und den USA im neunzehnten Jahrhundert," *Jahrbuch für Europäische Verwaltungsgeschichte,* no. 11 (Baden-Baden: Nomos, 1999), 24–28.
87. Cited in Zimmermann, "Die Entwicklung des Naturschutzes," 40.
88. Wilhelm Wetekamp, "Aus der Geschichte der staatlichen Denkmalpflege," *Mitteilungen der Brandenburgischen Provinzialkommission für Naturdenkmalpflege* 7 (1914): 207–218, here 208. Cited in Ott et al., "Über die Anfänge des Naturschutzgedankens," 25.
89. Hugo Conwentz, *Die Gefährdung der Naturdenkmäler und Vorschläge zu ihrer Erhaltung* (Berlin: Gebrüder Bornträger, 1904).
90. Ott et al., "Über die Anfänge des Naturschutzgedankens," 28.
91. Wettengel, "Staat und Naturschutz," 365–367.

92. Walter Mrass, *Die Organisation des staatlichen Naturschutzes und der Landschaftspflege im deutschen Reich und der Bundesrepublik Deutschland seit 1935* (Stuttgart: Verlag Eugen Ulmer, 1969).
93. Wettengel, "Staat und Naturschutz," 362; Verein Naturschutzpark e.V., *Naturschutzparke: Fünfzig Jahre Verein Naturschutzpark* (Stuttgart: Verlag des Vereins Naturschutparke, 1959); Andrea Kiendl, *Die Lüneburger Heide: Fremdenverkehr und Literatur* (Berlin: Reimer, 1993).
94. Conwentz, *Die Gefährdung der Naturdenkmäler,* 6.
95. Mitglieder des Provinzial Komitees (n.d.), ALVR 11120. For brief biographies of these individuals, see Horst Romeyk, *Die leitenden staatlichen und kommunalen Verwaltungsbeamten der Rheinprovinz, 1816–1945* (Düsseldorf: Droste, 1994).
96. For a useful overall survey of the Kaiserreich's various nature preservation organizations, see Dominick, *Environmental Movement in Germany,* 42–78, and Raymond Dominick, "Nascent Environmental Protection in the Second Empire," *German Studies Review* 9 (1986): 257–291.
97. On bird protection, see Wettengel, "Staat und Naturschutz," 368; Dominick, *Environmental Movement in Germany,* 10–11, 24–25, 53–54; Horst Hanemann and Jürgen M. Simon, *Deutscher Bund für Vogelschutz, e.V. Die Chronik eines Naturschutzverbandes von 1899–1984* (Wiesbaden: Wirtschaftsverlag, 1987).
98. Dominick, "Nascent Environmental Protection," 277.
99. Malcolm Nicolson, "Alexander von Humboldt, Humboldtian Science and the Origins of the Study of Vegetation," *History of Science* 25 (1987): 167–194; Donald Worster, *Nature's Economy: A History of Ecological Ideas* (Cambridge: Cambridge University Press, 1991), 133–138.
100. Malcolm Nicolson, "Humboldtian Plant Geography after Humboldt: The Link to Ecology," *British Journal of the History of Science,* 29 (1996): 289–310. The word *ecology* did not at this time carry the cultural, political, and public policy meanings it holds today. During the Kaiserreich, it referred to a minor branch of botany and zoology. It did not refer to the study of the impacts of pollution on human health and biotic diversity, nor to a philosophy that promotes a nonanthropocentric view of nature. The term *ecology* was coined by the German zoologist Ernst Haeckel in 1866 to refer to the study of the individual organism's relationship to its environment. Haeckel examined the role of the environment in the process of natural selection, including species' adaptability to their environment and their interactions with each other. While Haeckel focused on individual species, plant geographers offered a holistic vision of biotic communities that looked at the interdependent relationships between species and the association between those relationships and environmental factors. A "functional" ecological theory that could be used in land use planning and toxicological studies was not developed until after the Second World War. For a useful introduction to the history of ecology in Germany, see Eugene Cittadino, *Nature as the*

*Laboratory: Darwinian Plant Ecology in the German Empire, 1880–1900* (Cambridge: Cambridge University Press, 1990).

101. See VVS, *Geschäftsberichte* for the years 1911–1913, BAK B245/185.
102. Letter from Conwentz to Oberregierungsrat Ebbinghaus, 2 August 1913, 2, BAK B245/185, fol. 223.
103. Ibid., 2–3, fol. 222–223; memorandum from Reusch, 3 September 1913, BAK 245/185, fol. 221.
104. On the familiarity of nature in the *Heimat* tradition, see Confino, "The Nation as a Local Metaphor: Heimat, National Memory, and the German Empire, 1871–1918," *History and Memory* 5, no. 1 (Spring/Summer 1993): 42–86; on the relationship between this familiarity and environmental perception and care, see Rollins, *Greener Vision of Home*, 74–78.
105. Dr. M. Braetz, "Schutz den heimischen Kriechtieren und Lurchen!" *Naturdenkmäler: Vorträge und Aufsätze* 2, no. 11, ed. Staatliche Stelle für Naturdenkmalpflege (Berlin: Gebrüder Bornträger, 1915), 5–8; on holism in the natural world, see also Ludwig Ankenbrand, *Naturschutz und Naturschutz-Parke* (Munich: Melchior Kupperschmid, 1912).
106. Braetz, "Schutz den heimischen Kriechtieren," 9, 24.
107. Hugo Conwentz, *Die Heimatkunde in der Schule: Grundlagen und Vorschläge zur Forderung der naturgeschichtlichen und geographischen Heimatkunde in der Schule* (Berlin: Gebrüder Bornträger, 1904), 2–3. Cited in Dominick, *Environmental Movement in Germany*, 24.
108. Conwentz, *Die Gefährdung der Naturdenkmäler*, 14–22.
109. Wettengel, "Staat und Naturschutz," 364–372.
110. Ernst Rudorff, "Antrag auf Schutz der landschaftlichen Natur," *Alterthumsverein* 6, no. 8 (1888): 86. Cited in Knaut, "Ernst Rudorff," 27.
111. Knaut, "Ernst Rudorff," 23–24; Rollins, *Greener Vision of Home*, 74–82.
112. Ernst Rudorff, "Über das Verhältnis des modernen Lebens zur Natur," *Preussische Jahrbücher* 45 (1880): 261–276, here 276.
113. Ibid., 262. Cited in Rollins, *Greener Vision of Home*, 74.
114. Ernst Rudorff, *Heimatschutz*, 3rd ed. (Munich, 1904), 88. Cited in Wettengel, "Staat und Naturschutz," 60.
115. On the social background of *Heimatschutz* members, see Rollins, *Greener Vision of Home*, 102–112. On the ties to turn-of-the-century architectural reform, see Matthew Jefferies, "Back to the Future? The 'Heimatschutz' Movement in Wilhelmine Germany," *History* 77 (1992): 411–420, and Matthew Jefferies, *Politics and Culture in Wilhelmine Germany: The Case of Industrial Architecture* (Washington, D.C.: Berg, 1995); Stefan Muthesius, "The Origins of the German Conservation Movement," in *Planning for Conservation*, ed. Roger Kain (New York: St. Martin's Press, 1981), 31–48.
116. Rollins, *Greener Vision of Home*; Norbert Borrmann, *Paul Schultze-Naumburg, 1869–1949: Maler—Publizist—Architekt: Vom Kulturreformer der Jahrhundertwende zum Kulturpolitiker im Dritten Reich* (Essen: Rich-

ard Bacht, 1989), 62; Matthew Jefferies, "Heimatschutz: Environmental Activism in Wilhelmine Germany," in *Green Thought in German Culture: Historical and Contemporary Perspectives,* ed. Colin Riordan (Cardiff: University of Wales Press, 1997), 47–62, here 47–48.

117. Rollins, *Greener Vision of Home,* 141–143; Röhkrämer, *Andere Moderne?* 113.

118. "Die Laufenburger Stromschnellen," *Der Kunstwart* 18 (1904/05): 22. Cited in Borrmann, *Paul Schultze-Naumburg,* 8.

119. Karl Peter Wiemer, *Ein Verein im Wandel der Zeit: Der Rheinischer Verein für Denkmalpflege und Heimatschutz von 1906 bis 1970* (Cologne: Rheinischer Verein für Denkmalpflege und Landschaftsschutz, 2000), 58–60.

120. Rollins, *Greener Vision of Home,* 81, 87–91, 167–170, Klaus-Georg Wey, *Umweltpolitik in Deutschland: Kurze Geschichte des Umweltschutzes in Deutschland seit 1900* (Opladen: Westdeutscher Verlag, 1982), 132–135.

121. Rollins, *Greener Vision of Home,* 112; Margitta Bucher, "Denkmale am Rhein," in *Der Rhein,* ed. Boldt, 157–158; Wiemer, *Ein Verein im Wandel der Zeit,* 47–51, 60–65.

122. Grant Allen, *The European Tour* (New York: Dodd, 1899), 141. Cited in Karl Ortseifen et al., eds., *Picturesque in the Highest Degree . . . Americans on the Rhine: A Selection of Travel Accounts* (Tübingen: Gunter Narr Verlag, 1993).

123. On agrarian-romanticism in the *Heimatschutz* movement, see Klaus Bergmann, *Agrarromantik und Grossstadtfeindschaft* (Meisenheim am Glan: Verlag Anton Hain, 1970).

124. Conwentz, *Die Gefährdung der Naturdenkmäler,* 32–76. On the conceptual limitations of Conwentz's critique, see Wey, *Umweltpolitik in Deutschland,* 130–131.

125. Wettengel, "Staat und Naturschutz," 365.

126. Ibid., 366–367.

127. Borrmann, *Paul Schultze-Naumburg,* 12–15.

128. Jefferies, "Heimatschutz," 43–45.

129. Paul Schultze-Naumburg, *Kulturarbeiten,* 2nd ed. (Munich: Callwey, Kunstwart Verlag, 1901–1916), preface to vol. 1, repr. in vol. 3, i.

130. Ibid., vol. 1: *Hausbau* (1901), 2–3; vol. 3: *Dörfer und Kolonien* (1908), i–ii.

131. Ibid., vol. 7: *Die Gestaltung der Erde durch den Menschen* (1916), 1–5, 39–40, 51.

132. Ibid., vol. 4: *Städtebau* (1906), 23–30, 157.

133. See *Mitteilungen des Rheinischen Vereins für Denkmalpflege und Heimatschutz* 3, no. 1 (1909); 4, no. 1 (1910); 6, no. 2 (1912).

134. Cited in Borrmann, *Paul Schultze-Naumburg,* 32.

135. Ibid., 60; Jefferies, "Heimatschutz," 44–52.

136. Konrad Guenther, *Der Naturschutz* (Freiburg: Friedrich Ernst Fehlenfeld, 1912), iii–iv, 11.

137. Ibid., iii, 7–8, 13.

138. Ibid., 13.

139. Ibid., 11.

140. Jochen Zimmer, ed., *"Mit uns zieht die neue Zeit": Die Naturfreunde, zur Geschichte eines alternativen Verbandes in der Arbeiterbewegung* (Cologne: Pahl-Rugenstein, 1984), 12. On the Friends of Nature, see also Jochen Zimmer, "Soziales Wandern: Zur proletarischen Naturaneignung," in *Besiegte Natur,* ed. Brüggemeier and Rommelspacher, 158–167.

141. Heinz Hoffman and Jochen Zimmer, eds., *Wir sind die Grüne Garde: Geschichte der Naturfreundejugend* (Essen: Klartext, 1986), 142–143. Cited in Dominick, *The Environmental Movement in Germany,* 63.

142. Jürgen Reulecke, "Wo Liegt Falado? Überlegungen zum Verhältnis von Jugendbewegung und Heimatbewegung vor dem Ersten Weltkrieg," in *Antimodernismus und Reform,* ed. Klueting, 1–19.

143. Friedrich Wilhelm Bredt, *Jugendpflege und Heimatschutz* (Düsseldorf: L. Schwann, 1913), 35.

144. Wettengel, "Staat und Naturschutz," 373; Zimmermann, "Entwicklung des Naturschutzes," 42.

145. Hermann Löns, "Naturschutz und Rasseschutz," in *Hermann Löns' nachgelassene Schriften,* vol. 1, ed. Wilhelm Deimann (Leipzig, 1928), 486. Cited in Wettengel, "Staat und Naturschutz," 373.

146. Guenther, *Der Naturschutz,* 8–9.

147. Borrmann, *Paul Schultze-Naumburg,* 43.

148. On Germany's alternative modernities, see Rohrkrämer, *Andere Moderne?*

## 2 The Militarization of Nature and Heimat

1. Eifelverein, ed., *Die Eifel 1888–1988: Zum hundertjährigen Jubiläum des Eifelvereins* (Düren: Eifelverein, 1989), 307.

2. *Die Eifel 1888–1988,* 304, 319.

3. Rudy Koshar, *Germany's Transient Pasts: Preservation and National Memory in the Twentieth Century* (Chapel Hill: University of North Carolina Press, 1998), 79.

4. Dr. Bär, "Zur hundertjährigen Zugehörigkeit der Rheinlande zu Preussen," *Mitteilungen des Rhenischen Vereins für Denkmalpflege und Heimatschutz* (hereafter *MRVDH*) 9, no. 1 (1915): 7.

5. For similar sentiments in the Rhineland-Palatinate, see Celia Applegate, *A Nation of Provincials: The German Idea of Heimat* (Berkeley: University of California Press, 1990), 108–119.

6. Georg Kreuzberg, "Heimat, Schule, und Krieg," *MRVDH* 9, no. 1 (1915): 32.

7. Ibid., 33–34. On wartime *Heimat* activities, see also Applegate, *Nation of Provincials,* 109–116, and Koshar, *Germany's Transient Pasts,* 80.

8. Alon Confino, "The Nation as a Local Metaphor: Heimat, National Mem-

ory, and the German Empire, 1871–1918," *History and Memory* 5, no. 1 (Spring/Summer 1993): 42–86, here 65–66.

9. Wilhelm Bölsche, *Die Deutsche Landschaft in Vergangenheit und Gegenwart* (Berlin: Vita, 1915), 20.

10. Celia Applegate, "The Question of Heimat in the Weimar Republic," *New Formations* 17 (1992): 67.

11. Kreuzberg, "Heimat, Schule, und Krieg," 33.

12. Hugo Otto, "Betrachtungen über Natur- und Heimatschutz in Polen," *MRVDH* 9, no. 1 (1915): 80.

13. On *Heimat* and war imagery, see Raymond Dominick, *The Environmental Movement in Germany: Prophets and Pioneers, 1871–1971* (Bloomington: Indiana University Press, 1992), 86; Applegate, *Nation of Provincials,* 116–117.

14. George Mosse, *Fallen Soldiers: Reshaping the Memory of the World Wars* (Oxford: Oxford University Press, 1990), 5. On the image of soldiers as "swamp beings," see Ulrich Linse, *Zurück, o Mensch, zur Mutter Erde: Landkommunen in Deutschland, 1890–1933* (Munich: DTV, 1983), 91.

15. Waldemar Bonsels, *Die Heimat des Todes: Empfindsame Kriegsberichte* (Munich: Walter Schmidkunz, 1916), 43.

16. Linse, *Zurück, o Mensch,* 91.

17. Paul Berry and Alan Bishop, eds., *Testament of a Generation: The Journalism of Vera Britain and Winifried Holtby* (London, 1985). Cited in Mosse, *Fallen Soldiers,* 111–112.

18. Bonsels, *Heimat des Todes,* 48.

19. Mosse, *Fallen Soldiers,* 87–88.

20. Linse, *Zurück, o Mensch,* 91.

21. *Eifelvereinsblatt* (hereafter *EVB*) 1917, 37. Cited in *Die Eifel 1888–1988,* 313.

22. *EVB* 1914, 223. Cited in *Die Eifel 1888–1988,* 309.

23. *EVB* 1917, 37. Cited in *Die Eifel 1888–1988,* 311; Applegate, *Nation of Provincials,* 114.

24. *EVB* 1916, 133–134, 163. Cited in *Die Eifel 1888–1988,* 313–314.

25. Friedrich Wilhelm Bredt, "Vorwort: Von Krieg und Kunst," in *MRVDH* 8, no. 3 (1914): 184. On the RVDH response to the Reims Cathedral bombing, see Koshar, *Germany's Transient Pasts,* 80.

26. Bodo Ebhardt, "Deutsche Burgen als Vorbilder," in *Das eiserne Buch: Die führenden Männer und Frauen zum Weltkrieg 1914/15,* ed. Georg Gellert (Hamburg, 1915), 204. Cited in Applegate, *Nation of Provincials,* 117. See also Koshar, *Germany's Transient Pasts,* 93.

27. Applegate, "The Question of *Heimat,*" 69.

28. G. Wolfram, "Nationalitätsgrenze und Bauart in Lothringen," *MRVDH* 9, no. 3 (1915): 159–164. See also Koshar, *Germany's Transient Pasts,* 91.

29. Otto, "Betrachtungen über Natur- und Heimatschutz in Polen," 80–83.

30. William Rollins, *A Greener Vision of Home: Cultural Politics and Environ-*

*mental Reform in the German Heimatschutz Movement, 1904–1918* (Ann Arbor: University of Michigan Press, 1997), 256.

31. Friedrich Wilhelm Bredt, "Der Heimatschutz im Preussischen Landtage," *MRVDH* 9, no. 1 (1915): 27.
32. Ibid., 29. According to Koshar, planning in East Prussia also included garden cities designed for returning veterans, patterned on what were thought to be ancient Germanic models. See Koshar, *Germany's Transient Pasts,* 105.
33. *EVB* 1919, 39. Cited in *Die Eifel 1888–1988,* 348–349.
34. Doris Kaufmann, "Heimat im Revier? Die Diskussion über das Ruhrgebiet im Westfälischen Heimatbund während der Weimarer Republik," in *Antimodernismus und Reform: Zur Geschichte der deutschen Heimatbewegung,* ed. Edeltraud Klueting (Darmstadt: Wissenschaftliche Buchgesellschaft, 1991), 174.
35. Hermann Bartmann, *Heimatpflege, Denkmalpflege und Heimatschutz: Ihre Aufgaben, Organisation und Gesetzgebung* (Leipzig: B. G. Teubner, 1920), 3–5.
36. Gerhard Platz, *Vom Wandern und Weilen im Heimatland* (Dresden: Landesverein Sächsischer Heimatschutz, 1920), 6.
37. Konrad Guenther, *Heimatlehre als Grundlage aller Volksentwicklung: Ein Programm für den Wiederaufbau* (Freiburg: Theodor Fischer Verlag, 1920), 2, 4–5. Cited in Dominick, *The Environmental Movement in Germany,* 87.
38. Konrad Guenther, *Die Heimatlehre vom Deutschtum* (Leipzig: R. Voigtländer, 1932), 12. Cited in Dominick, *The Environmental Movement in Germany,* 242.
39. Detlev J. Peukert, *The Weimar Republic: The Crisis of Classical Modernity,* trans. by Richard Deveson (New York: Hill and Wang, 1989), 61.
40. Dieter Kastner and Vera Torunsky, *Kleine rheinische Geschichte 1815–1986* (Cologne: Rheinland, 1987), 52.
41. The best work in English on Rhenish separatism is Henry Nadler's *The Rhenish Separatist Movements during the Early Weimar Republic* (New York: Garland, 1987). Other useful works include Klaus Reimer, *Rheinland Frage und Rheinlandbewegung (1918–1933): Ein Beitrag zur Geschichte der regionalistischen Bewegungen* (Frankfurt am Main: Lang, 1979); Henning Köhler, *Autonomiebewegung oder Separatismus? Die Politik der kölnischen Volkszeitung 1918/1919* (Berlin: Colloquium, 1974).
42. On Minister Hoffmann's opposition in the Rhineland, see *Die Eifel 1888–1988,* 321.
43. Cited in Franziska Wein, *Deutschlands Strom—Frankreichs Grenze: Geschichte und Propaganda am Rhein, 1919–1930* (Essen: Klartext, 1992), 18.
44. Nadler, *Rhenish Separatist Movements,* 1.
45. For an analysis of similar policies in Rhineland-Palatinate, see Applegate, *Nation of Provincials,* 121–123.

46. Not all French historians accepted this argument. The famous *Annaliste* Lucien Febvre dismissed nationalist and racist arguments about the Rhine as inaccurate and misguided. The Rhineland, he maintained, had witnessed a blending of races and cultures for centuries that made it impossible to establish an ethnic boundary on the basis of geographic features. See Lucien Febvre, *Der Rhein und seine Geschichte,* trans. by Peter Schöttler (1935; Frankfurt: Campus, 1994).

47. Wein, *Deutschlands Strom,* 15–89.

48. Ibid., 150.

49. Both John Williams and Celia Applegate have spoken of a growing nationalization of *Heimat* rhetoric in the early 1920s. See John Williams, "'The Chords of the German Soul Are Tuned to Nature': The Movement to Preserve the Natural *Heimat* from the *Kaiserreich* to the Third Reich," *Central European History* 29, no. 3 (1996): 339–384, here 344; Applegate, "The Question of *Heimat,*" 69–70.

50. H. Helbok, "Mensch und Volk," in *Der deusche Heimatschutz: Ein Rückblick und Ausblick,* ed. Gesellschaft der Freunde des deutschen Heimatschutzes (Munich: Kastner and Callwey, 1930), 17–33, here 33.

51. See Applegate, *Nation of Provincials,* 129–132.

52. Cited in Wein, *Deutschlands Strom,* 105; see also her discussion on 97–107.

53. Reich Interior Ministry to Reichsrat minister Sperr, 26 January 1925, MK51152, Bayerisches Hauptstaatsarchiv Munich. Cited in Williams, "'Chords of the German Soul,'" 358. See also Applegate, *Nation of Provincials,* 130–132.

54. Wein, *Deutschlands Strom,* 107–110.

55. Rheinischer Heimatbund e.V., Der Zweck des Bundes, 1920, 1, ALVR 12718.

56. Ibid.

57. On the Bonn Regional Studies Institute, see Edith Ennen, "Hermann Aubin und die geschichtliche Landeskunde der Rheinlande," *Rheinische Vierteljahrsblätter* 34 (1970): 9–42, and Marlene Nikolay-Panther, Wilhelm Janssen, and Wolfgang Herborn, eds., *Geschichtliche Landeskunde der Rheinlande: Regionale Befunde und raumübergreifende Perspektiven* (Cologne: Böhlau, 1994).

58. Hermann Aubin, Theodor Frings, and Josef Müller, *Kulturströmungen und Kulturprovinzen in den Rheinlanden: Geschichte, Sprache, Volkskunde* (1926; Bonn: Ludwig Röhrscheid, 1966).

59. On the institute as a political tool, see Wein, *Deutschlands Strom,* 114–122.

60. *Die Eifel 1888–1988,* 327.

61. Quoted in Johannes Horion, *Die Rheinische Provinzialverwaltung: Ihre Entwicklung und ihr heutiger Stand* (Düsseldorf: L. Schwann, 1925), 54.

62. "Heimat in Note," in *Die Heimat* (1923). Cited in Kaufmann, "Heimat in Revier?" 175–176.

63. *Die Eifel, 1888–1988,* 330; Nadler, *Rhenish Separatist Movements,* 302–303.

64. On the Siebengebirge separatists, see Nadler, *Rhenish Separatist Movements*, 236–237; *Die Eifel 1888–1988*, 328–330; Jens Klocksin, *Separatisten im Rheinland: Siebzig Jahre nach der Schlacht im Siebengebirge, Ein Rückblick* (Bonn: Pahl-Rugenstein, 1993); Elmar Scheuren and Christoph Trapp, eds., *Separatisten im Siebengebirge: Die "Rheinische Republik" des Jahres 1923 und die "Schlacht" bei Aegidienberg* (16–17 November 1923), publication accompanying exhibition at Siebengebirgsmuseum der Stadt Königswinter, 16 November 1993–23 January 1994 (Bonn: P. R. Druck, 1993), 9–69. The separatists' demise in the Pfalz was far more violent; see Applegate, *Nation of Provincials*, 145–147.
65. Horion, *Die Rheinische Provinzialverwaltung*, 55; see also Nadler, *Rhenish Separatist Movements*, 267.

## 3 The Landscape of Modernity in the Weimar Era

1. Paul Kaufmann, *1000 Jahre Deutschtum an Rhein Ruhr Saar* (Berlin: Geschäftsstelle für Heimatliteratur Dormeyer and Kunst, 1925); Hermann Aubin et al., *Der Deutsche und das Rheingebiet* (Halle: Buchhandlung des Waisenhauses, 1926); Wilhelm Schellberg, ed., *Rheinland: Ein Volksbuch zur Tausendjahrfeier rheinischen Landes* (Düsseldorf: L. Schwann, 1925). For an excellent summary of the event in its political context, see Franziska Wein, *Deutschlands Strom—Frankreichs Grenze: Geschichte und Propaganda am Rhein 1919–1930* (Essen: Klartext, 1992), 123–142.
2. F. L. Lubszynski, ed., *Festbuch zur Jahrtausendfeier der Rheinlande 1925: Aus Anlass der Festwoche der Stadt Uerdingen am Rhein* (Uerdingen: George Fohrer, 1925), 7–8.
3. *Glühwein* is a type of mulled wine popular in the Rhineland.
4. Wein, *Deutschlands Strom*, 128–129.
5. Several festival writers tried to downplay the *völkisch* xenophobia that had reached its cresendo in 1923. The historian Erich Tross, for example, dismissed claims of "Nordic fanatics" that the Rhine marked a "racial" border between Germanic and Gallo-Roman blood, claiming instead that Rhenish strength stemmed from the racial mix in the area. See Erich Tross, *Der deutsche Rhein: Seine Germanisierung im weltgeschichtlichen Zusammenhang* (Frankfurt: Frankfurter Societät, 1925).
6. Lubszynski, *Festbuch zur Jahrtausendfeier*, 9.
7. W. Ewald and B. Kuske, eds., *Katalog der Jahrtausend Ausstellung der Rheinlande in Köln 1925* (Cologne: von M. Dumont Schauberg, 1925).
8. Edmund Renard, "Die Denkmalpflege in der Rheinprovinz," in *Rheinische Provinzialverwaltung: Ihre Entwicklung und Ihr heutiger Stand*, ed. Johannes Horion (Düsseldorf: L. Schwann, 1925), 443.
9. Ernst Tiedge, "Das Landschaftsbild von Xanten in Gefahr!" *Düsseldorfer Nachrichten*, 21 July 1926.
10. Raymond Dominick, *The Environmental Movement in Germany: Prophets*

*and Pioneers, 1871–1971* (Bloomington: Indiana University Press, 1992), 82.

11. On the scholarly debate concerning the irrational and antimodern tendencies of Weimar nature conservation, see John A. Williams, "'The Chords of the German Soul Are Tuned to Nature': The Movement to Preserve the Natural *Heimat* from the Kaiserreich to the Third Reich," *Central European History* 29, no. 3 (1996): 339–384, particularly 340–344. Works that emphasize these antimodern tendencies in Weimar include Hermann Bausinger, "Zwischen Grün und Braun: Volkstumsideologie und Heimatpflege nach dem Ersten Weltkrieg," in *Religions- und Geistesgeschichte der Weimarer Republik,* ed. Hubert Cancik (Düsseldorf: Patmos, 1982), 215–259, and Rolf-Peter Sieferle, *Fortschrittsfeinde? Opposition gegen Technik und Industrie von der Romantik bis zur Gegenwart* (Munich: C. H. Beck, 1984).

12. See David Thomas Murphy, *The Heroic Earth: Geopolitical Thought in Weimar Germany, 1918–1933* (Kent, Ohio: Kent State University Press, 1997), 27–28.

13. See Detlev Peukert, *The Weimar Republic: The Crisis of Classical Modernity,* trans. by Richard Deveson (New York: Hill and Wang, 1989).

14. Ibid., 83.

15. Edict of the Cultural Ministry and the Agricultural and Forestry Ministries auf Grund des Gesetzes vom 8. Juli 1920 zur Änderung des §34 des Feld- und Forstpolizeigesetzes vom 1. April 1880. Cited in Elmar Heinen, "Naturschutzgebiet Siebengebirge gestern—heute—morgen," *Rheinische Heimatpflege* 27 (1990): 112–121, here 117–118.

16. Williams, "'Chords of the German Soul,'" 355; Dominick, *Environmental Movement in Germany,* 84 .

17. Walther Schoenichen, "Aus der Entwicklung der Naturdenkmalpflege," in *Der deusche Heimatschutz: Ein Rückblick und Ausblick,* ed. Gesellschaft der Freunde des deutschen Heimatschutzes (Munich: Kastner and Callwey, 1930), 222–227, here 224. On Schoenichen's nature protection activities, see Dominick, *Environmental Movement in Germany,* 81–85; Michael Wettengel, "Staat und Naturschutz, 1906–1945: Zur Geschichte der Staatlichen Stelle für Naturdenkmalpflege in Preussen und der Reichstelle für Naturschutz," *Historische Zeitschrift* 257, no. 2 (October 1993): 355–399, here 376–380.

18. Karl Ditt, *Raum und Volkstum: Die Kulturpolitik des Provinzialverbandes Westfalen, 1923–1945* (Münster: Aschendorffsche, 1988), 60.

19. Staatliche Stelle für Naturdenkmalpflege, "Vierter Deutscher Naturschutztag in Berlin vom 8. bis 12. April," in *Beiträge zur Naturdenkmalpflege* 15, no. 1 (1932): 43–44.

20. Ditt, *Raum und Volkstum,* 18.

21. On Horion's life, see Sinnersdorfer Heimatkunde, ed., *Dr. Johannes Horion* (Pulheim: Gerhard Fensterer, 1983); Johannes Horion, *Die Rheinische*

*Provinzialverwaltung: Ihre Entwicklung und Ihr heutiger Stand* (Düsseldorf: L. Schwann, 1925), 395.

22. Horion, *Die Rheinische Provinzialverwaltung,* 56; see also "Rheinischer Verein für Denkmalpflege und Heimatschutz und die Rheinische Provinzialverwaltung," *Rheinische Heimatpflege* 2 (1931): 5–8.

23. "Parteifreunde des Rheinischen Zentrums!" *Kölnische Volkszeitung,* 8 November 1929.

24. Wein, *Deutschlands Strom,* 57–99.

25. On Weimar cultural plurality, see Peukert, *Weimar Republic,* 11; Ditt, *Raum und Volkstum,* 38–41. Horion's leadership made the Rhine Province more liberal in its interpretation of cultural politics than Westphalia, where Provincial Commissioner for Cultural Affairs Karl Zuhorn and the head of the Westphalian Heimat Association, Karl Wagenfeld, embraced a far more *völkisch* conception of the relationship between space and ethnic character. See Ditt, *Raum und Volkstum,* 53–70.

26. See miscellaneous files on hiking organizations in ALVR 12460.

27. Letter from Head President Fuchs to Provincial Governor Horion, 29 October 1925, ALVR 11121; Head President Fuchs to Horion, 20 May 1926, ALVR 12460.

28. Dr. Janssen, "Reklame am Rhein," *Nachrichtenblatt für rheinische Heimatpflege* 3, no. 1–2 (1931/32): 11–13.

29. Renard, "Die Denkmalpflege," 457; Senior Civil Servant Freiherr von Dungern, secretary of the Rhenish Provincial Office for Natural Monument Preservation, "Der Rheinsiche Naturschutz im Rechnungsjahre 1927/28," *Nachrichtenblatt für rheinische Heimatpflege* 1, no. 5–6 (1929): 6–9; Walther Schoenichen, *Die Naturschutzgebiete Preussens* (Berlin: Gebrüder Bornträger, 1926), 293–320.

30. Wiemer, *Ein Verein im Wandel der Zeit: Der Rheinische Verein für Denkmalpflege und Heimatschutz von 1906 bis 1970* (Cologne: Verlag des Rheinischen Vereins für Denkmalpflege und Landschaftsschutz, 2000), 88–90.

31. Robert Rein, "Wesen und Aufgabe der Naturdenkmalpflege," *Rheinische Jugend* 5, no. 20 (August 1932): 133–143; Dr. Schwab, "Naturschutz," in Official Exhibition Guide, *Der Rhein—Sein Werden und Wirken,* Koblenz 2 July to 31 August (Koblenz: Görresdrückerei, 1927), 78–79.

32. Wiemer, *Verein im Wandel der Zeit,* 78, 95–97.

33. "Landesplanung und Naturschutz im Rheinland," 23 July 1931, ALVR 11122.

34. Janssen, "Reklame am Rhein," 11.

35. Wiemer, *Verein im Wandel der Zeit,* 93–95, 237.

36. On the Eifel's economic state, see Eifelverein, ed., *Die Eifel 1888–1988: Zum hundertjährigen Jubiläum des Eifelvereins* (Düren: Eifelverein, 1989), 325.

37. Ibid., 332–334.

38. Horion, *Die Rheinische Provinzialverwaltung,* 504–508.
39. "Fremdenverkehr—die Hilfe für die Eifel?" *Kölnische Volkszeitung,* 29 March 1932. On Eifel tourism, see also Rudy Koshar, *Germany's Transient Pasts: Preservation and Memory in the Twentieth Century* (Chapel Hill: University of North Carolina Press, 1998), 145.
40. On Eifelverein tourism efforts, see *Die Eifel 1888–1988,* 373, 388–389, 390–396.
41. *Eifelvereinsblatt (EVB)* 1925, 90. Cited in *Die Eifel 1888–1988,* 372.
42. *EVB* 1920, 58. Cited in *Die Eifel 1888–1988,* 351–352.
43. *Die Eifel 1888–1988,* 351, 383.
44. *EVB* 1927, 136–137. Cited in *Die Eifel 1888–1988,* 388.
45. Dr. Schwab, "Das schönste Naturdenkmal der Eifel, der Laacher See, in Gefahr," in *EVB* 1925, 106–108. Cited in *Die Eifel 1888–1988,* 383–385.
46. Ernst Tiedge, "Bedeutung der Aufgaben des Naturschutzes in Unserer Zeit," *Zeitschrift des Rheinischen Vereins für Denkmalpflege und Heimatschutz* 18 (1925): 133–144, here 133. Many thanks to Karl Peter Wiemer for referring me to this important source, as well as to the Bislicher Island debate discussed below. See Wiemer's discussion of Tiedge in *Ein Verein im Wandel der Zeit,* 90–92.
47. Tiedge, "Bedeutung der Aufgaben des Naturschutzes," 134.
48. Ibid., 136.
49. Ibid., 135.
50. Ibid., 136–138.
51. Ibid., 133–135.
52. Schoenichen, "Aus der Entwicklung der Naturdenkmalpflage," 224. On holism in German ecological studies during the interwar era, see Eugene Cittadino, "Lebensraum and Lebensgemeinschaft: Ecology and Ideology in Interwar Germany," unpublished paper presented at the History of Science Society, Minneapolis, 28 October 1995; Anne Harrington, *Reenchanted Science: Holism in German Culture from Wilhelm II to Hitler* (Princeton: Princeton University Press, 1996).
53. Schoenichen, "Aus der Entwicklung der Naturdenkmalpflege," 224; Heinrich Rubner, *Deutsche Forstgeschichte, 1933–1945: Forstwirtschaft, Jagd, und Umwelt im NS-Staat* (St. Katharinen: Scripta Mecaturae, 1985), 27.
54. Hermann Bartmann, *Heimatpflege, Denkmalpflege und Heimatschutz: Ihre Aufgaben, Organisation und Gesetzgebung* (Leipzig: B. G. Teubner, 1920), 40.
55. Ibid., 40–54.
56. "Das Rheinsystem," in *Der Schaffende Rhein: Beiträge der Rheinfreunde* 8 (1932): 25.
57. August Reichensperger, "Zoologische Inseln in der Rheinlandschaft, ihre Tierformen und die Bedeutung ihres Schutzes," 320–325, and Dr. Menke, "Das Tal des Mittelrheins als Wanderstrasse von Pflanzen aus anderen Klimazonen," 328–331, in *Nachrichtenblatt für rheinische Heimatpflege* 3, no. 9–10 (1931/1932).

58. Murphy, *The Heroic Earth,* 1–28. On the history and political significance of geopolitics in Germany, see Mark Bassin, "Imperialism and the Nation State in Friedrich Ratzel's Political Geography," *Progress in Human Geography* 11, no. 4 (1987): 473–495 and "Race contra Space: The Conflict between German *Geopolitik* and National Socialism," *Political Geography Quarterly* 6, no. 2 (April 1987): 115–134; Henning Heske, "Karl Haushofer: His Role in German Geopolitics and in Nazi Politics," *Political Geography Quarterly* 6, no. 2 (April 1987): 135–144. On the Rhine in geopolitical thought, see Karl Haushofer, *Der Rhein: Sein Lebensraum, Sein Schicksal,* 3 vols. (Berlin-Grunewald: Kurt Vowinckel Verlag, 1928).

59. Murphy, *Heroic Earth,* 1–60; Wilhelm Pessler, *Deutsche Volkstumsgeographie* (Braunschweig: Georg Westermann, 1931).

60. Peter Zepp, "Die Siedlungen des Rheintales von Bingen bis Bonn in landschaftskundlicher Darstellung," *Nachrichtenblatt für rheinische Heimatpflege* 3, no. 9–10 (1931/32): 305–320.

61. Ibid., 308.

62. *Der Rhein: Sein Werden und Wirken,* 21.

63. Ibid., 255–257.

64. Ibid., 21.

65. Georg Räderscheidt, "Gegenwart und rheinische Kulturlandschaft," *Nachrichtenblatt für rheinische Heimatpflege* 3, no. 9–10 (1931/32): 299.

66. On the Bislicher Island campaign, see files in ALVR 11080.

67. See Günter van Endert, *Gegen die drohende Verunstaltung der Bislicher Insel und der Landschaft um Xanten* (Xanten, 1926), 1–19, here 19.

68. Ernst Tiedge, "Das Landschaftsbild von Xanten in Gefahr!" *Düsseldorfer Nachrichten,* 21 July 1926.

69. Ibid.

70. "Ablehnung der Erklärung der Bislicher Insel als Naturschutzgebiet," *Kölnische Zeitung,* 8 December 1926; "Trostlose Aussichten für den Heimatschutz," *Düsseldorfer Nachrichten,* 19 November 1926. On sacrifice to capitalist "mammon," see Hugo Otto, 24 April 1926, in Endert, *Gegen die drohende Verunstaltung der Bislicher Insel,* 35.

71. Report from Regierungsassassor Reeder to district president in Cologne, "Das Naturschutzgebiet Siebengebirge," 11 January 1927, BAK B245/185, 7–9, fol. 186–187.

72. August Reichensperger, "Der Kampf um die Sieben Berge," *Nachrichten aus der rheinischen Denkmalpflege,* vol. 1 (Düsseldorf: L. Schwann, 1919), 23–25.

73. "Prozess um den Naturschutz im Siebengebirge: Eine Klage ohne Vorgang," *Kölnische Zeitung,* 5 June 1931.

74. Reeder, "Das Naturschutzgebiet Siebengebirge," 9, fol. 186.

75. Hans Klose, *Fünfzig Jahre staatlicher Naturschutz: Ein Rückblick auf den Weg der deutschen Naturschutzbewegung* (Giessen: Brühlscher Verlag, 1957), 31. Cited in Dominick, *Environmental Movement in Germany,* 85; see also Klaus-Georg Wey, *Umweltpolitik in Deutschland: Kurze*

*Geschichte des Umweltschutzes in Deutschland seit 1900* (Opladen: Westdeutscher Verlag, 1982), 136–138.

76. "Landesplanung und Naturschutz," *Kölnische Volkszeitung*, 14 October 1930.

77. Heinz Günter Steinberg, "Die Entwicklung des Ruhrsiedlungsverbandes," in *Ruhrgebiet und Neues Land*, vol. 2: *Beiträge zur neueren Landesgeschichte des Rheinlandes und Westfalens*, ed. Walter Först (Cologne: Grote, 1968), 116–117.

78. On the war as an impetus for corporatist experimentation more broadly, see Charles S. Maier, *Recasting Bourgeois Europe: Stabilization in France, Germany, and Italy in the Decade after World War I* (Princeton: Princeton University Press, 1975); Thomas Rohkrämer, *Eine andere Moderne? Zivilisationskritik, Natur und Technik in Deutschland, 1880–1933* (Paderborn: Schöningh, 1999), 246–251.

79. Jürgen Brandt, *Landesplanung*, Deutscher Verein für Wohnungsreform, vol. 5 (Berlin: Carl Heymanns, 1929), 2.

80. Ibid., 2–19.

81. Stephan Praeger, "Landesplanung und Naturschutz," *Nachrichtenblatt für rheinische Heimatpflege* 3, no. 1–2 (1931): 13–19.

82. Brandt, *Landesplanung*, 13.

83. On this point, see Ulrich Linse, *Ökopax und Anarchie: Eine Geschichte der ökologischen Bewegungen in Deutschland* (Stuttgart: DTV, 1986), 26–36.

84. Hermann Zillig, "Der Naturschutz in der Rheinproviniz," 1929, 1, in BAK 245/181, fol. 230.

85. Albert Kloeckner, "Landesplanung und Landschaftsgestaltung," *Kölnische Volkszeitung*, 13 November 1930.

86. Joachim Wolschke-Bulmahn and Gert Groening, *75 Jahre Bund Deutscher Landschafts-Architekten BDLA, 1913–1988*, vol. 1: *Zur Entwicklung der Interessenverbände der Gartenarchitekten in der Weimarer Republik und im Nationalsozialismus* (Bonn: Köllen, 1989), 50–51.

87. "Bericht über den Studiengang für Landschaftsschutz und Landschaftsgestaltung vom 4.–7. Juli 1929 in Essen," *Nachrichtenblatt für rheinische Heimatpflege* 1, no. 5–6 (1929): 49–50; "Erster Deutscher Studiengang über Landschaftsschutz und Landschaftsgestaltung," *Rheinische-Westfälische Zeitung*, 4 July 1929.

88. See Walter Laqueur, *Weimar: A Cultural History* (New York: Putnam, 1974); Jeffrey Herf, *Reactionary Modernism: Technology, Culture and Politics in Weimar and the Third Reich* (Cambridge: Cambridge University Press, 1984).

89. Hans Schwenkel, "Gegner des Heimatschutzes," *Mitteilungen des Landesvereins Sächsicher Heimatschutz* 20, no. 9/12 (1931): 116–118.

90. Ibid. See also Linse, *Ökopax und Anarchie*, 25–35.

91. Werner Lindner, *Ingenieurwerk und Naturschutz* (Berlin: Hugo Bermühler, 1926), vii.

92. "Landesplanung und Naturschutz im Rheinland," 23 July 1931, ALVR 11122.

93. Steinberg, "Die Entwicklung des Ruhrsiedlungsverbandes," 121.
94. Doris Kaufmann, "Heimat im Revier? Die Diskussion über das Ruhrgebiet im Westfälischen Heimatbund während der Weimarer Republik," in *Antimodernismus und Reform: Zur Geschichte der deutschen Heimatbewegung*, ed. Edeltraud Klueting (Darmstadt: Wissenschaftliche Buchgesellschaft, 1991), 178–179; Tiedge, "Bedeutung der Aufgaben des Naturschutzes," 134.
95. "Tagung der Berzirkstelle für Naturdenkmalpflege im Ruhrbezirk," *Rheinische-Westfälische Zeitung*, 31 May 1927; "Natur- und Heimatschutz im Industriegebiet," *Kölnische Zeitung*, 15 June 1926.
96. On the Ruhr Settlement Association, see "Die Tätigkeit des Siedlungsverbandes Ruhrkohlenbezirks: Nach einem Vortrag der Verbandsleitung am 20 July 1926 vor dem Wohnungsausschuss des preussischen Landtages," ALVR 12466; Heinrich Hoebink, *Mehr Raum—Mehr Macht: Preussische Kommunalpolitik im rheinischen-westfälischen Industriegebiet* (Essen: Klartext, 1990); Kloeckner, "Landesplanung und Landschaftsgestaltung;" and Steinberg, "Die Entwicklung des Ruhrsiedlungsverbandes," 115–152.
97. Wey, *Umweltpolitik in Deutschland*, 141–146. Wey notes that, in practice, agricultural and forestry interests were able to water down the 1922 law's provisions; most permits to cut trees were granted so long as property owners replanted tree stands elsewhere.
98. Kloeckner, "Landesplanung und Landschaftsgestaltung."
99. On Ruhr pollution issues, see Dominick, *Environmental Movement in Germany*, 82; Rubner, *Deutsche Forstgeschichte*, 33–34; Gert Gröning and Joachim Wolschke-Bulmahn, *Die Liebe zur Landschaft*, vol. 1: *Natur in Bewegung: Zur Bedeutung natur- und freiraumorientierter Bewegungen der ersten Hälfte des zwanzigsten Jahrhunderts für die Entwicklung der Freiraumplanung* (Munich: Minerva, 1986), 90.
100. Garden and Landscape Consultant Meyer-Jungclaussen, "Von der Bedeutung des Mutterbodens im Landstrassenbau," *Der Strassenbau* 23, 10 August 1931. Reprinted in Fürst Pückler Society, pamphlet no. 1.
101. Meyer-Jungclaussen, "Landschaftliche Gestaltungsfragen im Braunkohlenbergbau-Gelände: Gedanken über Waldbau und Landschaftsbild," Fürst Pückler Society, pamphlet no. 5.
102. "Landesplanung und Naturschutz," *Kölnische Volkszeitung*, 14 November 1930.
103. Ulrich Linse, *Zurück, o Mensch, zur Mutter Erde: Landkommunen in Deutschland 1890–1933* (Stuttgart: DTV, 1983); see also Linse, *Ökopax und Anarchie*, 26–36.
104. On Weimar's framework for leisure, see Peukert, *Weimar Republic*, 75, and Gerhard Huck, ed., *Sozialgeschichte der Freizeit: Untersuchungen zum Wandel der Alltagskultur in Deutschland* (Wuppertal: Hammer, 1980).
105. On August Sander, see *August Sander: Rheinlandschaften. Photographien 1926–1946*, with text by Wolfgang Kemp (Munich: Schirmer/Mosel, 1975);

*August Sander: Landschaften,* with text by Olivier Lugon (Munich: Schirmer/Mosel, 1999); *August Sander: Photographs of an Epoch, 1904–1959* (Millerton, N.Y.: Aperture, 1980).

106. William Rollins, *A Greener Vision of Home: Cultural Politics and Environmental Reform in the German Heimatschutz Movement* (Ann Arbor: University of Michigan Press, 1997), 260.

107. Williams, "'Chords of the German Soul,'" 354–355.

108. Peter Zepp, "Landschafts- und Naturschutz, eine Volksangelegenheit," *Nachrichtenblatt für Rheinische Heimatpflege* 1, no. 5–6 (1929): 5.

109. Schoenichen, "Aus der Entwicklung der Naturdenkmalpflege," 226.

110. Williams, "'Chords of the German Soul,'" 352–355; Wey, *Umweltpolitik in Deutschland,* 136.

111. Schoenichen, "Aus der Entwicklung der Naturdenkmalpflege," 226.

112. See Walter Effenberger, "Die Photographie im Dienste des Naturschutzes," 158–178, and Georg E. F. Schulz, "Film und Naturschutz," 180–191, in *Wege zum Naturschutz,* ed. Walther Schoenichen (Breslau: Ferdinand Hirt, 1926).

113. Schulz, "Film und Naturschutz," 182–183.

114. Dr. Spies, "Programm für den Besucher," 1–4. Cited in Dr. Schwab, "Der Naturschutz im Rheinstromgebiet," *Beiträge zur Rheinkunde* 4 (1928): 31–34.

115. See files on 1931 Nature Protection Exhibition in Berlin, ALVR 3783.

116. Letter from Rolf vom Endt to Josef Busley, 20 October 1930; Oskar Karpa, "Niederschrift über die Sitzung betreffend Vorbereitung einer rheinischen Naturschutz-Ausstellung," 3 December 1930, ALVR 3873.

117. "Die Vogelwarte der Stadt Essen: Zur Eröffnung im Frühjahr 1930," BAK B245/182, fol. 269–279.

118. Hans Klose, *Die heimatliche Natur und der Volksbund Naturschutz* (Berlin-Lichterfelde, 1922). Cited in Joachim Wolschke-Bulmahn, *Auf der Suche nach Arkadien: Zu landschaftsidealen und Formen der Naturaneignung in der Jugendbewegung und ihrer Bedeutung für die Landespflege* (München: Minerva, 1990), 193.

119. "Schafft Bausteine zum Turmbau auf der Hohen Bracht im Sauerland!" in ALVR, Nachlass Horion 65.

120. August Reichensperger, "Der Kampf um die Sieben Berge," *Nachrichten aus der Rheinischen Denkmalpflege* 1 (1919): 24.

121. Peukert, *Weimar Republic,* 89; see also 89–95. John Williams argues that fears of youths also reflected their prominent role in the revolutions of 1918–19. See Williams, "'The Chords of the German Soul,'" 352–353.

122. Peukert, *Weimar Republic,* 90–91.

123. On the splits within the Naturfreunde, see Jochen Zimmer, *"Mit uns zieht die Zeit": Die Naturfreunde, zur Geschichte eines alternativen Verbandes in der Arbeiterbewegung* (Cologne: Pahl-Rugenstein, 1984), 66–75.

124. Karl Ditt, "'Mit Westfalengruss und Heil Hitler': Die Westfälische Heimat-

bewegung 1918–1945," in *Antimodernismus und Reform,* ed. Klueting, 189–215, here 197.

125. K. J. Fassbinder, "Jugend und Herberge," *Zeitschrift des Rheinischen Vereins für Denkmalpflege und Heimatschutz* (hereafter ZRVDH) 20, no. 3 (1927): 7.

126. On *wilde Cliquen,* see Peukert, *Weimar Republic,* 93.

127. Karl Stroebel, "Jugendwandern und Naturschutz," *Rheinische Jugend* 17, no. 11 (November 1929): 486–488. See also John A. Williams, "Steeling the Young Body: Official Attempts to Control Youth Hiking in Germany, 1913–1938," in *Occasional Papers in German Studies,* vol. 12 (July 1997).

128. Senior Civil Servant Brossner, "Die geistigen Grundlagen des Jugendherbergswerkes," *Rheinische Jugend* 17, no. 7 (July 1929): 50–51.

129. "Erlebtes und Erlauschtes von einem Fahrenden," *Rheinische Jugend* 16, no. 4 (April 1928): 193.

130. Karl Vossen, "Jugendpflege und Heimatschutz," 4, and Ernst Stahl, "Die neuen Jugendherbergen der Rheinprovinz," 102–158, in *ZRVDH* 20, no. 3 (1927). These essays were part of a special issue devoted to Rhenish youth hostels.

131. Wilhelm Münker, *Das deutsche Jugendherbergswerk: Seine Enstehung und Entwicklung bis 1933* (Bielefeld, 1944), 22. Cited in Wolschke-Bulmahn, *Auf der Suche,* 178.

132. Fassbinder, "Jugend und Herberge," 13.

133. Letter from Regierungspräsident in Düsseldorf to Landräte and Oberbürgermeister, 22 November 1928, BAK B245/181, fol. 243.

134. *Eifelkalender 1930,* 95; *Die Eifel, 1888–1988,* 349. On rules for hikers, see also Hermann Hesse, "Wandern und Naturschutz," *Rheinische Jugend* 16, no. 4 (April 1928): 206–207.

135. Schoenichen, "Aus der Entwicklung der Naturdenkmalpflege," 226.

136. Walther Schoenichen, "Naturschutz und Schule," in *Wege zum Naturschutz,* ed. Schoenichen, 192–209; Klaus Goebel, "Der Heimatkundeunterricht in den deutschen Schulen," in *Antimodernismus und Reform,* ed. Klueting, 90–111.

137. Reichsshulkonferenz 1920, "Leitsäzte über Schule und Heimat," 16 June 1920 and "Leistsätze der 5. Tagung des Reichsschulausschusses vom 27. bis 29. April 1922." Cited in Williams, "'Chords of the German Soul,'" 356. On the relationship between *Heimatkunde,* civic education, and republicanism, see Applegate, *Nation of Provincials,* 154–166.

138. Zepp, "Landschafts- und Naturschutz," 4–5.

139. Schoenichen, "Naturschutz und Schule," 204.

140. Ibid., 194–195, 201–205. On school excursions and their value in nature study, see K. Sturm, *Heimatscholle! Heimatleben! Kölner Schulwanderungen,* 2nd ed. (Cologne: Kommissions Verlag, 1929), 8–9.

141. Dominick, *Environmental Movement in Germany,* 83.

142. *Die Eifel 1888–1988,* 360–364, 378, 397, 400, 404.

143. Wolschke-Bulmahn, *Auf der Suche,* 137–139, 146–147, 155.

144. On social hiking, see ibid., 60–61; Jochen Zimmer, "Soziales Wandern: Zur proletarischen Naturaneignung," in *Besiegte Natur: Geschichte der Umwelt im neunzehnten und zwanzigsten Jahrhundert,* ed. Franz-Josef Brüggemeier and Thomas Rommelspacher (Munich: C. H. Beck, 1987), 158–167; Heinz Hoffman and Jochen Zimmer, eds., *Wir sind die Grüne Garde: Geschichte der Naturfreundejugend* (Essen: Klartext, 1986). On working-class alternatives to bourgeois nature protection, see Linse, *Ökopax und Anarchie,* 42–56.

145. Gröning and Wolschke-Bulmahn, *Liebe zur Landschaft,* 92; Wolschke-Bulmahn, *Auf der Suche,* 60–61.

146. Hugo Frohn, "Jugendwander an Berufsschulen," *Rheinische Jugend* 19, no. 3 (March 1931): 82.

147. Gröning and Wolschke-Bulmahn, *Liebe zur Landschaft,* 99–120.

148. Ernst Winkler, "Stadt und Land," *Der jugendliche Arbeiter* 28, no. 9 (1929): 4–7. Cited in Wolschke-Bulmahn, *Auf der Suche,* 61.

149. Wey, *Umweltpolitik in Deutschland,* 140.

150. Peter Zepp, "Denkschrift zur Lage und Neuorganisation der Natur-wissenschaftlichen Vereine in der Rheinprovinz," 16 June 1932, ALVR 11121.

151. Williams, "'Chords of the German Soul,'" 362–363.

152. Schoenichen, "Aus der Entwicklung der Naturdenkmalpflege," 226; see also Wolschke-Bulmahn, *Auf der Suche,* 171–173.

153. Reichensperger, "Zoologische Inseln," 320.

154. Winfried Speitkamp, "Denkmalpflege und Heimatschutz in Deutschland zwischen Kulturkritik und Nationalsozialismus," *Archiv für Kulturgeschichte* 70 (1988): 149–193.

155. Max Kästner-Falkenberg, "Vom Heimatgefühl," in *Naturschutz in Sachsen,* ed. Landesverein Sächsischer Heimatschutz (Dresden: Verlag Landesverein Sächsischer Heimatschutz, 1929), 9–16, here 9–10.

156. Ibid., 9.

157. Schoenichen, "Aus der Entwicklung der Naturdenkmalpflege," 227.

158. I provide a more detailed analysis of the Fighting League and Schultze-Naumburg's racism in the next chapter. On the relationship between racism and architectural criticism, see Barbara Miller Lane, *Architecture and Politics in Germany 1918–1945* (Cambridge, Mass.: Harvard University Press, 1968).

159. Karl Wagenfeld, "Heimatschutz Volkssache," in *Heimatschutz* 1, no. 2 (Winter 1925/1926): n.p. Cited in Williams, "'Chords of the German Soul,'" 363–364.

160. Karl Wagenfeld, "Industrie und Volkstum," in *Der deutsche Heimatschutz,* ed. Gesellschaft der Freunde des Naturschutzes, 73–74.

161. Williams, "'Chords of the German Soul,'" 367.

162. Cited in Gert Gröning and Joachim Wolschke-Bulmahn, "Politics, Planning and the Protection of Nature: Political Abuse of Early Ecological Ideas in Germany, 1933–1945," *Planning Perspectives* 2 (1987): 127–148.

163. Eugenic ideas were by no means the exclusive province of the National Socialist Party or the *völkisch* right wing. Many liberal and social democratic thinkers embraced these ideas as well. Urban planners in the 1920s had advocated confining the "hereditarily diseased" in asylums separated from the rest of the urban population. See Wolfgang Voigt, "The Garden City as a Eugenic Utopia," *Planning Perspectives* 4 (1989): 295–312.

164. Richard Klapheck, "Tradition und Gegenwart," *ZRVDH* 2 (1931).

165. Bausinger, "Zwischen Grün und Braun," 219.

166. "Aus der Geschichte der Juden im Rheinland: Jüdische Kult- und Kulturdenkmäler," *ZRVDH* 1 (1931); Wiemer, *Verein im Wandel der Zeit,* 96–97.

167. Schriftführer Risse, "Heimat und Rasse: Zwei Entgegnungen," *Die Westfälische Heimat* 12, no. 7 (1930): 195–196. Cited in Kaufmann, "Heimat im Revier," 189.

168. Johannes Horion, "Die Vernichtung des lebensunwerten Lebens," *Kölnische Volkszeitung,* 4 April 1931.

169. Staatliche Stelle für Naturschutz im Regierungsbezirk Koblenz, "Jahresbericht 1931," *Nachrichtenblatt für Rheinische Heimatpflege* 3, no. 9–10 (1931/1932): 345.

170. *EVB* 1933, 75. Cited in *Die Eifel, 1888–1988,* 403.

## 4 From Landscape to Lebensraum

1. VVS, *Jahresbericht 1933,* p. 1 in BAK, Bestand 245, no. 185, fol. 49.

2. "Die Lage des Eifelvereins: Wege und Aufgabe im nationalen Staat," *Kölnische Zeitung,* 13 June 1933. There is a large body of literature on the *Gleichschaltung* of local associations that cannot be cited in detail here. Useful examples include Karl Bracher, "The Stages of Totalitarian Integration *(Gleichschaltung),*" in *Republic to Reich: The Making of the Nazi Revolution,* ed. Hajo Holborn (New York: Pantheon, 1973), 30–42, and Rudy Koshar, *Social Life, Local Politics and Nazism, Marburg 1880–1935* (Chapel Hill: University of North Carolina Press, 1986), 251–262.

3. On *Heimatschutz* leader Ernst Rudorff's importance to National Socialist ideology, see letter from Heumann to Reich Office for Nature Protection, 15 September 1936, in BAK 245/50, fol. 30. Riehl's *Natural History of the German People,* first published in 1841, was included on Alfred Rosenberg's list of 400 "recommended" National Socialist titles and went through four new editions during the course of the Third Reich. See Raymond Dominick, *The Environmental Movement in Germany: Prophets and Pioneers, 1871–1971* (Bloomington: Indiana University Press, 1992), 85.

4. Thomas Childers, *The Nazi Voter: The Social Foundations of Fascism in Germany, 1919–1933* (Chapel Hill: University of North Carolina Press, 1983).

5. VVS, *Jahresbericht 1933,* 1.

6. Rhenish *Heimatschutz* and *Naturschutz* leaders, not surprisingly, distanced themselves from Nazism after the war, largely forgetting their earlier enthusiasm for the regime. See, for example, Rhenischer Verein für Denkmalpflege und Landschaftsschutz, ed., *Festschrift für Franz Graf Wolff Metternich* (Neuss: Verlag Gesellschaft für Buchdruckerei, 1974), 50, and Eifelverein, ed., *Die Eifel, 1888–1988: Zum hundertjährigen Jubiläum des Eifelvereins* (Düren: Eifelverein, 1989), 435, for a similar sentiment. Other regional associations, such as the Westphalian Provincial Association, also claimed that provincial self-administration was a site of "refuge" from Nazism; see Karl Ditt, *Raum und Volkstum: Die Kulturpolitik des Provinzialverbandes Westfalen, 1923–1945* (Münster: Aschendorffsche, 1988), 22.

7. On these ideological affinities, see Dominick, *Environmental Movement in Germany,* 89, and Raymond Dominick, "The Nazis and the Nature Conservationists," *Historian* 49 (1987): 508–538, here 510–511.

8. The literature on the modernity of the Third Reich is enormous and cannot be cited in detail here. For an analysis of Nazi environmental policy in light of questions of modernity, see Michael Prinz, "Die soziale Funktion moderner Elemente in der Gesellschaftspolitik des Nationalsozialismus," in *Nationalsozialismus und Modernisierung,* ed. Rainer Zitelmann and Michael Prinz (Darmstadt: Wissenschaftliche Buchgesellschaft, 1994), 297–327, here 315.

9. My view contrasts with those studies that argue that these two movements' shared *völkisch,* antimodern, and right-wing roots made *Gleichschaltung* relatively seamless. See, for example, Michael Wettengel, "Staat und Naturschutz, 1906–1945: Zur Geschichte der Staatlichen Stelle für Naturdenkmalpflege in Preussen und der Reichstelle für Naturschutz," *Historische Zeitschrift* 257, no. 2 (October 1993): 379–382; Winfried Speitkamp, "Denkmalpflege und Heimatschutz in Deutschland zwischen Kulturkritik und Nationalsozialismus," *Archiv für Kulturgeschichte* 70 (1988): 149–193. Dominick presents a more nuanced picture, noting that only some conservationists held *völkisch* views. See Dominick, "Nazis and Nature Conservationists," 510–513.

10. On the "polycracy" of the Third Reich, see Martin Broszat, *The Hitler State: The Foundation and Development of the Internal Structure of the Third Reich,* trans. by John W. Hiden (New York: Longman, 1981), and Ian Kershaw, *The Nazi Dictatorship: Problems and Perspectives of Interpretation,* 2nd ed. (London: Edward Arnold, 1989), 61–81. On local autonomy in the Third Reich, see Volker Dahm, "Nationale Einheit und partikuläre Vielfalt: Zur Frage der kulturpolitischen Gleichschaltung im Dritten Reich," *Vierteljahreshefte für Zeitgeshichte* 43, no. 2 (April 1995): 221–265.

11. On popular support for Nazism and the limits of ideological indoctrination, see Ian Kershaw, *Popular Opinion and Political Dissent in the Third Reich: Bavaria 1933–1945* (Oxford: Clarendon, 1983); Detlev Peukert, *Inside the Third Reich: Conformity, Opposition and Racism in Everyday Life,* trans. by Richard Devenson (1982; New Haven: Yale University Press, 1987); and Robert Gellately, *Backing Hitler: Consent and Coercion in Nazi Germany* (Oxford: Oxford University Press, 2001). I have also found Michel Foucault's conceptions of social discipline and self-policing fruitful for understanding preservationist groups' *Selbstgleichschaltung* in the early years of the Nazi regime. The uncoerced dissemination and replication of *Heimat* discourses, what Foucault would term the "capillary" effects of power, consolidated the Nazis' legitimacy at the local level. By shifting the focus from Berlin to the provinces, moreover, power was negotiated at multiple sites on the periphery, rather than from the center outward. On Foucauldian conceptions of power, see Michel Foucault, *Power/Knowledge: Selected Interviews and Other Writings, 1972–1977,* ed. Colin Gordon (New York: Pantheon, 1980).

12. Hans Klose, "Heimatschutz im nationalen Deutschland," *Naturdenkmalpflege und Naturschutz in Berlin und Brandenberg* 17, 205–207. Cited in Burkhardt Riechers, "Nature Protection during National Socialism," *Historical Social Research* 21, no. 3 (1996): 47.

13. On the Nazi "green wing," see Anna Bramwell "Ricardo Walther Darré: Was This Man 'Father of the Greens'?" *History Today* 34 (September 1984): 7–13; Anna Bramwell, *Blood and Soil: Walther Darré and Hitler's Green Party* (London: Kensal Press, 1985); Simon Schama, *Landscape and Memory* (New York: Knopf, 1995), 119–120.

14. Wettengel, "Staat und Naturschutz," 386. The Nazi regime achieved international renown for its *Dauerwald* policies, which represented a major reform of the country's traditional scientific forestry practices. See Franz Heske, *German Forestry* (New Haven: Yale University Press, 1938), and Heinrich Rubner, *Deutsche Forstgeschichte, 1933–1945: Forstwirtschaft, Jagd, und Umwelt im NS-Staat* (St. Katharinen: Scripta Mecaturae, 1985), 153–155.

15. I describe Seifert's work on the *Autobahn* in greater detail in Chapter 5; for a discussion of the roadways' "landscape friendly" design, see William Rollins, "Whose Landscape? Technology, Fascism, and Environmentalism on the National Socialist *Autobahn,*" *Annals of the Association of American Geographers* 85, no. 3 (1995): 498–504.

16. Wettengel, "Staat und Naturschutz," 381; Anna Bramwell, *Ecology in the Twentieth Century* (New Haven: Yale University Press, 1989), 196.

17. Quoted in Robert Procter, *Racial Hygiene: Medicine under the Nazis* (Cambridge, Mass.: Harvard University Press, 1988), 227. On animal protection in the Third Reich, see Boria Sax, *Animals in the Third Reich: Pets, Scapegoats, and the Holocaust* (New York: Continuum, 2000), 35, 175–182. Nazi law made it a criminal offense to torment or roughly mishandle an ani-

mal, to neglect a pet in one's ownership, to use dogs in the chase, or to perform a painful operation on an animal in an unprofessional manner, and it set strict guidelines for the use of animals in laboratory experiments. The law's definitions defined unnecessary cruelty as that "which served no rational, justified purpose."

18. Wettengel, "Staat und Naturschutz," 382–383.

19. On social Darwinism in the Nazi movement, see Daniel Gasman, *The Scientific Origins of National Socialism: Social Darwinism in Ernst Haeckel and the German Monist League* (New York: American Elsevier, 1971). On Haeckel's influence on ecological science, see Robert C. Stauffer, "Haeckel, Darwin and Ecology," *Quarterly Review of Biology* 32 (1957): 138–144.

20. Quoted in Robert Pois, *National Socialism and the Religion of Nature* (London: Croom Helm, 1986), 38. Pois aptly describes Nazism as a form of biological mysticism, though his emphasis on National Socialism as a response to secularization and Weberian rationalization neglects the scientific and bureaucratizing elements that characterized Nazi racial hygiene.

21. Quoted in ibid., 38.

22. Adolf Hitler, *Mein Kampf*, trans. Ralph Manheim (1925; Boston: Houghton Mifflin, 1971), 393.

23. Ibid., 286–287, 304.

24. Ibid., 264–265, 302. See also Jost Hermand, *Old Dreams of a New Reich: Volkisch Utopias and National Socialism* (Bloomington: Indiana University Press, 1992), 61.

25. On the social Darwinist foundations of German political geography, see Mark Bassin, "Race contra Space: The Conflict between German *Geopolitik* and National Socialism," *Political Geography Quarterly* 6, no. 2 (April 1987): 115–134, and "Imperialism and the Nation State in Friedrich Ratzel's Political Geography, *Progress in Human Geography* 11, no. 4 (1987): 473–495; Michael Fahlbusch, Mechtild Rössler, and Dominik Siegrist, "Conservatism, Ideology and Geography in Germany 1920–1950," *Political Geography Quarterly* 8, no. 4 (October 1989): 353–367.

26. I say popularize here because Darré borrowed the phrase Blood and Soil from August Winnig, the one-time Social Democrat who brought the phrase into political prominence. See Bramwell, *Blood and Soil,* 54–55.

27. Bramwell, *Blood and Soil,* 75–90. On Nazi agricultural reform, see Clifford Lovin, "Agricultural Reorganization in the Third Reich: The Reich Food Corporation (Reichsnährstand), 1933–1936," *Agricultural History* 43, no. 4 (1969): 447–461; J. E. Farquharson, *The Plough and the Swastika: The NSDAP and Agriculture in Germany, 1928–1945* (London: Sage, 1976); Gustavo Corni, *Hitler and the Peasants: Agrarian Policy of the Third Reich* (New York: Berg, 1990).

28. Bramwell, *Blood and Soil,* 86.

29. Darré outlines these connections between race and territory in several texts,

including *Das Bauerntum als Lebensquell der nordischen Rasse* (Munich: J. F. Lehmanns, 1933), *Neuadel aus Blut und Boden* (Munich: J. F. Lehmanns, 1935), *Um Blut und Boden: Reden und Aufsätze* (Munich: Zentralverlag der NSDAP, 1940). See also Bramwell, "Ricardo Walther Darré," 8, and Bramwell, *Blood and Soil,* 55.

30. Bramwell, "Ricardo Walther Darré," 8; Bramwell, *Ecology in the Twentieth Century,* 197–200.
31. See Bramwell, "Ricardo Walther Darré," 10.
32. On Darré's racism, see Dominick, *Environmental Movement in Germany,* 94–95.
33. See Dominick, "Nazis and Nature Conservationists," 521–522.
34. I do not have figures on how many Rhenish nature preservationists had joined or voted for the NSDAP before 1933, although, as Celia Applegate points out, it is unlikely that the Nazis had infiltrated *Heimat* organizations extensively before 1933 because of Nazi disdain for these groups' provincialism and elitism; see Celia Applegate, *A Nation of Provincials: The German Idea of Heimat* (Berkeley: University of California Press, 1990), 189. At the national level, Paul Schultze-Naumburg was the only major preservationist to join the party before 1933; of the many cultural organizations that affiliated with Alfred Rosenberg's Fighting League for German Culture by the end of 1930, none was a nature conservation society (see Dominick, *Environmental Movement in Germany,* 95–96). After the Nazi takeover in 1933, nationally renowned conservationists such as Walther Schoenichen and Konrad Guenther joined the party, as did several prominent Rhenish landscape preservationists, such as Karl Oberkirch in Essen. Nazi Party membership was not a prerequisite for attaining a *Naturschutz* office, however, and many preservationists appear to have voiced support without formally joining the NSDAP.
35. Dominick, *Environmental Movement in Germany,* 96–97; Matthew Jefferies, "Heimatschutz: Environmental Activism in Wilhelmine Germany," in *Green Thought in German Culture: Historical and Contemporary Perspectives,* ed. Colin Riordan (Cardiff: University of Wales Press, 1997), 42–54, here 51–52.
36. Paul Schultze-Naumburg, *Kunst und Rasse,* 2nd ed. (Munich: J. F. Lehmanns Verlag, 1935).
37. Norbert Borrmann, *Paul Schultze-Naumburg, 1869–1949: Maler— Publizist—Architekt: Vom Kulturreformer der Jahrhundertwende zum Kulturpolitiker im Dritten Reich* (Essen: Richard Bacht, 1989), 144–153, 182.
38. Cited in Barbara Miller Lane, *Architecture and Politics in Germany, 1918– 1945* (Cambridge, Mass.: Harvard University Press, 1968), 163.
39. *Völkischer Beobachter,* 11 November 1931. Cited in Dominick, *Environmental Movement in Germany,* 93.
40. Schultze-Naumburg, *Kunst und Rasse,* 145.

41. Paul Schultze-Naumburg, "Die Gestaltung der Landschaft," in *Der deutsche Heimatschutz: Ein Rückblick und Ausblick,* ed. Gesellschaft der Freunde des deutschen Heimatschutzes (Munich: Kastner and Callwey, 1930), 11–17, here 13–14.

42. Borrmann, *Paul Schultze-Naumburg,* 216; see also 135–150.

43. Hans Schwenkel, "Heimatschutz im nationalen Deutschland," *Mein Heimatland* 7/8, 231. Cited in Joachim Wolschke-Bulmahn, *Auf der Suche nach Arkadien: Zu landschaftsidealen und Formen der Naturaneignung in der Jugendbewegung und ihrer Bedeutung für die Landespflege* (Münich: Minerva, 1990), 69.

44. *Naturschutz* 15 (1933/1934): 8. Cited in Dominick, *Environmental Movement in Germany,* 99.

45. Walter Schoenichen, *Naturschutz im Dritten Reich: Einführung in Wesen und Grundlagen zeitgemässer Naturschutz-Arbeit* (Berlin, 1934), 1. Cited in Wettengel, "Staat und Naturschutz," 380.

46. Schoenichen, *Naturschutz im Dritten Reich,* 1. Cited in Wettengel, "Staat und Naturschutz," 379.

47. Walther Schoenichen, *Urdeutschland: Deutschlands Naturschutzgebiete in Wort und Bild,* vol. 1 (Berlin: J. Neumann, Neudamm, 1935), 11.

48. Gert Gröning and Joachim Wolschke-Bulmahn, "Politics, Planning and the Protection of Nature: Political Abuse of Early Ecological Ideas in Germany, 1933–1945," *Planning Perspectives* 2 (1987): 127–148, here 129–130.

49. Schoenichen, *Urdeutschland,* 1, 11.

50. Fritz Brennecke, *The Nazi Primer: Official Handbook for Schooling the Hitler Youth,* trans. Harwood L. Childs (New York: Harper, 1938; repr. New York: AMS Press, 1972), 59.

51. Josef Zimmermann, "Die Entwicklung des Naturschutzes, insbesondere in den rheinischen Gebieten, und Gedanken über eine allgemeine Geschichte des Naturschutzes," *Eifeljahrbuch* (1995): 33–50, here 43; Dominick, *Environmental Movement in Germany,* 107. In a letter from Klose to Professor Ernst Lehmann, 30 November 1948, Klose confirmed his crucial role in drafting the RNG, though because he was one quarter Jewish, Klose was not an NSDAP member. He described his role in the project as "overall in charge" and noted that he was directly responsible for the preamble. See BAK B245/253, fol. 57; Rubner, *Deutsche Forstgeschichte,* 82–84.

52. Hans Kornfeld, "Erste Sitzung der Rheinischen Provinzialstelle für Naturschutz," 12 December 1936, 1, in ALVR 11138.

53. Oskar Karpa, "Reichsnaturschutzgesetz und Landschaftsschutz des Rheintales," *Der Schaffende Rhein: Jahresbericht 1935 und Beiträge zur Rheinkunde* 12 (1936): 28–31.

54. On the ideological overlap between Nazism and *Heimat* organizations, see Ditt, *Raum und Volkstum,* 21, and Dominick, *Environmental Movement in Germany,* 85–90.

55. On Rhinelanders' enthusiasm for remilitarization, see Eifelverein, ed., *Die*

*Eifel 1888–1988: Zum hundertjährigen Jubiläum des Eifelvereins* (Düren: Eifelverein, 1989), 411.

56. Dominick, *Environmental Movement in Germany,* 85.
57. Richard Rein, "Die heimische Landschaft wird geschützt: Das neue Reichsnaturschutzgesetz und das Rheinland," *Düsseldorfer Nachrichten,* 28 July 1935.
58. Kornfeld, "Erste Sitzung," 1.
59. Wettengel, "Staat und Naturschutz," 385.
60. Karpa, "Reichsnaturschutzgesetz und Landschaftsschutz des Rheintales," 30.
61. The RNG protected native nongame animals, while the Reich Hunting Law (Reichsjadggesetz) regulated game species. The Hunting Law included different categories of protection. It forbade the hunting of certain species (e.g., bison, bears, beavers), restricted the hunting season for others (e.g., elk, deer, seals) and left others unregulated, including wild rabbits and sparrowhawks. See Graf Hoensbröch, "Was machtet ihr aus der Heimat? Das deutsche Volk, sein Wild und sein Wald—Kein sinnloser Raubbau!" *Westdeutscher Beobachter,* 23 October 1935; *General Anzeiger der Kölnische Zeitung,* "Wie wird unsere heimische Tierwelt geschützt?" 11 February 1941.
62. Rein, "Die heimische Landschaft wird geschützt"; Werner Weber, *Das Recht des Landschaftsschutzes* (Berlin: J. Neumann-Neudamm, 1938), 82; Hans Klose "Der Schutz der Landschaft nach §5 des Reichsnaturschutzgesetzes," in *Der Schutz der Landschaft nach dem Reichsnaturschutzgesetz,* ed. Hans Klose, Hans Schwenkel, and Werner Weber (Berlin: J. Neumann-Neudamm, 1937), 10–11, 17–18.
63. Kornfeld, "Erste Sitzung," 6.
64. Ibid., 1.
65. Werner Weber and Walther Schoenichen, "Das Reichsnaturschutzgesetz vom 26. Juni 1935 (RGBl. 1935 I, 82l) und die Verordnung zur Durchführung des vom 31 October 1935 nebst ergänzenden Bestimmungen und ausführlichen Erläuterungen Berlin 1936," 9. Cited in Wettengel, "Staat und Naturschutz," 385. On nature protection and Nazi social policy, see Walther Schoenichen, *Naturschutz als völkische und internationale Kulturaufgabe* (Jena: Gustav Fischer, 1942), 51, 55.
66. Schoenichen, *Urdeutschland,* 9; Kornfeld, "Erste Sitzung," 6.
67. "Naturschutz auch eine biologische Forderung," *Rheinische-Westfälische Zeitung,* 16 July 1943.
68. Schoenichen, *Internationale Kulturaufgabe,* 61, 85.
69. Heske, *German Forestry,* 41.
70. Wernher Witthaus, "Die ganze Landschaft soll es sein!" *Nachrichtenblatt für Rheinische Heimatpflege* 5, no. 5/7 (1933–34): 172.
71. See Weber, *Das Recht des Landschaftsschutzes,* 83.
72. "Landesplanungsgemeinschaft Rheinland," *Die Rheinprovinz,* 12 (September 1936): 596.

73. Rheinischer Verein für Denkmalpflege und Landschaftsschutz, ed., *Festschrift für Franz Graf Wolff Metternich*, 50.

74. Kornfeld, "Erste Sitzung," 1.

75. Rudolf Hoffmann, "Landschaftsschutz und Bauaufgaben im nationalsozialistischen Staat," *Die Rheinprovinz* (April 1936): 247–250, here 250.

76. Klose, "Der Schutz der Landschaft," 8; Hans Kornfeld, "Wünsche zur Erhaltung der Rheinlandschaft," *Die Rheinprovinz* (July 1936): 464.

77. Schoenichen, *Internationale Kulturaufgabe*, 29–30.

78. Alwin Seifert, "Heimat und Siedlung," *ZRVDH* 30, no. 2 (1937): 8.

79. Schoenichen, *Internationale Kulturaufgabe*, 85.

80. On the creation of the Reich Nature Protection Office, see Wettengel, "Staat und Naturschutz," 383–388.

81. Dominick, *Environmental Movement in Germany*, 102–103. On the incorporation of *Naturschutz* within the RVH, see Wettengel, "Staat und Naturschutz," 379–380.

82. Oskar Karpa, "Bericht über meine Teilnahme an der 20. Tagung für Naturdenkmalpflege in der Staatlichen Stelle für Naturdenkmalpflege zu Berlin," 12 December 1933, ALVR 11122.

83. Wettengel, "Staat und Naturschutz," 381.

84. Dominick, *Environmental Movement in Germany*, 107.

85. Quoted in Wettengel, "Staat und Naturschutz," 383.

86. Hans Kornfeld and Dr. Hartmann, "Niederschrift über die Arbeitstagung des Deutschen Bundes Heimatschutz im Provinzialständehaus zu Hannover am 4 October 1937," ALVR 11125.

87. On the reorganization of the DBH, see letter from Haake to Rhenish *Heimat* clubs (1938?), ALVR 11145; Karl Peter Wiemer, *Ein Verein im Wandel der Zeit: Der Rheinische Verein für Denkmalpflege und Heimatschutz von 1906 bis 1970* (Cologne: Verlag des Rheinische Vereins für Denkmalpflege und Landschaftsschutz, 2000), 112.

88. "Entwurf für die Rundfunk Reportage über die Forschungsstelle 'Rheinländer in aller Welt,'" n.d., 1, in ALVR Nachlass Haake 63. On the defense of regional autonomy as compatible with the *Führerprinzip*, see Ditt, *Raum und Volkstum*, 161–164.

89. Haake, speech before Frick at Prussian Gemeindetag meeting 5 April 1940, 1, in ALVR Nachlass Haake 86.

90. Ibid.

91. Ibid., 8–10.

92. "Landschaftliche Kulturpflege," *Kölnische Zeitung*, 29 August 1937.

93. Heinz Haake, speech on Rhenish art, Berlin 1940, 2, in ALVR Nachlass Haake 86.

94. Ibid.

95. Oskar Karpa, "Übersicht über den Aufbau des Naturschutzes in Preussen," 3 October 1934, in ALVR 11122.

96. "Beihilfe für den Naturschutz," 22 April 1937, and "Bericht über Ausgaben für Rechnungsjahr 1937," 21 April 1938, ALVR 11123. Unlike Westphalia, the Rhineland did not establish a provincial natural history museum to serve as the focal point for *Naturschutz* affairs. On the Westphalian museum and its activities under the Third Reich, see Karl Ditt, *Raum und Volkstum,* 327–347.

97. Rheinischer Verein für Denkmalpflege und Landschaftsschutz, ed., *Festschrift für Franz Graf Wolff Metternich,* 54.

98. Ibid.; "Lehrgang für Naturschutzkommissare," n.d., ALVR 11123.

99. Elmar Heinen, "Naturschutzgebiet Siebengebirge gestern—heute—morgen," *Rheinische Heimatpflege* 27 (1990): 112–121, here 119.

100. Rein, "Die heimische Landschaft wird geschützt."

101. Heinz Haake, speech at RVDH thirtieth anniversary, 1936, 1–3, in ALVR Nachlass Haake 62.

102. Heinz Haake, speech at the annual meeting of the Rheinischer Heimatbund in Trier, 1938, 3, in ALVR Nachlass Haake 85.

103. Haake, speech on Rhenish art, 3.

104. On the founding of the Rhenish Society for Regional Planning, see Pressenotiz: Landeshauptmann Heinrich Haake, April 1943, 2, in ALVR Nachlass Haake 43; "Landesplanungsgemeinschaft Rheinland," *Die Rheinprovinz* 12, no. 9 (September 1936): 593–596.

105. See Haake, speech before Frick, 6–8; "Landesplanung, Wohnung- und Siedlungswesen," *Die Rheinprovinz* (May 1937): 332–340; "Die Rheinische Provinzialverwaltung: Ein Bericht aus dem umfangreichen Arbeitsbereich in den Jahren 1933–1936," *Westdeutscher Landzeitung Geldern,* 10 June 1937.

106. Haake, speech before Frick, 5; "Landesplanungsgemeinschaft Rheinland," 593–594.

107. "Landesplanungsgemeinschaft Rheinland," 596. See also "Landesplanung, Wohnungs- und Siedlungswesen," 332. The Rhenish Regional Planning Society also assisted in drawing up the Four-Year Plan for the province, and in establishing military installations and strategic locations for sensitive industries.

108. Wilhelm Schürmann, "Siedlung und Landesplanung," *ZRVDH* 30, no. 2 (1937): 33–38.

109. On Freder's deurbanization plans, see Lane, *Architecture and Politics,* Rudy Koshar, *Germany's Transient Pasts: Preservation and National Memory in the Twentieth Century* (Chapel Hill: University of North Carolina Press, 1998), 156–157.

110. Schürmann, "Siedlung und Landesplanung," 31–33.

111. Kornfeld, "Wünsche zur Erhaltung der Rheinlandschaft," 462–469.

112. Ibid., 467.

113. Kornfeld, "Erste Sitzung," 5.

114. Schürmann, "Siedlung und Landesplanung," 34–38.

115. Kornfeld, "Erste Sitzung," 5. On Rhine tourism, see Josef Zepp, "Fremdenverkehr und Naturschutz," *Rheinische Heimatpflege* 8, no. 1 (1936): 105–115.

116. Zepp, "Fremdenverkehr und Naturschutz," 111.

117. Oskar Karpa, "Reichsnaturschutzgesetz und Landschaftsschutz des Rheintales," *Der Schaffende Rhein: Jahresbericht 1935 und Beiträge zur Rheinkunde* 12 (1936): 30–31.

118. Rheinischer Verein für Denkmalpflege und Landschaftsschutz, *Festschrift für Franz Graf Wolff Metternich*, 55–58.

119. Ibid., 55.

120. Final draft, "Verordnung zum Schutz der Landschaft des Mittelrheins" (1941?), ALVR 11241.

121. Rheinischer Verein für Denkmalpflege und Landschaftsschutz, *Festschrift für Franz Graf Wolff Metternich*, 55–56.

122. "Endgültiger Entwurf und Begründung einer für das Rheintal zu erlassenden Schutzverordnung nebst kritischer Würdigung des Entwurfes Becker und der Abänderungenanträge der beteiligten Behörden," 1941, ALVR 11241.

123. Rheinischer Verein für Denkmalpflege und Landschaftsschutz, *Festschrift für Franz Graf Wolff Metternich*, 58; "Verordnung zum Schutz der Landschaft des Mittelrheins" and "Begründung einer für das Rheintal zu erlassenden Schutzverordnung," ALVR 11241; Schoenichen, *Internationale Kulturaufgabe*, 33, 55.

124. Dominick, *Environmental Movement in Germany*, 104–105; Wiemer, *Verein im Wander der Zeit*, 184–185.

125. Dominick, *Environmental Movement in Germany*, 105.

126. A similar pattern of recasting *Heimatpflege* along racist lines occurred in the neighboring province of Westphalia, thus pointing to a larger pattern of regional racialization in the Third Reich. See Ditt, *Raum und Volkstum*, 151–205.

127. Heinz Haake, Cologne Gurzenich speech (1940?), 3, in ALVR Nachlass Haake 86.

128. Friedrich Metz, "Die rheinische Kulturlandschaft," in *Land und Leute: Gesammelte Beiträge zur deutschen Landes- und Volksforschung von Friedrich Metz*, ed. E. Meynen and R. Oehme (Stuttgart: W. Kohlhammer, 1961), 127.

129. Ibid., 130.

130. Seifert, "Heimat und Siedlung," 6–9.

131. "Arbeitstagung der staatlichen Kommissare für Naturschutz," *Düsseldorfer Nachrichten*, 10 April 1935.

132. Hans Schwenkel, "Aufgaben der Landschaftsgestaltung und der Landschaftspflege," *Der Biologe* 10, no. 4 (1941): 11.

133. Heinz Haake, "Begleitschrift der Lehrschau 'Die Schöne Stadt,'" 5, in ALVR Nachlass Haake 86.

134. F. Schmidt, "Heimatschutz und Siedlung," *ZRVDH* 30, no. 2 (1937): 10.
135. The German Labor Front was also responsible for many of the Rhineland's model Nazi housing complexes. See Günther Wohlers, "Der rheinische Siedler und sein Haus," *ZRVDH* 30, no. 2 (1937): 39–48.
136. Schmidt, "Heimatschutz und Siedlung," 15.
137. Wohlers, "Der rheinische Siedler und sein Haus," 45–46.
138. "Landesplanung, Wohnungs- und Siedlungswesen," 332–340; Wolfgang Voigt, "The Garden City as Eugenic Utopia," *Planning Perspectives* 4, no. 3 (1989): 295–312.
139. Robert Proctor's work demonstrates that Nazi racial hygiene also spurred doctors to investigate the detrimental effects of environmental toxins and pollutants on the population's "germ plasm," a point that deserves further scholarly investigation in studies of Nazi environmental history. Nazi doctors and health officials initiated studies of the long-term effects of chemicals such as the insecticide DDT; pharmaceuticals such as quinine, mercury, iodine, and arsenic; and commercial substances such as lead and benzene. Public health officials also sought to modify the population's consumption habits to ensure reproductive health. They began campaigns to reduce or eliminate Germans' intake of "hereditary poisons" such as alcohol and tobacco, and stressed the importance of a diet rich in fruit and fiber and the consumption of whole-grain bread. See Robert Proctor, *The Nazi War on Cancer* (Princeton: Princeton University Press, 1999).
140. Membership figures for *Naturschutz* leaders in the NSDAP indicate the limits to *Gleichschaltung.* Raymond Dominick's survey of eighteen nature conservation leaders indicates that only one, Paul Schultze-Naumburg, joined the party before 1933. By 1939 nine more had joined, indicating a participation rate of 59 percent. While this was a higher rater of participation than in most professional groups and in the adult male population in general, Dominick warns that party membership may have stemmed from membership in other professional bodies unrelated to nature protection. Many conservationists were civil servants and academics, who supported Hitler in overwhelming numbers. See Dominick, *Environmental Movement in Germany,* 112–115. Most important, these numbers say little about the movement's rank and file; while I do not have figures for how many Rhenish preservationists joined the NSDAP, their desire for institutional and ideological distance from the regime suggests that there were limits to the process of synchronization at the regional level.
141. Weber, *Das Recht des Landschaftsschutzes,* 80.
142. Wilhelm Lienenkämper, "Der Deutsche und seine Landschaft: Vom gegenwärtigen Stand der Naturschutzbewegung," *Heimatliebe—Heimatschutz* 80 (31 March 1934).
143. Rhenish officials were displeased by Schoenichen and welcomed his replacement in 1939 by the more moderate Klose. In 1935 Karl Oberkirch, the nature protection commissioner for the Ruhr Settlement Association, wrote of

local preservationists' disagreements with Schoenichen and remarked that Klose was "their man" in Berlin. Letter from Oberkirch to Oskar Karpa, 13 August 1935, ALVR 11122.

144. See, for example, P. J. Busch, "Ein Eifelmoor," and "Aus dem Rheinischen Naturschutz," *Rheinischer Naturfreund* 4, no. 1 (September 1940): 8–14, 36–41.

145. Hans Kornfeld, "Wünsche zur Erhaltung der Rheinlandschaft," *Die Rheinprovinz* (July 1936): 464.

146. Ibid., 469.

147. Ibid.

148. "Die Lage des Eifelvereins: Wege und Aufgabe im nationalen Staat," *Kölnische Zeitung*, 13 June 1933.

149. Heinz Haake, speech at fourty-eighth anniversary of Sauerländischer Gebirgsverein 1938, 2, AVLR Nachlass Haake 66.

150. Haake speech at Kaufmann's seventieth birthday (1933), 1, ALVR 11169.

151. Eifelverein, "Jahresbericht für das 47. Vereinsjahr 1934/35," ALVR 11169.

152. *Die Eifel 1888–1988*, 444.

153. Ibid., 447–448; "Die Lage des Eifelvereins: Wege und Aufgaben im nationalen Staat," *Kölnische Volkszeitung*, 13 June 1933.

154. The Eifelverein was headquarted in Mayen but established local branches *(Ortsgruppen)* throughout the Rhineland. It also had local groups in major German cities, such as Berlin, as well as in American cities, such as Chicago. On membership numbers, see Eifelverein, "Jahresbericht für das 47. Vereinsjahr"; "Die Eifel ruft: mit dem Wanderstab nach Daun," *Kölnische Volkszeitung*, 3 July 1935.

155. *Die Eifel 1888–1988*, 447. In 1938, Schramm replaced Kauffmann, who had served as Eifelverein chairman for thirty-four years.

156. "Im Dienste der Heimat, der Eifel: Tagung des Eifelvereins in Kyllburg," *Kölnische Volkszeitung*, 14 March 1939.

157. Peter Josef Weiss, *Der Eifeler und sein Verein, 1888–1973: 85 Jahre Eifelverein* (Düren: Eifelverein, 1973), 61.

158. Weiss, *Der Eifeler,* 59–60; *Die Eifel 1888–1988*, 438–439.

159. Weiss, *Der Eifeler,* 61–63.

160. See "Jugendherbergswerk marchiert: Jahresversammlung des Rheinischen Jugendherbergsverbandes in Düsseldorf—Fünf neue Heimstätten werden in diesem Jahre gebaut," *Nationale Zeitung*, 7 June 1937.

161. Weiss, *Der Eifeler,* 59–61; *Die Eifel 1888–1988*, 439. Haake was also an important promoter of sporting activities in the Rhineland. Noting the importance of sport for *Volksgesundheit*, he established new sporting areas throughout the Rhineland that included running tracks, fitness equipment, and swimming pools. See "Leibesübungen in den Erziehungsheimen," *Rheinische Landeszeitung*, 12 July 1937.

162. Weiss, *Der Eifeler,* 59–61; *Die Eifel 1888–1988*, 439.

163. "Reichstreffen der deutschen Wanderer: Der 46. Deutsche Wandertag in Mayen," *Nationalzeitung*, 19 July 1937.

164. Eifelverein, "Jahresbericht für das 47. Vereinsjahr 1934/35."
165. *Die Eifel* 1939, 68. Cited in *Die Eifel 1888–1988,* 440.
166. "Fünfzigjahrfeier des Eifelvereins," 19 June 1938, ALVR 11169.
167. *Die Eifel* 1937, 34. Cited in *Die Eifel 1888–1988,* 442.
168. Letter from Parteiamtliche Prüfungskommission der NSDAP zur Förderung des N. S. Schriftums to Eifelverein, 1 April 1937, ALVR 11169.
169. Letter from Kauffmann to Prüfungskommission, 23 March 1937, ALVR 11169.
170. Letter from Prüfungskommission to Eifelverein 29 April 1939, ALVR 11169.
171. Letter from Kauffmann to Kornfeld, 14 April 1939, 1, ALVR 11169.
172. Adam Wrede, "Grundzüge rheinischen Wesens: Frohsinn und Lebensfreude," in *Lebendiges Rheinland: Rheinische Landschaft, Rheinisches Volkstum, Rheinische Wirtschaft,* ed. A. Ahrens et al. (Düsseldorf: L. Schwann, 1940), 96–99.
173. *Eifel-Kalendar 1936,* 1.
174. "Eifelverein Jahresbericht 1940," 2, ALVR 11169.
175. Ibid., 4.
176. *Die Eifel* 1942, 31. Cited in *Die Eifel 1888–1988,* 453. The Rhineland's other recreation societies reported a similar loss of members after the war's outbreak. The VVS, for example, which experienced a modest gain in members between 1933 and 1938, saw its membership decline from 557 to 551 in 1939, and it continued its descent throughout the rest of the regime. See VVS, "Geschäftsbericht für das Jahr 1939," 12, in ALVR 11055.
177. *Die Eifel* 1939, 136. Cited in *Die Eifel 1888–1988,* 450–451.
178. *Die Eifel* 1940, 93. Cited in *Die Eifel 1888–1988,* 452–454.

## 5 Constructing Nature in the Third Reich

1. Hans Klose, head of the Reich Office for Nature Protection, referred to the period between 1935 and 1939 as the high point for *Naturschutz,* in his postwar historical chronicle of the movement. See Josef Zimmermann, "Die Entwicklung des Naturschutzes, insbesondere in den rheinischen Gebieten, und Gedanken über eine allgemeine Geschichte des Naturschutzes," *Eifeljahrbuch* (1995): 43.
2. Michael Wettengel, "Staat und Naturschutz, 1906–1945: Zur Geschichte der Staatlichen Stelle für Naturdenkmalpflege in Preussen und der Reichstelle für Naturschutz," *Historische Zeitschrift* 257, no. 2 (October 1993): 355–399, here 389; Walther Schoenichen, *Naturschutz als völkische und internationale Kulturaufgabe* (Jena: Gustav Fischer, 1942), 54–55.
3. "Landschaft als Lebensraum: Die Aufgaben des Landschaftsanwalts," *Rheinische-Westfälische Zeitung,* 9 September 1941. On Seifert's environmental ideas, see William Rollins, "Whose Landscape? Technology, Fascism and Environmentalism on the National Socialist *Autobahn,*" *Annals of the Association of American Geographers* 85, no. 3 (1995): 494–520.

4. Walther Schoenichen, *Urdeutschland: Deutschlands Naturschutzgebiete im Wort und Bild,* vol. 1 (Berlin: J. Neumann-Neudamm, 1935), 2.

5. Schoenichen, *Urdeutschland,* 2; Burkhardt Riechers, "Nature Protection during National Socialism," *Historical Social Research* 21, no. 3 (1996): 34–56, here 48–49.

6. Raymond Dominick has made a similar point, noting that Nazi public works projects undermined nature conservation efforts. See *The Environmental Movement in Germany: Prophets and Pioneers, 1871–1971* (Bloomington: Indiana University Press, 1992), 108–109.

7. Wettengel, "Staat und Naturschutz," 391; on the RNG's ineffectiveness, see also Riechers, "Nature Protection during National Socialism," 47. There is a need for further research on this point, especially with regard to conservation regions, which in many cases protected large-scale stretches of habitat for flora and fauna. John Williams has noted that toward the end of the Weimar Republic there were approximately 500 nature reserves in Germany, with about 300 of these located in Prussia (see "'The Chords of the German Soul Are Tuned to Nature': The Movement to Preserve the Natural *Heimat* from the *Kaiserreich* to the Third Reich," *Central European History* 29, no. 3 (1996): 339–384). Michael Wettengel's figure of 800 preservation regions in 1940 would indicate that the Third Reich added roughly 300 nature reserves, a relatively insignificant expansion over the Weimar years considering Nazi rhetoric about the republic's profligate waste of natural resources.

8. Heinrich Rubner, *Deutsche Forstgeschichte, 1933–1945: Forstwirtschaft, Jagd, und Umwelt im NS-Staat* (St. Katharinen: Scripta Mecaturae, 1985), 85.

9. Hans Klose, *Richtlinien für die Obliegenheiten des Kreisbeauftragten für Naturschutz* (Berlin: Reichstelle für Naturschutz, 1941), in ALVR 11135. See also Dominick, *Environmental Movement in Germany,* 108.

10. Wilhelm Lienenkämper, "Die Arbeit der Naturschutzbeauftragten: Planvolles Schaffen oder Armeleutebetrieb?" (n.d.), in Archiv des Landschaftsverbandes Westfalen (hereafter ALVW) C 70, no. 184, vol. 1, fol. 227.

11. Ibid., fol. 228.

12. Ibid.

13. Letter to Walter Schoenichen 15 March 1935, BAK 245/18, fol. 352.

14. Letter from commissioner for nature protection in Stadtkreis Bonn to district president in Cologne, 4 November 1939, BAK 245/18, fol. 80; letter from Graf Carl von Spee to Provincial Nature Protection Commissioner Oskar Karpa, 20 May 1935, ALVR 11137.

15. Rudy Koshar, *Germany's Transient Pasts: Preservation and Memory in the Twentieth Century* (Chapel Hill: University of North Carolina Press, 1998), 157–158.

16. On Nazi public housing projects, see Barbara Miller Lane, *Architecture and*

*Politics in Germany, 1918–1945* (Cambridge, Mass.: Harvard University Press, 1968), 205–211.

17. Eifelverein, ed. *Die Eifel 1888–1988: Zum hundertjährigen Jubiläum des Eifelvereins* (Düren: Eifelverein, 1989), 412–416.

18. Celia Applegate, *A Nation of Provincials: The German Idea of Heimat* (Berkeley: University of California Press, 1990), 225.

19. See Rudolf Hoffmann, "Landschaftsschutz und Bauaufgaben im nationalsozialistischen Staat," *Die Rheinprovinz* (April 1936): 249; Walther Schoenichen, "Ödlandaufforstung—Jawohl! Aber mit Bedacht," in *Naturschutz* 15 (1934): 80.

20. On regional concern about land reclamation, see memorandum from Karl Oberkirch, district commissioner for nature protection in the Ruhr Settlement Association to the association president, 22 November 1935, BAK B245/24, fol. 237–238; letter from Vogelschutzverein Haltern und Umgebung to Oberkirch, 15 November 1935, BAK245/24, fol. 239–240; letter from Dr. Menke to Herbert Iven, provincial commissioner for nature protection in the Rhine Province, 9 December 1942, ALVR 11136.

21. Memorandum from Hans Kornfeld concerning nature protection conference in the Oberpräsidium Koblenz on 16 May 1938, ALVR 11123.

22. Rudolf Hoffmann, "Landschaftsschutz und Bauaufgaben im nationalsozialistischen Staat," *Die Rheinprovinz* (April 1936): 247–250, here 249; Riechers, "Nature Protection during National Socialism," 47–49. Michael Wettengel has referred to 1936 as a "general break" in Nazi support of and tolerance for environmental protection measures; see "Staat und Naturschutz," 386.

23. On Darré's demise, see Anna Bramwell, *Blood and Soil: Walther Darré and Hitler's Green Party* (London: Kensal, 1985), 178–180, and Anna Bramwell, *Ecology in the Twentieth Century* (New Haven: Yale University Press, 1989), 201–205.

24. *Reichsministerialblatt der Forstverwaltung* 1, 1937, 343. Quoted in Wettengel, "Staat und Naturschutz," 386.

25. Rollins, "Whose Landscape?" 509.

26. Wettengel, "Staat und Naturschutz," 387.

27. Hans Klose, Hans Schwenkel, and Werner Weber, eds., *Der Schutz der Landschaft nach dem Reichsnaturschutzgesetz* (Berlin: J. Neumann-Neudamm, 1937), 14.

28. Ibid., 15–16.

29. Ibid., 8.

30. On the Wahner Heath, see letter from Herbert Iven to Dr. Gobbin concerning closure of hiking and recreation areas in the Rhine Province, 20 July 1939, BAK B245/18; on the Haard Forest, see BAK B245/24, fol. 63–69.

31. Correspondence between Dr. Schmeisser, Cologne district nature protection commission officer, and Reich Forestry Ministry, 28 November 1939, BAK 245/18, fol. 76–77.

32. Cited in Koshar, *Germany's Transient Pasts,* 156; see also Rollins, "Whose Landscape?" 494.

33. Provinzialbaurat Fehlemann, "Reichsautobahnplanung in der Rhein-provinz," *Die Rheinprovinz* (May 1936): 297–302. On Weimar highway planning, see Johannes Horion, *Denkschrift über den Ausbau der rechts- und linksrheinischen Durchgangstrassen zwischen Köln und Koblenz* (Düsseldorf: L. Schwann, 1930); Martin Kornrumpf, *HAFRABA e.V., Deutsche Autobahn-Planung, 1926–1934* (Bonn: Kirschbaum, 1990).

34. Thomas Zeller, *Strasse, Bahn, Panorama: Verkehrswege und Landschafts-veränderung in Deutschland von 1930 bis 1990* (Frankfurt: Campus, 2002), 48–52.

35. James D. Shand, "The Reichsautobahn: Symbol for the Third Reich," *Journal of Contemporary History* 19 (1984): 190–192. On the *Reichautobahn*'s economic effects, see also Rollins, "Whose Landscape?" 496; Zeller, *Strasse, Bahn, Panorama,* 62–66; Thomas Zeller, "'The Landscape's Crown': Land-scape, Perceptions, and Modernizing Effects of the German Autobahn Sys-tem, 1934 to 1941," in *Technologies of Landscape: From Reaping to Recy-cling,* ed. David E. Nye (Amherst: University of Massachusetts Press, 1999), 218–239, here 218–219; R. J. Overy, *The Nazi Economic Recovery, 1932–1938* (Cambridge: Cambridge University Press, 1996).

36. On the *Autobahn*'s propaganda value, see Rainer Stommer, ed., *Reichsautobahn—Pyramiden des Dritten Reiches: Analysen Zur Ästhetik eines unbewältigten Mythos* (Marburg: Jonas Verlag, 1982).

37. Fehlemann, "Reichsautobahnplanung in der Rheinprovinz," 300.

38. "Landschaft als Lebensraum," *Rheinische-Westfälische Zeitung,* 26 Sep-tember 1941.

39. Shand, "The Reichsautobahn," 196.

40. Paul Schultze-Naumburg, *Das Glück der Landschaft* (Berlin, 1942), 88. Cited in Norbert Borrmann, *Paul Schultze-Naumburg, 1869–1949: Maler—Publizist—Architekt: Vom Kulturreformer der Jahrhundertwende zum Kulturpolitiker im Dritten Reich* (Essen: Richard Bacht, 1989), 222.

41. Jeffrey Herf, *Reactionary Modernism: Technology, Culture and Politics in Weimar and the Third Reich* (Cambridge: Cambridge University Press, 1984), 204. On *Deutsche Technik,* see also Zeller, *Strasse, Bahn, Panorama,* 69–77.

42. Hoffmann, "Landschaftsschutz und Bauaufgaben," 248.

43. Fritz Todt, *Leistung und Schönheit: Der Technik im Dritten Reich: Bild-Beilage zur Zeitschrift 'Deutsche Technik'* (July 1939), 2. Cited in Herf, *Re-actionary Modernism,* 205.

44. See "Landschaft und Wasserstrassen: Der Ingenieur als Gestalter—Wasserbaukultur in Westdeutschland," *Kölnische Zeitung,* 15 January 1940.

45. On landscape advocates' background and roles, see Thomas Zeller, "'Landschaften des Verkehrs': Autobahnen im Nationalsozialismus und Hochgeschwindigkeitsstrecken für die Bahn in der Bunderepublik," *Technikgeschichte* 64, no. 4 (1997): 326, and Zeller, *Strasse, Bahn, Pan-orama,* 91–111. Zeller notes that Seifert did not have free rein in choosing

the landscape advocates; General Inspector Todt and the NSDAP chose several candidates.

46. Alwin Seifert, "Natur und Technik im Deutschen Strassenbau," in *Im Zeitalter des Lebendigen: Natur—Heimat—Technik,* ed. Seifert (Munich: Müllersche Verlagshandlung, 1943), 19–23.

47. Reinhold Hoemann, "Landschaft und Autobahn," *Rheinischer Naturfreund* 1, no. 3 (August 1939): 9; "Landschaftsgestaltung als Aufgabe," *National-Zeitung,* 26 September 1941.

48. "Landschaft als Lebensraum: Die Aufgaben des Landschafts-anwalts," *Rheinische-Westfälische Zeitung,* 26 September 1941; "Landschaft und Wasserstrassen: Der Ingenieur als Gestalter," *Kölnische Zeitung.*

49. See Wettengel, "Staat und Naturschutz," 392–393; Zeller, *Strasse, Bahn, Panorama,* 41–209.

50. Rollins, "Whose Landscape?" 495–496; 505–508; 511–513.

51. Schoenichen, *Urdeutschland,* 1: 2. See also Dietmar Klenke, "Autobahn und Naturschutz in Deutschland: Eine Liaison von Nationalpolitik, Landschaftspflege, und Motorisierungsvision bis zur ökologischen Wende der siebziger Jahre," in *Politische Zäsuren und gesellschaftlicher Wandel im 20. Jahrhundert,* ed. Matthias Frese and Michael Prinz (Paderborn: F. Schöningh, 1996), 465–498.

52. Hoffmann, "Landschaftsschutz und Bauaufgaben," 248–249.

53. Fehlemann, "Reichsautobahnplanung in der Rheinprovinz," 298; "Landschaftsgestaltung als Aufgabe," *National-Zeitung.*

54. "Landschaft als Lebensraum," *Rheinische-Westfälische Zeitung.*

55. "Landschaftsgestaltung als Aufgabe," *National Zeitung.*

56. Hoffmann, "Landschaftsschutz und Bauaufgaben," 248; Shand, "The Reichautobahn," 192.

57. Seifert, *Im Zeitalter des Lebendigen,* 20. Quoted in Rollins, "Whose Landscape?" 504.

58. Alwin Seifert, *Ein Leben für die Landschaft* (Düsseldorf: Eugen Diederichs, 1962), 10.

59. Ibid., 20.

60. Ibid., 155.

61. On *Autobahn* landscape design, see Seifert, "Natur und Technik," 18; Rollins, "Whose Landscape?"; and Claudia Windisch-Hojnacki, *Die Reichsautobahn: Konzeption und Bau, 1935–1945,* published diss. (Bonn: Rheinische Friedrich Wilhelms Universität, 1989).

62. Seifert, *Leben für die Landschaft,* 75–82. See also example in A. D. Genevriere, "Strassenneubau und Naturschutz im Rheintal," *Die Rheinprovinz* (October 1937): 661–663.

63. Seifert, "Natur und Technik," 19.

64. Ibid., 18–19.

65. Ibid., 16–19; Hoemann, "Landschaft und Autobahn," 10–11; Zeller, "Landschaften des Verkehrs," 328.

66. Seifert, "Natur und Technik," 19.

67. Seifert, *Leben für die Landschaft,* 57.
68. Seifert, "Natur und Technik," 17.
69. Zeller, "Landscape's Crown," 226–227.
70. Jeffrey Herf, *Reactionary Modernism: Technology, Culture and Politics in Weimar and the Third Reich* (Cambridge: Cambridge University Press, 1984), 189–216.
71. Rollins, "Whose Landscape?" 495.
72. Ibid., 513, note 2.
73. The Nazis did not realize their plans to mass produce the *Volkswagen,* the "people's car," during the Third Reich; the economy-size cars were not manufactured in appreciable numbers until after the war. See Hans Mommsen and Manfred Grieger, *Das Volkswagenwerk und seine Arbeiter im Dritten Reich* (Düsseldorf: ECON, 1996); Heidrun Edelmann, "Der Traum vom 'Volkswagen,'" in *Geschichte der Zukunft des Verkehrs: Verkehrskonzepte von der frühen Neuzeit bis zum einundzwanzigsten Jahrhundert,* ed. Hans-Liudger Dienel and Helmuth Trischler (Frankfurt/ New York: Campus, 1997), 280–288.
74. Shand, "The Reichsautobahn," 195. Shand notes that the Nazis believed the roadways would also boost foreign tourism, not only because the new roads made long-distance driving easier but also because their very novelty made them tourist attractions in their own right. See p. 190.
75. Rollins, "Whose Landscape?" 498–500; on the *Reichsautobahn'*s role in visual consumption, see Zeller, *Strasse, Bahn, Panorama,* 158–165.
76. Seifert, "Natur und Technik," 19.
77. On the primacy of linking cultural centers and improving views, see Zeller, "'Landschaften des Verkehrs,'" 327; Rollins, "Whose Landscape?" 498.
78. Seifert, *Leben für die Landschaft,* 83.
79. Alwin Seifert, "Reichsautobahn im Wald," in *Im Zeitalter des Lebendigen,* 109–118, here 109.
80. Seifert, "Die Versteppung Deutschlands," in *Im Zeitalter des Lebendigen,* 24–51, here 25.
81. Seifert, "Vom Lebendigen und vom Toten," in *Im Zeitalter des Lebendigen,* 82–89, here 82; Seifert, *Leben für die Landschaft,* 34–49. For a discussion of anthroposophy and soil preservation, see Bramwell, *Ecology in the Twentieth Century,* 198.
82. Seifert, *Leben für die Landschaft,* 121.
83. Ibid., 68–74.
84. Ibid., 34–35; Seifert, "Reichsautobahn im Wald," 110. On the principle of *Bodenständigkeit* in *Autobahn* design, see Rollins, "Whose Landscape?" 506; Zeller, *Strasse, Bahn, Panorama,* 165–175.
85. On Clements's work, see Ronald Tobey, *Saving the Prairies: The Life Cycle of the Founding School of American Plant Ecology, 1895–1955* (Berkeley: University of California Press, 1981); Eugene Cittadino, "Ecology and the Professionalization of Botany in America, 1890–1905," *Studies in the His-*

*tory of Biology* 4 (1980): 171–198. Interestingly, the concept of plant societies as superorganisms came under fire in America in the 1930s for its holistic and teleological leanings, which many scientists associated with fascist political tendencies. See Tobey, *Saving the Prairies,* 155–190.

86. Ecologists today would dispute Seifert's claim that natural systems achieve a state of homeostasis with their environmental conditions. On the new "nonlinear" ecology, see Donald Worster, "The Ecology of Order and Chaos," *Environmental History Review* 14, no. 1–2 (Spring/Summer 1990): 1–18; Daniel Botkin, *Discordant Harmonies: A New Ecology for the Twenty-First Century* (New York: Oxford University Press, 1991) and *Forces of Change: A New View of Nature* (Washington, D.C.: National Geographic Society, 2000).

87. Seifert, "Reichsautobahn im Wald," 112. On the principle of *Bodenständigkeit* in the landscape advocates' work, see Zeller, *Strasse, Bahn, Panorama,* 165–186.

88. Seifert, *Leben für die Landschaft,* 72.

89. Ibid.; Hoemann, "Landschaft und Autobahn," 10.

90. Seifert, *Leben für die Landschaft,* 67. Seifert's autobiography overlooks the intense conflict that erupted between himself and Todt over the costs and aesthetic impact of *bodenständig* plantings along the *Autobahnen.* See Zeller, *Strasse, Bahn, Panorama,* 176–187.

91. Seifert, "Reichsautobahn im Wald," 112.

92. Hoemann, "Landschaft und Autobahn," 11.

93. Seifert, *Leben für die Landschaft,* 17, 67.

94. Ibid., 89.

95. Seifert, *Die Heckenlandschaft,* Potsdamer Vorträge no. 8 (Potsdam: Eduard Stichnote, 1944), 9, 24–28.

96. Seifert, "Die Versteppung Deutschlands," 24–33.

97. Seifert, *Leben für die Landschaft,* 35, 100–105; Rollins, "Whose Landscape?" 506; Dominick, *Environmental Movement in Germany,* 110; Bramwell, *Ecology in the Twentieth Century,* 198.

98. Alwin Seifert, *Die Heckenlandschaft,* 57.

99. Bramwell, *Blood and Soil,* 173–174.

100. Seifert, "Natur und Technik," 10.

101. Ibid.

102. Alwin Seifert, "Heimat und Siedlung," *Zeitschrift des Rheinischen Vereins für Denkmalpflege und Heimatschutz* 30, no. 2 (1937): 6.

103. Seifert, *Die Heckenlandschaft,* 9–20.

104. Seifert, *Leben für die Landschaft,* 23.

105. Seifert, "Reichsautobahn im Wald," 112. On the parallels between nativist ecological rhetoric and Nazi racism, see also Gert Gröning and Joachim Wolschke-Bulmahn, "Politics, Planning and the Protection of Nature: Political Abuse of Early Ecological Ideas in Germany, 1933–1945," *Planning Perspectives* 2 (1987): 127–148, and Gert Gröning and Joachim Wolschke-

Bulmahn, *Die Liebe zur Landschaft,* vol. 1: *Natur in Bewegung: Zur Bedeutung natur- und freiraumorientierter Bewegungen der ersten Hälfte des zwangzigsten Jahrhunderts für die Entwicklung der Freiraumplanung* (Munich: Minerva, 1986), 188–204.

106. Seifert, "Natur und Technik," 11.

107. See Rollins, "Whose Landscape?"

108. Letter from Karl Oberkirch, district nature protection commissioner in the Ruhr Settlement Association to association president, 6 June 1942, BAK 245/184, fol. 9. On the tensions between landscape advocates and regional nature protection commissions, see Zeller, *Strasse, Bahn, Panorama,* 129–138.

109. Letter from Oberkirch to Ruhr Settlement Association president, fol. 9.

110. Letter from Oberkirch to Karl Friedrich Kolbow, provincial governor of Westphalia, 16 November 1941, 1, AVLR 12468. Fritz Todt attempted to orchestrate a similar shift in power by recommending that street building in general be removed from provincial control and placed under his direction in a giant national public works agency. See ALVR Nachlass Haake 44. On landscape advocates' attempts to usurp landscape design competencies, see Zeller, *Strasse, Bahn, Panorama,* 139–142; 198–202.

111. Reinhold Hoemann, "Aufgaben und Pflichten der Führer der Gemeinden betr. Landschaftspflege und Landschaftsgestaltung," 27 February 1942, 1, ALVR 11136.

112. Seifert, *Leben für die Landschaft,* 36.

113. Seifert, "Die Versteppung Deutschlands," 51.

114. Letter from Oberkirch to Wilhelm Münker, 7 September 1941, 1, and letter Oberkirch to Kolbow, 16 November 1941, 4, ALVR 12468.

115. Letter from Oberkirch to Münker, 7 September 1941, 3; see also letter from Oberkirch to Kolbow, 16 November 1941, 2, ibid.

116. Letter from Oberkirch to Kolbow, 16 November 1941, 5; see also letter from Oberkirch to Guido Erxleben, 16 November 1941, ibid.

117. Letter from Hans Schwenkel, Württemberg state commissioner for nature protection, to Hans Kornfeld, Rhineland provincial cultural affairs officer, 9 December 1941, ibid.

118. On this point see also Zeller, *Strasse, Bahn, Panorama,* 128–138, 198–202.

119. The contours of this debate were derived from several archival files, including BAK B245/18 and B245/185, and ALVR 11055, 11122–11123, and 11241.

120. Letter from Hans Klose, head of the Reich Office for Nature Protection, to Seifert, 5 November 1940, fol. 5–6; letter from VVS to Nature Protection Commissioner Lutz Heck in the Reich Forestry Ministry, 6 March 1939, fol. 24–27 in BAK B245/185. See also letter from Rhine Province nature protection commissioner Herbert Iven to Klose, 14 January 1941, fol. 169–170, B245/18.

121. Letter from Seifert to General Inspector Fritz Todt, 13 June 1939, fol. 174–177, BAK B245/18. Letter also available in ALVR 11241.

122. Ibid. On the creation of *Autobahn* landscapes for visual consumption, see Zeller, "'Landschaften des Verkehrs,'" 323–340.
123. Letter from Seifert to Todt, 13 June 1939.
124. Ibid. Seifert may have been drawing an unfavorable comparison here between the seemingly "wild" areas of his mountainous Bavarian *Heimat* and the Rhineland's industrial landscape. As I discussed in Chapter 1, however, the Conwentzian tradition of *Naturdenkmalpflege* had always recognized a variety of landscapes, including ones with limited economic activity, as *Naturschutzgebiete*. Germany's nature protection areas together amounted to about 2,500 square kilometers, or 1/200 of the German Reich in 1935; the Siebengebirge's 75 square kilometers placed it among the country's most important protection regions. Germany's total area of nature protection regions was still only one-third the area of Yellowstone Park alone. See Schoenichen, *Urdeutschland*, 5–6.
125. Letter from Seifert to Todt, 13 June 1939.
126. Letter from VVS chairman Eduard von Gartzen to Iven, 11 January 1941, 1, ALVR 11241.
127. Letter from Iven to Klose, 14 January 1941, fol. 170.
128. Letter from Schwenkel to Kornfeld, 9 December 1941, BAK 245/18.
129. Letter from Gartzen to Iven, 11 January 1941, 1, ALVR 11241.
130. Letter from Iven to Klose, 14 January 1941, B245/18, fol. 169–171.
131. Ibid.
132. Ibid.
133. The KdF was an NSDAP organization that sponsored low-cost leisure activities for factory workers, part of the Nazi attempt to overcome class barriers by making middle-class cultural amenities available to the masses. On the KdF, see Otis C. Mitchell, ed., *Nazism and the Common Man: Essays in German History 1929–1939,* 2nd ed. (Washington, D.C.: University Press of America, 1981); Hasso Spode, "Arbeiterurlaub im Dritten Reich," in *Angst, Belohnung, Zucht, und Ordnung: Herrschaftsmechanismen im Nationalsozialismus,* ed. Carola Sachse (Opladen: Westdeutscher Verlag, 1983), 277–279; Shelley Baranowski, "Strength through Joy: Tourism and National Integration in the Third Reich," in *Being There: Tourism, Consumer Culture and Identity in Modern Europe and North America,* ed. Shelley Baranowski and Ellen Furlough (Ann Arbor: University of Michigan Press, 2002). The KdF soon challenged local tourism promotion groups, since the National Socialists removed tourist promotion from the hands of local agencies and *Heimat* groups and placed it under centralized administration. Applegate, *Nation of Provincials,* 214; *Die Eifel 1888–1988,* 438.
134. "Umbau auf dem Drachenfels," *Kölnische Zeitung,* 15 September 1936.
135. Letter from VVS to Heck, 6 March 1939, B245/185, fol. 274.
136. Letter from Oberkirch to Münker, 7 September 1941.
137. Wilhelm Lienenkämper, "Der Deutsche und seine Landschaft," in *Heimatliebe-Heimatschutz,* 30 March 1934, in ALVW C70, No. 184.

138. *Düsseldorfer Nachrichten,* 20 April 1933, ALVR 11122.

139. A bridge was eventually constructed near this site between 1967 and 1969. See Bildarchiv der Pressestelle des Landschaftsverbandes Rheinland, Nos. 66/23/5, 68/1271, 73/1.

140. Koshar, *Germany's Transient Pasts,* 207. On the symbolism of trees, see also Bernd Weyergraf, *Waldungen: Die Deutschen und ihr Wald,* exhibition of the Akademie der Künste from 20 September to 15 November 1987 (Berlin: Die Akademie, 1987).

141. Alwin Seifert, "Die Zukunft der Ostdeutschen Landschaft," in *Im Zeitalter des Lebendigen,* 211–219. On Seifert's support for transforming these areas, see Rollins, "Whose Landscape?" 510–511.

142. On RKFDV resettlement policies, see Robert Koehl, *RKFDV: German Resettlement and Population Policy 1939–1945: A History of the Reich Commission for the Strengthening of Germandom* (Cambridge, Mass.: Harvard University Press, 1957). For Himmler's landscape planning guidelines, see Reichskommissariat für die Festigung deutschen Volkstums, "Allgemeine Anordnung über die Gestaltung der Landschaft in den eingegliederten Ostgebieten," 1940, BAK R49, No. 165, fol. 196–220.

143. On landscape planning in occupied Poland, see Gröning and Wolschke-Bulmahn, "Politics and Planning," and *Die Liebe zur Landschaft,* vol. 3: *Die Drang nach Osten* (Munich: Minerva, 1987); Mechtild Rössler, "Applied Geography and Area Research in Nazi Society: Central Place Theory and Planning, 1933–1945," *Environment and Planning D: Society and Space* 7 (1989): 419–431.

144. Quoted in Gröning and Wolschke-Bulmahn, "Politics and Planning," 139.

145. RKFDV, "Allgemeine Anordnung über die Gestaltung der Landschaft," 2.

146. Seifert, *Die Heckenlandschaft,* 57.

147. Heinrich Wiepking-Jürgensmann, "Der Mensch and die Pflanze," *Gartenflora* 84 (1935): 221–223. Quoted in Gröning and Wolschke-Bulmahn, "Politics and Planning," 137.

148. "Landschaftliche Kulturpflege: Eine universale Aufgabe—Ziele und Wege—Zum Tag für Denkmalpflege und Heimatschutz," *Kölnische Zeitung,* 20 August 1937.

149. Fritz Todt, *Der Strassenbau im nationalsozialistischen Staat* (Berlin, n.d.), 3. Quoted in Shand, "The Reichsautobahn," 197.

150. Reinhold Hoemann, "Aufgaben und Pflichten der Führer der Gemeinden," 1, in ALVR 11136.

151. Ibid., 18.

152. Hoemann, "Aufgabe und Pflichten der Führer der Gemeinden betr. Landschaftspflege und Landschaftsgestaltung," 18.

153. Zeller, *Strasse, Bahn, Panorama,* 111–128.

154. Zeller, "'Landscape's Crown,'" 225–233, and Zeller, *Strasse, Bahn, Panorama,* 142–198, 203–209.

155. Rollins, "Whose Landscape?" 509; Zeller, "Landschaften des Verkehrs," 330–336.

156. Colin Riordan, ed., *Green Thought in German Culture: Historical and Contemporary Perspectives* (Cardiff: University of Wales Press, 1997), 25.

157. See Benedict Anderson's discussion of messianic time in *Imagined Communities: Reflections on the Origins and Spread of Nationalism,* rev. ed. (London: Verso, 1991), 24.

158. Quoted in Hoemann, "Aufgaben und Pflichten der Führer der Gemeinden betr. Landschaftspflege und Landschaftgestaltung," 21.

## Conclusion

1. Horst Lademacher, "Die nördlichen Rheinlande von der Rheinprovinz bis zur Bildung des Landschaftsverbandes Rheinland," in *Rheinische Geschichte in drei Bänden,* vol. 2: *Neuzeit,* ed. Franz Petri and Georg Droege (Düsseldorf: L. Schwann, 1976), 604–616.

2. Stephen Spender, *European Witness* (New York: Reynal and Hitchcock, 1946), 15–16

3. Ibid., 24.

4. Arne Anderson, "Heimatschutz: Die bürgerliche Naturschutzbewegung," in *Besiegte Natur: Geschichte der Umwelt im neunzehnten und zwanzigsten Jahrhundert,* ed. Franz-Josef Brüggemeier and Thomas Rommelspacher, 2nd ed. (Munich: C. H. Beck, 1989), 156–157.

5. Spender, *European Witness,* 13–14.

6. Ibid., 7–8.

7. Celia Applegate, *A Nation of Provincials: The German Idea of Heimat* (Berkeley: University of California Press, 1990) 18–19.

8. The historical literature on post-1945 German environmental protection is too vast to be cited here in detail. Two useful surveys are Raymond Dominick, *The Environmental Movement in Germany: Prophets and Pioneers 1871–1971* (Bloomington: Indiana University Press, 1992), 119–214; Colin Riordan, ed., *Green Thought in German Culture: Historical and Contemporary Perspectives* (Cardiff: University of Wales Press, 1997), 26–30. On nature conservation and environmental protection in the Federal Republic, see Günther Zwanzig, *Die Fortentwicklung des Naturschutzrechts in Deutschland nach 1945* (Erlangen: Rudolf Merkel, 1962); Herbert Ant, "Entwicklung, Übersicht, und Gliederung der Naturschutzgebiete in der Bundesrepublik Deutschland," *Schriftenreihe für Landschaftspflege und Naturschutz* 6 (1971): 161–176; Gerhard Olschowy, ed., *Natur- und Umweltschutz in der Bundesrepublik Deutschland* (Hamburg: Parey, 1978); Christian Pfister, *Das 1950er Syndrom: Der Weg in die Konsumgesellschaft* (Bern: Verlag Paul Haupt, 1995); Sandra Chaney, "Visions and Revisions of Nature: From the Protection of Nature to the Invention of the Environment in the Federal Republic of Germany, 1945–1975, Ph.D. diss., University of North Carolina at Chapel Hill, 1997; and Monika Bergmeier, *Umweltgeschichte der Boomjahre 1949–1973: Das Beispiel Bayern* (Münster: Waxmann, 2002).

9. On Rhine River cleanup, see Mark Cioc, *The Rhine: An Ecobiography, 1815–2000* (Seattle: University of Washington Press, 2002), 173–201; Kenneth J. Langran, "International Water Quality Management: The Rhine River as a Study in Transfrontier Pollution Control," Ph.D. diss., University of Wisconsin–Madison, 1979; Marco Verweij, *Transboundary Environmental Problems and Cultural Theory: The Protection of the Rhine and the Great Lakes* (New York: Palgrave, 2000).

10. Dominick, *The Environmental Movement in Germany*, 140.

11. "Fischkatastrophe in der Ahr," *Westfälische Nachrichten*, 10 May 1957; "Der Rheinstrom ist gefährlich krank," *Düsseldorfer Nachrichten* 73 (1952).

12. Riordan, ed., *Green Thought in German Culture*, 30. On Green political theory and its relationship to the New Left, see Andrei Markovits, *The German Left: Red, Green, and Beyond* (New York: Oxford University Press, 1993); Helmut Wiesenthal, *Realism in Green Politics: Social Movements and Ecological Reform in Germany* (Manchester, U.K.: University of Manchester Press, 1993); Sabine von Dirke, *All Power to the Imagination! The West German Counterculture from the Student Movement to the Greens* (Lincoln: University of Nebraska Press, 1997).

13. "Unser Wasser," *Mitteilungen, Vereinigung Deutscher Gewässerschutz*, No. 10/11 (1956): 9.

14. On the movement from *Naturschutz* to *Umweltschutz*, see Dominick, *The Environmental Movement in Germany*, 138.

15. Quoted in Torsten Mick and Michael Tretter, "Der Rhein und Europa," in *Der Rhein: Mythos und Realität eines europäischen Stromes*, ed. Hans Boldt (Cologne: Rheinland, 1988), 35–46, here 46.

16. On Rhineland-Prussia tensions and the drive for regional autonomy, see Dieter Kastner and Vera Torunsky, *Kleine rheinische Geschichte 1815–1986* (Cologne: Rheinland, 1987), 11–16.

17. On the regionalization of cultural authority, see Horst Lademacher, *Von den Provinzialständen zum Landschaftsverband: Zur Geschichte der landschaftlichen Selbstverwaltung der Rheinlande* (Cologne: Rheinland, 1973), 7–18 and Karl Ditt, *Raum und Volkstum: Die Kulturpolitik des Provinzialverbandes Westfalen, 1923–1945* (Münster: Aschendorffsche, 1988).

18. See Ditt, *Raum and Volkstum*, on Westphalia, and Werner Hartung, *Konservative Zivilisationskritik und Regionale Identität: Am Beispiel der niedersächsischen Heimatbewegung 1895 bis 1919* (Hannover: Hahnsche Buchhandlung, 1991), on Lower Saxony.

19. The large number of works that deal with the American and British nature preservation movements and their nationalist ideals cannot be cited here in detail. On the American wilderness movement, see especially Roderick Nash's classic *Wilderness and the American Mind*, 4th ed. (New Haven: Yale University Press, 2001), and William Cronon, "The Trouble with Wilderness, or Getting Back to the Wrong Nature," in *Uncommon Ground: Rethinking the Human Place in Nature*, ed. Cronon (New York: W. W.

Norton, 1996), 69–90. On the British preservation movement, see Jan Marsh, *Back to the Land: The Pastoral Impulse in England from 1880 to 1914* (London: Quartet Books, 1982); David Evans, *A History of Nature Conservation in Great Britain* (New York: Routledge, 1991); and John Sheail, *Nature Conservation in Britain: The Formative Years* (London: Stationery Office, 1998). For comparative analyses, see Raymond Dominick, "The Roots of the Green Movement in the United States and West Germany," *Environmental Review* 13, no. 3 (Fall 1988): 1–30, and Karl Ditt, "Nature Conservation in England and Germany 1900–70: Forerunner of Environmental Protection?" *Contemporary European History* 5, no. 1 (1996): 1–28.

# Sources

*Primary Sources*

Archiv des Landschaftsverbandes Rheinland (ALVR), Brauweiler
    Provinzial Verwaltung der Rheinprovinz, Kulturabteilung
    Nachlass Heinrich Haake
    Nachlass Johannes Horion
Archiv des Landschaftsverbandes Westfalen-Lippe (ALVW), Münster
    C70 Provinzialverwaltung Westfalen
Archiv des Rheinischen Heimatbundes, Cologne
Bundesarchiv Koblenz (BAK)
    B245 Bundesforschungsanstalt für Landschaftsökologie und Naturschutz/
    Staatliche Stelle für Naturdenkmalpflege
    R2 Reichsfinanzministerium
    R49 Reichskommissariat für die Festigung deutschen Volkstums
    R113 Reichstelle für Raumordnung
Geheimes Staatsarchiv Preussischer Kulturbesitz, Berlin-Dahlem
    Rep I/84a Preussisches Justizministerium
    I/87b Preussisches Ministerium für Landwirtschaft, Domänen und Forsten
Nordrhein-Westfälisches Hauptstaatsarchiv
    NW60 Kultusministerium
    NW 132 Ministerium für Ernährung, Landwirtschaft, und Forsten

*Principal Journals and Newspapers*

*Beiträge zur Naturdenkmalpflege*
*Beiträge zur Rheinkunde*
*Düsseldorfer Nachrichten*

*Eifelkalendar*
*Eifelvereinsblatt*
*Heimatschutz: Mitteilungsblatt des Deutschen Bundes Heimatschutz*
*Kölnische Volks zeitung*
*Kölnische Zeitung*
*Mitteilungen des Rheinischen Vereins für Denkmalpflege und Heimatschutz*
*Nachrichtenblatt für Naturschutz*
*Nachrichtenblatt für rheinische Heimatpflege*
*Naturschutz: Monatsschrift für alle Freunde der Deutschen Heimat*
*Rheinische Heimat*
*Rheinische Heimatblätter*
*Rheinische Heimatpflege*
*Rheinische Jugend*
*Rheinischer Naturfreund*
*Rheinische Vierteljahresblätter*
*Rheinische Zeitung*
*Die Rheinprovinz: Amtliches Organ des Landeshauptmanns der Rheinprovinz*
*Die Strasse*
*Zeitschrift des Rheinischen Vereins für Denkmalpflege und Heimatschutz*

# *Acknowledgments*

The idea for this study emerged in the spring of 1993 in Seattle. At that time I was at the University of Washington, studying American environmental history with Richard White, European intellectual history with John Toews, and early twentieth-century German history with Elisabeth Domansky. Formulating a historical study that might bring together my love of European history and environmental history and engage questions raised by this trio of dynamic scholars seemed a daunting task at the time. Fortunately my intellectual and professional trajectory after I completed my master's degree brought me into contact with scholars in Germany and in the U.S. German Studies community whose support, encouragement, and criticism enabled me to synthesize these theoretical perspectives in this project, which investigates Germans' diverse and problematic engagement with environmental issues in the late nineteenth and early twentieth centuries. Their insights and questions have all informed this book. I want to take this opportunity to thank these individuals, the granting agencies that have supported my research, and the many family members, friends, and colleagues whose editorial advice and emotional support made this book possible.

This book began as a doctoral dissertation at the University of Wisconsin. I would like to thank my doctoral adviser, Rudy Koshar, dissertation readers Laird Boswell and Jim Steakley, and doctoral committee members Lynn Nyhart and Bill Cronon, whose excellent suggestions and critical insights helped to transform the dissertation into a more engaging and sophisticated book manuscript. This project would also not have been possible without the intellectual dialogue, personal support, and editorial advice of scholar friends such as Karen Till, Tim McMahon, Mark Cioc, Jami Moss, Thomas Zeller, Joe Lucchesi, and many others whom space does not permit me to thank individually but who helped to shape the manuscript as well. Special thanks go to my wonderful colleagues at the

University of South Carolina, Kay Edwards, Kasey Grier, and Lessie Jo Frazier. Karen Maloney in Instructional Support at the University of South Carolina spent many long hours on the map of the Rhine Province; I greatly valued her technical know-how and aesthetic sensibility. At Harvard University Press, thanks go as well to Kathleen McDermott, Elizabeth Gilbert, and Kathi Drummy, whose editorial advice has been invaluable. Manuscript editor Julie Hagen helped to make this a more polished and readable book; I greatly appreciated her suggestions. I also appreciated the comments of the two anonymous readers who reviewed the initial manuscript; though I was not able to incorporate all of their suggestions, they helped to improve the book immensely.

During my stays in Germany, I benefited greatly from conversations with numerous scholars and archivists who helped me locate materials and made me feel welcome. I am especially grateful to Michael Wettengel at the Bundesarchiv in Koblenz, whose immense knowledge of *Naturschutz* and whose kindness encouraged me early on in the project and helped to make the Rhineland a second *Heimat* for me. Franz-Josef Brüggemeier, Karl Ditt, Karl Peter Wiemer, and Elmar Heinen provided keen insights about German environmental history and Rhineland regional history that have enriched this manuscript. Many thanks also to the staff at the Landschaftsverband Archiv in Brauweiler, especially Stefanie Mauch, Wolfgang Schaffer, and Reinhardt Kahlfeld, who assisted me throughout my research and writing, and to Elmar Scheuren at the Siebengebirge Museum in Königswinter, who kindly offered last-minute help with names, dates, and photographs.

I would like to thank the many institutions whose financial support for research and writing made this book possible, including the Fulbright Commission, the National Endowment for the Humanities, the Council for European Studies, the German Academic Exchange Service, and the University of Wisconsin Alumni Research Fund. The University of South Carolina Strategic Programs and Research program and a College of Liberal Arts Scholarship Support award assisted me with postgraduate research grants, while the generous leave granted me by the History Department in the spring of 2001 helped in the final crucial phases of manuscript writing and preparation. I also could not have completed the project without additional love and support from my extended family: Jamie McCarthy, Joe Brunet, my sister, Laura, and my parents, Sandy and Tom Lekan.

# Index

Adenauer, Konrad, 88, 254, 255
Aesthetics: of landscape, 3–4, 11, 16, 23, 26, 43, 126, 143; as preservation standard, 47, 49, 53, 115; of environmental perception, 57, 58, 59, 65, 256–257. *See also* Landscape; Prussia, Disfigurement Laws
Agrarian romanticism, 11, 24, 63, 67, 126, 259. *See also Heimatschutz,* modernity of; Romanticism
Ahr region, 107, 108, 110, 256
Anthroposophy, 161, 226
Applegate, Celia, 7, 79, 83
Arndt, Ernst Mortiz, 2, 6, 27
Aubin, Hermann, 26, 93–94, 189
*Autobahnen:* in Nazi propaganda, 212–213, 214–215; environmental impact of, 213, 214, 250; in *Deutsche Technik,* 215; naturalistic design of, 220–224; in centralization of power, 224, 243; as reactionary modernism, 224–226, 250–251; for visual consumption, 225–226, 248; mitigation of environmental impact, 227–229; in environmental restoration, 229–230; in Nazi racial ideology, 246–247, 263; costs, 248. *See also* Landscape advocates; Seifert, Alwin

Balance of Nature, 4, 112, 115
Beautification Society for the Siebengebirge: tourism promotion, 30; membership, 40; in Siebengebirge preser-vation campaign, 40–46; eminent domain rights, 42, 48; leadership, 43; opposition to, 46–48, 121; support for National Socialists, 153, 154, 155; opposition to *Autobahn* bridge, 239–240. *See also* Siebengebirge; Society to Save the Siebengebirge
Billboards, 107, 108, 187
Bird protection, 52–53, 107, 119, 142
Bislicher Island, 119–121. *See also* Rhine Province, nature protection regions; Tiedge, Ernst
Blood and Soil, 2–3; as Nazi slogan, 152, 160, 162, 251; in landscape preservationist discourse, 157, 167, 177, 192, 204
*Bodenständigkeit,* 85, 188, 190, 234
Bonn, 28, 36, 37, 42, 211–212, 253, 256
Bredt, Friedrich Wilhelm, 108
Byron, Lord, 25–26

Cologne: restoration of cathedral, 28, 29; municipal support for Siebengebirge preservation, 42–43, 46, 47–48; *Jahrtausendfeier,* 99–100, 135; environmental impact of National Socialism, 208, 211
Conwentz, Hugo: on natural monument preservation, 21, 39, 51–58; in creation of State Office for Natural Monument Preservation, 50–51, 63–64, 70–71; use